National Audubon Society
Field Guide to
North American Wildflowers

A Chanticleer Press Edition

National Audubon Society
Field Guide to

North American Wildflowers

Eastern Region

Revised Edition

Revising Author
John W. Thieret
Professor Emeritus of Botany
Northern Kentucky University

Original Authors
William A. Niering
Professor of Botany
Connecticut College

and

Nancy C. Olmstead
Research Associate
Connecticut Arboretum

Alfred A. Knopf, New York

Prepared and produced by
Chanticleer Press, Inc., New York.

Printed and bound by Toppan Printing Co., Ltd.,
Tokyo, Japan.

Published July 1979
Second edition, fully revised, March 2001
Second printing, July 2002

Library of Congress Cataloging-in-Publication Data
available.
ISBN: 0-375-40232-2

CONTENTS

NATIONAL AUDUBON SOCIETY

The mission of NATIONAL AUDUBON SOCIETY, *founded in 1905, is to conserve and restore natural ecosystems, focusing on birds, other wildlife, and their habitats for the benefit of humanity and the earth's biological diversity.*

One of the largest, most effective environmental organizations, AUDUBON has nearly 550,000 members, numerous state offices and nature centers, and 500+ chapters in the United States and Latin America, plus a professional staff of scientists, educators, and policy analysts. Through its nationwide sanctuary system AUDUBON manages 160,000 acres of critical wildlife habitat and unique natural areas for birds, wild animals, and rare plant life.

The award-winning *Audubon* magazine, which is sent to all members, carries outstanding articles and color photography on wildlife, nature, environmental issues, and conservation news. AUDUBON also publishes *Audubon Adventures,* a children's newsletter reaching 450,000 students. Through its ecology camps and workshops in Maine, Connecticut, and Wyoming, AUDUBON offers nature education for teachers, families, and children; through *Audubon Expedition Institute* in Belfast, Maine, AUDUBON offers unique, traveling undergraduate and graduate degree programs in Environmental Education.

AUDUBON sponsors books and on-line nature activities, plus travel programs to exotic places like Antarctica, Africa, Baja California, the Galápagos Islands, and Patagonia. For information about how to become an AUDUBON member, subscribe to *Audubon Adventures,* or to learn more about any of our programs, please contact:

NATIONAL AUDUBON SOCIETY
Membership Dept.
700 Broadway
New York, NY 10003
(800) 274-4201
(212) 979-3000
http://www.audubon.org/

NATIONAL AUDUBON SOCIETY
FIELD GUIDE SERIES

Also available in this unique all-color,
all photographic format:

African Wildlife

Birds (Eastern Region)

Birds (Western Region)

Butterflies

Fishes

Fossils

Insects and Spiders

Mammals

Mushrooms

Night Sky

Reptiles and Amphibians

Rocks and Minerals

Seashells

Seashore Creatures

Trees (Eastern Region)

Trees (Western Region)

Tropical Marine Fishes

Weather

Wildflowers (Western Region)

THE AUTHORS

Revision author John W. Thieret is Professor Emeritus of Botany at Northern Kentucky University. He has written many technical and popular articles on botanical and other nature subjects and is the author or coauthor of several books. He specializes in the study of plants of eastern North America.

The authors of the original edition are the late William A. Niering, Professor of Botany at Connecticut College, Director of the Connecticut Arboretum, and a noted expert on wetlands ecology, and Nancy C. Olmstead, Research Associate at the Connecticut Arboretum.

ACKNOWLEDGMENTS

This revised guide builds upon the original edition's success in aiding the public to appreciate the marvelous wildflower diversity of eastern North America. I therefore wish to express my sincere appreciation to the late William A. Niering and his coauthor, Nancy C. Olmstead, and all of those whom they acknowledged in the first edition.

During my work on this book I received help and encouragement from David M. Brandenburg, John Kartesz, Robert F. C. Naczi, Mildred W. Thieret, and the staff of the Lloyd Library in Cincinnati. I made frequent use of the Herbarium of Northern Kentucky University.

Michael A. Vincent, curator of the W. S. Turrell Herbarium at Miami University in Ohio, reviewed manuscripts and provided many helpful comments and corrections, as did another esteemed colleague, Richard Spellenberg, who was simultaneously revising the companion volume for western wildflowers.

I am grateful to the fine staff at Chanticleer Press. I extend special thanks to Miriam Harris, senior editor, who guided this project to fruition, and to Lisa Lester, whose intensive editing work in the final months greatly improved the quality and useability of this guide. Photo editors Jennifer McClanaghan and Meg Kuhta did an outstanding job of gathering and sorting through thousands of images to find the accurate and beautiful photographs that are so essential to this field guide; illustrator Bobbi Angell contributed lovely renderings of many species; and art director Drew Stevens and designers Bernadette Vibar, Jennifer Dahl, and Michiyo Uno brought the text and images together splendidly. Tremendous assistance throughout the final stages of the project came from editorial assistant Mee-So Caponi, editors Lisa Leventer, Pamela Nelson, and Marian Appellof, and proofreader Linda Eger. Alicia Mills and Katherine Thomason saw the guide through the complex production and printing processes. In earlier stages of the project, Mary Sutherland helped with editing, and further assistance came from Edie Locke, Lauren Weiden-man, and Amy Oh. I thank Amy Hughes for getting this project off the ground during her tenure as editor-in-chief. Thanks also to her successor, George Scott, for shepherding it along to completion. Finally, to the photographers, thanks for your keen eyes and superb skills in obtaining beautiful photographs.

INTRODUCTION

What is a wildflower? What one person considers a wildflower may be a weed to another. All we can safely say is that wildflowers are wild plants with flowers and that they may be found almost anywhere, from cracks in city sidewalks to vast empty deserts, pristine forests, seashores, old fields, prairies, or mountain meadows. This guide is directed toward the reader whose interest in wildflowers is new as well as toward the nature devotee who knows many of the common or showy eastern wildflowers but desires to learn more. Because space in a single book is necessarily limited, only a portion of the thousands of eastern wildflowers can be discussed or illustrated. Therefore, it is the aim of this guide to cover most of the flowers of eastern North America that attract attention because they are showy or because of their unusual nature, to represent the floral diversity of all regions of the East more or less equally, to illustrate with at least one example most genera of eastern wildflowers, and to represent the variation found among species of some of the huge eastern families, such as asters, mints, and mustards.

Geographic Scope
Many field guides covering eastern and western North America use the 100th meridian as a dividing line between the two regions. We have chosen, instead, a more natural boundary (see map), which extends southeastward from the Arctic along the eastern base of the Rocky Mountains to the Big Bend region of Texas at the Mexican border. This line marks a pronounced change in the kinds of native plants, with few species extending very far beyond on either side. This guide covers the entire region from this line eastward to the Atlantic Coast.

Major Eastern Habitats
The topographical and biological variety of the eastern United States has resulted in a wide range of habitats, which accounts for the great number and diversity of native

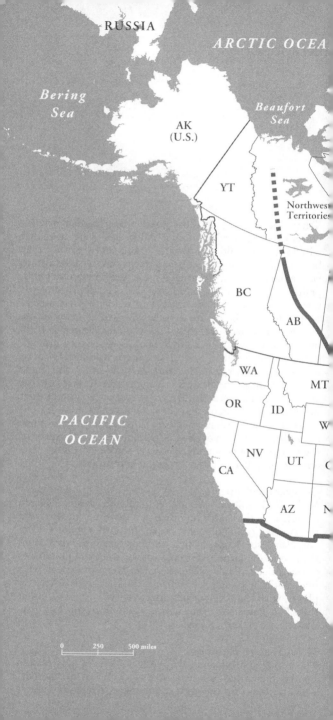

RUSSIA

ARCTIC OCEAN

*Bering
Sea*

AK
(U.S.)

*Beaufort
Sea*

YT

Northwest
Territories

*PACIFIC
OCEAN*

BC

AB

WA

MT

OR

ID

W

NV

UT

C

CA

AZ

N

0   250   500 miles

plants. The eastern sector includes the extensive deciduous forest region from the Atlantic Coast westward to Minnesota, eastern Iowa, southern Missouri, and eastern Texas. From the northeast the deciduous forest stretches southward through the Appalachians but is replaced on the coastal plains by extensive evergreen pine forests. The southern tip of Florida is subtropical and has many Caribbean species. With decreasing precipitation as one moves westward, forest vegetation is replaced by grassland with a rich diversity of prairie flowers. Although sporadic remnants of tall-grass prairie occur as far east as Ohio, the vast continuous grasslands begin in Kansas and Oklahoma. As aridity increases to the west, tall-grass prairie tends to give way to mid-height grasses and, ultimately, to short-grass plains near the Rocky Mountains.

Photographs

Although many flower books are illustrated with drawings or paintings, we have chosen to use color photographs because they show flowers as seen in nature, rather than as interpreted by an artist. In presenting the work of expert wildflower photographers, we believe we provide any naturalist, amateur and professional alike, an excellent means of arriving at an accurate identification of many of our eastern plants. A good photograph captures the true color of a wildflower in its natural setting, facilitating identification. In addition, the beauty of pictures taken by outstanding photographers makes this useful guide a delight to the eye.

The photographs we have chosen usually emphasize the flowers themselves, but leaves and other identifying features are also often shown. Where useful, line drawings are included among the text descriptions.

Captions

The caption under each photograph gives the plate number, the plant's main common name, height data for the plant, and one of the following dimensions: the approximate flower width (*w.*) or flower length (*l.*), or the approximate cluster length (*cl.*) or cluster width (*cw.*). This information is especially helpful for the photographs showing flowers larger or smaller than life-size. Plant height is not given for plants classified as aquatics, vines, or creepers (the term creeper is used here loosely to describe any trailing or sprawling plant). The caption ends with the page number of the species description in the text.

Arrangement by Color

Although we realize that any identification technique has its limitations, we have grouped the photographs of the flowers by color, since that is the feature most of us notice first. Note that colors may intergrade, that is, they may blend into one another, resulting in intermediate hues. Thus, if you are looking for a specific plant in the yellow color group and do not find it there, check the orange and green groups as well, since yellow often intergrades with these hues. The color groups are arranged in the following order:

Green
Green intergrades into white, yellow, and sometimes blue; intermediate-hued flowers should be sought here or among those colors.

White
White intergrades into many colors, particularly very pale pink, lavender, blue, green, and yellow. Pale pastel flowers should also be sought among those colors.

Yellow
Yellow intergrades especially into orange and green.

Orange
Orange intergrades into brown, red, and yellow.

Brown
Some eastern wildflowers are brownish, brown-maroon, or rust. These hues intergrade into purple (through maroon), red, orange, and occasionally yellow.

Red
Red intergrades into pink, orange, and purple.

Pink
Here, pink is considered to be a pastel red, without any blue hue to it. Nevertheless, it intergrades into purple through lavender, and as the color becomes denser it intergrades into red.

Purple
Among all the colors, purple is perhaps the most difficult to define. Colors mixing blue and red may be differently perceived from one person to the next. As used here, purple ranges from lavender through red-violet to violet-blue. Flowers with some mixture of red or pink, blue, or blue and violet may be grouped in the pink or the blue category.

Blue
Blue intergrades into purple or lavender and through pastel hues into white.

A plant that has flowers with more than one prominent color may be included in two different color sections; also, when a plant has a conspicuously colored or unusual fruit, the fruit may be shown as well.

Flower Subgroups
Within the color groups we have further organized the plants so that those that have flowers or flower clusters with similar structure occur together.

To accomplish this, we have devised six basic subgroups: radially symmetrical flowers; daisy- and dandelion-like flowers; bilaterally symmetrical flowers; elongated clusters; rounded clusters; and fruit. (Not all subgroups are present in every color group.) These subgroups are discussed in more detail in "How to Identify a Flower," below. First, however, we will review the structure of a flower and other parts of a plant so that the subgroups are better understood.

Flower Symmetry
The overall symmetry of a flower is evident when you look directly into its "face." If its flower parts are of equal length and radiate outward from the center, in spoke-like fashion, it is termed radially symmetrical, or regular (below, left); such a flower can be divided into equal halves along several lines that run through the center. If flower parts are of unequal length on one side relative to the other, and the flower can be divided into equal halves along only one line through the center, the flower is termed bilaterally symmetrical, or irregular (below, right). For accurate identification, it is most helpful to observe a flower's type of symmetry.

Flower Parts
Most flowers consist of four series of parts. The outer, often green series is the calyx, composed of sepals. The next, usually showy series is the corolla, composed of petals. Generally it is the corolla that most clearly reveals the symmetry of a flower. The calyx and the corolla together are called the perianth. In some plants sepals and petals may look alike. In others petals may be missing, and only green, sepal-like structures are present. In a very few plants there are no petals, but the sepals are petal-like and sometimes

Radially symmetrical

Bilaterally symmetrical

very showy, which is understandably confusing to the beginner. Even fewer flowers have neither sepals nor petals. Sepals may be joined to one another and form a dish, bell, or tube; petals may also be joined in such shapes. If petals are separate, a gentle tug on one will remove only it; if they are joined, all petals will be removed at once. In our description of a flower with separate petals, the number of petals is given; in a flower with joined petals, the number of lobes of the corolla is given.

Just inside the petals, and often attached to the corolla in plants with joined petals, are the stamens. Each stamen consists of a relatively slender stalk (filament) and a pollen-bearing body called the anther. In the very center of the flower is at least one pistil. The pistil has a swollen basal portion, the ovary, containing ovules, each ovule harboring an egg; ovules grow into seeds. All these flower parts may be attached at the top of the ovary or at its base. The ovary matures into a dry or fleshy fruit. Above the ovary is a stout or slender, sometimes branched style, topped by a pollen-receiving stigma. The pollen inside the anther is transferred to the stigma by insects or other animals (e.g., hummingbirds), wind, or water. This is pollination. Soon the pollen will produce the sperm that fertilizes the egg deep within the flower.

Flower Clusters

Flowers may be borne singly at the end of the stem (terminal) or singly all along the stem in the leaf axils (the angle formed by the stem and the upper side of the leaf). Frequently, flowers are arranged in clusters (inflorescences) set apart from the rest of the plant. These clusters may be flat-topped, elongated, or more or less round, and they may be relatively loose or dense. Technical names for flower clusters have been avoided in our text wherever possible, but some are very helpful in identification. For example, in the carrot family (Apiaceae) the flower cluster usually has a number of branches all attached at one point, an inflorescence called an umbel. Also, many members of the aster family (Asteraceae) have a cluster of tiny flowers, some forming the button-like, central disk, others forming the petal-like rays; all are collectively called the head, which resembles a single radially symmetrical flower. Reduced leaves near the flower or in or near the flower cluster are called bracts. (Commonly used botanical terms are explained in the Glossary and also appear in labeled drawings.)

Leaves

Leaves can be an important aid in identifying a wildflower. Each leaf has two parts, a stalk (petiole) and a blade. A leaf may be simple, with the blade all in one piece, or it may be compound. In a compound leaf the blade is composed of separate parts, the leaflets, either arranged along a central

Parts of a Flower

Generalized Flower

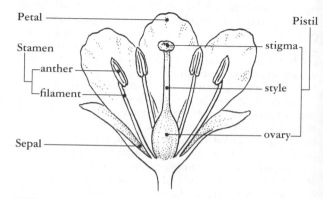

Petal

Stamen
- anther
- filament

Sepal

Pistil

stigma

style

ovary

Flowers in a Composite Head

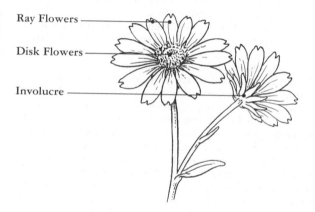

Ray Flowers

Disk Flowers

Involucre

Disk Flower

Ray Flower

Stigma
Anther

Petals (fused)

Pappus

Ovary

Pea Flower

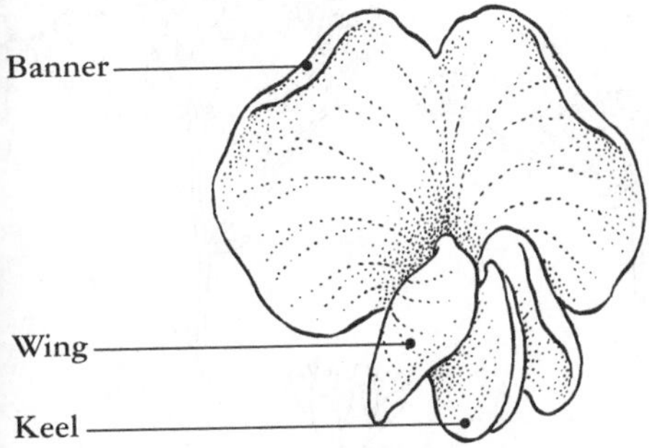

Banner

Wing

Keel

Iris

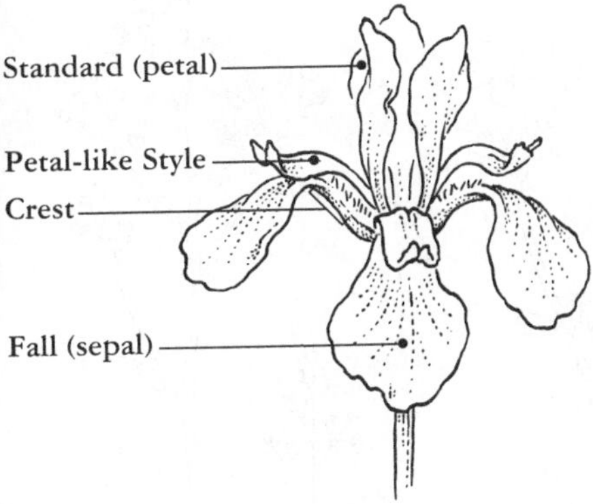

Standard (petal)

Petal-like Style

Crest

Fall (sepal)

Arum

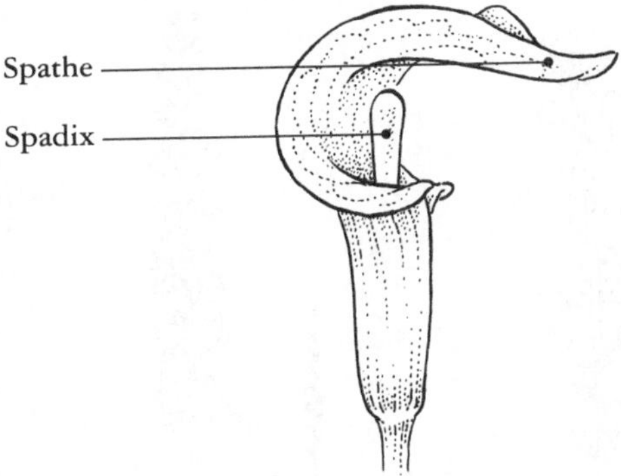

Spathe

Spadix

Flower Cluster Types

Umbel

Corymb

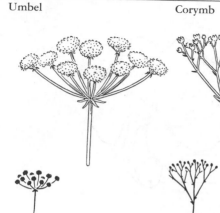

Cyme

Panicle

Raceme

Spike

stalk (pinnately compound), or attached at the end of a stalk, spreading like the fingers of a hand (palmately compound). The edges of leaves and leaflets may be smooth, toothed, or more or less deeply lobed.

There are several common arrangements of leaves on plants. In the most common arrangement, called alternate, each leaf is attached at a different level on the stem. If two leaves are attached at one level but on opposite sides of the stem, they are said to be opposite. If three or more are attached in a ring, at one level and equally spaced, the leaves are described as whorled. Leaves that appear at ground level are called basal; if there are many, they form a basal rosette. In the text, if the leaf arrangement is not mentioned, you may assume it is alternate.

Classification and Names

Common names of plants are highly variable and often differ from one region to the next. A geographically widespread plant may have several common names or, if well known, perhaps just one, whereas a plant that has a more restricted distribution may have no common name at all. In addition, the same name often refers to more than one species, which may or may not resemble one another. Each plant, however, has only one scientific name. In the mid–18th century, the great Swedish botanist Carl von Linné (Carolus Linnaeus) developed the scientific nomenclature in use today. The names are structured in Latin, and many have Greek roots. The first part of the scientific name is the genus (plural, genera); it is always capitalized and is usually assigned to a number of species with many characteristics in common. The second part is the species name; it is not capitalized and often tells something about the particular plant, such as its flower color, size, where it grows, or whom its name honors. The two parts together form the plant's scientific name, which is used uniformly around the world. (In some cases, there is debate among authorities about which genus certain species belong to.) Just as species may be grouped in genera according to shared characteristics, so genera may be grouped in larger aggregations called families.

The scientific names in this book are based primarily on modern regional sources, books that compile, describe, and often illustrate all the plants that grow naturally within a defined geographic region.

The terms subspecies and variety refer to formal categories below the species level. These subdivisions mean about the same thing biologically; the categories are maintained for historical and practical purposes. Both terms refer

Leaves

Parts of a Leaf

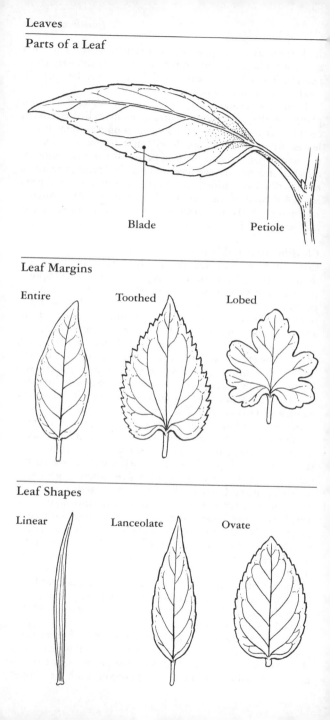

Blade   Petiole

Leaf Margins

Entire   Toothed   Lobed

Leaf Shapes

Linear   Lanceolate   Ovate

Leaf Arrangements

Simple Leaves

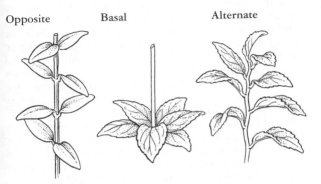

Opposite   Basal   Alternate

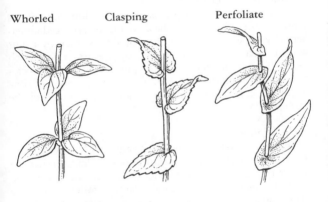

Whorled   Clasping   Perfoliate

Compound Leaves

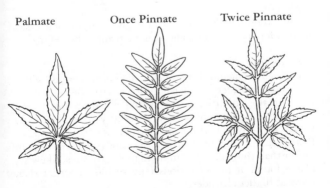

Palmate   Once Pinnate   Twice Pinnate

to geographic populations of a given species that differ somewhat from one another genetically, but not enough to warrant the designation of each as a separate species.

Informal terms such as race, phase, form, and variant are descriptive of population structure or geographic variation and relate to differences that are not represented in formal classification. Race refers to a population of a given species that differs genetically from other populations of the same species. Phase, a very casual term, signifies some alternate condition in a plant's appearance (for example, a yellow-flowered individual in a normally orange-flowered species). The terms form and variant, used in a nontechnical sense, simply refer to the appearance of an individual plant or of a particular population that may differ from that of another individual plant or population of the same species.

Wildflower Descriptions

The text contains descriptions of each wildflower species shown in the color plates. The accounts are arranged alphabetically by scientific name, first by family, then by genus within each family, and finally, by species within each genus. This arrangement tends to put closely related species near one another, thus allowing for easy comparison of similar species. The following details are given in each of the species accounts:

Description

The entry for each species begins with a statement describing the conspicuous features of the plant, so that the user of this guide can quickly decide whether he or she is on the right track. Detailed information then follows about the plant's flowers, leaves (in the case of cacti, stems and spines), and fruit (if applicable). As an additional aid, diagnostic features of the plant are italicized.

Height

The overall height of the plant is given, or, in some cases, such as for trailing vines and aquatic plants, the length.

Flowering

Each entry includes the plant's blooming period, which may vary considerably depending on latitude, elevation, and climatic conditions. The period given applies to the entire geographic range; in one locality, the plant may flower for only a portion of the time stated in the text. Plants that occur in southern locations tend to bloom earlier than those growing in more northerly sites; likewise, plants found at low elevations tend to bloom earlier than those at higher altitudes.

Habitat

Knowing the general environment in which a plant occurs is often very helpful in its identification, for most plants grow only in certain situations. For example, Skunk Cabbage *(Symplocarpus foetidus)* and Marsh Marigold *(Caltha palustris)* prefer wetlands; Queen Anne's Lace *(Daucus carota)* is found mainly in open sunny fields; and Pink Lady's Slipper *(Cypripedium acaule)* is typical of shady woods. This section may also mention commonly associated trees or shrubs; it helps to become familiar with these to fully understand some habitat descriptions.

Range

The geographic range of each species is usually given from north to south, beginning in Canada or the northeastern United States and moving clockwise: that is, southward, westward, and then northward again. The plant's range lies within the area described by this "circle." (When the range is given as "Throughout," this indicates that the plant occurs across the East, as defined in "Geographic Scope," above.)

Comments

These notes give additional items of interest about the plant, such as whether it is native to North America or was introduced from Europe or Asia, other related or similar species, the origin of the plant's names, its uses, and various legend and lore. This may include mention that a certain plant or some part of it is poisonous. However, because this book is not intended as a guide to edible plants, information about toxicity is not always given, and some plants that are poisonous may not be noted as such. Thus, we must urge that you never ingest any part of a wild plant unless you are absolutely certain of its identification and know that you are not allergic or otherwise sensitive to it.

This section may also include information as to whether the plant or its relatives are rare and/or endangered. Populations of many native wildflowers have been depleted because of land development, lumbering, farming, intensive grazing, and, in a few instances, by private and commercial collecting. By 1973, humankind's impact on the environment had become so severe that Congress passed, and has since repeatedly renewed, the Endangered Species Act to give some protection to plants and other organisms faced with extinction. State laws, which vary widely, offer additional protection for many plants and are often strictly enforced. Therefore, the reader is advised to check the laws of his or her state carefully before removing any plant from the environment. Conscience is the best guide if we are to save our rarest wildflowers from extinction.

How to Identify a Flower

First determine which of the major color groups the flower of the plant you are observing belongs to. (To make it easy to locate each color group, and the flower shapes within them, thumb tabs showing the color and shape are provided within the color plate section.) Then turn to that color section and look for a photograph that matches the flower; if you do not find it there, check the color groups into which the flower may intergrade (see "Arrangement by Color," above).

The color sections are further divided into subgroups according to flower or flower cluster shape and fruit. Flowers are complicated structures and not every flower will fit precisely into any one grouping; therefore, if you fail to find your flower in one likely subgroup, try another subgroup in the same color category. The subgroups are:

Radially Symmetrical Flowers

These flowers are mostly borne separately among or above the foliage; when viewed face on (looking into the center of the flower), they have the symmetry of a wheel. The individual flower parts are equal in size and radiate out from the center, and the flower can be divided into equal halves along several lines running through the center.

Daisy- and Dandelion-like Flowers

A daisy-like flower appears to be a single radially symmetrical flower but is actually composed of many tiny flowers forming a button-like, central disk from which radiate numerous showy, petal-like flowers. A dandelion-like flower is similarly constructed but lacks the button-like center; here the central flowers are surrounded by larger petal-like flowers.

Bilaterally Symmetrical Flowers

These flowers are mostly borne separately among or above the foliage; when viewed face on (looking into the center of the flower), one vertical half forms the mirror image of the other, and there is only one dividing line that gives equal halves. Most often the flower parts on the lower side of the flower are longer than those on the upper, but exceptions occur.

Elongated Clusters

For the most part these flowers are held above the foliage and are arranged loosely or tightly in an elongated mass on a central stalk. Even if among the foliage, the central stalk and the flower cluster are apparent. Often the cluster is very tight, the individual flowers packed together and sometimes almost individually indistinguishable. Flowers may be radially or bilaterally symmetrical.

Rounded Clusters

For the most part, these flowers are held above the foliage and are arranged loosely or tightly in a rounded (sometimes flat-topped) mass atop a main stalk. Even if among the foliage, the main stalk and flower cluster are apparent. When the cluster is loose, the slender stalks of the individual flowers all attach at a common point, or nearly so, atop the main stalk. Often the cluster is very tight, the individual flowers packed together and sometimes almost individually indistinguishable. Flowers may be radially or bilaterally symmetrical.

Fruit

Some plants are spectacular when in fruit, during which time the dry or fleshy, mature, seed-bearing portion of the flower is evident.

If the photograph and the plant you have found seem to match, read the caption beneath the picture and refer to the text description to confirm your identification.

An inexpensive hand lens is useful in studying wildflowers, and will also expand your appreciation of the minute structure and beauty of the individual flower parts.

HOW TO USE THIS GUIDE

Example 1: Blue Flower in a Floodplain

On a plain along a river you have found a plant with pink buds and blue, trumpet-shaped, radially symmetrical flowers in rounded clusters.

Turn to the color plates labeled Blue Rounded Clusters and look for a flower with the form described. You note several flowers of this type, all grouped together, but do not see one that matches your specimen. Since the buds on its flower cluster are pink, turn to the color plates labeled Pink Rounded Clusters. Virginia Bluebells seems to be the closest match. The caption under the photograph gives information about the plant height and the size of the flower, as well as the page number of the text description.

You check the text description and find that your plant matches Virginia Bluebells *(Mertensia virginica),* which is a plant that grows along floodplains.

Example 2: Yellow Flower in a Wetland

In a wet area you have found a plant with yellow, star-like flowers grouped together in an elongated cluster and with lance-shaped, opposite leaves.

Turn to the color plates labeled Yellow Elongated Clusters. Among these, your flower most closely resembles the photograph of Swamp Candles *(Lysimachia terrestris)*. Upon reading the species description in the text, you confirm that your example is a match.

Example 3: Red, Berry-like Fruit in Moist Woods

In a moist wooded area you have found a bright red, berry-like fruit on a trailing plant growing close to the ground with round, shiny, green, opposite leaves.

Turn to the color plates labeled Red Fruit. Among the many plants with red, berry-like fruits in this section, only two are labeled as creepers: Partridgeberry *(Mitchella repens)* and Cranberry *(Vaccinium macrocarpon)*. Closer examination of the photographs shows that Partridgeberry has round, shiny green, opposite leaves.

Reading the species description confirms your identification.

PART I
COLOR PLATES

The color plates on the following pages are divided into nine color groups (see "Arrangement by Color" on page 19 of the Introduction for explanation):

Green
White
Yellow
Orange
Brown
Red
Pink
Purple
Blue

Within the color groups, the flowers are further divided by shape and form into up to five subgroups:

Radially Symmetrical Flowers
Daisy- and Dandelion-like Flowers
Bilaterally Symmetrical Flowers
Elongated Clusters
Rounded Clusters

Thumb Tabs

Each subgroup is indicated by a colored symbol on a thumb tab at the left edge of each double-page of plates. The red and white color groups have an additional thumb tab for fruit.

Symbol	Subgroup
	Radially Symmetrical Flowers Viewed face-on, flowers have a wheel-like symmetry, with individual parts radiating from center, so that they can be divided into equal halves along several lines. Usually 4–5 petals, occasionally 3 or 6.
	Daisy- and Dandelion-like Flowers Flower head with a button-like center and many radiating, strap-like petals (actually ray flowers), or with many ray flowers and no button-like center.
	Bilaterally Symmetrical Flowers Viewed face-on, flowers have a bilateral symmetry: One half forms mirror image of other, so that they can be divided into equal halves only along one line through the center. Usually 4–5 petals or lobes, sometimes 3 or 6.
	Elongated Clusters Elongated masses of flowers arranged along a central stalk. Cluster is often very dense, with individual flowers packed tightly together. Individual flowers may be radially or bilaterally symmetrical.
	Rounded Clusters Rounded masses of flowers atop a central stalk. Cluster is often so dense that individual flowers, which may be radially or bilaterally symmetrical, are almost indistinguishable.
	Fruit The dried or fleshy, seed-bearing part of the flower.

Examples

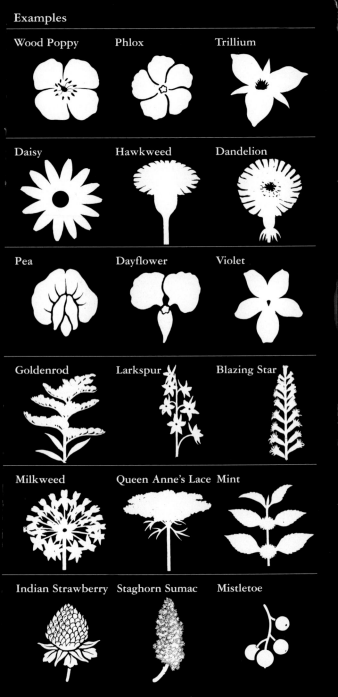

Wood Poppy

Phlox

Trillium

Daisy

Hawkweed

Dandelion

Pea

Dayflower

Violet

Goldenrod

Larkspur

Blazing Star

Milkweed

Queen Anne's Lace

Mint

Indian Strawberry

Staghorn Sumac

Mistletoe

How to Read the Captions Under the Plates

Example:
301   Downy Yellow Violet, 6–16″, *w.* ¾″, *p. 821*
1—— 2 ———————————— 3 — 4—— 5 ——

w. (width)	Refers to average *width* of the flower. In sunflowers and clovers it is the width of the entire flower head.
l. (length)	Refers to average *length* of the flower. Given for some tubular and nodding or hanging flowers as well as some extremely recurved flowers where the length of the flower in profile is its most noticeable dimension. In sunflowers and clovers it is the length of the entire flower head.
cw. (cluster width)	Refers to range of *cluster width.* Given for broad clusters, usually umbels, compound umbels, corymbs, and cymes.
cl. (cluster length)	Refers to range of *cluster length.* Given for elongated clusters, usually spikes, racemes, and panicles.

1 Plate number.
2 Common name of plant.
3 Height of typical mature plant. Usually a range is given; if only one figure is shown, it refers to maximum height.
4 Dimensions of the flower (see chart below left).
5 Page number of species description.

Sunflower

Lily

Bunchberry

Coneflower

Orchid (lip)

Bellwort

Dwarf Ginseng

Queen Anne's Lace

Sensitive Brier

Smartweed

False Hellebore

White Sweet Clover

1   Indian Cucumber Root, 1–2½′, *l.* ½″, *p. 609*

2   Blue Cohosh, 1–3′, *w.* ½″, *p. 437*

3 Spanish Moss, *epiphyte, l. ½–¾", p. 444*

4 Smooth Solomon's Seal, 8–84", *l. ½–¾", p. 610*

5   Green Violet, 1–3′, *l.* ¼″, *p.* 817

6   Small Whorled Pogonia, 4–10″, *l.* ¾″, *p.* 659

7   **Greenfly Orchid,** 2½–16″, *w.* ⅜″, *p.* 657

8   **Large Twayblade,** 4–10″, *l.* ½″, *p.* 660

9 Great Ragweed, 2–15′, *cl.* 1–10″, *p.* 365

10 Common Ragweed, 1–5′, *cl.* 1–6″, *p.* 364

11 Winged Sumac, 3½–23′, *cl. 6″, p. 333*

13   **Staghorn Sumac,** 3–30′, *cl. 8″, p. 335*

15 Poison Sumac, 6–20′, *l.* ⅛″, *p.* 336

16 False Hellebore, 2–7′, *w.* ½″, *p.* 620

17   False Nettle, 1½–3′, *cl.* 1½″, *p. 811*

18   Stinging Nettle, 2–4′, *l.* ¹⁄₁₆″, *p. 812*

19 Wood Nettle, 1½–4′, *l.* ⅛″, *p. 811*

21 Lamb's-quarters, 1–6′, *w.* 1/16″, *p.* 477

23　Thorny Pigweed, 1–4′, *cl.* 6″, *p. 330*

24　Eastern Bottlebrush Grass, 2–5′, *cl.* 10″, *p. 686*

25   Timothy, 1½–3′, *cl. 8″, p. 687*

26   Little Barley, 4–20″, *cl. ¾–3″, p. 686*

27   Smooth Brome, 16–46″, *cl.* 4–12″, *p.* 683

29   Water Pennywort, 2', *w.* 1/16", *p. 342*

31 Black Snakeroot, 1–4', *p. 343*

32 Marijuana, 3–16', *w. ⅛", p. 455*

33 Alumroot, 2–3′, *l.* ¼″, *p.* 775

34 Carrion Flower, *vine, w.* ½″, *p.* 802

35 Cocklebur, 1–6′, *l.* ½–1½″, *p. 423*

36 Bur Reed, 1–3′, *cw.* 1″, *p. 808*

37 Large-flowered Trillium, 8–18″, *w.* 2–4″, *p. 616*

38 Catesby's Trillium, 8–20″, *w.* 2–3″, *p. 613*

39 Nodding Trillium, 6–24", *w.* 1½", *p. 614*

41 Horse Nettle, 1–3′, *w.* ¾–1¼″, *p. 805*

43 Starflower, 4–8″, *w.* ½″, *p.* 716

44 Bowman's Root, 2–3′, *w.* 1½″, *p.* 749

45   Bunchberry, 3–8″, *w.* 1½″, *p.* 488

46   Wood Anemone, 4–8″, *w.* 1″, *p.* 724

47   Rue Anemone, 4–8″, *w.* 1″, *p.* 741

48   Thimbleweed, *2–3′, w. 1″, p.* 725

49   False Rue Anemone, *4–16″, w. ½″, p.* 732

50   Swamp Dewberry, *creeper, w. ¾″, p.* 757

51   Common Strawberry, *creeper, w. ¾", p. 748*

52   False Violet, *creeper, w. ½", p. 745*

53   Pyxie, *creeper, w. ¼", p. 499*

54 Diapensia, 1–3″, *w.* ½″, *p.* 498

55 Grass-of-Parnassus, 6–20″, *w.* 1″, *p.* 777

57 Sea Milkwort, 2–12″, *w.* ⅛–¼″, *p.* 712

58 Goldthread, 3–6″, *w.* ½″, *p.* 730

60   Bloodroot, 10″, *w.* 1½″, *p. 674*

61   Fragrant Water Lily, *aquatic, w.* 3–5″, *p. 642*

62   Goldenseal, 12–15″, *w.* ½″, *p. 733*

63 Cheeses, *creeper, w.* ½–¾", *p. 630*

64 Oconee Bells, 2–8", *w.* 1", *p. 500*

65 White Prickly Poppy, 1–3′, *w.* 3″, *p. 672*

67 Mayapple, 1–1½′, *w.* 2″, *p. 428*

69 Teaberry, *creeper, l. ⅜", p. 508*

70 Cranberry, *creeper, l. ½", p. 519*

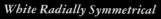

71   White Campion, 1–3', *w.* 1", *p.* 472

72   Bladder Campion, 8–30", *w.* 1", *p.* 474

73 **Starry Campion, 2–3′, w. ¾″, p. 472**

75 Jimsonweed, 1–5′, *w. 3–4″, p. 803*

77   Indian Pipe, 3–9″, *l.* ½–1″, *p.* 637

78   Sessile Bellwort, 6–12″, *l.* 1″, *p.* 618

79   Daisy Fleabane, 1–5′, *w.* ½″, *p. 387*

80   Philadelphia Fleabane, 6–36″, *w.* ½–1″, *p. 388*

381 Bushy Aster, 12–40″, *w.* ½–¾″, *p.* 370

83 Oxeye Daisy, 1–3′, *w.* 1–2″, *p. 406*

85 Small-flowered White Aster, 2–6½′, *w.* ⅜″, *p. 374*

86 Shepherd's Needle, 12–40″, *w.* 1″, *p. 379*

87 Flat-topped White Aster, 1–7′, *w.* ½–¾″, *p.* 376

88 Calico Aster, 1–5′, *w.* ½″, *p.* 371

89   White Wood Aster, 12–40″, *w.* 1″, *p. 369*

90   Panicled Aster, 2–5′, *w.* ¾–1″, *p. 374*

91   Sweet White Violet, 3–5″, *w.* ½″, *p. 817*

92   Canada Violet, 8–16″, *w.* ¾–1″, *p. 818*

93   Tartarian Honeysuckle, 4–10′, *l.* ¾″, *p. 460*

4 Japanese Honeysuckle, *vine, l. 1½″, p. 457*

5 Naked Broomrape, *3–10″, l. ¾″, p. 668*

97 Japanese Bamboo, 3–7′, *cl.* 2–3″, *p. 702*

99   Goatsbeard, 3–6′, *w.* ⅛″, *p. 745*

100   False Goatsbeard, 2–6′, *l.* ⅛″, *p. 774*

101   Culver's Root, 3–7′, *cl.* 2–6″, *p. 801*

102   Lizard Tail, 2–5′, *cl.* 6″, *p. 773*

103   Devil's Bit, 1–4′, *l.* ⅛″, *p. 600*

104 Common Plantain, 6–18″, *l.* 1/16″, *p.* 679

105 Canadian Burnet, 1–5′, *cl.* 6″, *p.* 759

107 Horseweed, 1–7′, *w.* ¼″, *p. 385*

109   Silver-rod, 1–3′, *l.* ¼″, *p. 414*

110   Meadowsweet, 2–5′, *w.* ¼″, *p. 760*

111   Fly Poison, 1–4′, *w.* ½″, *p.* 599

112   White Baneberry, 1–2′, *w.* ¼″, *p.* 721

113　**Bur Cucumber,** *vine, w.* ½–⅝", *p. 492*

115 Foam Flower, 6–12″, *w.* ¼″, *p. 780*

117   Titi, 25′, *cl.* 2½–6″, *p.* 497

119 Pokeweed, 10′, w. ¼″, p. 677

120 Maleberry, 3–12′, l. ⅛–¼″, p. 512

122   Shinleaf, 5–10″, *w.* ⅝″, *p.* 718

123   Leatherleaf, 1–4′, *l.* ¼″, *p.* 506

125   Featherfoil, *aquatic, l. ⅜", p. 712*

27   Black Cohosh, 3–8′, *w.* ½″, *p.* 727

28   Beetleweed, 1–2½′, *w.* ⅛″, *p.* 498

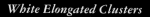

129   Northern Bedstraw, 8–36″, *w.* ¼″, *p.* 764

130   Sweet Pepperbush, 3–10′, *w.* ⅜″, *p.* 480

131 Death Camas, 1–2½′, w. ½″, p. 622

133 White Lettuce, 2–5′, l. ½″, p. 410

134 Lawn Orchid, 2–7″, l. ¼″, p. 666

136   Yucca, 2–10′, *w.* 1½″, *p. 326*

137   Ragged Fringed Orchid, 1–2′, *l.* ½″, *p. 663*

139   Nodding Ladies' Tresses, 6–24″, *l.* ½″, *p.* 665

141   Colicroot, 1–3′, *l.* ¼–½″, *p. 594*

143 White Sweet Clover, 3–8′, *cl. 8″, p. 541*

145   Slender Vervain, 2–4′, *w.* ¼″, *p. 815*

146   Lopseed, 1–3′, *cl.* 6″, *p. 814*

147   Canada Mayflower, 2–6″, *l.* ⅛″, *p. 608*

148   Arrowhead, *aquatic, w.* ⅝″, *p. 328*

149   Springcress, 6–24″, *w.* ½″, *p. 439*

150 **Thyme-leaved Speedwell**, 2–10″, *w.* ⅛″, *p. 800*

151 **Common Speedwell**, *creeper, w.* ¼″, *p. 800*

153   Boneset, 2–4', *w.* ¼", *p. 389*

55 Sweet Everlasting, 1–2′, *l.* ¼″, *p. 392*

157   Water Parsnip, 2–6′, *cw.* 2–3″, *p. 344*

158   Cow Parsnip, 4–9′, *cw.* 4–8″, *p. 341*

159   Queen Anne's Lace, 1–3½', *cw. 3–5", p. 340*

160   Water Hemlock, 3–6½', *cw. 3", p. 338*

161   Poison Hemlock, 2–10′, *cw.* 1½–2″, *p. 338*

63 Wild Raisin, 3–12', *cw. 4"*, *p. 464*

165   Red Osier, 3–10′, *cw.* 1–2″, *p.* 489

166   Elderberry, 3–12′, *cw.* 2–10″, *p.* 461

167 Hobblebush, 3–10′, *cw.* 2–6″, *p. 465*

168 Maple-leaved Viburnum, 3–10′, *cw.* 2–3″, *p. 463*

169   Wild Sarsaparilla, 8–20″, *cw.* 1½–2″, *p. 355*

171   Dwarf Ginseng, 4–8″, *w.* ¹⁄₁₆″, *p. 356*

173   Sweet Cicely, 1½–3', w. ¹⁄₁₆", p. 342

174   Bastard Toadflax, 6–16", w. ⅛", p. 769

175 White Milkweed, 1–3′, *cw.* 2½–3″, *p. 362*

177 **Pearly Everlasting**, 1–3′, *w.* ¼″, *p. 366*

178 **Plantainleaf Pussytoes**, 4–16″, *l.* ⅜″, *p. 366*

179   Common Pipewort, *aquatic, cw. ½", p. 521*

181 Turkey Beard, 2–4′, *w.* ½″, *p.* 620

182 Buttonbush, 3–10′, *cw.* 1½″, *p.* 763

183 Tawny Cotton Grass, 1½–4′, *cw.* 1″, *p.* 494

184 Prairie Mimosa, *2–4′*, *cw. ½″*, *p. 535*

185 White Clover, *creeper, cw. ¾″, p. 549*

186 Groundsel Tree, *3½–10′*, *l. ½″*, *p. 377*

187 Garlic Mustard, 1–3′, *l.* ¼″, *p.* 434

188 Watercress, *aquatic, w.* ⅛″, *p.* 442

90 Whitlow Grass, 8″, *w.* ⅛″, *p.* 440

191 Flowering Spurge, 10–36″, *cw.* 1–10″, *p.* 522

193   Enchanter's Nightshade, 1–3′, *cl.* 8″, *p. 644*

194   Wild Madder, 1–3′, *w.* ⅛″, *p. 765*

195   Cleavers, 8–36″, *w.* ⅛″, *p. 763*

196   Hoary Mountain Mint, 1–3′, *cw.* 1½″, *p. 584*

197 Water Horehound, 6–24", *l.* ¹⁄₁₆", *p.* 578

199 Peppergrass, 6–24″, *w*. ¹⁄₁₆″, *p. 441*

200 Shepherd's Purse, 6–18″, *l*. ¹⁄₁₆″, *p. 438*

201   Blue Ridge Phacelia, 8–16″, *w.* ½″, *p. 563*

202   Multiflora Rose, 6–15′, *w.* ¾–1½″, *p. 754*

203   Mountain Laurel, 3–15′, *w.* ¾–1″, *p. 510*

204   Great Laurel, 5–35′, *w.* 1½–2″, *p. 516*

205 Floating Heart, *aquatic, w.* ½–¾", *p. 635*

206 Mountain Sandwort, 2–5", *w.* ½", *p. 470*

207 Venus Flytrap, 4–12″, w. 1″, p. 500

209   Chickweed, 3–8″, *w.* ¼″, *p.* 474

210   Star Chickweed, 6–16″, *w.* ½″, *p.* 475

211 Virgin's Bower, *vine, w.* 1″, *p.* 729

212 Buckbean, *aquatic, w.* ½″, *p.* 634

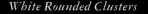

213   Tread Softly, 6–36″, *w.* 1″, *p. 522*

214   Swamp Honeysuckle, 3–9′, *l.* 1½–2″, *p. 517*

215 Swamp Lily, 3′, *w.* 4″, *p.* 331

216 Spider Lily, 1½′, *w.* 7″, *p.* 331

217   White-topped Sedge, 8–24″, *cw.* ⅝″, *p. 495*

218   Three-birds Orchid, 3–12″, *l.* ¾″, *p. 665*

219   Pennywort, 3–8″, *l.* ½″, *p.* 557

220   Early Saxifrage, 4–16″, *w.* ¼″, *p.* 780

221   Dodder, *vine, w.* ⅛″, *p. 484*

222   Early Meadow Rue, *8–30″, l.* ¼″, *p. 739*

23 Cutleaf Toothwort, 8–16", *w.* ¾", *p. 439*

225 Nodding Mandarin, 8–24″, *l.* 1″, *p. 602*

226 Bluebead Lily, 6–15″, *l.* ¾–1″, *p. 601*

227 Highbush Blueberry, 5–15′, *l.* ¼–½″, *p. 518*

228 Bearberry, *creeper, l.* ¼″, *p. 505*

229   Yaupon, 5–15′, *l.* ¼″, *p. 349*

230   Winterberry, 3–10′, *cw.* ¼–½″, *p. 348*

231   Common Snowberry, 1–4′, *l.* ¼″, *p. 462*

233   Canadian Dwarf Cinquefoil, 2–6″, *w.* ½–⅝″, *p.* 7

234   Rough-fruited Cinquefoil, 1–2′, *w.* ¾″, *p.* 752

235   Dwarf Cinquefoil, ½–2″, *w.* ⅜″, *p.* 752

236   Silverweed, *creeper, w.* ½–1″, *p.* 750

237   Indian Strawberry, *creeper, w.* ¾″, *p.* 746

238   Seedbox, 2–3′, *w.* ½″, *p.* 646

239   Barren Strawberry, 3–8″, *w.* ½″, *p.* 761

240   Frostweed, 8–18″, *w.* ¾–1½″, *p.* 479

242   Yellow Wood Sorrel, 6–15″, *w.* ½″, *p.* 671

243   Celandine, 1–2′, *w.* ⅝″, *p.* 673

244   Wood Poppy, 1–1½′, *w.* 1½–2″, *p.* 675

245   Whorled Loosestrife, 1–3′, *w.* ½″, *p. 715*

246   Garden Loosestrife, 2–3′, *w.* ¾″, *p. 714*

247 Fringed Loosestrife, 1–4′, *w.* ¾″, *p. 713*

248 Moneywort, *creeper, w.* 1″, *p. 714*

249   Swamp Buttercup, 1–3′, *w.* 1″, *p.* 738

250   Common Buttercup, 2–3′, *w.* 1″, *p.* 736

251   Marsh Marigold, 1–2′, *w.* 1–1½″, *p.* 727

52 Kidneyleaf Buttercup, 6–24″, *w.* ¼″, *p. 735*

253 Yellow Globeflower, 12–20″, *w.* 1–1½″, *p. 741*

254 Bulbous Buttercup, 1–2′, *w.* 1″, *p. 737*

255   Puncture Weed, *creeper, w. ½″, p. 824*

256   Pineweed, *4–20″, w. ⅛–¼″, p. 565*

57 Common Purslane, *creeper, w. ¼", p. 708*

259   Velvetleaf, 1–6′, *w.* 1″, *p. 627*

260   American Lotus, *aquatic, w.* 6–10″, *p. 639*

261   Yellow Water Lily, *aquatic, w. 4–5", p. 641*

263   Prickly Pear, 1′, *w.* 2–3″, *p. 446*

264   Plains Prickly Pear, 2–24″, *w.* 2–3″, *p. 447*

65   Sessile Bellwort, 6–12″, *l.* 1″, *p. 618*

266   Trout Lily, 4–10″, *w.* 1″, *p. 603*

267   Yellow Jessamine, *vine, l.* 1½″, *p. 624*

268   Trumpets, 1½–3½′, *w.* 3–5″, *p. 770*

69 Hooded Pitcher Plant, 6–24″, *w. 2″, p.* 772

271 Prairie Coneflower, 1½–5′, *w.* 1½–3½″, *p. 411*

272 Black-eyed Susan, 1–3′, *w.* 2–3″, *p. 412*

273 Oxeye Sunflower, 2–5′, *w.* 1½–3″, *p. 398*

274   Jerusalem Artichoke, 5–10′, *w. 3″, p. 398*

275   Woodland Sunflower, 3–7′, *w. 2½–3½″, p. 397*

276   Giant Sunflower, 3–12′, *w. 1½–3″, p. 396*

277   Common Sunflower, 3–10', w. 3–6", p. 394

278   Maximilian's Sunflower, 3–10', w. 2–3", p. 396

279   Hairy Golden Aster, 1–2′, *w.* 1″, *p.* 399

280   Camphorweed, 1–3′, *w.* ½–¾″, *p.* 399

281   Nodding Bur Marigold, 1–3′, *w.* 2″, *p. 378*

282   Tickseed Sunflower, 1–5′, *w.* 1–2″, *p. 378*

283   Golden Star, 3–15″, *w.* 1–1½″, *p. 382*

284   Golden Ragwort, 1–2′, *w.* ¾″, *p. 412*

285   Compass Plant, 3–12′, w. 3″, p. 413

286   Lance-leaved Coreopsis, 1–2′, w. 2–2½″, p. 386

287 Garden Coreopsis, 2–4', w. 1¼", p. 386

288 Sneezeweed, 2–5', w. 1–2", p. 394

289   Yellow Goatsbeard, 1–3′, *w.* 1–2½″, *p.* 420

290   Elecampane, 2–6′, *w.* 2–4″, *p.* 403

291 Curlycup Gumweed, 6–36″, *w*. 1″, *p*. 393

292 Yellow Hawkweed, 1–3′, *w*. ½″, *p*. 401

293   Coltsfoot, 3–18″, *w.* 1″, *p. 421*

294   Two-flowered Cynthia, 1–2′, *w.* 1½″, *p. 403*

295 Common Dandelion, 2–18″, *w.* 1½″, *p. 419*

296 Mouse-ear Hawkweed, 3–12′, *w.* 1″, *p. 401*

297   **Spiny-leaved Sow Thistle**, 1–6′, *w.* 1″, *p. 418*

299 Prickly Lettuce, 2–5′, *w.* ¼″, *p. 405*

300 Wild Lettuce, 2–10′, *w.* ¼″, *p. 404*

301 Downy Yellow Violet, 6–16″, *w.* ¾″, *p. 821*

302 Lesser Celandine, 5–10″, *w.* 1–1½″, *p. 738*

303 Yellow Butterwort, 5–18″, *w.* ¾–1½″, *p. 591*

04 Muskflower, 8–16″, *l.* ¾″, *p. 790*

05 Pale Touch-me-not, 3–6′, *l.* 1½″, *p. 425*

306 Large Yellow Lady's Slipper, 8–28″, *l.* 2″, *p. 655*

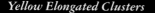

307 Smooth False Foxglove, 1–5′, *w.* ¾″, *p. 783*

308 Downy False Foxglove, 1–5′, *w.* 1″, *p. 784*

309   Common Mullein, 2–7′, *w.* ¾–1″, *p.* 798

310   Moth Mullein, 2–4′, *w.* 1″, *p.* 797

Yellow Elongated Clusters

311 Yellow Rattlebox, 4–31″, *l.* ½″, *p.* 795

312 Butter-and-eggs, 1–3′, *l.* 1″, *p.* 788

313 Showy Rattlebox, 2–3′, *l.* 1″, *p.* 533

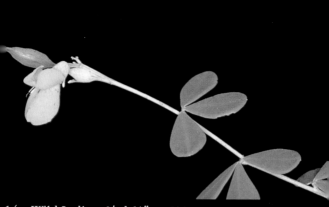

14   Wild Indigo, 3′, *l.* ½″, *p. 530*

15   Bush Pea, 1–4½′, *l.* ½″, *p. 546*

16   Yellow Fringed Orchid, 1–2½′, *l.* ¾″, *p. 661*

317   Swamp Candles, 1–3′, *w.* ½″, *p.* 716

318   Horse Balm, 2–4′, *l.* ⅜–½″, *p.* 576

319   Agrimony, 1–6′, *w.* ¼″, *p.* 744

320 Swamp Saxifrage, 1–3′, *w.* ⅛″, *p.* 779

321 Seaside Goldenrod, 1–8′, *l.* ⅜″, *p.* 417

322 Blue-stemmed Goldenrod, 1–3′, *l.* ¼″, *p.* 415

323   Rough-stemmed Goldenrod, 1–6′, *l*. ⅛″, *p*. 416

324   Sweet Goldenrod, 2–3′, *l*. ⅛″, *p*. 415

325   Tall Goldenrod, 2–7′, *l*. ⅛″, *p*. 414

326 Stiff Goldenrod, 1–5′, *l.* ³⁄₈″, *p. 416*

327 Showy Goldenrod, 2–7′, *l.* ¼″, *p. 417*

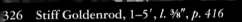

328 Yellow Sweet Clover, 2–5′, *cl.* 6″, *p. 542*

329   Squawroot, 3–10″, *l.* ½″, *p. 667*

330   Pussy Willow, 2–20′, *cl.* 2–2½″, *p. 768*

331   Water Arum, 6–12″, *cl.* 1″, *p. 351*

32 Golden Club, *aquatic, cl. 1–2", p. 352*

333 Green Dragon, *1–3', cl. 4–8", p. 350*

335   Common St. John's Wort, 1–2½′, *w.* ¾–1″, *p. 567*

336   Kalm's St. John's Wort, 2–3′, *w.* ¾–1½″, *p. 566*

338 Evening Primrose, 2–5′, *w.* 1–2″, *p.* 647

339 Yellow Star Grass, 3–6″, *w.* ¾″, *p.* 332

340 Birdsfoot Trefoil, 6–24″, *l.* ½″, *p.* 539

341   Swollen Bladderwort, *aquatic, w.* ⅝″, *p. 593*

342   Horned Bladderwort, 2–12″, *l.* ¾″, *p. 592*

43 Bluebead Lily, 6–15", *l.* ¾–1", *p. 601*

345 Common Barberry, 3–10′, *w.* ¼″, *p.* 426

47 Ditch Stonecrop, 8–24″, *w.* ⅛″, *p.* 778

48 Golden Alexanders, 1–3′, *cw.* 2″, *p.* 345

349   Lance-leaved Goldenrod, 2–4′, *l.* ¼″, *p. 390*

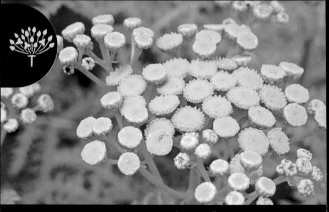

350   Common Tansy, 2–3′, *w.* ½″, *p. 418*

351   Cypress Spurge, 6–12″, *cw.* ¾–4″, *p. 524*

52 Broom Snakeweed, 6–20″, *w.* ¼″, *p. 393*

353 Yellow Thistle, 1–5′, *w.* 2½″, *p. 383*

354 Witch Hazel, 10–15′, *l.* ¾″, *p. 561*

355 Southern Bush Honeysuckle, 4–5′, *l.* ¾″, *p.* 456

356 Hop Clover, 6–18″, *cw.* ½–1″, *p.* 547

357 Wild Senna, 3–6′, *w.* ¾″, *p.* 545

358 Common Wintercress, 1–2′, *w.* ⅜″, *p. 436*

359 Black Mustard, 2–3′, *w.* ½″, *p. 437*

360 Hoary Puccoon, 6–18″, *w.* ⅓″, *p. 431*

361 Canada Lily, 2–5′, w. 2–3″, p. 606

362 Wood Lily, 1–3′, w. 2″, p. 606

63   Turk's-cap Lily, 3–7′, *l.* 2½″, *p. 607*

364   Orange Hawkweed, 1–2′, *w.* ¾″, *p. 400*

365 Spotted Touch-me-not, 2–5′, *l.* 1″, *p.* 424

366 Little Bluestem, 1½–4½′, *cl.* 2½″, *p.* 689

367   Butterfly Weed, 1–2½′, *cw. 2″, p. 361*

369   Flame Azalea, 15′, *w.* 1½–2″, *p. 513*

71　Orange Milkwort, 6–12″, *cw.* ¾″, *p.* 697

373 Wild Ginger, 6–12", *w.* 1½", *p. 358*

374 Red Iris, 2–5', *w.* 3", *p. 570*

76 Dutchman's Pipe, *vine, l. 2″, p. 357*

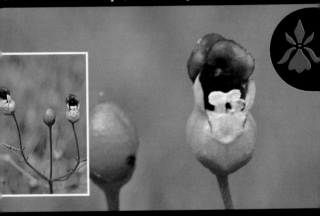

377 Maryland Figwort, *3–8′, l. ¼″, p. 796*

379   Striped Coral Root, 8–20″, *l.* 1¼″, *p. 653*

381   Jack-in-the-pulpit, 1–3′, *cl.* 2–3″, *p. 350*

382   Common Cattail, 3–9′, *cl.* 6″, *p. 809*

383   Wool Grass, 3–5′, *cl.* ¼″, *p. 495*

384   Sea Oats, 3–7′, *cl.* 8–16″, *p. 691*

385   Grama Grass, 6–20″, *cl.* 2″, *p. 682*

86 Giant Reed, 5–15′, *cl.* 1′, *p. 688*

87 Sweet Vernal Grass, 12–28″, *cl.* 3″, *p. 682*

88 Indian Grass, 3–8′, *cl.* 10″, *p. 690*

Brown Elongated Clusters

389 Barnyard Grass, 6–48″, *cl.* 4–12″, *p. 685*

390 Tussock Sedge, 2–3′, *p. 493*

391 Skunk Cabbage, 1–2′, *cl.* 1″, *p.* 354

392 Tawny Cotton Grass, 1¼–4′, *cl.* 1″, *p.* 494

393   Leafy Three-square, 1–5′, *cl.* 1½″, *p. 496*

394   Shining Cyperus, 4–16″, *cl.* ½″, *p. 493*

95 Soft Rush, 1½–4′, *l.* ¼″, *p.* 573

96 Wood Rush, 6–16″, *l.* ¾″, *p.* 574

397   Fire Pink, 6–24″, *w.* 1½″, *p.* 473

398   Hibiscus, 3–10′, *w.* 6–8″, *p.* 627

399   Scarlet Pimpernel, 4–12″, *w.* ¼″, *p.* 710

00 Maltese Cross, 2–3′, *w.* 1″, *p. 469*

01 Indian Blanket, 8–16″, *w.* 1–3″, *p. 391*

402 Carolina Mallow, *creeper, w.* ½″, *p. 630*

403   Small Red Morning Glory, *vine, w.* ¾", *p.* 485

404   Wild Columbine, 1–2', *l.* 1–2", *p.* 725

05 Purple Trillium, 8–16″, *w.* 2½″, *p.* 615

06 Wild Poinsettia, 2–3′, *cw.* 1½″, *p.* 523

407   Northern Pitcher Plant, 8–24″, *w. 2″, p. 772*

408   Crimson Pitcher Plant, 2–3′, *w. 2–3″, p. 771*

09 Slender Glasswort, 6–18", *cw.* ⅛", *p.* 478

411   Curly Dock, 2–4', *l.* ⅛", *p.* 704

13 Cardinal Flower, 2–4', *l.* 1½", *p. 451*

415   Common Mugwort, 2–4′, *l.* ⅛–¼″, *p. 368*

417   Scarlet Gilia, 2–6′, *l.* 1″, *p. 692*

418   Trumpet Honeysuckle, *vine, l.* 1–2″, *p. 459*

419   Bee Balm, 2–5′, *l.* 1½″, *p.* 581

420   Indian Paintbrush, 1–2′, *l.* 1″, *p.* 785

21   Indian Pink, 1–2′, *w.* 1″, *p. 624*

22   Trumpet Creeper, 20′, *l.* 2½″, *p. 430*

423　Pinesap, 4–16″, *l.* ½″, *p. 636*

424　Wild Coffee, 2–4′, *l.* ¾″, *p. 462*

25   Wood Betony, 6–18″, *l.* ¾″, *p. 792*

427　Winterberry, 3–10′, *cw.* ¼–½″, *p. 348*

428　Yaupon, 5–15′, *l.* ¼″, *p. 349*

30 Red Chokeberry, *3–12', w. ½", p. 753*

431 Climbing Bittersweet, *vine, cl. 4", p. 476*

433 **Amur Honeysuckle,** 3–30′, *l.* ½–1″, *p. 458*

434 **Redberry Elder,** 2–10′, *w.* ¼″, *p. 461*

36 Indian Strawberry, *creeper, w. ¾", p. 746*

37 Rosary Pea, *vine, l. ⅝", p. 526*

439 Musk Mallow, 8–24″, *w.* 1½″, *p.* 629

441   Seashore Mallow, 1–3′, *w.* 1½–2½″, *p. 629*

442   Wild Geranium, 1–2′, *w.* 1–1½″, *p. 559*

443 Showy Evening Primrose, 8–24″, *w.* 2½–3″, *p.* 6∢

444 Saltmarsh Pink, 6–18″, *w.* ¾–1½″, *p.* 557

45 **Spring Beauty,** 6–12″, *w.* ½–¾″, *p.* 707

447   Deptford Pink, 6–24", *w. ½", p. 468*

49 Common Corn Cockle, 1–3′, *w. 2″, p. 466*

451   Rose Moss, 2–8″, *w.* ⅝″, *p.* 709

53 Virginia Meadow Beauty, 1–2′, w. 1–1½″, p. 631

54 Stork's Bill, 6–12″, w. ½″, p. 558

455   Rugosa Rose, 4–6′, *w.* 2–3″, *p.* 755

456   Virginia Rose, 1–6′, *w.* 2–3″, *p.* 756

57 Prairie Rose, 2', *w.* 2", *p.* 754

459   Common Morning Glory, *vine, l. 2–3", p. 486*

61   Hedge Bindweed, *vine, l. 2–3″, p. 483*

463   Twinflower, *creeper, l. ½", p. 456*

465 Mountain Cranberry, *creeper, l. ¼″, p. 520*

466 Dwarf Clematis, 1–2′, *l. 1–2″, p. 728*

467 Showy Lady's Slipper, 1–3′, *l.* 1–2″, *p. 656*

468 Calypso, 3–8″, *l.* 1½–2″, *p. 651*

469 Pink Lady's Slipper, 6–15″, *l.* 2½″, *p. 653*

470 Rose Pogonia, 3–24", *l.* 1¾", *p.* 664

471 Rosebud Orchid, 1–2', *l.* 2", *p.* 652

473   Fireweed, 2–6′, *w. 1″, p. 643*

474   Thread-leaved Sundew, 4–12″, *w. ½″, p. 504*

476　Grass Pink, 6–20″, *l.* 1½″, *p.* 650

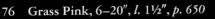

477　Showy Orchis, 5–12″, *l.* 1″, *p.* 657

479 Goat's Rue, 1–2′, *cl.* 3″, *p. 546*

480 Slender Bush Clover, 1–3′, *l.* ¼″, *p. 539*

82　Purple Locoweed, 8–12″, *l.* ¾″, *p. 543*

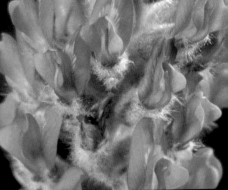

83　Showy Locoweed, 4–12″, *cl.* 1½–7″, *p. 543*

485   Illinois Tick Trefoil, 2–5′, *l.* ½″, *p. 536*

486   Obedient Plant, 1–4′, *cl.* 4–8″, *p. 583*

88 Swamp Pink, 1–3′, *cl.* 1–3″, *p. 604*

89 Large Blazing Star, 1–5′, *w.* 1″, *p. 408*

491 Pennsylvania Smartweed, 1–4′, *cl.* ½–2½″, *p.* 76

93 Lady's Thumb, 8–31″, *cl. ½–2″, p.* 703

94 Swamp Smartweed, *aquatic* or 2–3′, *cl.* 1½–7″, *p.* 700

495 Violet Wood Sorrel, 4–8″, *w.* ¾″, *p. 671*

496 Dame's Rocket, 1–4′, *l.* ¾″, *p. 441*

97 Annual Phlox, 8–18″, *w.* 1″, *p.* 693

499 Rose Vervain, 6–18″, *w.* ½–¾″, *p.* 814

301 Marsh St. John's Wort, 8–24″, *w.* ½–¾″, *p. 568*

503   Wild Garlic, 8–24″, *w.* ½″, *p.* 595

05   Nodding Onion, 8–24″, *l*. ¼″, *p. 596*

507   *Wild Mint, 6–24″, w. ⅛″, p. 579*

509   Swamp Milkweed, 1–4′, *w.* ¼″, *p. 360*

510   Common Milkweed, 2–6′, *cw.* 2″, *p. 360*

511   Alpine Azalea, *creeper, w. ¼", p. 512*

512   Sheep Laurel, 1–3′, *w. ⅜–½", p. 509*

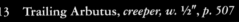
13 Trailing Arbutus, *creeper, w. ½″, p. 507*

515 Lapland Rosebay, 4–12″, *w.* ⅝″, *p. 515*

17 Rhodora, 1–3′, *l.* ½–¾″, *p. 514*

519   Southern Gaura, 2–5′, *w.* ¼″, *p. 646*

520   Hog Peanut, *vine, l.* ½″, *p. 528*

22 Virginia Bluebells, 8–24", *l.* 1", *p. 432*

23 Wild Bleeding Heart, 10–18", *l.* ¾", *p. 553*

525   Creeping Bush Clover, *creeper, l. ¼", p. 538*

526   Beach Pea, *vine, l. ¾", p. 538*

28 Wild Bergamot, 2–4′, *l.* 1″, *p.* 582

29 Swamp Loosestrife, 8′, *l.* ½″, *p.* 625

531 Crown Vetch, 1–2′, *cw. 1″, p. 532*

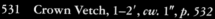

532 Red Clover, 6–24″, *cw. ½–1″, p. 548*

34 Peppermint, 1–3′, *cw.* ½–¾″, *p. 580*

35 Rabbit-foot Clover, 6–18″, *cl.* ¾″, *p. 547*

537   **Climbing Boneset,** 13′, *w. ¼″, p. 409*

538   **Saltmarsh Fleabane,** 1–5′, *w. ¼″, p. 409*

40 Canadian Thistle, 1–5′, *w. 1″, p. 383*

41 Musk Thistle, 2–9′, *w. 1½–2½″, p. 380*

543   Ivy-leaved Morning Glory, *vine, w.* 1½", *p.* 485

544   Purple Saxifrage, ¾–4", *w.* ½", *p.* 778

46 Periwinkle, 6–8″, *w.* 1″, *p. 347*

47 Purple-flowering Raspberry, 3–6′, *w.* 1–2″, *p. 758*

549   American Sea Rocket, 6–20″, *w.* ¼″, *p. 438*

551 Purple Passionflower, *vine, w.* 1½–2½", *p.* 676

553   Boltonia, 1–5′, *w.* ¾–1¼″, *p.* 379

55 Purple Coneflower, 1–5′, *w.* 2½–4″, *p. 387*

557 New England Aster, 3–7′, *w.* 1–2″, *p.* 372

559 Showy Aster, 1–3′, *w.* 1½″, *p.* 375

561 Birdsfoot Violet, 4–10″, *w.* 1½″, *p.* 820

563   Common Blue Violet, 3–8″, *w.* ½–¾″, *p. 821*

564   Fringed Polygala, 3–7″, *l.* ¾″, *p. 697*

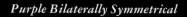

565   Common Butterwort, 2–6″, *w.* ⅜″, *p.* 591

566   Monkeyflower, 1–3′, *l.* 1″, *p.* 790

569　Purple Loosestrife, 2–4′, *w.* ½–¾″, *p. 626*

1 Indigobush, 5–17′, *l.* ¼–⅜″, *p.* 527

573 Purple Prairie Clover, 1–3′, *cl. 2″*, *p. 534*

574 Cow Vetch, *vine, l. ½″*, *p. 549*

'6   Hairy Beardtongue, 1–3', *l.* 1", *p.* 794

77   Large-flowered Beardtongue, 2–4', *l.* 2", *p.* 794

579 Eyebright, 4–15″, *l.* ⅜–½″, *p.* 787

580 Blue Toadflax, 6–24″, *l.* ¼–½″, *p.* 791

82 Spiked Lobelia, 1–4′, *l.* ³⁄₈–½″, *p.* 453

83 Spring Larkspur, 4–24″, *w.* ¾″, *p.* 731

84 Indian Tobacco, 1–3′, *l.* ¼″, *p.* 451

585 Common Speedwell, *creeper, w. ¼″, p. 800*

586 Large Purple Fringed Orchid, 2–4′, l. 1″, p. 663

87 Wild Hyacinth, 6–24″, *w. 1″, p. 600*

589 Prairie Blazing Star, 2–5′, *w.* ½″, *p.* 407

591 **Blue Vervain,** 2–6′, *w.* ⅛″, *p. 816*

592 **Kentucky Bluegrass,** 1–3′, *cl.* 6″, *p. 689*

593   Monkshood, 2–4′, *l.* ¾″, *p.* 720

594   Hyssop Skullcap, 1–2½′, *l.* 1″, *p.* 587

595   Motherwort, 2–4′, *w.* ³⁄₈″, *p.* 578

597 Ground Ivy, *creeper, l. ½–¾", p. 576*

599 Greek Valerian, 1–1½′, *w.* ½″, *p.* 695

601 Seaside Gentian, 1–3′, *w.* 1½″, *p.* 554

603 Water Willow, *aquatic, l. ½", p. 323*

605 Virginia Waterleaf, 1–2½′, *l.* ¼–½″, *p.* 562

7   Tall Ironweed, 3–7′, *w.* ¼″, *p. 422*

609 Fringed Gentian, 1–3′, *l.* 2″, *p. 556*

610 Venus's Looking Glass, 6–18″, *w.* ¾″, *p. 453*

2 Crested Dwarf Iris, 4–9″, *w.* 2½″, *p.* 569

13 Blue-eyed Grass, 4–20″, *w.* ½″, *p.* 572

615 Bluets, 3–6″, *w.* ½″, *p.* 765

17   **Blue Dogbane**, 1–3′, *w.* ½–¾″, *p.* 346

619 Scarlet Pimpernel, 4–12", *w.* ¼", *p. 710*

623   Stiff Aster, 4–24″, *w.* 1″, *p.* 372

25   Common Blue Violet, 3–8″, *w.* ½–¾″, *p. 821*

627   Tall Bellflower, 2–6′, *cl.* 1–2′, *p. 450*

29   Corn Speedwell, 2–16″, *w.* ¼″, *p.* 799

631   Blue Salvia, 2–5′, *l.* ½–1″, *p.* 585

633 Water Hyacinth, *aquatic, l. 2″, p. 705*

634 Wild Lupine, 8–24″, *l. ⅝″, p. 540*

635   True Forget-me-not, 6–24″, *w.* ¼″, *p. 433*

636   Closed Gentian, 1–2′, *l.* 1–1½″, *p. 555*

37 Blue-eyed Mary, 6–18″, *l.* ½″, *p.* 787

PART II
FAMILY AND SPECIES DESCRIPTIONS

ACANTHUS FAMILY
Acanthaceae

Herbs or shrubs with showy flowers often held in large, often showy bracts.

Flowers: Usually bilaterally symmetrical. Sepals 4–5; petals 4–5, united, usually forming 2-lobed upper lip and 3-lobed lower lip; stamens 2 or 4; all these parts attached at base of ovary.
Leaves: Opposite, simple, often with pale streaks or bumps, sometimes with smooth edges.
Fruit: 2-celled capsule, with seeds borne on characteristic small, hooked stalks.

There are about 230 genera and 2,500 species, native to temperate and tropical regions. Many are cultivated as ornamentals. Several plants are used medicinally, particularly in the Old World. In the West, most species are restricted to the warmer parts of the southwestern United States.

---

603 Water Willow
Justicia americana

Description:	An aquatic with *bicolored flowers* in dense, head-like or spike-like clusters on long slender stalks rising from leaf axils.
Flowers:	To ½″ (1.5 cm) long; calyx shorter than corolla; lower corolla lip 3-lobed, white, spotted with purple; upper corolla lip pale violet or white, arching over lower lip; *stamens 2, with purplish-red anthers.*
Leaves:	3–6″ (7.5–15 cm) long, narrow, opposite, *willow-like.*
Fruit:	Brown capsule.
Height:	Aquatic; 1–3′ (30–90 cm) above water.
Flowering:	June–October.
Habitat:	Wet shorelines and shallow water.
Range:	Ontario and Quebec; New York south to Florida, west to Texas, and north to Kansas, Iowa, Wisconsin, and Michigan.
Comments:	This colony-forming plant has underground stems. Loose-flowered Water Willow (*J. ovata*), a similar species found from Virginia south to Florida and Alabama, has more loosely flowered spikes.

545 Wild Petunia; Stalked Ruellia
Ruellia pedunculata

Description: Violet, *trumpet-shaped flowers* on short hairy stems from leaf axils.

Flowers: To 2″ (5 cm) long; *calyx with 5 long, thread-like lobes* to ¹⁄₁₆″ (1 mm) wide, pa of *leaf-like bracts* below each flower.

Leaves: To 2″ (5 cm) long, opposite, elliptical, short-stalked, downy.

Height: 1–2′ (30–60 cm).

Flowering: June–September.

Habitat: Rich woods, especially limestone sites.

Range: South Carolina south to Florida and we to Texas; also in Illinois and Missouri.

Comments: Among the seven other members of thi genus occuring in the East, this one is recognized by the long-pointed calyx lobes and bracts under the flower. The flowers of *Ruellia* recall garden petunias *(Petunia)* of the nightshade family (Solanaceae).

SWEETFLAG FAMILY
Acoraceae

Erect, aromatic, wetland plants with leaves borne edge t edge in a fan-like arrangement and inconspicuous flowers i a dense, finger-like cluster jutting from side of a 3-angle leaf-like stalk.

Flowers: Bisexual. Sepals 6; petals absent; stamens 6; a these parts attached at base of ovary.
Leaves: Basal, sword-like, each with an off-center midvein.
Fruit: Berry, becoming hard and dry.

There is only 1 genus with 1 or 2 species, found in th northern temperate regions of North America and Eurasi Members of Acoraceae are sometimes placed in the arur family (Araceae).

---

334 Sweetflag; Calamus
Acorus calamus

Description: Growing in water or wet soil, with iris-like leaves and an outward-jutting, finger-like cluster of greenish to yellowish or brownish flowers.

Sweetflag

Flowers: About ⅛″ (3 mm) long; densely grouped in diamond-shaped patterns in a cylindrical cluster 2–3½″ (5–9 cm) long.

Leaves: 1–4′ (30–120 cm) long, stiff, light green, sword-like, parallel-veined, each with an off-center midvein.

Fruit: Small, gelatinous berry, becoming dry.

Height: 1–4′ (30–120 cm).

Flowering: May–August.

Habitat: Swamps, marshes, meadows, riverbanks, and small streams.

Range: Throughout East, except Florida and Arctic; also in West.

Comments: According to some authorities, there are two species called Sweetflag in North America. One is native; the other was introduced from Eurasia. They are difficult to tell apart. The range given above is for the entire genus in North America. The thick rhizome of this plant, covered with the bases of old leaves, has a distinctive odor and flavor. The candied rhizome, called calamus, is an old-fashioned confection with a unique taste. This species is sometimes grown in wetland gardens.

AGAVE FAMILY
Agavaceae

Stout plants, with woody stems or stem-bases, often ta
or even tree-like, with stout, rapidly growing flower stal
rising from crowded rosettes of long narrow leaves at ste
or branch ends.

Flowers: Usually radially symmetrical. Sepals and petals
each, colored alike, often thick and fleshy, separate
united to form a tube at base; stamens 6; all these par
attached at top of ovary in some genera, at base of ova
in others.
Leaves: Strongly thickened, leathery, or firm-succule
(rarely soft-succulent), parallel-veined, usually ve
fibrous, often prickly or with stout teeth on edges, ofte
with a sturdy, terminal spine.
Fruit: Usually a capsule, sometimes a firm berry.

There are about 20 genera and 700 species, found in tro
ical or warm regions, often where it is arid. Some supp
valuable fiber, such as sisal hemp from Sisal *(Agave sisalana*
Despite their common name, century plants *(Agave)* do n
take 100 years to flower, but it may take several decades t
store enough food reserves to supply the rapidly growir
flower stalk and mature the seeds, after which time th
rosette dies. The liquors pulque, mescal, sotol, and tequi
are made from fermented extracts of the large fleshy bases
Agave species in Mexico. Members of Agavaceae are some
times included in the complex lily family (Liliaceae).

136 Yucca; Adam's Needle
Yucca filamentosa

Description: A tall stout stem rising from a rosette o
rigid, sword-like leaves and bearing a loos
cluster of *white, nodding, bell-shaped
flowers well above foliage.*
Flowers: 1½" (4 cm) wide; sepals 3, petal-like;
petals 3; stamens 6.
Leaves: To 2½' (75 cm) long, 2½" (6.5 cm)
wide, spoon-shaped, tapering, *with loose
threads along edges.*
Fruit: Many-seeded capsule.
Height: 2–10' (60–300 cm).
Flowering: June–September.
Habitat: Sandy beaches, dunes, and old fields.
Range: Ontario; New York and Connecticut
south to Florida, west to Texas, and

north to Nebraska, Missouri, Illinois, and Wisconsin.

Comments: Although yuccas are more typical of western deserts and grasslands, some are native in the East. This species escapes from cultivation in the northern part of its range. Soapweed (*Y. glauca*) is a typical species of the western Plains, found east to Iowa, Missouri, and Arkansas; its rigid, bayonet-like leaves have hairy edges, and the flowering stalk, reaching a height of 4′ (1.2 m), bears a flower cluster, the base of which is reached by the leaf tips. Spanish Bayonet (*Y. aloifolia*), found from North Carolina south to Florida and Alabama, has toothed leaves with hairless edges. Yucca fruit can be cooked and eaten after the seeds are removed; the large petals are used in salads. Yuccas depend on the Yucca Moth as their agent of pollination, and these moths depend on yuccas for food. At flowering time the female moth gathers a mass of pollen from the anthers of the yucca and then flies to another yucca flower, where she deposits a number of eggs into the ovary among the ovules (immature seeds). Next, she places the pollen mass on the stigma of the flower, thus ensuring pollination and subsequent development of the ovules into seeds. As the seeds enlarge, they become the food source for the moth larvae. Many of the seeds remain uninjured and are eventually dispersed, potentially producing new plants. At maturity, the larvae leave the seed capsule, drop to the ground, and pupate. The adult moth emerges next season as the yuccas begin to flower.

WATER PLANTAIN FAMILY
Alismataceae

Aquatic or marsh herbs with long-stalked, simple, basal leaves and a leafless stalk bearing whorls of small flowers in a raceme or an often much-branched panicle.

Flowers: Radially symmetrical. Sepals 3, green; petals 3, de͏ cate, white or pinkish; stamens 6 to many; all these pa͏ attached at base of 6 to many separate pistils.
Leaves: Prominently veined, with bases sheathing stem.
Fruit: Hard, 1-seeded; in clusters.

There are about 12 genera and 75 species, widely distri͏ uted in shallow freshwater, brackish, or muddy habitats warm and temperate climates. Many provide food f͏ wildlife.

---

108 Water Plantain
Alisma subcordatum

Description: A tall, *spindly, many-branched aquatic*
with small white (rarely pink) *flowers in͏ whorls.*

Flowers: ⅛" (4 mm) wide; sepals 3, green;
petals 3.

Leaves: Basal, long-stalked, blades 2–10"
(5–25 cm) long, olive green, distinctly
veined, elliptical.

Height: Aquatic; 4–36" (10–90 cm) above wate͏

Flowering: June–October.

Habitat: Shallow, freshwater marshes, sluggish
streams, ponds, and lakes.

Range: Manitoba east to New Brunswick, sout͏
to Georgia, west to Texas, and north to
North Dakota; also in parts of West.

Comments: In this typical emergent aquatic, the
lower part is often submerged, while th͏
upper part is exposed. Leaves formed
underwater are ribbon-like and soon rot
they are seldom seen on adult plants.
The bulb-like base of several species of
Alisma was dried and eaten by Native
Americans.

---

148 Arrowhead; Wapato
Sagittaria latifolia

Description: An aquatic with a tall stalk rising from
large basal leaves and bearing white
flowers in whorls of 3.

Flowers: ⅝" (16 mm) wide; petals 3, white; sepal
3; stamens 7–10.

Leaves: Long-stalked, blades 2–16" (5–40 cm)

long, arrowhead-shaped, varying from broad to narrow, unlobed to lobed with 2 long, backward-projecting lobes.

Height: Aquatic; 1–4' (30–120 cm) above water.

Flowering: July–September.

Habitat: Wet sites or shallow water along lake and stream edges, marshes, and swamps.

Range: Throughout East, except far north; also in much of West.

Comments: This aquatic is closely related to Water Plantain *(Alisma subcordatum)*. Several similar species with arrowhead-shaped leaves are distinguished from one another by technical features. Beneath the muck, rhizomes produce edible, starchy tubers, utilized by ducks and muskrats and known as "duck potatoes." Native Americans are said to have opened muskrat houses to get at their cache of tubers.

AMARANTH FAMILY
Amaranthaceae

Mostly herbs with inconspicuous flowers, usually in spike-like or head-like clusters, often with brightly colored bracts.

Flowers: Unisexual or bisexual, radially symmetrical. Calyx with 2–5 scale-like sepals, often brightly colored; petals absent; stamens 5 or fewer; all these parts attached at base of ovary.

Leaves: Alternate or opposite, simple.

Fruit: Small, seed-like.

There are about 65 genera and 900 species, most abundant in warm regions. Some with conspicuous colored bracts, such as cockscombs *(Celosia)*, are cultivated; others may be considered troublesome, allergy-causing weeds. Certain species of *Amaranthus* are grown for their edible, seed-like fruits.

22 Pigweed; Green Amaranth
Amaranthus retroflexus

Description: A rough hairy stem with clusters of tiny, greenish flowers.

Flowers: In terminal panicles to 2½" (6.5 cm)

long and in clusters in leaf axils; flower intermingled with elongated, bristle-like bracts.

Leaves: 3–6" (7.5–15 cm) long, oval to lanceolate, stalked, untoothed.

Height: 2–4' (60–120 cm).

Flowering: August–October.

Habitat: Waste places, roadsides, and cultivated soil.

Range: Throughout much of North America, except Arctic.

Comments: Native to tropical America, this plant grows prolifically over a broad range of habitats.

23 Thorny Pigweed
Amaranthus spinosus

Description: Tiny, yellow-green flowers on a stout, much-branched, sometimes reddish stem.

Flowers: Male flowers mostly in slender, terminal spikes to 6" (15 cm) long; female flower mostly in dense, round clusters; flowers *intermingled with bristly bracts* as long as sepals.

Leaves: 1–3" (2.5–7.5 cm) long, ovate to lanceolate; *pair of rigid spines* in each leaf axil.

Height: 1–4' (30–120 cm).

Flowering: July–October.

Habitat: Waste places, disturbed ground, and cultivated soil.

Range: Manitoba and Ontario; Maine south to Florida, west to Texas, and north to Minnesota.

Comments: *Amaranthus* species, though regarded as common weeds, produce tremendous numbers of seed-like fruit, which are an important food for many songbirds.

AMARYLLIS FAMILY
Amaryllidaceae

Herbs, or rarely woody plants, growing from underground stems or bulbs, with narrow, basal leaves and a long leafless flower stalk.

owers: Radially symmetrical. Sepals and petals 3 each, colored alike, united below into a tube, sometimes with additional parts in center forming a crown; stamens 6; all these parts attached at top of ovary.

eaves: Grass-like or strap-shaped, sometimes with few teeth.

ruit: Capsule or berry.

There are about 65 genera and 900 species, mostly native to tropical and warm regions. Daffodils and jonquils (both of which are groups in the genus *Narcissus*) as well as species of *Amaryllis* are highly prized ornamentals. Members of Amaryllidaceae are sometimes included in the complex lily family (Liliaceae).

---

215 Swamp Lily
Crinum americanum

Description:	A small cluster of fragrant, *stringy, white flowers* on a leafless stalk rising from basal leaves.
Flowers:	4″ (10 cm) wide; petal-like parts 6, narrow, attached to a long green tube; stamens 6, with *reddish-purple filaments.*
Leaves:	To 4′ (1.2 m) long, 1–3″ (2.5–7.5 cm) wide, strap-like.
Height:	To 3′ (90 cm).
Flowering:	Periodically throughout year, chiefly spring–fall.
Habitat:	Marshes and streambanks.
Range:	Along coastal plain from South Carolina south to Florida and west to Texas.
Comments:	Despite its common name, this beautiful flower is not a true lily. Its flower parts are attached above the ovary rather than below as in lilies.

---

216 Spider Lily
Hymenocallis liriosme

Description:	Few *spidery, white flowers on a 2-edged stalk* rising from basal leaves.
Flowers:	To 7″ (17.5 cm) wide; petal-like parts 6, radiating, attached to a long slender tube; stamens 6, projecting from a cup or crown of white gauzy tissue inside tube.

Leaves:	To ¾" (2 cm) wide, at least 1' (30 cm) long, strap-like, deeply grooved.
Height:	1½' (45 cm).
Flowering:	March–May.
Habitat:	Marshes and ditches.
Range:	Alabama west to Texas and Oklahoma.
Comments:	The crown (the "hymen" or membrane from which the stamens arise) of this showy plant is distinctive, as is the spidery appearance of the long, narrow, petal-like parts. The species name means "fragrant lily." There are several species of *Hymenocallis* in the southeastern United States.

339 Yellow Star Grass
Hypoxis hirsuta

Description:	A small, grass-like plant with *star-shaped, yellow flowers* (often in 3s) at tip of a hairy stem.
Flowers:	¾" (2 cm) wide, 6-pointed; petals and sepals 3 each, similar; stamens 6.
Leaves:	4–12" (10–30 cm) long, basal, narrow, hairy, grass-like.
Height:	3–6" (7.5–15 cm).
Flowering:	March–September.
Habitat:	Open woods and dry meadows.
Range:	Saskatchewan east to New England, south to Florida, west to New Mexico, and north to North Dakota.
Comments:	This small plant, which contrasts sharply with the large showy amaryllis, can easily be confused with a grass unless its distinctive flower is seen.

59 Easter Lily; Atamasco Lily; Zephyr Lily
Zephyranthes atamasco

Description:	Several flat leaves growing from an underground bulb and a leafless stalk, usually about as tall as leaves, bearing a *white, pink-tinged, lily-like flower*.
Flowers:	3½" (9 cm) wide; petal-like parts 6, widest toward tip, curving outward slightly; stamens shorter than style.

Leaves:	To 14″ (35 cm) long, basal, narrow, sharp-edged.
Height:	To 1′ (30 cm).
Flowering:	April–June.
Habitat:	Rich woods and damp clearings.
Range:	Maryland south to Florida and west to Louisiana.
Comments:	The genus name alludes to Zephyrus, in Greek myth the god of the west wind and husband of Chloris, goddess of flowers. The species name, derived from a Native American word meaning "stained with red," describes the flower. This plant generally blooms around Eastertime, hence one of its common names. The leaves and bulbs are poisonous, as are the bulbs of many members of the amaryllis family.

CASHEW FAMILY
Anacardiaceae

Shrubs or small trees with resinous or milky sap.

Flowers: Bisexual or unisexual, mostly radially symmetrical. Sepals and petals usually 5 each; stamens 5 or 10; all these parts attached at base of ovary.
Leaves: Simple or pinnately compound.
Fruit: Berry-like.

There are about 70 genera and 600 species, mostly in the tropics but also in temperate regions. Some species are grown as ornamentals for landscape decoration and some for their nuts (including the cashew, which is produced by *Anacardium occidentale*). Others, such as Poison Ivy (*Toxicodendron radicans*), can cause severe skin irritation. Anacardiaceae has also been known as the sumac family.

11 Winged Sumac
Rhus copallina

Description:	A shrub or small tree with *hairy twigs, milky sap,* and small greenish flowers.
Flowers:	Cluster to 6″ (15 cm) long, dense, pyramidal, terminal.
Leaves:	Hairy, compound, pinnately divided into generally 7–21 untoothed or slightly toothed, shiny leaflets, each

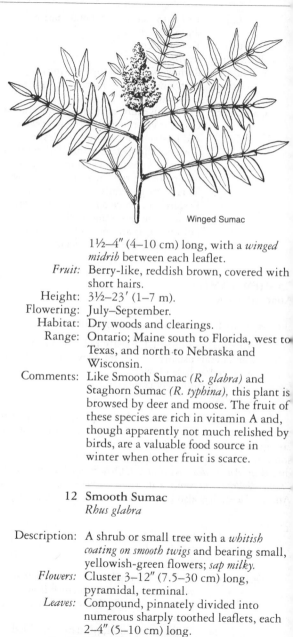

Winged Sumac

1½–4" (4–10 cm) long, with a *winged midrib* between each leaflet.

Fruit: Berry-like, reddish brown, covered with short hairs.

Height: 3½–23' (1–7 m).

Flowering: July–September.

Habitat: Dry woods and clearings.

Range: Ontario; Maine south to Florida, west to Texas, and north to Nebraska and Wisconsin.

Comments: Like Smooth Sumac *(R. glabra)* and Staghorn Sumac *(R. typhina),* this plant is browsed by deer and moose. The fruit of these species are rich in vitamin A and, though apparently not much relished by birds, are a valuable food source in winter when other fruit is scarce.

12 Smooth Sumac
Rhus glabra

Description: A shrub or small tree with a *whitish coating on smooth twigs* and bearing small, yellowish-green flowers; *sap milky.*

Flowers: Cluster 3–12" (7.5–30 cm) long, pyramidal, terminal.

Leaves: Compound, pinnately divided into numerous sharply toothed leaflets, each 2–4" (5–10 cm) long.

Fruit: Berry-like, reddish brown, velvety, clustered.

Height:	2–40′ (0.6–12 m).
Flowering:	June–July.
Habitat:	Dry soil.
Range:	Throughout much of East; also in western United States and British Columbia.
Comments:	Fragrant Sumac *(R. aromatica)* has only three leaflets, bears brilliant red fruit, and occurs from southeastern Quebec and western Vermont south to northwestern Florida, west to eastern Texas, and north to Nebraska.

13, 432 Staghorn Sumac
Rhus typhina

Description:	A shrub or small tree with *branches and twigs covered with velvety hairs* and small green to brownish flowers in terminal clusters; *sap milky, yellowish.*
Flowers:	Cluster to 8″ (20 cm) long, pyramidal.
Leaves:	Compound, pinnately divided into generally 11–25 opposite, lanceolate, toothed leaflets, each 2–5″ (5–12.5 cm) long, dark green above, paler below.
Fruit:	Berry-like, reddish brown, *covered with bright red hairs.*
Height:	3–30′ (90–900 cm).
Flowering:	June–July.
Habitat:	Fields, clearings, and dry soil.
Range:	Ontario east to Nova Scotia, south to Georgia, west to Mississippi and Kansas, and north to South Dakota and Minnesota.
Comments:	The soft hairy covering on the branches, resembling that on a deer's antlers when in velvet, accounts for the common name. The species name indicates the supposed resemblance of the branches to cattails *(Typha).* Its bark and leaves are a source of tannin, and the downy fruits are eaten by many songbirds and game birds, particularly in winter. False Poison Sumac *(R. michauxii),* a southern species found from Virginia to Florida, resembles a dwarf Staghorn Sumac, but its leaflets are green and downy on the underside.

14 Poison Ivy
Toxicodendron radicans

Description:
An upright, climbing, or trailing shrub bearing small, yellowish-white or yellowish-green flower clusters; old stems covered with fibrous roots, appearing hairy.

Flowers: ⅛" (3 mm) wide; cluster 1–3" (2.5–7.5 cm) long, loose, in leaf axils.

Leaves: Compound, divided into *3 glossy or dull green leaflets,* each 2–5½" (5–14 cm) long

Fruit: To ¼" (6 mm) wide, white to straw-colored, berry-like, *clustered;* appearing August–November, persisting through winter.

Height:
Erect plants to 8' (2.5 m); or climbing vines to 150' (45 m) long.

Flowering:
May–July.

Habitat:
Open woods, thickets, fencerows, roadsides, and waste places.

Range:
Ontario east to Nova Scotia, south to Florida, west to Texas, and north to South Dakota and Minnesota.

Comments:
All parts of this plant can cause severe skin inflammation, itching, and blistering on direct contact or if borne by sooty smoke. Washing thoroughly with soap or swabbing with alcohol immediately after exposure may remove the oil irritant. Poison Ivy is extremely variable in form, occurring as a groundcover along roadsides, an erect shrub (especially in sandy, coastal areas), or a large vine on trees. Its colorful fall foliage is especially conspicuous. Valuable winter forage for wildlife, its fruit is eaten by many songbirds and game birds with no harmful effects.

15 Poison Sumac
Toxicodendron vernix

Description:
A tall shrub or small tree with smooth, gray, black-speckled branches bearing small, yellowish-green flowers on purplish stalks in loose clusters rising from lower leaf axils.

Flowers:	Less than ⅛" (4 mm) long.
Leaves:	To 1' (30 cm) long, compound, divided into 7–15 pointed, *untoothed leaflets.*
Fruit:	*Straw-colored, berry-like;* in drooping clusters.
Height:	6–20' (1.8–6 m).
Flowering:	May–July.
Habitat:	Swamps, marshes, bogs, and wet depressions.
Range:	Ontario east to Nova Scotia, south to Florida, west to Texas, and north to Tennessee, Wisconsin, and Minnesota.
Comments:	Touching this poisonous plant can result in serious skin irritation, causing inflammation, itching, and blistering, which is easily spread from one part of the body to another, as well as to other people. Easily recognized by its straw-colored fruit and restriction to wet sites, Poison Sumac is a valuable winter food source for many songbirds and game birds, as the fruit persists when other food is scarce.

CARROT FAMILY
Apiaceae

Usually aromatic herbs with hollow stems, sometimes fern-like leaves, and small flowers usually in umbels, further grouped into compound umbels.

Flowers: Radially symmetrical; those near edge of compound umbel sometimes bilaterally symmetrical. Sepals 5, small, or absent; petals 5; stamens 5; all these parts attached at top of ovary.
Leaves: Simple or pinnately or palmately compound.
Fruit: Splitting into halves, each 1-seeded.

There are about 300 genera and 3,000 species, mostly in the Northern Hemisphere. Nearly a quarter of the genera are native to the United States, with several large genera in the West. The family is important for such food as carrots (*Daucus carota*), parsnips (*Pastinaca sativa*), and celery (*Apium graveolens*), and such spices and seasonings as coriander seeds and cilantro (both obtained from *Coriandrum sativum*), caraway (*Carum carvi*), anise (*Pimpinella anisum*), parsley (*Petroselinum crispum*), and dill (*Anethum graveolens*). Certain native species, some of which very closely resemble

domesticated plants, are quite poisonous. Flower cluste
often resemble umbrellas. Apiaceae has also been known
the parsley family (Umbelliferae).

160   Water Hemlock
Cicuta maculata

Description:	A smooth, erect, highly branched plan with sturdy, *magenta-streaked stems and dome-shaped, loose compound umbels of smal white flowers.*
Flowers:	About ⅛" (4 mm) long; compound umbel 3" (7.5 cm) wide, flattened, without bracts beneath.
Leaves:	Lower ones to 1' (30 cm) long, doubly divided, sharp-pointed, leaflets toothed with *veins ending at notches between teeth.*
Fruit:	Round, flat, with thick ridges.
Height:	3–6½' (90–200 cm).
Flowering:	June–September.
Habitat:	Wet meadows, thickets, and freshwater swamps.
Range:	Throughout East, except Newfoundlan and Arctic; also in much of West.
Comments:	A very small quantity of this highly poisonous plant can cause death. Its roots have been mistaken for parsnips and other common root crops, with fata results; cattle, horses, and sheep have died from grazing on it. The similar, and equally deadly, western *C. douglasii* is also called Water Hemlock. Neither species is related to true hemlocks *(Tsuga)* but to Poison Hemlock *(Conium maculatum).*

161   Poison Hemlock
Conium maculatum

Description:	A tall, usually much-branched, imposing plant with *purple-spotted stems,* compound leaves, and *small compound umbels of white flowers.*
Flowers:	1/16" (2 mm) long; sepals absent; petals 5; compound umbel 1½–2" (4–5 cm) wide, with inconspicuous bracts beneath.

Leaves:	Much-divided, triangular in overall outline, numerous leaflets deeply lobed, with *veins running to tips of teeth;* stalks of upper leaves shorter than those of lower.
Fruit:	⅛" (3 mm) long, seed-like, with roughened surface.
Height:	2–10' (60–300 cm).
Flowering:	June–August.
Habitat:	Waste places, weedy areas, and woodland borders.
Range:	Throughout East, except Newfoundland and Arctic; also in much of West.
Comments:	All parts of this plant are poisonous, containing the toxic alkaloid coniine (the first alkaloid synthesized in the laboratory). Judging from the symptoms, it was an extract of this hemlock that was used to execute Socrates and others in ancient Greece. Death results from the eventual paralysis of the respiratory nerves, leading to suffocation. A European native, Poison Hemlock has now spread worldwide. It is usually a biennial, producing a cluster of attractive ferny leaves the first year. The flower stalk appears the second year; then, after flowering and fruiting, the plant dies. The conspicuous dead stalks may persist throughout much of the winter. The leaves resemble parsley and indeed have been mistaken for it, with deadly results. Poison Hemlock resembles water hemlocks *(Cicuta)* but has leaflets that are deeply lobed and toothed rather than simply toothed; its leaflet veins run to the tips of the lobes or teeth rather than to the notches between them. This plant is not related to the cone-bearing trees known as hemlocks.

192 Honewort; Wild Chervil
Cryptotaenia canadensis

Description:	Small, uneven compound umbels of tiny white flowers on stalks of unequal length.
Flowers:	About ⅛" (3 mm) wide, lacking visible sepals.

Leaves: 3–6" (7.5–15 cm) long, palmately
divided into 3 toothed, often deeply
lobed leaflets.
Fruit: Blackish, oblong, *ribbed*.
Height: 1–3' (30–90 cm).
Flowering: June–September.
Habitat: Moist woods and thickets.
Range: Manitoba east to New Brunswick, south
to Florida, west to Texas, and north to
North Dakota.
Comments: Although not a showy wildflower
because of its minute, irregularly
clustered flowers, this plant does have
distinctive fruit. Its young leaves and
stems may be used as a seasoning like
parsley or as boiled greens, and the root
may be cooked and eaten like parsnips,
but caution is advised because many
similar species of the carrot family are
deadly poisonous.

159 Queen Anne's Lace; Wild Carrot
Daucus carota

Description: Lacy, *flat-topped compound umbels of tiny,
cream-white flowers, with 1 dark reddish-
brown to purplish flower* usually at center
of each umbel.
Flowers: Compound umbel 3–5" (7.5–12.5 cm)
wide, with stiff, *3-forked, leaf-like bracts*
beneath.
Leaves: 2–8" (5–20 cm) long, very finely cut,
fern-like, with a carrot-like odor when
crushed.
Fruit: *Bristly,* not barbed.
Height: 1–3½' (30–100 cm).
Flowering: May–October.
Habitat: Dry fields and waste places.
Range: Throughout East, except Arctic; also in
much of West.
Comments: Native to Europe, this plant is the
ancestor of the garden carrot; its long,
first-year taproot can be cooked and
eaten. Although it is an attractive, hairy
biennial, it is considered a troublesome
weed. When mature, the compound
umbel curls inward, resembling a bird's

nest. The plant has been reproduced from one embryonic cell in tissue culture and has actually flowered, with even the usual differently colored central flower present.

180 Rattlesnake Master
Eryngium yuccifolium

Description: Smooth rigid stems bearing heads composed of many small, greenish-white flowers intermingled with pointed bracts.

Flowers: Head ¾" (2 cm) wide, slightly ovoid, surrounded by large pointed bracts.

Leaves: To 3' (90 cm) long, linear, sharp-pointed, parallel-veined, with spiny edges, clasping stem.

Height: 2–6' (60–180 cm).

Flowering: July–August.

Habitat: Prairies, open woods, and thickets.

Range: Minnesota east to Michigan and Virginia, south to Florida, west to Texas, and north to Nebraska; also in Connecticut.

Comments: Spiny leaves make walking through clumps of this plant difficult and also make it unpalatable to grazing livestock. It was once credited with a variety of curative powers. The flower heads develop a bluish cast with maturity.

158 Cow Parsnip
Heracleum lanatum

Description: A very tall plant with *huge leaves, compound umbels of numerous white flowers,* and grooved, woolly, hollow stems.

Flowers: To ½" (1.5 cm) wide; petals 5, asymmetrical, notched, often tinged with purple; compound umbel 4–8" (10–20 cm) wide, flattened.

Leaves: Divided into *3 segments,* each 3–20" (7.5–50 cm) wide, lobed and toothed; whole leaf with *inflated sheath* at stalk base.

Fruit: Broad, flat, oval.
Height: 4–9' (1.2–2.7 m).
Flowering: June–August.
Habitat: Moist ground.
Range: Alberta east to Newfoundland, south to Georgia, west to Tennessee and Kansas, and north to North Dakota; also in much of West.
Comments: The young stems, leafstalks, and roots of this plant can be cooked and eaten, but because the flowers resemble those of water hemlocks *(Cicuta),* which are extremely poisonous, great care must be taken, as with many members of the carrot family.

29   Water Pennywort
Hydrocotyle americana

Description: A creeping or weakly erect marsh plant with *small clusters of tiny, greenish-white flowers* rising from leaf axils.
Flowers: About ¹⁄₁₆" (2 mm) wide, 5-petaled; in clusters of 1–5.
Leaves: ½–1¾" (1.5–4.5 cm) wide, simple, *roundish,* doubly scalloped, with deep basal notch.
Height: Creeper; to 2' (60 cm) long, with runners rising from leaf axils.
Flowering: June–September.
Habitat: Damp woods and meadows.
Range: Ontario east to Nova Scotia, south to South Carolina, west to Tennessee, and north to Indiana, Wisconsin, and Minnesota.
Comments: There are about eight pennywort species in our range. Their distinctive, rounded "penny-like" leaves, on stems that creep or float, account for the common name.

173   Sweet Cicely
Osmorhiza claytonii

Description: A hairy plant with *small sparse compound umbels of white flowers.*
Flowers: Less than ¹⁄₁₆" (2 mm) wide, 5-petaled.
Leaves: *Fern-like,* divided into blunt-toothed or

lobed leaflets, each ½–3½" (1.5–9 cm)
long.

Fruit: Tapered, blackish, covered with stiff,
clinging hairs; style to ¹⁄₁₆" (2 mm),
persistent.

Height: 1½–3' (45–90 cm).

Flowering: May–June.

Habitat: Woods.

Range: Saskatchewan east to Nova
Scotia, south to Georgia, west to
Arkansas and Kansas, and north to
Minnesota.

Comments: The roots of this plant have an
anise-like odor when bruised. Several
species of this genus occur in our
range, among them Anise Root
(*O. longistylis*), which has styles to ¼"
(4 mm) long.

31 Black Snakeroot
Sanicula canadensis

Description: Inconspicuous, greenish flowers in
small, uneven *compound umbels on stalks
of unequal length.*

Flowers: Sepals 5, each ¹⁄₁₆" (2 mm) long, narrow,
lanceolate, extending beyond 5 tiny
white petals; leafy bracts beneath
compound umbel.

Leaves: *Palmately divided* into 3–5 wedge-
shaped to narrow, oblong, *sharply
toothed* leaflets, each to 3" (7.5 cm)
long.

Fruit: Small, oval, covered with hooked
bristles.

Height: 1–4' (30–120 cm).

Flowering: May–July.

Habitat: Dry open woods.

Range: Ontario and Quebec south to Florida,
west to Texas, and north to South
Dakota and Minnesota.

Comments: The genus name of this widely
distributed species, derived from
the Latin *sanare* ("to heal"), refers to
its once-reputed medicinal powers.
Several closely related species are
distinguished only by minor technical
characteristics.

157 **Water Parsnip**
Sium suave

Description: An aquatic or wetland plant with *strongly ridged stems* and compound umbels of *tiny, dull white flowers.*

Flowers: Compound umbel 2–3" (5–7.5 cm) wide, with *narrow, leaf-like bracts beneath.*

Leaves: 4–10" (10–25 cm) long, pinnately compound; basal leaves often submerged, finely divided into 5–17 lanceolate, toothed leaflets, each 2½–5½" (6.5–14 cm) long.

Fruit: Tiny, ovate, with prominent ribs.

Height: 2–6' (60–180 cm).

Flowering: July–September.

Habitat: Wet meadows and thickets and muddy shorelines.

Range: Throughout East, except Arctic; also in much of West.

Comments: The roots of this plant can be boiled and eaten as a cooked vegetable, but because the plant is somewhat similar to the deadly water hemlocks *(Cicuta),* it is best left alone.

Water Parsnip

348 Golden Alexanders
Zizia aurea

Description: Flat-topped *compound umbels of small, bright yellow flowers,* with 1 stalkless flower at center of each umbel.

Flowers: Compound umbel about 2″ (5 cm) wide.

Leaves: Twice divided, with usually 3–13 long, pointed, *toothed leaflets,* each 1–2″ (2.5–5 cm) long.

Height: 1–3′ (30–90 cm).

Flowering: April–June.

Habitat: Meadows, shorelines, moist woods, and thickets.

Range: Manitoba east to Nova Scotia, south to Florida, west to Texas, and north to North Dakota.

Comments: Other yellow-flowered members of the carrot family include *Z. aptera,* also known as Golden Alexanders, with simple, heart-shaped, basal leaves, and Yellow Pimpernel *(Taenidia integerrima),* with compound leaves and untoothed leaflets. Meadow Parsnip *(Thaspium trifoliatum)* is in a different genus but is sometimes called Golden Alexanders as well; it has only three lanceolate, toothed leaflets.

DOGBANE FAMILY
Apocynaceae

Herbs or shrubs (trees in tropical regions) with flowers borne singly or in clusters and often with milky sap.

Flowers: Radially symmetrical. Calyx with 5 united sepals; corolla with 5 united petals; corolla lobes often twisted in bud; stamens 5; all these parts attached at base of ovary.

Leaves: Opposite, whorled, or alternate; simple.

Fruit: 2 pods, often attached at tips by style.

There are about 200 genera and 2,000 species, most abundant in the tropics and subtropics. Oleander *(Nerium oleander)* and several species of periwinkle *(Vinca)* are popular ornamentals. Many, including Oleander, are poisonous. Some species are sources of medicine and others produce valuable fruit or commercial rubber.

617   Blue Dogbane
Amsonia tabernaemontana

Description: *Sky blue, star-shaped flowers* in much-branched clusters; corolla downy on outside.

Flowers: Petals 5, each ¼–⅜" (6–10 mm) long, narrow, rising from funnel-like tube.

Leaves: Lanceolate to elliptical, short-stalked, alternate but often very close and appearing opposite.

Fruit: *Paired slender pods,* each 3–4½" (9–12.5 cm) long, opening along one side.

Height: 1–3' (30–90 cm).

Flowering: April–July.

Habitat: Moist or wet woods and streambanks.

Range: New York and Massachusetts south to Florida, west to Texas, and north to Kansas and Ohio.

Comments: The species name commemorates the 16th-century German herbalist Jakobus Theodorus Tabernaemontanus.

514   Spreading Dogbane
Apocynum androsaemifolium

Description: A bushy plant with numerous small, pink, *nodding, bell-like, fragrant flowers,* striped inside with deeper pink; broken stems and leaves exude *milky sap.*

Flowers: ⅜" (8 mm) wide; clustered at top or rising from leaf axils.

Leaves: 2–4" (5–10 cm) long, smooth, opposite, ovate, blue-green.

Fruit: Paired slender pods, each 3–8" (7.5–20 cm) long, opening along one side, with seeds ending in tufts of hair.

Height: 1–4' (30–120 cm).

Flowering: June–August.

Habitat: Woodland borders, thickets, fields, and roadsides.

Range: Nearly throughout East, except Arctic; also in much of West.

Comments: Indian Hemp *(A. cannabinum),* a slightly smaller species with erect clusters of greenish-white flowers, is also found in fields and, like our other *Apocynum* dogbanes, is poisonous. Clasping-leaved

Dogbane *(A. sibiricum)*, found widely throughout the Northeast in sandy or gravelly habitats such as streambanks, has stalkless or nearly stalkless leaves. Spreading Dogbane is a relative of milkweeds *(Asclepias)*.

546, 618 Periwinkle; Myrtle
Vinca minor

Description: A low, evergreen, *trailing plant* with *purplish-blue (rarely white) flowers* borne singly in leaf axils.

Flowers: To 1″ (2.5 cm) wide; corolla funnel-shaped, 5-lobed, with a *whitish star* in center.

Leaves: 1¼–2″ (3–5 cm) long, *shiny, dark green, opposite.*

Fruit: Paired, short, cylindrical pods, each ½–1¼″ (1.5–3 cm) long.

Height: 6–8″ (15–20 cm).

Flowering: April–May.

Habitat: Woodland borders, roadsides, abandoned sites, and cemeteries.

Range: Ontario east to Nova Scotia, south to Florida, west to Texas, and north to Nebraska and Minnesota; sparingly escaped in West.

Comments: This introduced plant, now escaped from cultivation, frequently forms extensive patches. The Latin word *pervinca* (from the root "to bind") is the source of both the genus name and the common name Periwinkle. In the Southeast the related Madagascar Periwinkle *(Catharanthus roseus)*, with either pink or white flowers, is naturalized.

HOLLY FAMILY
Aquifoliaceae

Evergreen or deciduous trees or shrubs with sometimes toothed leaves and very small, solitary or clustered flowers.

Flowers: Male and female flowers on separate plants. Sepals 4–9; petals 4–9; stamens 4–9; petals and sepals attached at base of ovary.

Leaves: Simple, with minute dark stipules at base of ea
stalk; leathery in evergreen species.
Fruit: Berry-like, red, yellow, or black, with 1–9 seeds.

There are 4 genera and about 370 species, widely distri
uted. Many species are popular plants for landscape decor
tion, especially those with evergreen leaves and bright
colored fruits.

230, 427   Winterberry; Black Alder
Ilex verticillata

Description: *A deciduous shrub with clusters of very
small, white flowers* in leaf axils.

Flowers: Cluster ¼–½" (6–13 mm) wide; sepals,
petals, and stamens 4–8 each.

Leaves: 2" (5 cm) long, elliptical, *toothed but not
spiny.*

Fruit: Berry-like, *showy red (rarely yellow),* less
than ¼" (6 mm) wide; on very short
stalks, singly or in small clusters along
branches.

Height: 3–10' (90–300 cm).

Flowering: June–August.

Habitat: Swamps, damp to dry thickets, and
pondsides.

Range: Ontario east to Newfoundland, south to
Florida, west to Texas, and north
through Arkansas to Minnesota.

Comments: This shrub is extremely showy in late

Winterberry

fall and early winter, when covered with bright fruits. Birds are readily attracted to them. The southern Possum Haw (*I. decidua*), found in thickets and moist sites from Virginia to Texas, also has distinctive red fruit. In total, four other similar deciduous species and six evergreen species occur in the Southeast.

229, 428 **Yaupon**
Ilex vomitoria

Description: *A shrub or small tree with evergreen leaves* and clusters of numerous *tiny, greenish-white flowers.*

Flowers: Male plant with flowers in stalked clusters of 3–9; female plant with flowers in unstalked clusters of 1–3; sepals, petals, and stamens 4 each.

Leaves: ¾–1½" (2–4 cm) long, leathery, lanceolate to ovate, smooth, finely toothed, *dark green and shiny above, pale green below.*

Fruit: Berry-like, bright red, translucent, about ¼" (5 mm) wide.

Height: 5–15' (1.5–4.5 m), occasionally to 45' (14 m).

Flowering: March–May.

Habitat: Swamps and wet woods, rarely on sand hills.

Range: Virginia south to Florida and west to Texas and Oklahoma.

Comments: This distinctive native shrub bears decorative red berries seldom eaten by birds. The species name alludes to the fact that an infusion made from the leaves was used by Native Americans as a laxative and in emetic purification rites. The common name derives from a Catawba word for "small tree."

ARUM FAMILY
Araceae

Erect, prostrate, or climbing herbs with numerous small flowers crowded on a fleshy spike (spadix), usually surrounded by an often showy bract (spathe).

Flowers: Bisexual or unisexual. Sepals and petals absent, represented by 4–6 segments (tepals); stamens usually 4–6; all these parts attached at base of ovary.
Leaves: Simple or compound, mostly long-stalked.
Fruit: Usually a berry.

There are about 110 genera and 1,800 species, found in shady, damp or wet places, most numerous and varied in the tropics. Many, such as Calla Lily (*Zantedeschia aethiopica*), *Philodendron* species, and *Dieffenbachia picta* and *D. seguine*, both known by the common name Dumbcane, are cultivated as ornamentals. Without proper treatment, many species are poisonous. Once treated, the roots of some tropical species are an important starch supply; for instance, the root of Taro (*Calocasia esculenta*) is the source of Hawaiian poi.

---

333 Green Dragon
Arisaema dracontium

Description: 1 greenish, *long-tipped spadix* (the "dragon's tongue") protruding several inches beyond a *narrow green spathe*.
Flowers: Spadix 4–8" (10–20 cm) long, with tiny greenish-yellow, unisexual flowers at base.
Leaves: *1, compound, long-stalked,* with 5–15 pointed, dull-green leaflets, central one to 11" (28 cm) long.
Fruit: Orange-red and green, clustered berries.
Height: 1–3' (30–90 cm).
Flowering: May–June.
Habitat: Wet woodlands, low rich ground, and streambanks.
Range: Ontario and Quebec south through New Hampshire to Florida, west to Texas, and north to Nebraska and Minnesota.
Comments: As with Jack-in-the-pulpit (*A. triphyllum*), the swollen, underground stem of this plant can severely irritate the mouth if ingested uncooked. Green Dragon is considered comparatively rare.

---

381 Jack-in-the-pulpit; Indian Turnip
Arisaema triphyllum

Description: An upright, ridged, *curved spathe enveloping an erect, yellowish, club-shaped spadix* beneath large leaves.

Flowers:	Spathe (the "pulpit") green or purplish brown, often streaked or mottled; spadix ("Jack") 2–3″ (5–7.5 cm) long, with separate, tiny, male and female flowers at base.
Leaves:	Usually 2 (sometimes 1), long-stalked, 3-parted, veined, dull green.
Fruit:	Shiny, red, clustered berries, on spadix; fruiting in late summer and fall.
Height:	1–3′ (30–90 cm).
Flowering:	April–June.
Habitat:	Damp woods and swamps.
Range:	Manitoba east to Nova Scotia, south to Florida, west to Texas, and north to North Dakota.
Comments:	Some authorities recognize one species, and others distinguish three, based on minor differences in leaves, spathe, and size. Because of needle-like calcium oxalate crystals and perhaps other acrid substances in the swollen, underground stem, it is peppery to the taste and causes a strong burning reaction if eaten raw; this unpleasant property can be eliminated by cooking. Native Americans gathered the fleshy corms for food.

331 Water Arum; Wild Calla
Calla palustris

Description:	*A broad white spathe around a spadix of tiny, yellow flowers,* growing in water or muck among oblong, *heart-shaped leaves.*
Flowers:	Spadix 1″ (2.5 cm) long; spathe 2″ (5 cm) long, with rolled edge.
Leaves:	Commonly to 6″ (15 cm) long, numerous, long-stalked, glossy, dark green.
Fruit:	Red, clustered berries; fruiting in late summer.
Height:	6–12″ (15–30 cm) above water or muck.
Flowering:	Late May–August.
Habitat:	Cool boggy wetlands and pondsides.
Range:	Alaska east to Newfoundland, south to Maryland, west to Iowa, and north to Minnesota and North Dakota.
Comments:	This perennial, a more northerly species than the other arums in our range, is also found in northern Eurasia. It is very

showy when in flower and, later, when
bearing its fruit. The genus name, its
meaning uncertain, was used by Pliny
the species name means "of marshes."

---

332 Golden Club
Orontium aquaticum

Description: An aquatic with long-stalked leaves an
a stalked, *golden yellow, club-shaped spad*

Flowers: Minute, clustered on spadix 1–2"
(2.5–5 cm) long; sepals 4–6; stamens
4–6; *underdeveloped spathe appears as
narrow, tubular leaf surrounding base of
spadix stalk.*

Leaves: Blades 5–12" (13–30 cm) long,
elliptical, veined, dark green, extendin
above or floating on water.

Fruit: Blue-green, clustered berries.

Height: Aquatic; 1–2' (30–60 cm) above water

Flowering: April–June.

Habitat: Shallow waters of marshes, swamps, an
ponds.

Range: New York and Massachusetts south to
Florida and west to Texas, chiefly along
coastal plain, and inland to Tennessee,
Kentucky, and West Virginia.

Comments: This emergent perennial is strikingly
beautiful, especially when seen against
the backdrop of dark open waters in
southern swamps. The genus name
derives from a plant that grows in the
Orontes River of Syria.

---

126 Arrow Arum
Peltandra virginica

Description: An aquatic or wetland plant with large,
long-stalked, fleshy leaves and a *green to
white, wavy-edged, tapering, leaf-like spath
curled around a rod-like, green to pale yellou
spadix.*

Flowers: Spathe 4–7" (10–17.5 cm) long; female
flowers at base of club-like spadix,
below male flowers.

Leaves: 1–2' (30–60 cm) long, *arrowhead-shaped*
with prominent veins.

Fruit:	Black, blackish-green, or brownish, clustered berries, surrounded by base of spathe.
Height:	Aquatic; 1–2′ (30–60 cm) above water.
Flowering:	May–June.
Habitat:	Shallow waters of ponds and slow-moving rivers, swamps, and marshes.
Range:	Ontario and Quebec south to Florida, west to Texas, and north through Missouri to Minnesota.
Comments:	This species is especially common in and along shallow waterways, where it may occur in large colonies. The genus name derives from the Greek *pelte* ("small shield") and *aner* ("stamen"), referring to the shield-like contour of the stamens. The common name derives from the arrowhead-shaped leaves.

30 Water Lettuce
Pistia stratiotes

Description:	A small, *floating aquatic* with inconspicuous green to white flowers on a spadix embedded in a *rosette of green leaves.*
Flowers:	Female flowers at base of spadix, below male flowers; spathe about ½″ (1.5 cm) long, greenish white.
Leaves:	2–10″ (5–25 cm) long, velvety, parallel-ribbed; rosette about 6″ (15 cm) wide.
Height:	Aquatic; to 10″ (25 cm) above water.
Flowering:	April.
Habitat:	Still waters of ponds, ditches, and swamps and slow-moving streams.
Range:	North Carolina south to Florida and west to Texas and beyond; occurrences north of this range may be from aquarium discards and perhaps do not persist.
Comments:	This aggressive plant rapidly covers vast expanses of open water in southern wetlands, especially Bald Cypress swamps. Its growth is so dense and compact that it gives the illusion that it can be walked upon. It is sometimes used as an aquarium plant.

391 Skunk Cabbage
Symplocarpus foetidus

Description: Emerging from moist soil in early
spring, a large, *brownish-purple and
green, mottled, shell-like spathe enclosing
a knob-like, yellowish to dark red-purple
spadix* covered with tiny flowers; by
late spring, a tight roll of fresh green
leaves beside spathe unfolding to form
huge, dark green leaves.

Flowers: Spathe 3–6″ (7.5–15 cm) long.

Leaves: 1–2′ (30–60 cm) long, to 1′ (30 cm)
wide, veined, on stalks rising directly
from ground.

Height: 1–2′ (30–60 cm).

Flowering: February–May.

Habitat: Open swamps and marshes, wet
woodlands, and streamsides.

Range: Ontario east to Nova Scotia, south
to North Carolina, west to Tennessee,
and north to Illinois, Iowa, and
Minnesota.

Comments: This distinctive plant sprouts early
in spring, and the heat of cellular
respiration resulting from its rapid
growth actually melts snow or ice
around it. Its strong fetid odor,
especially when the plant is bruised,
resembles that of skunk (hence its
common name) and lures insects that
pollinate it. The huge leaves of mature
plants may dominate an area.

GINSENG FAMILY
Araliaceae

Trees, shrubs, vines, or herbs with sometimes simple b
usually compound leaves, and small flowers in umbels
head-like clusters.

Flowers: Bisexual or unisexual, radially symmetrical. Caly
reduced to 4–5 points, or absent; petals and stamer
usually 5 each; all these parts attached at top of ovary.

Leaves: Alternate or whorled, generally pinnately
palmately compound.

Fruit: Berry or drupe.

There are about 70 genera and 700 species, found in tem-
rate and tropical regions. Some species, such as English
y *(Hedera helix),* are cultivated as ornamentals and some
e important drug or flavoring sources.

---

169 Wild Sarsaparilla
Aralia nudicaulis

Description: A leafless stalk topped with rounded
clusters of *greenish-white flowers beneath 1
large, umbrella-like leaf.*

Flowers: Cluster 1½–2″ (4–5 cm) wide; petals 5,
sharply reflexed, tiny; stamens 5, green.

Leaves: 8–20″ (20–50 cm) long, long-stalked,
rising above flower stalk, divided into 3
sections, each with 3–5 ovate, finely
toothed leaflets.

Fruit: Purple-black, clustered berries.

Height: 8–20″ (20–50 cm).

Flowering: July–August.

Habitat: Upland woods.

Range: Alberta east to Newfoundland, south to
Georgia, and northwest to Nebraska and
North Dakota; also in northwestern
United States and British Columbia.

Comments: The aromatic rhizomes of this plant are
dried and used as a substitute for
sarsaparilla. The species name, from the
Latin *nudus* ("naked") and *cauli* ("stalk"),
refers to the leafless flower stalk. Devil's
Walkingstick *(A. spinosa),* a small tree or
large shrub, has leaves and stems covered

Wild Sarsaparilla

with spines. Bristly Sarsaparilla *(A. hispida)*, which grows to a height of 4′ (1.2 m), is bristly only at the base. Spikenard *(A. racemosa)* lacks spines and has linden-like leaflets and numerous flower umbels in large clusters.

429   American Ginseng
Panax quinquefolius

Description: An umbel of *small, greenish-white or yellow-green, fragrant flowers* rising from whorl of *3 large, palmately compound leaves.*
Flowers: About ¹⁄₁₆″ (2 mm) wide; petals 5.
Leaves: 5–12″ (12.5–30 cm) long, each with 5 pointed, toothed leaflets.
Fruit: Red, clustered berries.
Height: 8–24″ (20–60 cm).
Flowering: May–August.
Habitat: Cool moist woods.
Range: Ontario east to Quebec, south to Georgia, west to Louisiana and Oklahoma, and north to South Dakota and Minnesota.
Comments: The flowers of this species smell like those of Lily-of-the-valley *(Convallaria majalis)*. Its root is highly prized by the Chinese as an alleged aphrodisiac and heart stimulant. It is also in demand as a tonic which has resulted in overcollection, so that the plant is now considered rare. It is classified as a threatened species in 3 eastern states. The genus name is from the Greek *panakeia* ("panacea" or "cure-all"). The common name, a corruption of the Chinese *Jin-chen* ("man-like"), refers to the resemblance of the roots to a human body.

171   Dwarf Ginseng
Panax trifolius

Description: An umbel of *tiny, dull white (fading to pink) flowers* rising from a *whorl of 3 compound leaves.*
Flowers: About ¹⁄₁₆″ (2 mm) wide; petals 5.

Leaves:	Leaflets 3–5, stalkless, toothed, ovate, each 1–1½″ (2.5–4 cm) long.
Fruit:	Yellowish, clustered berries.
Height:	4–8″ (10–20 cm).
Flowering:	April–June.
Habitat:	Moist woods and damp clearings.
Range:	Ontario east to Nova Scotia, south to Georgia, and northwest to Kentucky, Indiana, and Minnesota.
Comments:	This tiny, woodland perennial looks like a small version of American Ginseng (*P. quinquefolius*). Its distinctive tuber can be eaten raw or boiled.

BIRTHWORT FAMILY
Aristolochiaceae

Herbs or woody vines with commonly heart-shaped leaves and medium to large, bizarre, often carrion-scented flowers.

Flowers: Bilaterally or radially symmetrical. Calyx 3-lobed or bent, with red, purple, or brown, united sepals; petals absent; stamens usually at least 6; all these parts attached at top of ovary.
Leaves: Alternate or basal, stalked, commonly with smooth edges.
Fruit: Capsule, with 4–6 chambers.

There are about 10 genera and 600 species, widely distributed in tropical and temperate regions. Some are aromatic; a few are cultivated.

376 Dutchman's Pipe
Aristolochia macrophylla

Description:	A high-climbing vine with pipe- or *S-shaped, purplish-brown flowers* on a stalk with a heart-shaped bract.
Flowers:	2″ (5 cm) long; calyx flared into 3 short lobes.
Leaves:	6–15″ (15–38 cm) long, large, untoothed, *heart-shaped,* undersurface green.
Fruit:	Cylindrical capsule, 2½–4″ (6.5–10 cm) long, with many winged seeds.
Height:	Vine; climbing to 65′ (20 m).
Flowering:	April–June.
Habitat:	Rich moist woods and streambanks.

Range: Ontario and Michigan southeast to
Massachusetts, south to Georgia and
Alabama, and north to Kentucky.

Comments: A characteristic plant of the southern
Appalachian hardwood forests,
Dutchman's Pipe is often cultivated
outside its native range. Flowers of this
genus were once used as an aid in
childbirth, since they were thought to
resemble a human fetus. The similar
Pipe Vine *(A. tomentosa)* has a bractless
flower stalk, a yellowish calyx that is
purple around the opening, and downy
and whitish leaf undersurfaces.

373 Wild Ginger
Asarum canadense

Description: 1 darkish *red-brown to green-brown flower
growing at ground level* in angle between
leafstalks.

Flowers: 1½" (4 cm) wide, cup-shaped, with 3
pointed lobes.

Leaves: 1 pair, each 2–6" (5–15 cm) wide, *large
hairy, heart-shaped*, overshadowing
flower.

Fruit: Round capsule, about ½" (13 mm) long

Height: 6–12" (15–30 cm).

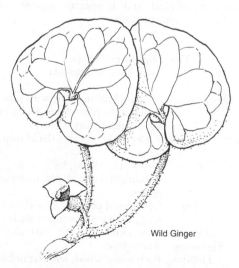

Wild Ginger

Flowering: April–May.
Habitat: Rich woods.
Range: Manitoba east to New Brunswick, south to Florida, west to Louisiana and Arkansas, and north to North Dakota.
Comments: The rhizome of this spring flower has a strong, ginger-like odor; when cooked with sugar, it can be used as a substitute for ginger. A southern species with greenish-purple flowers, Little Brown Jugs *(A. arifolium),* has more triangular, evergreen leaf blades.

MILKWEED FAMILY
Asclepiadaceae

Herbs, shrubs, or vines usually with thick milky sap, opposite or whorled leaves, flowers in flat or round, umbel-like clusters (cymes), and tufted seeds in pods.

Flowers: Radially symmetrical. Sepals 5; corolla of 5 united petals, with reflexed lobes; stamens 5, united with style to form a central columnar structure; often a central crown (corona) of 5 inflated sacs or scoop-shaped hoods between petals and stamens (*Asclepias* species with hoods usually enclosing a curved, horn-like appendage); all these parts attached at base of 2 ovaries.
Leaves: Simple, mostly opposite or in whorls.
Fruit: 2 pods, often joined at tips by style, containing many silky-haired seeds.

There are about 250 genera and 2,000 species, widely distributed but most abundant in tropical and subtropical regions. The rather elaborate central crown is especially characteristic of milkweed flowers. Several popular houseplants, such as those in the genera *Hoya* and *Stapelia,* belong to this family. Some species are a source of commercial rubber. In milkweeds *(Asclepias)* and others, the unusual structure of the flower regulates pollination. Pollen, contained in minute masses located in slits in the side of the central column, becomes attached to an insect when one of its legs enters a slit; as the insect visits another flower, the pollen must be left in precisely the right place on the column for pollination to be successful. This complicated mechanism may explain why so few fruits develop from each many-flowered cluster. Insects unable to pull free die trapped on the flower.

509   Swamp Milkweed
Asclepias incarnata

Description: *Deep pink or white flowers* clustered atop
tall branching stem with numerous
narrow, lanceolate leaves.

Flowers: ¼" (6 mm) wide; petals 5, recurved;
elevated central crown divided into 5
hoods.

Leaves: To 4" (10 cm) long, opposite.

Fruit: Elongated pod, 2–4" (5–10 cm) long,
opening along one side.

Height: 1–4' (30–120 cm).

Flowering: June–August.

Habitat: Swamps, shorelines, and thickets.

Range: Manitoba east to Nova Scotia, south to
Florida, west to Texas, and north to Nor
Dakota; also in Rocky Mountain states

Comments: The sap of this wetland milkweed is les
milky than that of other species, but it
flowers are typical of milkweeds. The
genus was named in honor of Asklepios
the Greek god of medicine, undoubted
because some species have long been
used to treat a variety of ailments. The
species name means "flesh-colored."

510   Common Milkweed
Asclepias syriaca

Description: A tall *downy plant* with slightly
drooping, *purplish to pink flower clusters.*

Flowers: ½" (1.5 cm) wide; petals 5, reflexed;
conspicuous central crown divided into
5 hoods; cluster 2" (5 cm) wide.

Leaves: 4–10" (10–25 cm) long, opposite,
broad-oblong, light green with *gray
down beneath;* exuding milky sap when
bruised.

Fruit: Rough-textured pod, opening along on
side, containing many overlapping
seeds, each with a tuft of silky hairs.

Height: 2–6' (60–180 cm).

Flowering: June–August.

Habitat: Old fields, roadsides, and waste places.

Range: Saskatchewan east to Nova Scotia, south
to Georgia, west to Texas, and north to
North Dakota.

Comments: This species differs from the similar
Showy Milkweed *(A. speciosa)* in its
longer hoods, which are ¼–⅜″ (6–9 mm)
long; those of Showy Milkweed are ½–⅝″
(11–16 mm) long. The plant contains
cardiac glycosides, allied to those in
Foxglove *(Digitalis purpurea)* of the
figwort family (Scropulariaceae), used in
treating some heart diseases. These
glycosides, when absorbed by Monarch
butterfly larvae whose sole source of food
is milkweed foliage, make the larvae and
adult butterflies toxic to birds and other
predators. Linnaeus, who named this
species, mistakenly thought that it was
from Syria, hence the species name.

367 Butterfly Weed; Orange Milkweed; Chigger Flower
Asclepias tuberosa

Description: Small, *bright orange, clustered flowers* atop
a leafy, hairy stem.
  Flowers: ⅜″ (9 mm) wide; petals 5, reflexed;
central crown divided into 5 erect
hoods; cluster about 2″ (5 cm) wide.
  Leaves: 2–6″ (5–15 cm) long, alternate, oblong,
narrow; exuding *watery, not milky, sap
when bruised.*
  Fruit: Hairy pod, 3–4½″ (7.5–12 cm) long.
  Height: 1–2½′ (30–75 cm).

Butterfly Weed

Flowering: June–September.
Habitat: Dry open soil, roadsides, and fields.
Range: Ontario and Quebec south to Florida, west to Texas, and north to South Dakota and Minnesota; also in southwestern U.S. and California.
Comments: Unusual among *Asclepias* in having alternate leaves and non-milky sap, this showy plant is frequently grown in home gardens. Its brilliant flowers attract butterflies, hence one of its common names. Because its tough root was chewed by Native Americans to treat pleurisy and other pulmonary ailments, it is also called Pleurisy Root.

175   White Milkweed
Asclepias variegata

Description: *Small white flowers with purplish centers* crowded into round, terminal clusters.
Flowers: ¼–½" (6–13 mm) long; petals 5; elevated central crown divided into 5 hoods; cluster 2½–3" (6.5–7.5 cm) wide.
Leaves: 3–6" (7.5–15 cm) long, *dark green above, pale beneath,* opposite, oval to oblong.
Fruit: Spindle-shaped pod, ¾" (2 cm) thick.
Height: 1–3' (30–90 cm).
Flowering: May–June.
Habitat: Open woods and thickets.
Range: New York and Connecticut south to Florida, west to Texas and Oklahoma, and northeast to Illinois and Ohio.
Comments: The stem of this plant has the milky sap typical of most milkweeds. The species name describes the bicolored flowers, which are quite showy in masses.

ASTER FAMILY
Asteraceae

Herbs, sometimes shrubs or vines, rarely trees, with simple or compound, alternate or opposite leaves, some species with milky sap; flowers small and often organized into larger, flower-like heads resembling 1 radially symmetrical flower cupped by a ring of bracts (involucre).

ower-like heads: Tiny, radially symmetrical flowers (disk flowers) forming a central disk; larger, strap-shaped, petal-like flowers (rays) surrounding central disk; flower head may be composed of all disk flowers (as in ragweeds) or all rays (as in dandelions).

owers: Calyx absent or represented by hairs, bristles, scales, or a crown, often persisting atop fruit; corolla with 4–5 united petals; stamens 4–5; all these parts attached at top of ovary.

aves: Opposite, alternate, or whorled; simple or compound.

uit: 1-seeded, seed-like, with a hard shell; often topped with a pappus.

There are about 1,100 genera and 20,000 species in this rge, worldwide family, making it and the orchid family Orchidaceae) the two largest plant families. Many garden arieties of Common Sunflower *(Helianthus annuus)*, horticultural variants of species in the genera *Cosmos, Zinnia,* and *Dahlia,* and several other plants are grown as ornamentals. Many kinds of lettuce seen in the grocery store are obtained om *Lactuca sativa,* and artichokes are from *Cynara scolymus.* Common Sunflower provides sunflower oil and sunflower eeds; Safflower *(Carthamus tinctorius)* is the source of safower oil. Pollen from ragweeds *(Ambrosia)* is a major cause f hay fever. When ingested, a number of species are poisonous to grazing animals; among these are snakeroots *Eupatorium),* broomweeds *(Gutierrezia),* certain sneezeweeds *(Dugaldia* and *Helenium),* bitterweeds *(Hymenoxys),* nd groundsels *(Senecio).* The family contributes tremendously to the diversity, and thus to the stability, of arid voodland and shrubland ecosystems throughout the world, s in the sagebrush-dominated areas of the western United tates. Asteraceae has also been known as the daisy or sunlower family (Compositae).

156 Yarrow; Milfoil
Achillea millefolium

Description:	*Flat-topped clusters of small whitish flower heads* atop a gray-green, leafy, usually hairy stem.
Flowers:	Head about ¼" (6 mm) wide; rays 4–6, surrounding tiny disk flowers.
Leaves:	6" (15 cm) long, *very finely dissected, gray-green, fern-like,* aromatic when crushed, lanceolate in outline, stalkless; basal leaves longer.

Yarrow

Height: 1–3' (30–90 cm).
Flowering: June–September.
Habitat: Old fields and roadsides.
Range: Throughout North America.
Comments: Yarrow was formerly used medicinally t
break a fever by increasing perspiration,
to treat hemorrhaging, and as a poultice
for rashes. A tea used by Native
Americans to cure stomach disorders
was made by steeping the leaves.

---

10 Common Ragweed
Ambrosia artemisiifolia

Description: A coarse, hairy-stemmed annual with
inconspicuous disk flowers in *elongated
clusters of separate male and female flower
heads;* some plants with hundreds of
heads.
Flowers: Male heads of yellow-green disk flowers,
stalked, upside down, in slender clusters
1–6" (2.5–15 cm) long, atop plant and
on side branches; female heads of green
disk flowers, stalkless, solitary or in
smaller clusters in axils of bracts or
small leaves at base of male clusters.
Leaves: To 4" (10 cm) long, highly dissected,
light green.

Fruit:	Small, top-shaped, tipped with a stout projection encircled by 4–9 short points.
Height:	1–5′ (30–150 cm).
Flowering:	July–October.
Habitat:	Cultivated fields, old fields, waste places, and roadsides.
Range:	Throughout North America, except far north.
Comments:	This plant, not goldenrods *(Solidago),* is a cause of hay fever. Pollination is by wind, as indicated by the drabness of the flower heads, which do not attract insects. The best control is to permit perennial plants to crowd out this annual. Since the fruits persist into winter and are numerous and rich in oil, they are relished by songbirds and upland game birds.

9 Great Ragweed
Ambrosia trifida

Description:	A tall, rough, hairy plant with *elongated, terminal clusters of nodding male flower heads above few clusters of female flower heads;* some plants with hundreds of heads.
Flowers:	Male heads of yellow-green disk flowers, stalked, upside down, in slender clusters 1–10″ (2.5–25 cm) long, atop plant and on side branches; female heads of green disk flowers, stalkless, solitary or in smaller clusters in axils of bracts or small leaves at base of male clusters.
Leaves:	To 8″ (20 cm) long, opposite, unlobed or with 3–5 lobes.
Fruit:	Top-shaped, tipped with a stout projection encircled by 4–10 short points.
Height:	2–15′ (60–450 cm).
Flowering:	June–October.
Habitat:	Waste places, fields, and roadsides.
Range:	Throughout much of North America, except far north.
Comments:	This is the giant among the ragweeds. The pollen of ragweeds is spread by the wind and is a principal cause of hay fever.

177 Pearly Everlasting
Anaphalis margaritacea

Description: An erect plant with a white woolly stem bearing a *flat cluster of white, globe-shaped rayless flower heads.*

Flowers: Head about ¼" (6 mm) wide; bracts petal-like.

Leaves: 3–5" (7.5–12.5 cm) long, alternate, narrow, *greenish white above, with dense white wool below.*

Height: 1–3' (30–90 cm).

Flowering: July–September.

Habitat: Dry pastures, roadsides, and waste places.

Range: Throughout much of North America, except southeastern United States and Arctic.

Comments: The pure white flowers of this showiest of everlastings are used in dried flower arrangements. Male and female flowers grow on separate plants.

178 Plantainleaf Pussytoes
Antennaria plantaginifolia

Description: A low, *colony-forming plant,* spreading by runners, with basal leaves and erect stems, each bearing a terminal cluster of *fuzzy, rayless flower heads.*

Flowers: Head to ⅜" (1 cm) long; disk flowers bristly; bracts green, white-tipped, sometimes pinkish toward base.

Leaves: To 2½" (6 cm) long, 1½" (4 cm) wide; those at base and at ends of runners largest, with usually 3 or 5 obvious veins, in rosettes, densely white-woolly below, much less so or even hairless above, ovate to obovate; those on stem scattered, much narrower.

Fruit: Seed-like, tipped with bristles.

Height: 4–16" (10–40 cm).

Flowering: April–June.

Habitat: Dry open woodlands, meadows, and rocky places.

Range: Quebec and Maine south to Florida, west to Louisiana, and north to Minnesota.

Comments: The crowded flower heads are thought to resemble a cat's paw, hence the common name. Male and the showier female flowers are on different plants. In some species of pussytoes the male flower heads are rare, even unknown, the female flower heads producing seeds without pollination. Most of our many species of *Antennaria* are difficult to identify, but Plantainleaf Pussytoes is not a problem, nor is the similar-leaved Single-head Pussytoes *(A. solitaria)*, found from Pennsylvania west to Illinois and south to the Gulf of Mexico; as its common name indicates, each stem bears a single flower head.

82 Mayweed; Stinking Chamomile
Anthemis cotula

Description: A daisy-like, malodorous plant bearing flower heads with *white rays surrounding a dome-shaped, yellow central disk.*

Flowers: Head to 1″ (2.5 cm) wide.
Leaves: 1–2½″ (2.5–6.5 cm) long, *finely dissected, fern-like.*
Height: 1–2′ (30–60 cm).
Flowering: June–October.
Habitat: Waste places and roadsides.
Range: Throughout North America, except Arctic.

Mayweed

Comments: This bushy, introduced plant is native
to Europe. Its foliage may cause skin
irritation when handled. Mayweed
resembles a plant from which
chamomile tea is made, hence the
common name Stinking Chamomile.
The similar Corn Chamomile *(A.
arvensis)* has flower heads to 1½″ (4 cm)
wide and grayish, hairy stems but is
scentless. Yellow Chamomile *(A.
tinctoria),* with yellow rays, occurs
sporadically from Quebec south to
New Jersey and west to Minnesota.

539 Common Burdock
Arctium minus

Description: A large bushy plant with round, *prickly,
pink to lavender, rayless flower heads.*
Flowers: Head ¾″ (2 cm) wide; disk flowers
numerous, tubular; bracts green,
overlapping, with hooked tips.
Leaves: To 18″ (45 cm) long, ovate, lower ones
heart-shaped, dark green above, woolly
below, with hollow leafstalks.
Height: 1–5′ (30–150 cm).
Flowering: July–October.
Habitat: Old fields and waste places.
Range: Throughout much of North America,
except far north.
Comments: The prickly flower heads of this
Eurasian weed easily catch on fur and
clothing, thus providing an excellent
mechanism for seed dispersal. Its young
leaves and leafstalks, roots, and flower
stalks can all be prepared in various
ways and eaten. Great Burdock
(A. lappa), a larger plant growing to
9′ (2.7 m) tall, has bigger flower heads
on solid grooved leafstalks.

415 Common Mugwort
Artemisia vulgaris

Description: A weedy, invasive plant with *deeply
divided, aromatic leaves densely silvery
downy beneath.*

Flowers: Head ⅛–¼" (3–5 mm) long, small, erect, *dull red, of all disk flowers;* crowded in elongated panicles.

Leaves: Green above, simple to variously dissected; strongly resembling foliage of hardy chrysanthemums.

Height: 2–4' (60–120 cm).

Flowering: July–October.

Habitat: Fields, roadsides, and waste places.

Range: Alberta east to Newfoundland, south to Florida, west to Louisiana, and north to Kansas, Iowa, and Minnesota; also widespread in northwestern United States to Alaska.

Comments: Naturalized from Europe, this plant is difficult to eradicate; it grows from stout, horizontal rhizomes that must be pulled or dug out if the plant is to be eliminated.

89 White Wood Aster
Aster divaricatus

Description: Often zigzag stems bearing somewhat flat-topped clusters of *flower heads with white rays.*

Flowers: Head to 1" (2.5 cm) wide; rays 6–10; *central disk yellow to bronzy-purple;* bracts whitish, with green tips.

Leaves: 2–7" (5–17.5 cm) long, stalked, *heart-shaped,* long-tapering, coarsely toothed.

Fruit: Dry, seed-like, tipped with whitish bristles.

Height: 12–40" (30–100 cm).

Flowering: July–October.

Habitat: Dry open woods.

Range: Virginia southwest to Tennessee and Alabama, west to Texas, and north to Nebraska.

Comments: This white aster is a typical late summer–early fall bloomer in open woodlands. Among the related species in our range, the taller Largeleaf Aster (*A. macrophyllus*) has lavender rays, rough, glandular flower stalks, and large, thick, rough leaves that, when very young, may be cooked and eaten as greens.

81 Bushy Aster
Aster dumosus

Description: *A rather stiff plant* with leafy branches bearing *numerous terminal flower heads with white or pale lavender rays* surrounding a pale yellow or brownish central disk.

Flowers: Head ½–¾" (1.5–2 cm) wide, relatively long-stalked.

Leaves: Those on stem 1–3" (2.5–7.5 cm) long, firm, sessile, linear to narrowly lanceolate, with rough edges; those on branches *smaller, numerous, bract-like*.

Fruit: Dry, seed-like, tipped with bristles.

Height: 12–40" (30–100 cm).

Flowering: August–October.

Habitat: Sandy, open sites and occasionally marshy ground.

Range: Ontario; New Brunswick south mainly along coast to Florida and west to Texas and north through Missouri and Iowa to Wisconsin.

Comments: This aster is most widely found in southern states; elsewhere it is more locally restricted to shoreline areas, such as around the Great Lakes.

Bushy Aster

560 Smooth Aster
Aster laevis

Description: A *smooth-leaved* perennial bearing flower heads with *many rich lavender-blue rays* surrounding a yellow central disk; stem with a *light grayish-white bloom.*

Flowers: Head to 1″ (2.5 cm) wide; bracts green-tipped.

Leaves: 1–4″ (2.5–10 cm) long, thick, slightly toothed, elliptical or lanceolate; lower ones stalked; upper ones unstalked, clasping stem.

Fruit: Dry, seed-like, tipped with often reddish bristles.

Height: 2–4′ (60–120 cm).

Flowering: August–October.

Habitat: Fields, open woods, and roadsides.

Range: Throughout much of North America, except Florida, California, and far north.

Comments: One of the most attractive blue asters, this species has bright green foliage that is very smooth to the touch. At least 11 other related *Aster* species are found within our range.

88 Calico Aster
Aster lateriflorus

Description: Several small flower heads with *white or pale purple rays surrounding a yellow or purplish-red central disk* along one side of straggly, divergent branches.

Flowers: Less than ½″ (1.5 cm) wide; rays 9–15; bracts with greenish midrib.

Leaves: 2–6″ (5–15 cm) long, lanceolate to elliptical, coarsely toothed; basal ones stalked, often soon dropping off; upper ones sessile.

Fruit: Dry, seed-like, tipped with bristles.

Height: 1–5′ (30–150 cm).

Flowering: August–October.

Habitat: Fields and thickets.

Range: Manitoba east to Nova Scotia, south to Florida, west to Texas, and north to South Dakota and Minnesota.

Comments: This is one of a group of closely related white, narrow-leaved asters, which

presumably interbreed and are difficult
to distinguish. The common name refe
to the fact that the disk flowers are at
first yellow and later turn purplish red,
so that flowers on one plant and even a
single head may include both colors at
the same time.

623   Stiff Aster; Bristly Aster
Aster linariifolius

Description: A *stiff leafy stalk* terminated by several
flower heads with *often pale blue rays
surrounding a yellow central disk turning
bronzy.*

Flowers: Head to 1″ (2.5 cm) wide.

Leaves: To 1½″ (4 cm) long, dark green, *linear,*
numerous.

Fruit: Dry, seed-like, tipped with tawny
bristles.

Height: 4–24″ (10–60 cm).

Flowering: August–October.

Habitat: Dry clearings and rocky banks.

Range: Quebec and New Brunswick south to
Florida, west to Texas, and north to
Iowa.

Comments: Numerous short stems form a mound of
flowers in colors ranging from deepest
lavender to shades of pink and white.

557   New England Aster
Aster novae-angliae

Description: A large, stout, hairy, leafy plant bearing
*flower heads with bright lavender to
purplish-blue rays clustered at branch ends.*

Flowers: Head 1–2″ (2.5–5 cm) wide, on a *stalk
with glandular, sticky hairs;* rays 35–45;
disk flowers yellowish; bracts narrow,
hairy, sticky.

Leaves: 1½–5″ (4–12.5 cm) long, lanceolate,
toothless, *clasping large stem.*

Fruit: Dry, seed-like, tipped with tawny
bristles.

Height: 3–7′ (90–210 cm).

Flowering: August–October.

Habitat: Wet thickets, meadows, and swamps.

New England Aster

Range: Manitoba east to Nova Scotia, south to Georgia, west to Oklahoma, and north to North Dakota; also in parts of western United States.

Comments: There are many color forms of this species, with rays ranging from lavender to purple to white. A pink form is sometimes grown commercially.

558 New York Aster
Aster novi-belgii

Description: A branching plant with slender, mostly smooth stems bearing narrow leaves and numerous *flower heads with blue-violet to rose (sometimes white) rays surrounding a yellow or reddish central disk.*

Flowers: Head 1–1¼" (2.5–3 cm) wide; rays 20–40; bracts whitish green, with *spreading or backward-curving tips.*

Leaves: 2–6" (5–15 cm) long, oblong to linear-lanceolate, more or less clasping stem.

Fruit: Dry, seed-like, tipped with bristles.

Height: 8–54" (20–140 cm).

Flowering: July–October.

Habitat: Shorelines, damp thickets, and meadows.

Range: Quebec, Newfoundland, and Nova Scotia south to South Carolina, mostly near coast.

Comments: This large aster is abundant in low area
along the coast. There are many color
forms, including those with white or
rose rays. The species name, Latin for "c
New Belgium," is from an early name
for New York.

85 Small-flowered White Aster
Aster racemosus

Description: Numerous *flower heads with white rays*
surrounding a yellowish to pinkish
central disk; *heads mostly clustered along
one side of widely diverging branches* on a
smooth, slender, purple-tinged stem.

Flowers: Head about ⅜" (8 mm) wide; rays
15–30; bracts green-tipped.

Leaves: Those on stem 3–5" (7.5–12.5 cm) long
sessile, linear to lanceolate, sometimes
slightly toothed; those on branches
smaller.

Fruit: Dry, seed-like, tipped with bristles.

Height: 2–6½' (60–200 cm).

Flowering: August–October.

Habitat: Dry to moist fields, meadows, forests,
and shorelines.

Range: Quebec and New Brunswick south to
Florida, west to Texas, and northeast to
Missouri, Illinois, and Ohio.

Comments: The many small-flowered asters found ir
our range are often difficult to
distinguish from one another, as are
many of the large-flowered species.

90 Panicled Aster
Aster simplex

Description: A tall stem bearing a panicle of flower
heads with *numerous white (occasionally
violet-tinged) rays.*

Flowers: Head ¾–1" (2–2.5 cm) wide; central
disk yellowish to pinkish; bracts narrow,
green-tipped.

Leaves: Lanceolate, sharp-pointed, sometimes
toothed, sessile or short-stalked; lower
ones 3–6" (7.5–15 cm) long, upper ones
smaller.

Fruit:	Dry, seed-like, tipped with bristles.
Height:	2–5′ (60–150 cm).
Flowering:	August–October.
Habitat:	Damp thickets, meadows, and shorelines.
Range:	Throughout much of North America, except far north.
Comments:	This colony-forming species spreads by rhizomes. It has several varieties, differing in color, ray size, and leaf shape and serration.

559 Showy Aster
Aster spectabilis

Description:	Open clusters of showy flower heads with *bright lavender rays surrounding a yellow central disk;* stem stiff, rough, often branched toward top.
Flowers:	Head to 1½″ (4 cm) wide; bracts oblong, sticky, with spreading green tips.
Leaves:	Lower ones 3–5″ (7.5–12.5 cm) long, light green, elliptical, stalked, with shallow teeth; upper ones linear, oblong, sessile, mostly untoothed.
Fruit:	Dry, seed-like, tipped with bristles.
Height:	1–3′ (30–90 cm).
Flowering:	August–October.
Habitat:	Dry clearings and sandy woods.
Range:	New York and Massachusetts south to Georgia and Alabama.
Comments:	This very showy, large-flowered, short-stemmed aster is easily cultivated and makes a fine display in late summer. Its distribution is mainly coastal, especially in pine barrens.

84 Saltmarsh Aster
Aster tenuifolius

Description:	A weak straggly plant with widely spreading branches, slender rhizomes, and *few flower heads with numerous white or pale purple rays.*
Flowers:	Head ½–1″ (1.5–2.5 cm) wide; central disk yellowish to pinkish.

Leaves:	To 6″ (15 cm) long, sparse, *fleshy,* untooted, narrow, tapering at both ends
Fruit:	Dry, seed-like, tipped with bristles.
Height:	12–27″ (30–70 cm).
Flowering:	August–October.
Habitat:	Salt or brackish marshes.
Range:	Maine south along coast to Florida, and west to Texas.
Comments:	Although this perennial aster has few flowers, it forms conspicuous masses in the brackish tidal marshes where all other large-flowered species are absent. Annual Saltmarsh Aster *(A. subulatus)* has many smaller flower heads, ¼–½″ (6–13 mm) wide.

87 Flat-topped White Aster
Aster umbellatus

Description:	A rigid, upright stem bearing a *flat-topped cluster of flower heads with white rays.*
Flowers:	Head ½–¾″ (1.5–2 cm) wide; rays 10–15, tending to curve downward or backward; central disk yellowish to pinkish.
Leaves:	To 6″ (15 cm) long, lanceolate or elliptical, tapering at both ends, *untoothed.*
Fruit:	Dry, seed-like, tipped with bristles.
Height:	1–7′ (30–210 cm).
Flowering:	August–September.
Habitat:	Moist thickets, woods, and swamp edges.
Range:	Alberta east to Newfoundland, south to Georgia and Alabama, and northwest to Missouri, Nebraska, and North Dakota.
Comments:	This conspicuous aster of wet meadows is one of the first asters to bloom; it has an extremely wide, flat top, almost 1′ (30 cm) wide.

554 Wavy-leaved Aster
Aster undulatus

Description:	A stiff, very rough stem bearing spreading branches and loose clusters of *flower heads with lavender, violet, or pale blue rays.*

Flowers:	Head about ¾" (2 cm) wide; rays 12–20; disk flowers yellow; bracts pale, downy, green-tipped.
Leaves:	2–6" (5–15 cm) long, with *wavy or shallowly toothed edges,* ovate, somewhat hoary; lower ones often with *dilated leafstalk bases* clasping stem; upper ones stalkless.
Fruit:	Dry, seed-like, tipped with tan to whitish bristles.
Height:	1–3½' (30–105 cm).
Flowering:	August–November.
Habitat:	Dry woods, thickets, and clearings.
Range:	Ontario; Nova Scotia and Maine south to Florida, west to Louisiana, and north to Tennessee and Illinois.
Comments:	There are several varieties of this plant, differing only in the outline of the leaves. The broadly winged leafstalks are particularly noteworthy.

186 Groundsel Tree
Baccharis halimifolia

Description:	A saltmarsh shrub with *greenish-white, rayless flower heads and angled twigs.*
Flowers:	Head ½" (1.5 cm) long, in clusters of 1–5; male and female flowers on separate plants.
Leaves:	To 2½" (6.5 cm) long, *alternate,* ovate; lower ones irregularly and bluntly toothed, upper ones untoothed.
Fruit:	Seed-like, those of female plants with very *white-silky* bristles.
Height:	3½–10' (1–3 m).
Flowering:	August–September.
Habitat:	Saltmarsh borders.
Range:	New York and Massachusetts south along coast to Florida, west to Texas and Oklahoma, and north to Kansas; also in southwestern and Pacific states.
Comments:	The female plants are especially showy in the fall due to the silky bristles of the numerous fruits. Groundsel Tree is one of two shrubs associated with coastal wetlands. The other is Marsh Elder *(Iva frutescens),* an opposite-leaved shrub that

often forms a belt at the edge of the marsh and invades even the marsh itself along mosquito ditches.

282 Tickseed Sunflower
Bidens aristosa

Description: Slender, leafy, much-branched stems bearing several *yellow, daisy-like flower heads.*

Flowers: Head 1–2" (2.5–5 cm) wide; rays long in relation to width of central disk.

Leaves: To 6" (15 cm) long, opposite, *pinnately divided,* segments toothed.

Fruit: Seed-like, *flat,* ovoid, usually with *2 barbed spines.*

Height: 1–5' (30–150 cm).

Flowering: August–October.

Habitat: Wet meadows, roadside ditches, abandoned fields, and low ground.

Range: Ontario; New England south to Georgia, west to Texas, and north to Nebraska, Iowa, and Minnesota.

Comments: The prickly fruit of *Bidens* species are known as beggars'-ticks, the very common, 2-pronged "stickers" that cling to one's clothing during autumn walks. They can be removed easily with the flat edge of a knife blade.

281 Nodding Bur Marigold
Bidens cernua

Description: Numerous *yellow flower heads nodding* increasingly as flowers mature.

Flowers: Head to 2" (5 cm) wide; rays usually 6–8, occasionally absent, short in relation to width of central disk; disk flowers darker yellow.

Leaves: 2–6" (5–15 cm) long, *simple,* smooth, opposite, stalkless, *narrowly lanceolate to elliptical.*

Fruit: Seed-like, with 2–4 barbed spines.

Height: 1–3' (30–90 cm).

Flowering: August–October.

Habitat: Swamps, streambanks, and wet ground.

Range: Throughout much of North America,
except Texas, Alabama, Florida, South
Carolina, and Arctic.

Comments: The species name is Latin for "nodding."
The seed-like fruit is sometimes eaten
by ducks. Where the range of this
species and Smooth Bur Marigold
(*B. laevis*) overlap in coastal areas, the
latter is much more prevalent.

86 Shepherd's Needle
Bidens pilosa

Description: A *square-stemmed* plant bearing flower
heads with *white to pale yellow or
purplish rays* surrounding a yellow
central disk.

Flowers: Head to 1" (2.5 cm) wide, on stalk
rising from leaf axils.

Leaves: Opposite, divided into lanceolate to
ovate, toothed segments, each 1–4"
(2.5–10 cm) long.

Fruit: Dry, seed-like, spindle-shaped, with
2–3 barbed spines.

Height: 12–40" (30–100 cm).

Flowering: March–frost.

Habitat: Waste places, roadsides, and lawns.

Range: Ontario; Massachusetts south to Florida
and west to California.

Comments: The barbed fruit of *Bidens* species
adhere to clothing and the fur of
animals, thus providing an excellent
means of dispersal. This plant is found
in warm areas worldwide.

553 Boltonia
Boltonia asteroides

Description: Broad flat clusters of generally small
flower heads with *white to pink, purple, or
blue rays surrounding a dome-shaped, yellow
central disk.*

Flowers: Head ¾–1¼" (2–3 cm) wide.

Leaves: 1–5" (2.5–12.5 cm) long, smooth, thick,
narrow, usually untoothed.

Fruit: Seed-like, usually with 2–4 very short
spines and several shorter bristles.

Boltonia

Height: 1–5′ (30–150 cm).
Flowering: July–October.
Habitat: Sandy or gravelly, moist to wet places.
Range: Saskatchewan and Manitoba; Maine
south to Florida, west to Texas, and
north to North Dakota.
Comments: This plant escapes from cultivation and
establishes itself locally. Its fruit has
spines somewhat like those of beggars'-
ticks (*Bidens*).

---

541 **Musk Thistle; Nodding Thistle;
Bristle Thistle**
Carduus nutans

Description: *Nodding, dark pink to rose-purple (rarely
white), thistle-like, rayless flower heads*
along a long stalk at end of main stem
and its branches; stem sometimes with a
cobweb-like covering.
Flowers: Head 1½–2½″ (4–6.5 cm) wide; *bracts
broad, pointed, purple,* outer ones curving
outward.
Leaves: To 10″ (25 cm) long, lanceolate, deeply
lobed, *very spiny,* with bases extending
up and down stem as *prickly wings.*
Fruit: Seed-like, with long, white, minutely
barbed bristles.

Height: 2–9' (60–270 cm).
Flowering: June–October.
Habitat: Waste places and fields.
Range: Throughout much of North America, except far north.
Comments: This ferociously spiny, European introduction has spread rapidly. It is considered a noxious weed in several states, since cattle may refuse to graze where it grows densely. Although very similar, this species differs from the closely related *Cirsium* thistles in lacking white matted hairs on the leaves and in having outward-pointing bracts around the flower heads.

606 Spotted Knapweed
Centaurea maculosa

Description: A highly branched, wiry-stemmed plant with *lavender, rayless flower heads* atop stems with soft hairs.
Flowers: Head to 1" (2.5 cm) wide; *bracts harsh, prickly, black-tipped.*
Leaves: Those at base 4–8" (10–20 cm) long, smaller above, highly dissected into linear segments.
Height: 2–4' (60–120 cm).
Flowering: June–August.
Habitat: Fields, waste places, and roadsides.
Range: Alberta; Ontario east to Nova Scotia, south to Florida, west to Louisiana, and north to Minnesota and North Dakota; also widely distributed in West.
Comments: There is some recent evidence that the correct name for this introduced species is *C. biebersteinii,* there being possibly a nomenclatural mix-up of plants in these two variable European species. Spotted Knapweed is considered a noxious weed in many western states. Its spiny, thistle-like involucre is a prominent feature. Two similar annuals are Cornflower (*C. cyanus*), with bright blue disk flowers, and Basket-flower (*C. americana*), a showy southwestern species with purple to pink flower heads 1½–3" (4–8 cm) wide.

283 Golden Star
Chrysogonum virginianum

Description: A showy plant with *yellow, daisy-like flower heads* on very hairy stems.
Flowers: Head 1–1½" (2.5–4 cm) wide; rays 5, each 1–1½" (2.5–4 cm) wide, petal-like.
Leaves: 1–3" (2.5–7.5 cm) long, long-stalked, egg-shaped or oblong, with round toothed edges.
Height: 3–15" (7.5–38 cm).
Flowering: March–July.
Habitat: Moist shady woodlands.
Range: New York south to Florida, west to Louisiana, and northeast to Ohio.
Comments: Each flower head resembles a yellow or golden star, and the stems have distinctive spreading, glandular hairs. It is the only species in this genus.

624 Chicory
Cichorium intybus

Description: A stiff stem bearing several stalkless, showy, *blue (sometimes pink or white) flower heads with square-tipped, fringed rays.*
Flowers: Head to 1½" (4 cm) wide, of all rays; style 2-parted, surrounded by dark blue fused anthers.
Leaves: Those at base 3–6" (7.5–15 cm) long, dandelion-like; those on stem much smaller, oblong to lanceolate, clasping.
Height: 12–52" (30–130 cm).
Flowering: June–October.
Habitat: Fields, roadsides, and waste places.
Range: Throughout North America, except far north.
Comments: Only a few flower heads open at a time, and each lasts only a day. While in some places this European weed has proliferated to become a plant pest, it is also sought for its food uses. The roots can be roasted and ground as a coffee substitute or additive; a European form is cultivated for this purpose, and millions of pounds are used here and abroad. Closely related to Chicory is the salad plant Endive (*C. endivia*).

540 Canadian Thistle
Cirsium arvense

Description:	Numerous fragrant, *pale magenta, lavender, or white, rayless flower heads* atop a highly branched, smooth-stemmed plant.
Flowers:	Head 1″ (2.5 cm) wide; bracts spine-tipped.
Leaves:	5–8″ (12.5–20 cm) long, gray-green, with matted hairs, *spiny,* lanceolate, deeply cut, wavy-edged, mostly stalkless.
Fruit:	¼″ (5 mm) long, seed-like, tipped with many feathery bristles.
Height:	1–5′ (30–150 cm).
Flowering:	June–October.
Habitat:	Pastures, roadsides, and waste places.
Range:	Throughout North America, except much of far north and southeastern United States.
Comments:	This European introduction, a pernicious weed that is classified as noxious in most states, reached the United States by way of Canada, hence the common name. Its smaller flowering heads and non-spiny stem distinguish it from Bull Thistle (*C. vulgare*).

353 Yellow Thistle
Cirsium horridulum

Description:	A tall branching stem with large, *yellow or red-purple, rayless flower heads* and very *spiny, clasping leaves.*
Flowers:	Head 2½″ (6.5 cm) wide; disk flowers tiny, 5-parted, tubular; bracts weakly spined.
Leaves:	6–10″ (15–25 cm) long, lanceolate in outline, pinnately lobed, stalkless and clasping stem, with spiny edges and tips; erect, narrow, spiny, bract-like leaves surrounding flower head.
Fruit:	¼″ (5 mm) long, seed-like, tipped with many feathery bristles.
Height:	1–5′ (30–150 cm).
Flowering:	May–August.

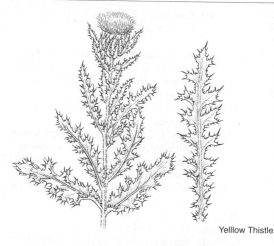

Yelllow Thistle

Habitat: Shorelines, marshes, and sandy or peaty
            fields.

Range: Maine south to Florida and west to
          Texas and Oklahoma.

Comments: Often found along the edges of salt
             marshes, this plant is also a pasture
             weed in the South, where its flower
             heads may be red-purple instead of
             yellow. The species name aptly describes
             the spiny nature of the plant. Prairie
             Thistle *(C. canescens)*, also with yellow
             flowers, has leaves white and velvety
             beneath, grayish above, with leaf
             bases extending wing-like down the
             stem; it is common in overgrazed
             pastures in the West.

542 Bull Thistle
Cirsium vulgare

Description: A very *prickly* plant with a *spiny-winged
               stem and large, rose-purple (occasionally
               white), rayless flower heads* surrounded
               by spiny, yellow-tipped bracts.

Flowers: Head 1½–2″ (4–5 cm) wide.

Leaves: 3–6″ (7.5–15 cm) long, coarsely
           pinnately lobed, spiny.

Fruit: About ¼″ (5 mm) long, seed-like,
          tipped with numerous feathery
          bristles.

Height: 2–6′ (60–180 cm).
Flowering: June–September.
Habitat: Roadsides, pastures, and waste places.
Range: Throughout North America, except parts of far north.
Comments: This native of Eurasia is our spiniest *Cirsium* thistle; it should be handled only with gloves. A biennial, it produces a rosette of leaves the first year and an upright flowering stalk the second year. The thistledown, or bristles on the fruits, serve as "parachutes" to carry the light seeds. Within the East, 15 additional biennial thistles with purple flower heads occur; Bull Thistle differs from these in its spine-tipped bracts and its spiny-winged stems.

107 Horseweed
Conyza canadensis

Description: *A coarse weedy plant* with an erect, bristly-haired stem and branching *clusters of small, cup-like flower heads* rising from upper leaf axils.
Flowers: Head less than ¼″ (6 mm) wide; rays white, inconspicuous; disk flowers numerous, yellow.
Leaves: 1–4″ (2.5–10 cm) long, dark green, linear to narrowly lanceolate, hairy, usually slightly toothed.
Fruit: Tiny, 1-seeded, with numerous bristles.
Height: 1–7′ (30–210 cm).
Flowering: July–November.
Habitat: Fields, roadsides, and waste places.
Range: Throughout North America, except parts of far north.
Comments: Originally a North American plant, Horseweed has spread to Europe, where it colonizes in open, disturbed sites. Its seed-like fruit is dispersed by the wind. An annual that thrives on bare soil, it is soon crowded out as perennials become established. Native Americans and early settlers used a preparation of its leaves to treat dysentery and sore throat.

286 Lance-leaved Coreopsis; Tickseed
Coreopsis lanceolata

Description: *Yellow, daisy-like flower heads* on long
stalks.

Flowers: Head 2–2½" (5–6.5 cm) wide; rays 8,
each with *3–5 notches at tip;* disk flower
numerous; outer bracts shorter than
inner ones, dissimilar.

Leaves: Lower and basal ones 3–6" (7.5–15 cm
long, short-stalked, elliptical to linear,
occasionally lobed; upper ones few,
opposite, unstalked, linear to oblong.

Fruit: 1-seeded, dry, winged, with 2 terminal
scales.

Height: 1–2' (30–60 cm).

Flowering: May–July.

Habitat: Sandy or rocky soil and disturbed areas

Range: Throughout East, except northern Plai
states and Prairie Provinces; also in
much of West.

Comments: This native species has escaped from
cultivation. It has branching stems at
the base and often forms sizable colonie
along roadsides and in old fields. A
southern species, Greater Tickseed
(*C. major*), is 2–3' (60–90 cm) tall; it
has sunflower-like flower heads 1–2"
(2.5–5 cm) wide and opposite leaves
deeply segmented into three parts,
appearing to be in whorls of six. Withi
the East, 11 other yellow-flowered
perennial species of *Coreopsis* occur.

287 Garden Coreopsis
Coreopsis tinctoria

Description: Numerous smooth, slightly angled
branches bearing showy, daisy-like
flower heads with *yellow rays surrounding
a reddish-purple central disk.*

Flowers: Head to 1¼" (3 cm) wide; rays 5–7, eacl
3-toothed, blotched *with reddish brown a
base;* outer bracts shorter than inner
ones, dissimilar.

Leaves: 2–4" (5–10 cm) long, opposite, highly
dissected into linear segments.

Height: 2–4' (60–120 cm).

Flowering: June–September.
   Habitat: Low ground, roadsides, and waste places.
   Range: Throughout East, except Maritime
        Provinces and far north; also in much of
        West.
Comments: This prevailingly western annual has
        escaped from cultivation in the East. It
        is widespread in the West and the South
        in disturbed areas, such as moist ditches.
        Because of its showiness, the flower is
        cultivated extensively, hence its
        common name.

555 Purple Coneflower
Echinacea purpurea

Description: An attractive perennial with *purple
        (rarely white), drooping rays* surrounding a
        spiny, brownish central disk.
   Flowers: Head 2½–4″ (6.5–10 cm) wide.
   Leaves: Rough, long-stalked, ovate, with 3–5
        major veins, edges often serrated.
   Height: 1–5′ (30–150 cm).
Flowering: June–October.
   Habitat: Dry open woods and prairies.
   Range: Quebec, New York, and Massachusetts
        south to Florida, west to Texas, and
        north to Kansas, Iowa, and Wisconsin.
Comments: The genus name is from the Greek
        echino, meaning "hedgehog," an allusion
        to the spiny, brownish central disk. The
        flowers of *Echinacea* species are used to
        make an extremely popular herbal tea,
        purported to help strengthen the
        immune system; an extract is also
        available in tablet or liquid form in
        pharmacies and health food stores. Often
        cultivated, Purple Coneflower is a
        showy, easily grown garden plant.

79 Daisy Fleabane
Erigeron annuus

Description: An erect *stem covered with spreading hairs*
        and bearing *flower heads with at least 40
        tightly packed, white to pale pink rays*
        surrounding a yellow central disk.

Flowers:	Head ½" (1.5 cm) wide; *rays short in relation to width of central disk;* bracts of equal length.
Leaves:	To 5" (12.5 cm) long, 2" (5 cm) wide, hairy, lanceolate, toothed.
Height:	1–5' (30–150 cm).
Flowering:	June–October.
Habitat:	Fields, roadsides, and waste places.
Range:	Throughout East, except far north; also in much of West.
Comments:	The common name fleabane originated from a belief that the dried flower heads of these plants could rid a dwelling of fleas. A similar weedy species, White-top Fleabane *(E. strigosus),* has narrower leaves to 1" (2.5 cm) wide and shorter hairs pressed against the stem.

80 Philadelphia Fleabane
Erigeron philadelphicus

Description:	Small, aster-like flower heads with *numerous narrow, white to pink rays* surrounding a large yellow central disk.
Flowers:	Head ½–1" (1.5–2.5 cm) wide.
Leaves:	Hairy; those at base to 6" (15 cm) long, oblong to narrowly ovate; those on stem smaller, toothed, *clasping.*
Height:	6–36" (15–90 cm).
Flowering:	April–August.
Habitat:	Rich thickets, fields, and open woods.
Range:	Throughout East, except Arctic; also in much of West.
Comments:	The genus name, from the Greek *eri* ("early") and *geron* ("old man"), presumably refers to the fact that the plants flower early and have a hoary down suggesting an old man's beard. Robin's Plaintain *(E. pulchellus),* mostly a woodland plant, is slightly shorter and has fewer, but larger, lilac or violet flower heads, as well as stem leaves that are sparse and stalkless but do not clasp the stem; it spreads actively by runners.

530 Spotted Joe-Pye Weed
Eupatorium maculatum

Description: A large, *purplish-pink, flat-topped cluster of fuzzy, rayless flower heads* atop a sturdy, *purple or purple-spotted stem,* hairy above.

Flowers: Head ⅜″ (8 mm) wide; cluster 4–5½″ (10–14 cm) wide.

Leaves: 2½–8″ (6.5–20 cm) long, *in whorls of* 3–5, thick, lanceolate, coarsely toothed.

Height: 2–6½′ (60–200 cm).

Flowering: July–September.

Habitat: Damp meadows, thickets, and shorelines.

Range: Alberta east to Newfoundland, south to North Carolina, west to Kansas, and north to North Dakota; also in parts of West.

Comments: This is one of several similar species found in our range. Sweet Joe-Pye Weed (*E. purpureum*) has a greenish stem, a dome-shaped cluster of dull pink flower heads, and foliage that smells like vanilla when crushed. Hollow Joe-Pye Weed (*E. fistulosum*) has a hollow stem. Coastal Plain Joe-Pye Weed (*E. dubium*) is a smaller species with ovate leaves. According to folklore, a Native American named Joe Pye used this plant to cure fevers, and early American colonists used it to treat an outbreak of typhus.

153 Boneset
Eupatorium perfoliatum

Description: A hairy plant with dense, *flat-topped clusters of many dull white, rayless flower heads.*

Flowers: Head to ¼″ (6 mm) long.

Leaves: 4–8″ (10–20 cm) long, opposite, lanceolate, wrinkled, sessile, toothed; usually united at base and *completely surrounding stem.*

Height: 2–4′ (60–120 cm).

Flowering: July–October.

Habitat: Low woods and wet meadows.

Range: Throughout East, except far north.

Comments: As suggested by the species name, the stem appears to be growing through the pairs of united leaves. Its leaves were wrapped with bandages around splints to help set broken bones. The dried leaves have also been used to make a tonic, boneset tea, thought to be effective in treating colds, coughs, and constipation. Upland Boneset (*E. sessilifolium*) is somewhat similar, but its leaves are not united at the base.

154 White Snakeroot
Eupatorium rugosum

Description: Solitary or clustered, firm stems bearing *flat-topped clusters of small, fuzzy, rayless, white flower heads.*

Flowers: Head about ¼" (5 mm) long, ⅛" (4 mm) wide.

Leaves: 2½–7" (6.5–18 cm) long, opposite, ovate, *stalked,* sharply toothed.

Fruit: Tiny, seed-like, with white bristles.

Height: 1–3' (30–90 cm).

Flowering: July–October.

Habitat: Woods and thickets.

Range: Saskatchewan east to Nova Scotia, south to Florida, west to Texas, and north to North Dakota.

Comments: This plant is toxic to cows. Humans who drink milk from the poisoned animals may get milk sickness, a disease that can be fatal. Smaller White Snakeroot (*E. aromaticum*), a non-aromatic plant despite its species name, has bluntly toothed leaves, the upper ones nearly stalkless. Late-flowering Thoroughwort (*E. hyssopifolium*) has very narrow leaves in whorls of 3–4 or some in pairs.

349 Lance-leaved Goldenrod
Euthamia graminifolia

Description: A smooth or finely downy stem branching above midstem, each branch bearing *1 flat-topped cluster of small yellow flower heads.*

Flowers:	Head about ¼" (5 mm) long; rays 10–20; disk flowers 8–12.
Leaves:	2¾–5" (7–12.5 cm) long, *narrow, elongated, pointed,* with 3–5 veins.
Height:	2–4' (60–120 cm).
Flowering:	July–October.
Habitat:	Roadsides, fields, and thickets.
Range:	Alberta east to Newfoundland, south to South Carolina, southwest to Louisiana, and northwest to Oklahoma and North Dakota; also in parts of West.
Comments:	The flat-topped flower arrangement and narrow leaves of this goldenrod are distinctive. Slender Fragrant Goldenrod (*E. tenuifolia*) has grass-like leaves with tiny resin dots and only one main vein. The similar, still smaller Narrow-leaved Bushy Goldenrod (*E. caroliniana*) has leaves less than ⅛" (3 mm) wide, with tufts of minute leaves in the axils.

401 Indian Blanket; Gaillardia; Firewheel
Gaillardia pulchella

Description:	Branching, hairy stems, each bearing 1 flower head with *reddish rays, tipped with yellow,* surrounding a reddish central disk.

Indian Blanket

Flowers:	Head 1–3″ (2.5–7.5 cm) wide; rays occasionally all yellow; disk flowers same color as rays.
Leaves:	1–3″ (2.5–7.5 cm) long, bristly-hairy o downy, mostly stalkless; lower ones bluntly lobed, upper ones lanceolate.
Height:	8–16″ (20–40 cm).
Flowering:	June–July.
Habitat:	Prairies, sandy fields, and roadsides.
Range:	Ontario, Quebec, and Maine south to Florida, west to Texas, and north to South Dakota and Minnesota; also in southwestern United States and California.
Comments:	This lovely plant may produce many color variants and combinations in the red-pink-yellow range. It is an easily grown garden ornamental. If rays are absent, entire flower heads may consist of enlarged disk flowers. Another common name for the species is Showy Gaillardia.

155 Sweet Everlasting; Catfoot
Gnaphalium obtusifolium

Description:	An erect, *cottony stem* bearing branched clusters of *white or yellowish-white, round, rayless, fragrant flower heads.*
Flowers:	Head about ¼″ (6 mm) long; disk flowers tiny, tubular, with bristles; bracts overlapping, white or tinged with yellow, persistent.
Leaves:	1–4″ (2.5–10 cm) long, whitish-woolly beneath, narrow, pointed, stalkless.
Height:	1–2′ (30–60 cm).
Flowering:	August–November.
Habitat:	Dry clearings, fields, and edges of woods
Range:	Alberta east to Nova Scotia, south to Florida, west to Texas, and north to Nebraska and Minnesota.
Comments:	The genus name, derived from the Greek *gnaphallon* ("tuft of wool"), refers to the woolly nature of the plants. This species is one of the more common among the 12 *Gnaphalium* within our range. Pussytoes (*Antennaria*) are similar but have mostly basal leaves.

291 Curlycup Gumweed; Stickyheads
Grindelia squarrosa

Description: A stout erect stem with several branches bearing *yellow, daisy-like flower heads.*

Flowers: Head about 1" (2.5 cm) wide; disk flowers darker than rays; *bracts pointed, curling outward, sticky, green.*

Leaves: 1–2½" (2.5–6.5 cm) long, oblong, stalkless, toothed, covered with translucent dots.

Height: 6–36" (15–90 cm).

Flowering: July–September.

Habitat: Prairies and waste places.

Range: Throughout much of North America, except far north and from North Carolina to Louisiana.

Comments: This tough but short-lived perennial is a common invader of heavily grazed rangeland in the West; because the plant has a bitter taste, it is not usually eaten by cattle. It has now spread to dry waste places in the East. Native Americans used its flowers and leaves for treating bronchitis and asthma and for healing sores. The powdered flower heads were once used in cigarettes to relieve asthma.

352 Broom Snakeweed; TurpentineWeed; Snakeweed
Gutierrezia sarothrae

Description: A sticky, bushy plant with *tiny, oblong, yellow flower heads* in clusters at ends of hairless branches.

Flowers: Head ¼" (6 mm) wide, in clusters of 2–5.

Leaves: About 1½" (4 cm) long, alternate, narrow, untoothed.

Height: 6–20" (15–50 cm).

Flowering: July–September.

Habitat: Dry plains and prairies.

Range: Alberta east to Manitoba and south through Minnesota and the Dakotas to Texas; also throughout western United States.

Comments: The fine brittle stems of this shrubby perennial are somewhat broom-like, hence common names such as Broom

Snakeweed and Broomweed; the stems
may die back nearly to the ground each
year. The plant is also known as
Matchweed and Matchbush, in referenc
to its numerous thin branches. The
plant is toxic to grazing animals. Since
it tends to increase in heavily grazed
areas, its abundance often indicates
deteriorating rangeland.

288 Sneezeweed
Helenium autumnale

Description: A *winged stem* bearing yellow, daisy-like
flower heads with fan-shaped, *drooping
rays;* disk flowers forming a conspicuou
greenish-yellow, ball-like structure at
center of head.

Flowers: Head 1–2″ (2.5–5 cm) wide; *rays 3-lobea*
Leaves: To 6″ (15 cm) long, alternate, lanceolate
toothed, with bases forming winged
extensions down stem.
Height: 2–5′ (60–150 cm).
Flowering: August–November.
Habitat: Swamps, wet meadows, and roadsides.
Range: Throughout North America, except
Maritime Provinces and far north.
Comments: As the species name implies,
Sneezeweed flowers in late summer or
fall. The common name is based on the
former use of its dried leaves in making
snuff, inhaled to cause sneezing that
would supposedly rid the body of evil
spirits. Other *Helenium* species include
Purple-head Sneezeweed *(H. flexuosum),*
with a purplish-brown ball of disk
flowers, and Slender-leaved Sneezeweed
(H. amarum), with stems covered with
almost thread-like leaves.

277 Common Sunflower
Helianthus annuus

Description: A rough erect stem bearing 1 to several
terminal flower heads with overlapping,
*yellow rays surrounding a brownish central
disk.*

Flowers:	Head 3–6″ (7.5–15 cm) wide; bracts at least ⅛″ (4 mm) wide, edged with bristles.
Leaves:	3–12″ (7.5–30 cm) long, *ovate to nearly triangular,* pointed, with rough stiff hairs, mostly alternate.
Fruit:	Dry, seed-like, with a white seed inside; produced by disk flowers.
Height:	3–10′ (90–300 cm).
Flowering:	July–November.
Habitat:	Prairies, waste places, and roadsides.
Range:	Throughout much of temperate North America.
Comments:	This native annual is appreciably smaller than the familiar cultivated variety Russian Giant, which has one large head to 1′ (30 cm) wide, usually drooping because of its weight; it is grown for its seed-like fruits, a popular snack. Native Americans ground sunflower seeds for bread flour and for oil used in cooking and for dressing hair. In the 19th century it was believed that growing Common Sunflower near the home would protect the occupants from malaria. Recent uses include silage (cattle feed) and oil for cooking and soap. The closely related Prairie Sunflower *(H. petiolaris),* found throughout the Great Plains, has bracts less than ⅛″ (4 mm) wide.

Common Sunflower

276 Giant Sunflower; Tall Sunflower
Helianthus giganteus

Description: A tall, rough, reddish stem bearing several to many *light yellow flower heads.*

Flowers: Head 1½–3″ (4–7.5 cm) wide; rays 10–20; disk flowers numerous; bracts narrow, thin, green.

Leaves: 3–7″ (7.5–17.5 cm) long, *rough, lanceolate, pointed, finely toothed,* mostly alternate, occasionally opposite.

Height: 3–12′ (90–360 cm).

Flowering: July–October.

Habitat: Swamps, wet thickets, and meadows.

Range: Alberta east to Nova Scotia, south to Georgia, west to Louisiana, and north to Illinois and Minnesota.

Comments: Despite this plant's names, its flower heads are comparatively small; the common and species names actually refer to the plant's overall height.

278 Maximilian's Sunflower
Helianthus maximilianii

Description: *Yellow flower heads* rising from upper half of stalk on rough stems.

Flowers: Head 2–3″ (5–7.5 cm) wide; rays darker yellow at base.

Leaves: 4–6″ (10–15 cm) long, stiff, *narrow, tapering at both ends, rough on both sides,* often folded lengthwise and curved downward at tips, mostly alternate.

Height: 3–10′ (90–300 cm).

Flowering: July–October.

Habitat: Prairies.

Range: Alberta east to Quebec, south through Maine to South Carolina and Mississippi, west to Texas, and north to North Dakota; also in much of West.

Comments: A native prairie perennial, this sunflower is a desirable range plant, eaten by many livestock. A heavy crop of seeds is produced, thus it is also a valuable plant for wildlife. It was named for the naturalist Prince Maximilian of Wied-Neuwied, Germany, who led an expedition into the American West in

the 1830s. Another bluegrass prairie species, Willow-leaved Sunflower *(H. salicifolius)*, has numerous long, narrow, drooping leaves covered with soft hairs and a purple-brown central disk; it is typical of rocky outcrops with heavy soil.

275 Woodland Sunflower
Helianthus strumosus

Description:	*Yellow flower heads* on branches of a smooth or slightly rough stem.
Flowers:	Head 2½–3½" (6.5–9 cm) wide; rays 9–15.
Leaves:	3–8" (7.5–20 cm) long, mostly opposite, ovate to broadly lanceolate, shallowly toothed or untoothed, rough above, *pale to whitish and somewhat hairy below.*
Height:	3–7' (90–210 cm).
Flowering:	August–September.
Habitat:	Woods, thickets, and clearings.
Range:	Ontario east to New Brunswick, south to Florida, west to Texas, and north to Kansas, Minnesota, and North Dakota.
Comments:	This is one of about 20 species of *Helianthus* with yellow disk flowers in our range.

Woodland Sunflower

274 Jerusalem Artichoke
Helianthus tuberosus

Description: Stout, rough, branching stems bearing *large, golden yellow flower heads.*

Flowers: Head to 3" (7.5 cm) wide; rays 10–20; bracts narrow, spreading.

Leaves: To 4–10" (10–25 cm) long, ovate to lanceolate, *thick, rough-toothed,* with *winged stalks, 3 main veins;* lower ones opposite, upper ones alternate.

Height: 5–10' (1.5–3 m).

Flowering: August–October.

Habitat: Roadsides, fields, and fencerows.

Range: Throughout East, except far north; also in northwestern United States.

Comments: This large coarse species was cultivated by Native Americans. The edible tubers are highly nutritious; unlike potatoes, they contain no starch but rather carbohydrate in a form that is metabolized into natural sugar. In 1805 Lewis and Clark dined on the tubers in what is now North Dakota. Today the tubers are sold in produce markets and health food stores and can be boiled or roasted like potatoes. Raw, they have a sweet, nut-like taste. Jerusalem in the common name is a corruption of the Italian *girasole,* meaning "turning to the sun."

273 Oxeye Sunflower; False Sunflower
Heliopsis helianthoides

Description: Resembling a small version of a yellow sunflower with a *cone-shaped central disk and opposite, toothed, simple leaves.*

Flowers: Head 1½–3" (4–8 cm) wide; rays persistent, becoming dry and papery.

Leaves: Larger leaves long-stalked.

Height: 2–5' (60–150 cm).

Flowering: July–September.

Habitat: Open woods and thickets.

Range: Throughout East, except Nova Scotia and far north.

Comments: As the species name implies, this plant

looks like true sunflowers (*Helianthus*).
Unlike sunflowers, its rays persist on the
flower heads; the rays of sunflowers
wither and fall away. It is placed in
Heliopsis due to its cone-shaped central
disk. Oxeye Sunflower is hardy and
easily grown as a showy garden
perennial in dry sites.

279 Hairy Golden Aster;
Prairie Golden Aster
Heterotheca camporum

Description:	Stiff, rough, hairy, leafy stems bearing few flower heads with *golden yellow rays surrounding a slightly darker central disk.*
Flowers:	Head at least 1″ (2.5 cm) wide; disk flowers becoming brown with age.
Leaves:	1–3″ (2.5–7.5 cm) long, oblong to lanceolate, covered with short hairs; upper leaves stalked, lower leaves narrowing to short stalks.
Fruit:	Seed-like, *ovate, tipped with soft hairs.*
Height:	1–2′ (30–60 cm).
Flowering:	July–September.
Habitat:	Dry plains, prairies, fields, and roadsides.
Range:	Iowa east through Michigan to New Jersey, south to North Carolina, and west to Alabama, Mississippi, Arkansas, and Missouri.
Comments:	The height of this species varies greatly with environmental conditions. Typically a midwestern prairie plant, it has in recent years been spreading its range eastward. At least four related species occur in the eastern United States.

280 Camphorweed
Heterotheca subaxillaris

Description:	*Yellow, daisy-like flower heads* on tall hairy stems; plant often appearing lopsided, unbalanced.
Flowers:	Head ½–¾″ (1.5–2 cm) wide.

Leaves: Alternate, oblong; basal ones 2–3″
(5–7.5 cm) long, stalked; *upper ones
smaller, wavy-edged, clasping stem.*
Height: 1–3′ (30–90 cm).
Flowering: July–November.
Habitat: Prairies, waste places, and roadsides in
sandy soil.
Range: Iowa east to New York and Connecticut
south to Florida, west to Texas, and
north to Nebraska; also in southwestern
United States and California.
Comments: This native annual or biennial has been
extending its range northward. It is
unpalatable to grazing livestock on
open rangeland.

---

364 Orange Hawkweed;
Devil's Paintbrush
Hieracium aurantiacum

Description: A slender, hairy, usually leafless stalk
bearing *dandelion-like, orange flower
heads;* sap milky.
Flowers: Head ¾″ (2 cm) wide, *of all rays;* each
ray with 5 teeth (tips of united petals);
bracts green, covered with *black, gland-
tipped hairs.*
Leaves: 2–5″ (5–12.5 cm) long, in a basal
rosette, elliptical, coarsely hairy.
Height: 1–2′ (30–60 cm).
Flowering: June–August.
Habitat: Fields, clearings, and roadsides.
Range: Alberta east to Newfoundland, south
to Florida, west to Arkansas, and north
to South Dakota and Minnesota;
scattered farther west.
Comments: This showy hawkweed, often
abundant and spectacular, is native to
Europe. It is found across the northern
part of our range, particularly in New
England. Farmers, who saw it as a
troublesome weed, named it Devil's
Paintbrush. The genus name is from
the Greek word for "hawk"; the
Roman naturalist Pliny believed that
these birds ate the plant to strengthen
their eyesight.

292   Yellow Hawkweed; King Devil
Hieracium caespitosum

Description: A hairy, mostly leafless stalk bearing several *bright yellow flower heads;* sap milky.

Flowers: Head ½″ (1.5 cm) wide, *of all rays;* bracts covered with gland-tipped, *black hairs.*

Leaves: Basal leaves 2–10″ (5–25 cm) long, oblong, untoothed, covered with stiff hairs.

Height: 1–3′ (30–90 cm).

Flowering: May–August.

Habitat: Pastures and roadsides.

Range: Ontario east to Newfoundland, south to Georgia, west to Tennessee, and north to Minnesota.

Comments: This perennial is similar to Orange Hawkweed *(H. aurantiacum),* differing primarily in flower color. Both introduced from Europe, they are considered weeds by farmers since they spread quickly by leafy runners. Meadows covered with a mixture of both flowers, however, are a beautiful sight. The very similar *H. floribundum,* found from Newfoundland to Virginia and west to Minnesota, differs in having upper leaf surfaces with only a few hairs near the edge. Tall Hawkweed *(H. piloselloides),* occurring from Newfoundland south to North Carolina and northwest to Ontario and Iowa, has no runners, essentially smooth leaves, and few black hairs on the bracts. These last two species are also European introductions.

296   Mouse-ear Hawkweed
Hieracium pilosella

Description: A small plant with *1 yellow, dandelion-like flower head* on a leafless, *hairy, glandular stalk; sap milky.*

Flowers: Head 1″ (2.5 cm) wide, *of all rays;* bracts covered with black hairs and glands.

Leaves:	Basal leaves 1–5" (2.5–12.5 cm) long, oblong, covered with stiff long hairs, *white bloom on underside.*
Fruit:	Small, seed-like, with slender bristles.
Height:	3–12' (90–360 cm).
Flowering:	June–September.
Habitat:	Pastures, fields, and lawns.
Range:	Ontario east to Newfoundland and Nova Scotia, south to Georgia, and northwest to Tennessee, Ohio, Michigan, and Minnesota.
Comments:	This European introduction has also been reported in British Columbia, Washington, and Oregon. The plant spreads rapidly by leafy runners, as well as by its numerous seeds. The common name and the species name refer to the hairy nature of the leaves. Large Mouse-ear Hawkweed *(H. flagellare),* which has 2–5 flower heads and leaves with green undersides, occurs from Prince Edward Island south to Virginia and west to Michigan.

298 Rattlesnake Weed
Hieracium venosum

Description:	Numerous yellow, *dandelion-like flower heads* in open clusters atop a long, usually leafless flower stalk; sap milky.
Flowers:	Head ½–¾" (1.5–2 cm) wide, *of all rays.*
Leaves:	Basal leaves 1½–6" (4–15 cm) long, elliptical, green with *reddish-purple veins.*
Fruit:	Seed-like, with yellowish bristles.
Height:	1–2½' (30–75 cm).
Flowering:	May–September.
Habitat:	Dry open woods, thickets, and clearings.
Range:	Ontario; New England south to Florida, west to Louisiana, and north to Missouri and Michigan.
Comments:	This native woodland flower is relatively widespread but most common in parts of our range where rattlesnakes occur, hence the common name. Within the East, 11 other yellow-flowered species of *Hieracium* occur, nine of them native.

290   Elecampane
Inula helenium

Description: Yellow, sunflower-like flower heads with long, *narrow, straggly rays surrounding a darker central disk* atop a tall hairy stem.

Flowers: Head 2–4″ (5–10 cm) wide.

Leaves: Large, rough, toothed, white-woolly beneath; *stem leaves stalkless, clasping stem;* basal leaves to 20″ (50 cm) long, with long stalks.

Height: 2–6′ (60–180 cm).

Flowering: July–September.

Habitat: Fields and roadsides.

Range: Ontario east to Newfoundland, south to North Carolina, west to Missouri, and north to Minnesota; also along the Pacific Coast from British Columbia southward.

Comments: Perhaps of Asian origin, Elecampane was introduced to America by early colonists. In the 19th century a tincture of its roots was thought useful in reducing fevers and as a diuretic, but it may have caused more illness than it cured.

294   Two-flowered Cynthia
Krigia biflora

Description: *Yellow-orange, dandelion-like flower heads* atop a smooth forking stem; sap milky.

Flowers: Head to 1½″ (4 cm) wide, *of all rays;* 2–6 heads per stalk.

Leaves: 1 (occasionally 2) on stem, small, oval, *clasping stem below fork;* basal leaves 2–7″ (5–17.5 cm) long, elliptical, stalked.

Height: 1–2′ (30–60 cm).

Flowering: May–August.

Habitat: Open woods and meadows.

Range: Manitoba and Ontario; New York and Massachusetts south to Georgia, west to Oklahoma and Missouri, and north to Minnesota.

Comments: This native perennial is related to hawkweeds *(Hieracium).* The smaller Dwarf Dandelion *(K. virginica),* found in

sandy sites, has a solitary flower head rising from a set of toothed or lobed basal leaves and is less than 1' (30 cm) tall. Potato Dandelion *(K. dandelion),* which has a large, solitary flower head on a leafless stem and a tuber ½–1" (1.5–2.5 cm) long just below the surface, is found from southern New Jersey south to Florida, west to Texas, and north to Missouri.

300   Wild Lettuce
Lactuca canadensis

Description: A *tall plant* with milky sap and an elongated cluster of small, *pale yellow flower heads;* slight bloom on stem and leaves.

Flowers: Head ¼" (6 mm) wide, *of all rays.*

Leaves: To 1' (30 cm) long, nearly toothless and lanceolate to deeply lobed, stalkless; exude milky sap when crushed.

Fruit: Dry, flat, 1-seeded, with "parachute" of bristles aiding in seed dispersal.

Height: 2–10' (60–300 cm).

Flowering: July–September.

Habitat: Clearings, thickets, and edges of woods.

Range: Throughout much of North America, except far north.

Comments: This large biennial is frequently found in disturbed sites. Its flower heads are

Wild Lettuce

inconspicuous, and the leaves lack the
spines of the similar Prickly Lettuce
(*L. serriola*). Young leaves can be used
in salads or as cooked greens but have a
slightly bitter taste. Wild Lettuce is
related to garden lettuce; if the latter is
allowed to go to seed, the resemblance of
the flower heads can be seen.

630 Florida Lettuce; False Lettuce
Lactuca floridana

Description: A loose cluster of numerous *blue
(sometimes whitish) flower heads* atop a
leafy stem; sap milky.

Flowers: Head ¼–½" (6–13 mm) wide,
composed of 11–17 rays.

Leaves: Blades 4–12" (10–30 cm) long, deeply
cut, dandelion-like; terminal segment
triangular, lateral segments lanceolate to
oval, all toothed.

Fruit: 1-seeded, crowned with *shiny white hairs.*

Height: 2–9' (60–270 cm).

Flowering: August–October.

Habitat: Rich woods, thickets, and clearings.

Range: Manitoba and Ontario; Massachusetts
south to Florida, west to Texas, and
north to South Dakota and Minnesota.

Comments: There are several species of lettuce with
blue flower heads, among them a more
western species, Large-flowered Blue
Lettuce (*L. pulchella*), with larger and
fewer flower heads than this species and
foliage covered with white waxy bloom.
Tall Blue Lettuce (*L. biennis*), found
from southern Canada south to North
Carolina and west to Iowa, has crowded
clusters of flower heads and tan fruit
bristles.

299 Prickly Lettuce
Lactuca serriola

Description: Loose clusters of *small, yellow, dandelion-
like flower heads* on an *erect stem with very
prickly leaves;* foliage exudes milky sap
when broken.

Flowers:	Head ¼″ (6 mm) wide, composed of usually 16–24 rays.
Leaves:	2–12″ (5–30 cm) long, oblong, lobed or unlobed, *prickly edged,* bristly beneath along midrib, clasping stem at base.
Fruit:	Dry, 1-seeded, with white bristles aiding in seed dispersal.
Height:	2–5′ (60–150 cm).
Flowering:	June–October.
Habitat:	Roadsides and waste places.
Range:	Throughout much of North America, except far north.
Comments:	The leaves of this originally European species are arranged distinctively, often twisting at the base so that they are oriented vertically. It was once mistakenly thought that its sap could be used as a substitute for opium.

83 Oxeye Daisy
Leucanthemum vulgare

Description:	The common white-and-yellow field daisy, with *1 flower head on each slender, erect stem.*
Flowers:	Head 1–2″ (2.5–5 cm) wide; *rays white,* all female; *disk flowers yellow,* both male and female; disk depressed at center.
Leaves:	Dark green, coarsely toothed or pinnately lobed; basal ones to 6″ (15 cm long, upper ones to 3″ (7.5 cm) long.
Height:	1–3′ (30–90 cm).
Flowering:	June–August.
Habitat:	Waste places, meadows, pastures, and roadsides.
Range:	Throughout much of North America, except arctic Canada; less abundant southward.
Comments:	An extremely common, even weed-like species, Oxeye Daisy was originally introduced to North America from Europe. This species—the "day's eye" —is disliked by farmers because it can produce an unwanted flavor in milk if eaten by cattle.

590 Rough Blazing Star
Liatris aspera

Description: A spike of rounded, *rayless, pinkish to lavender (sometimes white)* flower heads along stiff erect stems covered with grayish hairs.

Flowers: Head about ¾" (2 cm) wide; *bracts broadly rounded,* flaring, with pinkish, translucent edges.

Leaves: Rough, lanceolate to linear; lower ones 4–12" (10–30 cm) long, upper ones progressively smaller.

Height: 16–48" (40–120 cm).

Flowering: August–October.

Habitat: Open plains and thin woods in sandy soil.

Range: Ontario and New York south to Florida, west to Texas, and north to North Dakota.

Comments: This species is distinguished by its roughness and rounded bracts. The origin of the genus name is unknown; the species name is Latin for "rough."

589 Prairie Blazing Star
Liatris pycnostachya

Description: A spike of *rayless, rose-purple (rarely white), cylindrical, stalkless flower heads* densely crowded on a coarse, hairy, very leafy stem.

Flowers: Head about ½" (1.5 cm) wide; bracts with *long-pointed, purplish tips, spreading or bent backward.*

Leaves: Linear, rough, with translucent dots; lower ones 4–12" (10–30 cm) long, upper ones much smaller.

Height: 2–5' (60–150 cm).

Flowering: July–October.

Habitat: Damp prairies.

Range: North Dakota east to Massachusetts, southwest through Tennessee to Alabama and Mississippi, west to Texas and Oklahoma, and north to South Dakota.

Comments: One of the most popular of the blazing stars, this is sometimes grown as an ornamental. The species name, from the

Greek for "crowded," describes both the leaves and the flower heads. A species found in dry prairies, Dotted Blazing Star *(L. punctata)*, has leaves covered with resinous dots and long, pointed, flat bracts beneath the flower heads.

---

489 Large Blazing Star
Liatris scariosa

Description:	A spike of *rayless, pink-lavender flower heads in interrupted clusters* on a tall, smooth or downy stem.
Flowers:	Head to 1″ (2.5 cm) wide, on diverging stalks; bracts overlapping.
Leaves:	To 10″ (25 cm) long, numerous, soft-hairy to rough; lower ones ovate to lanceolate; upper ones smaller, linear.
Height:	1–5′ (30–150 cm).
Flowering:	August–September.
Habitat:	Dry woods and clearings.
Range:	Wisconsin east to New York and Maine, south to Georgia, west to Arkansas, and north to Missouri and Illinois.
Comments:	The flower heads and broad leaves with well-separated stalks are characteristic of the very similar *Liatris* species in our range; these may eventually prove to be variants of a single species.

---

490 Dense Blazing Star; Gay Feather
Liatris spicata

Description:	A tall spike of *rayless, rose-purple (sometimes white), closely set flower heads.*
Flowers:	Head ¼″ (6 mm) wide, stalkless; long styles protruding beyond corolla lobes; bracts thin, scale-like, blunt, with purple edges; spike at least 1′ (30 cm) long.
Leaves:	*Numerous, linear, crowded;* those at base at least 1′ (30 cm) long, upper ones progressively smaller.
Height:	1–6′ (30–180 cm).
Flowering:	July–September.
Habitat:	Moist low ground in meadows and prairies.

Range: Ontario and Quebec south through New
York and Massachusetts to Florida, west
to Louisiana, and north to Illinois and
Wisconsin.

Comments: The species name describes the
elongated inflorescence, with its
crowded, stalkless flower heads. The
protruding styles give the flower an
overall feathery appearance, hence its
occasional alternate name, Gay Feather.

537 Climbing Boneset;
Climbing Hempweed
Mikania scandens

Description: *A twining vine* with flat-topped clusters
of *white or pinkish flower heads* rising from
leaf axils.

Flowers: Head about ¼" (6 mm) wide, composed
of 4 disk flowers; bracts scale-like.

Leaves: 1–3" (2.5–7.5 cm) long, opposite, ovate
to triangular, with wavy-toothed or
untoothed edges.

Fruit: Tiny, dry, seed-like, with a tuft of
whitish bristles.

Height: Vine; to 13' (4 m) long.

Flowering: July–October; throughout year in
southern part of range.

Habitat: Streambanks, moist thickets, and
swamps.

Range: Ontario; New England south to Florida,
west to Texas, and northeast to Illinois
and Ohio.

Comments: This species forms a sizable growth over
other plants in moist woods and thickets.
Its flower heads resemble those of Boneset
(*Eupatorium perfoliatum*). The similar
Florida Keys Hempweed (*M. cordifolia*)
is found from Florida west to Texas.

538 Saltmarsh Fleabane
Pluchea odorata

Description: An erect annual with *flat-topped clusters of
pink-lavender, rayless flower heads;* plant
has a strong, somewhat camphor-like
odor.

Flowers: Head about ¼" (5 mm) wide; bracts pink or purple.

Leaves: 2–6" (5–15 cm) long, short-stalked or stalkless, ovate to lanceolate, slightly toothed, scalloped, or smooth.

Fruit: Tiny, dry, 1-seeded, with a circle of bristles.

Height: 1–5′ (30–150 cm).

Flowering: July–October.

Habitat: Saline to brackish marshes.

Range: Ontario; Maine south to Florida, largely along coast, west to Texas, and north to Kansas, Illinois, and Michigan; also in southwestern United States and California.

Comments: This brackish-marsh plant adds a flash of pink to marsh grasses at the end of the growing season. Its dense pinkish flower masses can be used in dried flower arrangements.

133   White Lettuce; Rattlesnake Root
Prenanthes alba

Description: A tall slender perennial with smooth stems lined with *clusters of white or pinkish, drooping flower heads;* stem usually purplish with whitish bloom, exudes milky sap when crushed.

Flowers: Head about ½" (1.5 cm) long, composed of 8–12 rays; stamens prominent, cream-colored.

Leaves: To 8" (20 cm) long, smooth; lower ones triangular, lobed or unlobed; upper ones often lanceolate.

Fruit: Dry, seed-like, with tan or reddish-brown bristles.

Height: 2–5′ (60–150 cm).

Flowering: August–September.

Habitat: Rich woods and thickets.

Range: Saskatchewan east to Quebec, south to North Carolina, west to Arkansas, and northwest to North Dakota.

Comments: The common name Rattlesnake Root suggests the plant was used as a remedy for snakebite. A bitter tonic was made from the roots and thought useful in

treating dysentery. This is one of
several similar species in our area,
all of which have drooping flower
heads, distinctly lobed leaves, and
milky sap. Lion's Foot *(P. serpentaria)*
is similar but its fruit has white bristles
and its stem lacks bloom. Gall-of-
the-earth *(P. trifoliolata)* has very
deeply divided, 3-parted leaves and
a waxy, reddish stem. Tall White
Lettuce *(P. altissima),* also known as
Tall Rattlesnake Root, has only
five main bracts surrounding the
flower head. Smooth White Lettuce
(P. racemosa), also known as Purple
Rattlesnake Root, has pinkish to purple
flower heads in a spike, elongated leaves
that clasp the stem, and yellow bristles.

271 Prairie Coneflower; Gray-headed Coneflower
Ratibida pinnata

Description:	A slender, hairy-stemmed plant bearing flower heads with *drooping, yellow rays surrounding a roundish to ellipsoid, grayish central disk darkening to brown* as rays drop off.
Flowers:	Rays 1–2½″ (2.5–6.5 cm) long; central disk ⅜–1″ (1–2.5 cm) high.
Leaves:	About 5″ (12.5 cm) long, compound, pinnately divided into lanceolate, coarsely toothed segments.
Height:	1½–5′ (45–150 cm).
Flowering:	June–September.
Habitat:	Dry woods and prairies.
Range:	Ontario; Vermont south to Florida, west to Louisiana and Oklahoma, and north to South Dakota and Minnesota.
Comments:	A similar species, Red-spike Mexican Hat *(R. columnifera),* is a shorter plant; its central disk is columnar, 2–4½ times as long as thick. Because these species are palatable to livestock, the plants tend to diminish with heavy grazing of rangeland. When bruised, the central disk exudes an anise scent.

272   Black-eyed Susan
Rudbeckia hirta

Description: A coarse, rough-stemmed plant bearing
daisy-like flower heads with showy,
*golden yellow rays surrounding a brown,
cone-shaped central disk.*

Flowers: Head 2–3" (5–7.5 cm) wide.

Leaves: 2–7" (5–17.5 cm) long, lanceolate to
ovate, rough, hairy; lower ones
untoothed or scantily toothed, with 3
prominent veins and winged stalks.

Fruit: Tiny, dry, seed-like, lacking bristles.

Height: 1–3' (30–90 cm).

Flowering: June–October.

Habitat: Fields, prairies, and open woods.

Range: Throughout much of North America,
except Nevada, Arizona, and far
north.

Comments: This native prairie biennial forms a
rosette of leaves the first year, followed
by flowers the second year. It is covered
with hairs that give it a rough texture.
Greenhead Coneflower *(R. laciniata)*
has yellow rays pointing downward,
a greenish-yellow central disk, and
irregularly divided leaves. A double-
flowered form of *R. laciniata,* called
Goldenglow, is an old-fashioned garden
ornamental.

284   Golden Ragwort
Senecio aureus

Description: A smooth plant with *yellow, daisy-like
flower heads in flat-topped clusters.*

Flowers: Head ¾" (2 cm) wide; rays 8–12.

Leaves: Basal leaves ½–6" (1.5–15 cm) long,
heart-shaped, long-stalked, with rounded
teeth; upper leaves 1–3½" (2.5–9 cm)
long, pinnately lobed.

Height: 1–2' (30–60 cm).

Flowering: April–July.

Habitat: Wet meadows, swamps, and moist
woods.

Range: Manitoba east to Newfoundland, south
to Florida, west to Texas, and north to
Missouri and Minnesota.

Comments: Of the 16 *Senecio* species, Round-leaved
Ragwort *(S. obovatus)* has spatulate
leaves tapering at the base. To the west,
on dry bluffs and prairies, Prairie
Ragwort *(S. plattensis)* has basal leaves
woolly on the underside. Woolly
Ragwort *(S. tomentosus),* found in open
woods and fields along the coastal plain
from New Jersey to Texas, has long,
narrow, woolly, basal leaves, especially
when young.

285 Compass Plant
Silphium laciniatum

Description: A tall plant bearing *yellow flower heads
with large, hairy-edged, green bracts; stem
exudes resinous sap.*
Flowers: Head to 3″ (7.5 cm) wide.
Leaves: 12–18″ (30–45 cm) long, alternate,
rough, *large, deeply divided,* unstalked
or short-stalked.
Height: 3–12′ (90–360 cm).
Flowering: July–September.
Habitat: Prairies.
Range: Ontario and New York south to
Virginia, Tennessee, and Alabama,
west to Texas, and north to North
Dakota.
Comments: Compass Plant is one of a group of tall,
mostly prairie sunflowers, some with
very large leaves. The common name
refers to the plant's deeply incised
leaves, which tend to be oriented in a
north–south direction. The hardened
sap of this plant can be chewed like
gum. Rosinweed *(S. integrifolium)*
has opposite, very rough, stalkless,
untoothed or slightly toothed leaves
and is 2–5′ (60–150 cm) tall. Cup Plant
(S. perfoliatum) has opposite leaves that
envelop its square stem, each leaf
forming a "cup" around it. Prairie Dock
(S. terebinthinaceum) has large, ovate or
heart-shaped, basal leaves to 2′ (60 cm)
long; the sparsely leaved flower stalk
sometimes reaches a height of nearly
10′ (3 m).

325 Tall Goldenrod
Solidago altissima

Description: *Small yellow flower heads on outward-arching branches* forming a pyramidal cluster atop a *grayish, downy stem.*

Flowers: Head about ⅛" (3 mm) long.

Leaves: Lanceolate, rough above, hairy below, sometimes toothed; lower ones to 6" (15 cm) long, upper ones smaller.

Height: 2–7′ (60–210 cm).

Flowering: August–November.

Habitat: Thickets, roadsides, and clearings.

Range: Throughout East, except Newfoundland and far north; also in parts of West.

Comments: Two other similar species with arching flower stalks are Late Goldenrod *(S. gigantea),* smooth-stemmed, often with whitish bloom, and with flower heads to ¼" (6 mm) long, and Canada Goldenrod *(S. canadensis),* with sharply toothed leaves and very small flower heads only ⅛" (3 mm) long.

109 Silver-rod; White Goldenrod
Solidago bicolor

Description: *An elongated spike of short-stalked flower heads with white to yellowish-white rays* surrounding a yellow central disk atop a hairy, grayish stem.

Flowers: Head about ¼" (6 mm) long; rays 7–9.

Leaves: Basal and lower leaves 2–4" (5–10 cm) long, oblong, stalked, toothed; upper ones smaller, narrower, often without stalks or teeth.

Height: 1–3′ (30–90 cm).

Flowering: July–October.

Habitat: Thin woods and clearings.

Range: Manitoba east to Nova Scotia, south to Georgia, west to Louisiana, and north to Illinois and Wisconsin.

Comments: This is the only *Solidago* with white rays in our area. Hairy Goldenrod *(S. hispida)* has yellow rays; it is found from New England south to Georgia, west to Arkansas, and north to Illinois and Minnesota.

322 Blue-stemmed Goldenrod; Wreath Goldenrod
Solidago caesia

Description: A smooth, *purplish,* frequently arching stem covered with *whitish bloom* and bearing *scattered clusters of yellow flower heads* in leaf axils; terminal cluster largest.

Flowers: Head about ¼" (6 mm) long.

Leaves: 2½–5" (6.5–12.5 cm) long, stalkless, elliptical, tapering at both ends, toothed, sharply pointed.

Height: 1–3' (30–90 cm).

Flowering: August–October.

Habitat: Woods, thickets, and clearings.

Range: Ontario east to Nova Scotia, south to Florida, west to Texas and Oklahoma, and north to Wisconsin.

Comments: Other goldenrods with scattered flower clusters include Wand Goldenrod *(S. stricta),* found in sandy sites from New Jersey southward, with a wand-like flower stalk and narrow, scale-like leaves pressed against the stem; Zigzag Goldenrod *(S. flexicaulis),* with a zigzag stem and broad ovate leaves; and Downy Goldenrod *(S. puberula),* found in dry sites in the Atlantic and Gulf Coast states and in the Appalachians, with a very leafy stem covered with fine spreading hairs.

324 Sweet Goldenrod; Anise-scented Goldenrod
Solidago odora

Description: A smooth, tall, *anise-scented* plant bearing *crowded, cylindrical clusters of yellow flower heads* along one side of slightly arching branches.

Flowers: Head about ⅛" (4 mm) long.

Leaves: 1–4" (2.5–10 cm) long, smooth, narrow, stalkless, with small, translucent dots.

Height: 2–3' (60–90 cm).

Flowering: July–September.

Habitat: Dry fields and open woods.

Range: Nova Scotia; New Hampshire and

Vermont south to Florida, west to Tex
and north to Missouri, Kentucky, and
Ohio.

Comments: The crushed leaves of Sweet Goldenroc
give off an anise scent that readily
identifies this widespread species. A te
can be brewed from its leaves and driec
flowers.

---

326 Stiff Goldenrod;
Hard-leaved Goldenrod
Solidago rigida

Description: A tall, coarse, hairy stem bearing a dens
*rounded or flat-topped, terminal cluster of
dark yellow, bell-shaped flower heads.*
Flowers: Head about ⅜" (8 mm) long; rays 7–1(
disk flowers 20–30.
Leaves: Basal ones rough, elliptical, long-stalke
with blades to 10" (25 cm) long; upper
leaves oval, clasping, *rigid, rough.*
Height: 1–5' (30–150 cm).
Flowering: August–October.
Habitat: Prairies, thickets, and open woods.
Range: Alberta east to Ontario, south through
New York to Georgia, west to Texas,
and north to North Dakota.
Comments: This is a deep-rooted and handsome
species. There are similar species with
relatively broad leaves and flat-topped
clusters in our area, but this is the only
one with hairy stems.

---

323 Rough-stemmed Goldenrod
Solidago rugosa

Description: A tall, *rough, hairy stem bearing divergent
or arching branches with small, light yellou
flower heads* mostly on upper side.
Flowers: Head about ⅛" (4 mm) long; rays 6–11
disk flowers 4–7.
Leaves: 1½–5" (4–12.5 cm) long, rough, sharpl
toothed, very hairy, wrinkled.
Height: 1–6' (30–180 cm).
Flowering: July–October.
Habitat: Fields, roadsides, and edges of woods.
Range: Alberta east to Ontario and Connecticu

south to Florida, west to Texas, and
north to North Dakota.

Comments: This highly variable goldenrod can form
large masses in fields that were once
cultivated. Goldenrods have been
popularly blamed for causing hay fever,
but this condition is actually caused by
ragweeds *(Ambrosia)* and various other
wind-pollinated plants, whose pollen is
abundant when goldenrod is in flower.
As suggested by their showy flowers,
goldenrods are insect-pollinated.

---

321 Seaside Goldenrod
Solidago sempervirens

Description: A succulent-leaved saltmarsh plant
with *bright yellow flower heads in clusters
along one side of arching branches.*
Flowers: Head about ⅜″ (8 mm) long; rays 7–10.
Leaves: *Fleshy,* lanceolate to oblong, toothless;
upper ones 2–8″ (5–20 cm) long; basal
ones to 1′ (30 cm) long.
Height: 1–8′ (30–240 cm).
Flowering: July–November.
Habitat: Sandy places and edges of saline or
brackish marshes.
Range: Ontario east to Newfoundland, south to
Florida, and west along Gulf Coast to
Texas; inland in Illinois, Ohio, and
Michigan.
Comments: Plants found from Florida to Texas are
recognized by some authorities as a
different species *(S. mexicana),* but others
consider them to represent the variety of
S. sempervirens. Seaside Goldenrod also
hybridizes regularly with Rough-
stemmed Goldenrod *(S. rugosa).*

---

327 Showy Goldenrod
Solidago speciosa

Description: A stout stem, smooth below and rough
above, bearing a dense, *pyramidal or club-
shaped, terminal cluster of small yellow
flower heads.*
Flowers: Head about ¼″ (6 mm) long.

Leaves: Elliptical, obscurely toothed; lower an
basal ones 4–10" (10–25 cm) long,
stalked; upper ones much smaller,
unstalked.
Height: 2–7' (60–210 cm).
Flowering: August–October.
Habitat: Open woods, prairies, and thickets.
Range: Ontario and New Hampshire south to
Georgia, west to Texas, and north to
North Dakota.
Comments: This is one of the showiest of about
125 species of goldenrod that occur
throughout the United States; they
are most common in the East.

---

297   Spiny-leaved Sow Thistle
Sonchus asper

Description: *Yellow, dandelion-like flower heads* on a
smooth angled stem containing *milky
sap.*
Flowers: Head 1" (2.5 cm) wide, of all rays; brac
lanceolate, green-edged.
Leaves: To 10" (25 cm) long, *prickly edged,*
usually deeply lobed with 2 rounded
lobes at base.
Fruit: Soft, *white,* with hair-like bristles.
Height: 1–6' (30–180 cm).
Flowering: June–October.
Habitat: Waste places and roadsides.
Range: Throughout North America, except
parts of far north.
Comments: This annual closely resembles Commor
Sow Thistle *(S. oleraceus),* which has tw
pointed lobes at the base of its leaves.
Field Sow Thistle *(S. arvensis)* is a
perennial with flower heads 1¼–2"
(3–5 cm) wide, with or without numerou
gland-tipped hairs on the bracts. All
sow thistles can be used as potherbs.

---

350   Common Tansy
Tanacetum vulgare

Description: An erect perennial with flat-topped
clusters of *bright orange-yellow, button-lik
flower heads.*

Flowers: Head ½" (1.5 cm) wide, of all disk
flowers, with occasional ray-like
extensions developing from marginal
flowers.

Leaves: 4–8" (10–20 cm) long, pinnately
divided into linear, toothed segments,
strongly aromatic.

Height: 2–3' (60–90 cm).

Flowering: July–September.

Habitat: Roadsides, edges of fields, waste places,
and shorelines.

Range: Throughout much of North America,
except Texas, South Carolina to
Alabama, and Arctic.

Comments: Originally from Europe, this plant
often escapes from gardens. It was
used medicinally for centuries to
induce miscarriages; the results
were sometimes fatal, as the bitter-
tasting leaves and stem contain
tanacetum, an oil toxic to humans
and animals. The inflorescences are often
dried for use in winter bouquets. Eastern
Tansy *(T. huronense)*, with long-hairy
leaves and larger flower heads, is found
on northern beaches and shorelines
across Canada and in Wisconsin,
Michigan, and Maine.

295 Common Dandelion
Taraxacum officinale

Description: A slender stalk bearing 1 flower head
composed of *numerous yellow rays;* stems
with milky sap.

Flowers: Head about 1½" (4 cm) wide; *rays with
5 tiny teeth at tip;* bracts narrow, pointed,
outer ones bent backward.

Leaves: Basal leaves 2–16" (5–40 cm) long,
deeply and irregularly toothed and
lobed.

Fruit: Dry, 1-seeded, topped with "parachute"
of long white bristles; fruiting mass
becoming a silky, downy, round head
when ripe.

Height: 2–18" (5–45 cm).

Flowering: March–September.

Habitat: Fields, roadsides, and lawns.

Range: Throughout North America, but
rare in extreme southeastern United
States.

Comments: This species, a native of Eurasia and a
cosmopolitan weed in temperate areas
worldwide, is probably known by mos
as a much-maligned lawn weed. The
seed-like fruits, with their attached
"parachute" of bristles, are carried far
and wide by the wind. The young leav
are used as greens. The word dandelior
refers to the likeness of the plant's leaf
teeth to those of a lion.

289 Yellow Goatsbeard
Tragopogon dubius

Description: A smooth stem bearing grass-like leave
and *1 yellow flower head* opening in
morning and usually closing by noon;
stems swollen just below heads, with
milky sap.

Flowers: Head 1–2½" (2.5–6.5 cm) wide, of all
rays; *bracts long-pointed, green.*

Leaves: To 1' (30 cm) long, broad at base wher
clasping stem, then narrowing to long
sharp tip.

Fruit: Seed-like, with "parachute" of bristles;
forming a round, *feathery head* to about
3" (7 cm) wide.

Height: 1–3' (30–90 cm).

Flowering: May–August.

Habitat: Fields and waste places.

Range: Throughout much of temperate North
America, except Arctic and parts of
southeastern United States.

Comments: The basal leaves of this originally
European plant can be eaten raw in
salads or as cooked greens. The genus
name, derived from the Greek *tragos*
("goat") and *pogon* ("beard"), refers to th
resemblance of the fruiting heads to a
goat's beard. The closely related Meado
Salsify *(T. pratensis),* found from Nova
Scotia south to Georgia, west to
Missouri and Kansas, and north to
Ontario, lacks swelling on its stem.

556 Salsify; Oyster Plant
Tragopogon porrifolius

Description: A showy plant with branched stems, each topped by *1 large purple flower head;* stem swollen and hollow just below head, with milky sap.

Flowers: Head 2–4″ (5–10 cm) wide, of all rays; bracts long-pointed, longer than rays.

Leaves: To 1′ (30 cm) long, linear, grass-like, clasping stem.

Fruit: Seed-like, with *feathery bristles* 2″ (5 cm) long.

Height: 2–4′ (60–120 cm).

Flowering: May–July.

Habitat: Fields and roadsides.

Range: Throughout much of North America, except far north and parts of southeastern United States.

Comments: Wide-ranging over much of North America except the far north, this species is a European native that has escaped from vegetable gardens. It is a most striking plant when in fruit, with its beige ball of fluff. When boiled, its roots taste somewhat like oysters. The spring leaves can be used in salads or cooked as greens.

293 Coltsfoot
Tussilago farfara

Description: A low, rhizomatous plant with *1 yellow flower head atop a scaly stalk.*

Flowers: Head 1″ (2.5 cm) wide; rays thin, surrounding disk flowers.

Leaves: Basal leaves 2–7″ (5–17.5 cm) long, broad, *heart-shaped,* slightly toothed, upright, *whitish beneath.*

Height: 3–18″ (8–45 cm).

Flowering: February–June.

Habitat: Roadsides and waste places.

Range: Ontario east to Newfoundland and Nova Scotia, south to North Carolina, west to Tennessee, and northwest to Minnesota.

Comments: The flower heads of this European introduction recall those of dandelions

(*Taraxacum*), but they are composed of
both rays and disk flowers. The common
name refers to the supposed resemblance
of the leaf to a colt's foot. The genus
name, from the Latin *tussis* ("a cough")
alludes to the plant's reputation as a cure
for coughs. An extract of fresh leaves can
be used for making cough drops or hard
candy, and its dried leaves can be steeped
for a tea.

607 Tall Ironweed
Vernonia gigantea

Description: A tall erect stem bearing *rayless, deep
purple-blue flower heads* in loose, terminal
clusters.

Flowers: Head about ¼" (6 mm) wide; disk
flowers 13–30, each 5-lobed; bracts
blunt-tipped, usually purple.

Leaves: 6–10" (15–25 cm) long, thin,
lanceolate, pointed, *downy beneath.*

Fruit: Seed-like, with double set of purplish
bristles.

Height: 3–7' (90–210 cm).

Flowering: August–October.

Habitat: Meadows, open woods, and pastures.

Range: Ontario and New York south to Florida,
west to Texas, and north to Kansas,
Iowa, Illinois, and Michigan.

Comments: The common name ironweed refers to
the toughness of the stem. Until
recently this species was known as *V.
altissima.* The genus name honors the
English botanist William Vernon, who
did fieldwork in North America. At
least six additional species of *Vernonia*
are found in the East; some were once
used for treating stomach ailments.

608 New York Ironweed
Vernonia noveboracensis

Description: A tall erect stem branching toward top,
each branch bearing a cluster of *rayless,
deep lavender to violet flower heads;* clusters
together forming a loose spray.

Flowers: Head about ⅜" (8 mm) wide; disk flowers 30–50, each 5-lobed; bracts with *long, hair-like tips;* cluster 3–4" (7.5–10 cm) wide.

Leaves: 4–8" (10–20 cm) long, alternate, finely toothed, lanceolate, pointed.

Fruit: Seed-like, with double set of purplish bristles.

Height: 3–6' (90–180 cm).

Flowering: August–October.

Habitat: Moist low ground and streambanks.

Range: New Hampshire and New York south to Florida, west to Alabama, and north to Kentucky and West Virginia.

Comments: This is a common plant in wet, open, bottomland fields. It typically has more flowers per head than Tall Ironweed *(V. altissima).*

---

35 Cocklebur; Clotbur
Xanthium strumarium

Description: A rough-stemmed plant with greenish, *separate male and female flower heads.*

Flowers: Female flower heads forming *ovoid burs* ½–1½" (1.5–4 cm) long, covered with *hooked prickles;* male flower heads on short spikes.

Leaves: 2–6" (5–15 cm) long, maple-like, coarsely toothed, long-stalked.

Height: 1–6' (30–180 cm).

Flowering: August–October.

Habitat: Waste places, roadsides, and low ground.

Range: Throughout much of temperate North America.

Comments: Each of the animal-dispersed burs contains two seeds. The young seedlings are poisonous to animals that ingest them; as the plants grow their toxicity decreases. The only other cocklebur in our area is Spiny Cocklebur *(X. spinosum),* which has tapering, shiny, veined leaves and distinctive 3-branched, orangish spines at the point of each leaf attachment.

TOUCH-ME-NOT FAMILY
Balsaminaceae

Often soft and somewhat succulent herbs with leafy, pa
translucent stems and usually nodding flowers.

Flowers: Bilaterally symmetrical. Sepals 3–5, often resem
bling petals, 1 forming a backward-projecting, necta
bearing spur; petals 5, side pairs united, lower ones larg
than upper ones; stamens 5, joined and forming a c
over pistil; all these parts attached at base of ovary.
Leaves: Alternate, opposite, or whorled; simple.
Fruit: 5-chambered capsule, opening explosively and d
pelling seeds.

There are 2 genera and about 450 species. Several speci
of *Impatiens* are grown as ornamentals.

---

365 Spotted Touch-me-not; Jewelweed
Impatiens capensis

Description:	A tall leafy plant with *succulent, translucent stems* bearing nodding, *usuall golden-orange flowers* splotched with reddish brown.
Flowers:	1″ (2.5 cm) long; calyx with 3 sepals, 1 sepal same color as petals and forming a *sharply spurred sac* ¼″ (6 mm) long, 2 sepals green; corolla with 5 petals, each side pair united and appearing as a single petal.
Leaves:	1½–3½″ (4–9 cm) long, alternate, thin ovate, pale beneath.
Fruit:	Swollen capsule; exploding at maturity, expelling seeds.
Height:	2–5′ (60–150 cm).
Flowering:	July–October.
Habitat:	Shaded wetlands and woods.
Range:	Alberta east to Newfoundland, south to Florida, west to Texas, and north to North Dakota; also in northwestern United States and Canada.
Comments:	An annual that often occurs in dense stands, this species is especially adapted to hummingbird visitation, but bees and butterflies are also important pollinators. If the leaves are submerged, they take on a silvery look. The sap of the stems and leaves is said to relieve itching from

Poison Ivy and nettles (with which it often grows) and has also been used to treat athlete's foot; scientific data confirm the fungicidal qualities.

305 Pale Touch-me-not; Jewelweed
Impatiens pallida

Description: A tall leafy plant with *succulent, translucent stems* bearing nodding, *usually pale yellow flowers* occasionally splotched with reddish brown.

Flowers: 1½" (4 cm) long; calyx tube ending in a *short hooked spur.*

Leaves: 1–4" (2.5–10 cm) long, alternate, thin, ovate, toothed.

Fruit: Fragile, swollen, elliptical capsule; exploding at maturity, expelling seeds.

Height: 3–6' (90–180 cm).

Flowering: June–October.

Habitat: Wet woods and meadows; often on mountainsides in wet, shady, limestone or neutral sites.

Range: Ontario east to Nova Scotia, south to Georgia, west to Oklahoma, and north to North Dakota.

Comments: This soft-stemmed annual is less common than the very similar Spotted Touch-me-not *(I. capensis)*. The sensitive triggering of seeds from the ripe capsule inspired these species' (as well as the family's) common name touch-me-not. Policeman's Hat *(I. glandulifera),* a large, purple-flowered species with mostly whorled or opposite leaves, is found from Ontario east to Nova Scotia and south to Massachusetts.

BARBERRY FAMILY
Berberidaceae

Herbs or shrubs with often spiny stems and/or leaves and flowers borne singly or in clusters or racemes.

Flowers: Radially symmetrical. Sepals 4–6, often petal-like; petals 4–6; stamens 4–18, in 2 circles, with anthers opening by little flaps; all these parts attached at base of ovary.

Leaves: Simple or compound.
Fruit: Berry or capsule.

There are about 13 genera and 650 species. A few speci
are cultivated as ornamentals, including Heavenly Bambc
(*Nandina domestica*). Roots of the eastern Mayapp
(*Podophyllum peltatum*) have drastic purgative and emet
properties. Common Barberry (*Berberis vulgaris*) is a nece
sary host in the complex life cycle of wheat rust (*Puccinia*
a destructive parasitic fungus.

345   Common Barberry
Berberis vulgaris

Description: A *spiny, gray-twigged shrub* with clustere
leaves and *hanging clusters of small yellow
flowers;* spines 3-branched.

Flowers: About ¼" (6 mm) wide; sepals 6; petals
6, each with 2 glandular spots inside;
stamens 6; stigma circular, depressed.

Leaves: 1–3" (2.5–7.5 cm) long, bristle-toothec

Fruit: Elliptical *berry, scarlet when mature.*

Height: 3–10' (90–300 cm).

Flowering: May–June.

Habitat: Pastures, fencerows, and thickets.

Range: Manitoba east to Newfoundland, south
to North Carolina, west to Kansas, and
north to Minnesota; also in parts of
northwestern United States and western
Canada.

Comments: Common Barberry is native to Europe.
Its fruits can be made into jams and
jellies, and their juice makes a pleasant
drink. Two other species of barberry
grow wild in the eastern United States:
American Barberry (*B. canadensis*), with
bristle-toothed leaves, notched petals,
and 3-branched spines, found from Wes
Virginia south to Georgia and west to
Tennessee, Kentucky, and Missouri, and
Japanese Barberry (*B. thunbergii*), a
common hedge plant, with unbranched
spines and leaves with smooth edges,
widely naturalized in our area except the
Deep South. Barberries are susceptible
to black stem rust, a destructive
parasitic fungus. The fungus spends part
of its life cycle on wheat and part on

barberry. To disrupt the life cycle, and thus control the disease, millions of barberry bushes have been destroyed in North America.

2 Blue Cohosh
Caulophyllum thalictroides

Description: Inconspicuous, *purplish-brown to yellow-green flowers* in a loosely branched cluster.

Flowers: ½" (1.5 cm) wide; sepals 6, pointed; petals 6, smaller, hood-shaped.

Leaves: 2 per plant, compound; lower leaf large, usually highly divided into 27 leaflets, each 1–3" (2.5–7.5 cm) long; upper leaf small, divided into 9–12 leaflets, with 3–5 pointed lobes at tip; young plants covered with white waxy bloom.

Fruit: Capsule, opening to expose *1–2 deep blue, berry-like seeds;* on a small, *inflated stalk.*

Height: 1–3' (30–90 cm).

Flowering: April–June.

Habitat: Moist woods.

Range: Manitoba east to Nova Scotia, south to Georgia, west to Oklahoma, and north to North Dakota.

Comments: The six stamens and central pistil of this early spring flower mature at different times, assuring cross-pollination. The petals bear fleshy nectar glands that are visited by early solitary bees. The ovary is eventually ruptured by the developing seeds within it; the seeds are thus exposed, an unusual condition among flowering plants. The seeds have reportedly been used as a coffee substitute. The foliage resembles meadow rues *(Thalictrum),* hence the species name.

66 Twinleaf
Jeffersonia diphylla

Description: *1 white flower* atop a leafless stalk.

Flowers: 1" (2.5 cm) wide; sepals 4, dropping off; petals 8.

Leaves: 3–6" (7.5–15 cm) long, basal, long-stemmed, *divided lengthwise into wing-li*
halves.

Fruit: Large, dry, pear-shaped capsule, with a tiny hinged lid.

Height: 5–10" (12.5–25 cm) when in flower; increasing to 1½' (45 cm) as fruit matures.

Flowering: April–May.

Habitat: Rich, damp, open woods; usually in limestone soil.

Range: Ontario and New York south to Georgi
and Alabama and northwest to Iowa an
Minnesota.

Comments: The solitary flower somewhat resembles
that of Bloodroot (*Sanguinaria
canadensis*), but the latter species has
palmately compound leaves with 5–9
lobes. Although both common and
species names suggest a plant with two
leaves, there are actually more; each leaf
is divided into two nearly separate
leaflets. The genus was named in honor
of Thomas Jefferson by his friend and
fellow botanist William Bartram. Only
one other species of twinleaf occurs in
the world: *J. dubia,* found in Japan.

67 Mayapple; Mandrake
Podophyllum peltatum

Description: *1 nodding flower* in angle between a *pair
of large, deeply lobed leaves.*

Flowers: 2" (5 cm) wide, fragrant; petals 6–9,
waxy, white.

Leaves: To 1' (30 cm) wide.

Fruit: Large, fleshy, *lemon-colored berry.*

Height: 1–1½' (30–45 cm).

Flowering: April–June.

Habitat: Rich woods and damp shady clearings.

Range: Ontario east to Nova Scotia, south to
Florida, west to Texas, and north to
Nebraska and Minnesota.

Comments: The common name refers to the May
blooming of its apple-blossom-like
flower. Although the leaves, roots, and
seeds are poisonous if ingested in large

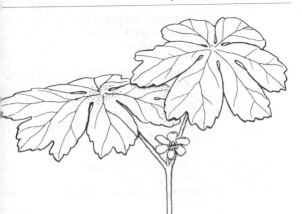

Mayapple

quantities, the roots were used as a cathartic by Native Americans. When ripe, the edible fruit can be used in jellies and for juice or eaten fresh. The common name Mandrake rightfully belongs to *Mandragora officinarum* of the nightshade family (Solanaceae), an unrelated Eurasian plant with a similar root.

TRUMPET CREEPER FAMILY
Bignoniaceae

Trees, shrubs, or woody vines, occasionally herbs, with large, showy, clustered flowers.

Flowers: Bilaterally symmetrical; in clusters at ends of branches or in leaf axils. Calyx 5-lobed; corolla funnel-shaped, bell-shaped, or tubular, 5-lobed and often 2-lipped; stamens 2 or 4; all these parts attached at base of ovary.
Leaves: Usually opposite; simple or pinnately or palmately compound.
Fruit: 2-valved capsule.

There are about 100 genera and 800 species, found mostly in the tropics. Some plants are cultivated as handsome ornamentals, such as those in the genera *Catalpa, Jacaranda,* and *Tecoma.*

422 Trumpet Creeper; Devil's Shoestrings; Hellvine
Campis radicans

Description: *A woody vine with trumpet-shaped, orange red to yellowish flowers.*
Flowers: 2½" (6.5 cm) long; corolla 5-lobed.
Leaves: Pinnately compound, with 7–11 toothed, ovate, pointed leaflets, each about 2½" (6.5 cm) long.
Fruit: Capsule, 6" (15 cm) long.
Height: Vine; to 20' (6 m) long.
Flowering: July–September.
Habitat: Low woods, fallow fields, fencerows, and thickets.
Range: Ontario east to New Hampshire, south to Florida, west to Texas, and north to North Dakota.
Comments: This attractive vine is often cultivated. It climbs by means of aerial rootlets on the stem and can be undesirably aggressive in the South. In fallow fields its prostrate stems—for which it is sometimes called Devil's Shoestrings—stretch for many feet, sometimes tripping unwary walkers. Another common name, Hellvine, reflects the opinion of some people regarding the plant.

BORAGE FAMILY
Boraginaceae

Generally herbs, often covered with bristly hairs.

Flowers: Radially symmetrical; often borne along one side of branches or at tip of stem coiled like a fiddleneck. Sepals 5, united at base; petals 5, united into a narrow tube and an abruptly flared top, usually with 5 small pads around small entry to corolla tube; stamens 5; all these parts attached at base of ovary.
Leaves: Simple.
Fruit: Divided into usually 4 hard, seed-like sections (nutlets); rarely a berry.

There are about 100 genera and 2,000 species, found mostly in warm or temperate regions. Some species are grown as ornamentals. Alkanet, a red dye used as a stain and to color medicine, wine, and cosmetics, is obtained from the

ot of the European species Common Bugloss *(Anchusa
icinalis).* Boraginaceae has also been known as the forget-
e-not family.

---

632 Viper's Bugloss; Blueweed
Echium vulgare

Description: A hairy plant with showy, *tubular, blue
flowers,* each with *protruding red stamens,*
in 1-sided clusters on lateral branches;
clusters uncoiling as flowers bloom.

Flowers: ¾" (2 cm) long; corolla 5-lobed;
stamens 5.

Leaves: 2–6" (5–15 cm) long, hairy, oblong to
lanceolate.

Fruit: Rough nutlets.

Height: 1–2½' (30–75 cm).

Flowering: June–October.

Habitat: Fields, roadsides, and waste places; often
in limestone soil.

Range: Alberta east to Newfoundland, south to
Georgia, west to Tennessee, Arkansas,
and Texas, and north to South Dakota
and Minnesota; also in parts of West.

Comments: A European species introduced as early
as 1683, this plant is considered a weed
by some and a desirable wildflower by
others. Its stiff hairs can penetrate the
skin. The origin of the name Viper's
Bugloss is uncertain: The resemblance of
the nutlets to snake heads may account
for "viper," which may also refer to the
dried plant's use as an alleged remedy
for snakebite, while "bugloss" is from
the ancient Greek for "ox tongue,"
which the plant's leaves were thought to
resemble.

---

360 Hoary Puccoon
Lithospermum canescens

Description: A *hairy, grayish* plant with terminal
clusters of *yellow-orange, tubular flowers;*
leaves and stems covered with fine soft
hairs, giving plant a hoary look.

Flowers: ½" (1.5 cm) wide; corolla with 5 flaring
lobes.

Leaves: ½–1½" (1.5–4 cm) long, narrow, most stalkless.
Fruit: 4 or fewer white to pale brown nutlets.
Height: 6–18" (15–45 cm).
Flowering: March–June.
Habitat: Dry, rocky or sandy sites and borders of grasslands.
Range: Saskatchewan east to Ontario and Pennsylvania, south to Georgia, west to Texas, and north to North Dakota.
Comments: Puccoon is a Native American word for a number of plants that yield dyes. Among the other species in our range, Hairy Puccoon (*L. caroliniense*) has harsher, longer hairs; Corn Gromwell (*L. arvense*), originally European but now found throughout the United States, is an annual with inconspicuous white flowers among its upper leaf axils

---

522 Virginia Bluebells; Virginia Cowslip
Mertensia virginica

Description: An erect plant with *smooth, gray-green foliage* and nodding clusters of pink bud opening into *light blue, trumpet-shaped flowers.*
Flowers: About 1" (2.5 cm) long; corolla 5-lobed
Leaves: Basal ones 2–8" (5–20 cm) long; those on stem smaller, oval, untoothed.
Height: 8–24" (20–60 cm).
Flowering: March–June.
Habitat: Floodplains and moist woods, rarely meadows.
Range: Ontario east to Maine, south to Georgia, west to Arkansas, and north to Minnesota.
Comments: When it grows in masses, this species makes a spectacular show, especially in the Midwest. Species of *Mertensia* are often called lungworts, after a European species that was believed to be a remedy for lung disease. A smaller, trailing, rosy-pink-flowered species, Sea Lungwort (*M. maritima*), occurs on coastal beaches from Labrador to Massachusetts. Tall Lungwort (*M. paniculata*), a species with a hairy

Virginia Bluebells

stem, ranges from Alberta east to
Quebec, south to Michigan and Iowa,
and in the Pacific Northwest. The genus
name honors the German botanist Franz
Karl Mertens (1764–1831).

635 True Forget-me-not
Myosotis scorpioides

Description:	A sprawling plant with several tiny, *light blue, tubular flowers with golden centers* growing on small, curving, divergent branches uncoiling as flowers bloom.
Flowers:	¼″ (6 mm) wide; corolla 5-lobed.
Leaves:	1–2″ (2.5–5 cm) long, oblong, blunt, hairy, mostly stalkless.
Height:	6–24″ (15–60 cm).
Flowering:	May–October.
Habitat:	Streamsides and wet places.
Range:	Manitoba east to Newfoundland, south to Georgia, west to Arkansas, and north to South Dakota and Minnesota; also in much of West.
Comments:	Introduced from Europe and once extensively cultivated, this species is now naturalized around lakes, ponds, and streams. In bud, the tightly coiled flower cluster resembles the tail of a scorpion, hence the species name. Tufted Forget-me-not *(M. sylvatica)* is now commonly cultivated and is becoming

established in drier habitats of the northeastern United States. Smaller Forget-me-not *(M. laxa),* with much smaller flowers, is native to North America and common in wet places.

MUSTARD FAMILY
Brassicaceae

Herbs often with peppery-tasting sap and flowers in racemes

Flowers: Usually radially symmetrical. Sepals 4, separate petals 4, separate, arranged as a cross, petal bases often long and slender; stamens usually 6, outer 2 shorter than inner 4; all these parts attached at base of ovary.
Leaves: Usually simple, sometimes pinnately compound rarely palmately compound.
Fruit: Pod, either long and narrow (silique) or short and relatively broader (silicle), divided into 2 chambers by parchment-like partition, sometimes many-seeded.

There are about 350 genera and 3,000 species, mostly in cooler regions of the Northern Hemisphere. The family is economically important, providing vegetables, spices, and ornamentals. Thirty percent of the vegetable acreage of some European countries is planted with species of this family. Kale, cabbage, broccoli, Brussels sprouts, cauliflower, and kohlrabi are all agricultural variants of *Brassica oleracea.* Some species are unwelcome weeds, and a few are poisonous to livestock. The family's traditional name Cruciferae, means "crossbearer," referring to the shape of the flower.

---

187 Garlic Mustard
Alliaria petiolata

Description: An erect plant, sometimes slightly branched, with *kidney-shaped to triangular leaves and white flowers* clustered at stem tips.
Flowers: About ¼" (6 mm) long; petals 4.
Leaves: 1–6" (2.5–15 cm) long, long-stalked, toothed; *exude a garlic odor when crushed.*
Fruit: Many-seeded, narrow pod, 1–2½" (2.5–6.5 cm) long.
Height: 1–3' (30–90 cm).
Flowering: April–June.

Habitat: Waste places and woods.
Range: Ontario east to New Brunswick, south to Georgia, west through Tennessee to Oklahoma, and north to North Dakota; also in parts of West.
Comments: A biennial native to Europe, this species was first recorded in the United States in 1868 in New York. Spreading rapidly, it is now known in at least 38 states and four Canadian provinces. Especially invasive in forests, it can become so abundant as to dominate the ground layer, adversely affecting the native species. The garlic-flavored leaves are edible.

189 Lyre-leaved Rockcress
Arabis lyrata

Description: An erect stem rising from a *rosette of basal leaves* with a terminal cluster of small, *white or greenish-white flowers.*
Flowers: About ¼" (6 mm) wide; petals 4.
Leaves: Basal, ¾–1½" (2–4 cm) long, *deeply lobed,* stem linear or spatulate.
Fruit: Narrow, up-curving pod, to 1¼" (3 cm) long.
Height: 4–16" (10–40 cm).
Flowering: April–May.

Lyre-leaved Rockcress

Habitat: Cliffs, ledges, and in gravelly or sandy soil.

Range: Alberta east to Quebec, south to North Carolina, west through Tennessee to Missouri, and north to Minnesota.

Comments: Other common members of this genus are Hairy Rockcress *(A. hirsuta),* with a basal rosette of hairy, oblong leaves, clasping stem leaves, and pods that are erect or pressed against the stem; and Smooth Rockcress *(A. laevigata),* with smooth, lanceolate, clasping leaves and down-curved or horizontal pods.

358 Common Wintercress
Barbarea vulgaris

Description: A tufted plant with elongated clusters of small, *bright yellow flowers* atop erect, leafy stems.

Flowers: ⅜" (8 mm) wide; petals 4; stamens 6.

Leaves: Lower ones 2–5" (5–12.5 cm) long, stalked, *pinnately divided into 5 segments, terminal segment large, rounded;* upper leaves lobed, clasping stem.

Fruit: Erect pod, ¾–1½" (2–4 cm) long, with a short beak.

Height: 1–2' (30–60 cm).

Flowering: April–August.

Habitat: Moist fields, meadows, brooksides, and waste places.

Range: Manitoba east to Newfoundland, south to Florida, west to Oklahoma, and north to North Dakota; also in much of West.

Comments: This early-blooming mustard, introduced from Eurasia, frequently forms showy, yellow patches in open fields. The young leaves and broccoli-like clusters of flower buds can be used in salads or cooked as greens. Another introduced species, Early Wintercress *(B. verna),* has lower leaves with 4–10 lobes and longer pods; now naturalized in much of the East and in the far western states and British Columbia, it is sometimes grown as a winter salad green called Scurvygrass.

359 Black Mustard
Brassica nigra

Description: A widely branched plant with *deeply lobed lower leaves and narrow clusters of small yellow flowers* near top of stem.

Flowers: About ½" (1.5 cm) wide; petals 4.

Leaves: 1½–3" (4–7.5 cm) long, with a *large terminal lobe* and usually 4 lateral lobes; upper leaves lanceolate, toothed, not lobed.

Fruit: Beaked, 4-sided pod, ½" (1.5 cm) long, *closely pressed to stem.*

Height: 2–3' (60–90 cm).

Flowering: June–October.

Habitat: Fields and waste places.

Range: Throughout much of North America, except far north; rare in southeastern United States.

Comments: This European immigrant is a member of the genus that includes some common garden vegetables: cabbage, cauliflower, kale, broccoli, and Brussels sprouts. When cooked, its very young lower leaves and unopened flower buds can be eaten. The seeds are used for seasoning in pickle recipes and in making the condiment mustard; they are favored by songbirds and sometimes sold as food for caged birds. At least six species of *Brassica* occur in our range.

Black Mustard

549 American Sea Rocket
Cakile edentula

Description: A low, *fleshy*, branching plant with *pale lavender flowers.*

Flowers: ¼" (6 mm) wide; petals 4.

Leaves: 3–5" (7.5–12.5 cm) long, ovate to lanceolate, wavy-toothed or lobed.

Fruit: *2-jointed pod,* to ¾" (2 cm) long, with upper joint longer than lower, ovoid, *with a short beak.*

Height: 6–20" (15–50 cm).

Flowering: July–September.

Habitat: Beaches.

Range: Greenland and Labrador south along coast to Florida and west to Louisiana; local around Great Lakes; also along Pacific Coast.

Comments: This annual, the commonest of our native species of sea rocket, is found on the windblown sand of beaches behind the high-tide line. The common name derives from *roquette,* the French name for this and related plants. The succulent young stems and leaves have a pungent taste somewhat like horseradish. European Sea Rocket *(C. maritima),* introduced from Europe and occurring along the East's Atlantic and Gulf beaches and on the Pacific Coast, has very deeply lobed leaves.

200 Shepherd's Purse
Capsella bursa-pastoris

Description: An erect plant with *triangular pods* and terminal clusters of *tiny white flowers.*

Flowers: ⅟₁₆" (2 mm) long; petals 4; stamens 6.

Leaves: Those of basal rosette 2–4" (5–10 cm) long, deeply toothed, *dandelion-like;* those on stem smaller, arrowhead-shaped, clasping.

Fruit: Triangular pod, ¼–½" (6–13 mm) wide, indented at tip.

Height: 6–18" (15–45 cm).

Flowering: March–December.

Habitat: Disturbed areas, cultivated land, lawns, and waste places.

Range: Throughout much of North America, except parts of far north.

Comments: This annual weed is probably a European native but is now found all over the world. The distinctive wedge-shaped fruit pods, slightly puffed out along the sides, resemble a medieval shepherd's purse, hence the common and species names. The young leaves can be used for greens.

---

149 Springcress; Bittercress
Cardamine bulbosa

Description: *Small white flowers in clusters* atop smooth erect stems.

Flowers: ½″ (1.5 cm) wide; sepals 4; petals 4, much longer than sepals; stamens 6.

Leaves: Those at base 1–1½″ (2.5–4 cm) long, oval or roundish, with long stalks; those on stem oblong to lanceolate, usually toothed, without stalks.

Fruit: *Erect, narrow pod,* 1″ (2.5 cm) long.

Height: 6–24″ (15–60 cm).

Flowering: March–June.

Habitat: Along springs and brooks, swamps, and wet clearings.

Range: Manitoba east to Nova Scotia, south to Florida, west to Texas, and north to North Dakota.

Comments: Cuckoo Flower *(C. pratensis),* with white or pinkish flowers, has pinnately divided leaves. Pennsylvania Bittercress *(C. pensylvanica),* with very tiny flowers, also has pinnately divided leaves. Mountain Watercress *(C. rotundifolia),* also white-flowered, has oval leaves with tiny projections on the leafstalks.

223, 521 Cutleaf Toothwort
Cardamine concatenata

Description: Terminal clusters of white or pink flowers on an erect stem with *deeply cleft leaves.*

Flowers: ¾″ (2 cm) wide; petals 4.

Leaves:	2–5″ (5–12.5 cm) wide, deeply lobed, sharply toothed, in *whorls of 3* above midstem.
Fruit:	Narrow, upward-angled pod.
Height:	8–16″ (20–40 cm).
Flowering:	April–May.
Habitat:	Moist low woodlands and damp thickets.
Range:	Ontario east to New Brunswick, south to Florida, west to Texas, and north to North Dakota.
Comments:	This species was formerly known as *Dentaria lacinata.* Twoleaf Toothwort (*C. diphylla,* formerly *Dentaria diphylla)* has only two nearly opposite, deeply dissected stem leaves, each with three toothed lobes. Toothworts bloom in the spring; the common name refers to the tooth-like projections on the underground stems.

190 Whitlow Grass
Draba verna

Description:	A tiny plant with slender, leafless stalks rising from a *rosette of basal leaves* and bearing *miniature, white flowers.*
Flowers:	⅛″ (4 mm) wide; petals 4, very deeply notched, appearing as 8.
Leaves:	½–1″ (1.5–2.5 cm) long, hairy, oblong to spatulate.
Fruit:	Elliptical pod, on stalk longer than pod.
Height:	To 8″ (20 cm).
Flowering:	March–June.
Habitat:	Fields, roadsides, and open places.
Range:	Ontario east to Nova Scotia, south to Georgia, west to Mississippi, and north to Iowa and Wisconsin; also in parts of West.
Comments:	The species name suggests the early spring (vernal) blooming of this very small, introduced Eurasian annual; it is often seen in garden soils. The plant was reputedly useful in treating finger sores known as "whitlows," hence its common name. Within our range occur 10 other species of *Draba,* all native.

496 Dame's Rocket
Hesperis matronalis

Description: An erect plant, usually branched above, with terminal racemes of fragrant, *purple, pink, or white flowers.*

Flowers: About ¾″ (2 cm) long, on stalks ½″ (1.5 cm) long; sepals 4, hairy; petals 4; stamens 6, outer 2 shorter than inner 4.

Leaves: 2–6″ (5–15 cm) long, lanceolate, inconspicuously to obviously toothed; upper ones stalkless or short-stalked, lower ones short- to long-stalked.

Fruit: Long, slender pod, 2–4″ (5–10 cm) long, with many seeds in 1 row on each side; pod somewhat constricted between seeds.

Height: 1–4′ (30–120 cm).

Flowering: April–August.

Habitat: Roadsides, open woods, woodland borders, thickets, and waste places.

Range: Throughout East, except Gulf states and Arctic; also in much of West.

Comments: An old-fashioned, biennial or perennial, European garden plant, Dame's Rocket is now widely naturalized in North America as far west as Alaska and California. A double-flowered form is sometimes seen. The genus name, from the Greek *hesperos* ("evening"), alludes to the fragrance of the flowers, which is most pronounced at the close of day. The species name, meaning "matronly," refers to several traditional names for the plant, including Mother-of-the-evening. As do certain other members of the mustard family, Dame's Rocket has both unbranched and branched hairs, which can be seen with a hand lens.

199 Peppergrass; Poor-man's Pepper
Lepidium virginicum

Description: Elongated clusters of *tiny white flowers* with 4 petals and *2 (rarely 4) stamens.*

Flowers: ¹⁄₁₆″ (2 mm) wide.

Leaves: Those at base about 2″ (5 cm) long, toothed, with large, terminal lobe and

several small side lobes; those on stem lanceolate, without stalks, or lower one with stalks.

Fruit: Dry, *rounded, flattened pod,* slightly notched at tip.

Height: 6–24" (15–60 cm).

Flowering: June–November.

Habitat: Waste places and roadsides.

Range: Throughout much of North America, except Prairie Provinces and parts of fa north.

Comments: Most of our species of peppergrass are quite similar. This species, a prolific weed, is one of the most common. The seeds of its fruit pod have a peppery taste and can be used to season food, especially soups and stews; the young leaves are used in salads or cooked as greens. Field Peppergrass *(L. campestre),* a European introduction, has six stamens, leaves that clasp the stem, frui pods that are longer than they are broac and a conspicuously hairy stem. Clasping Peppergrass *(L. perfoliatum),* also originally European, is a striking species with minute, yellow flowers, basal and lower leaves that are finely cu and fern-like, and circular upper leaves that wrap around the stem.

---

188 Watercress
Rorippa nasturtium-aquaticum

Description: An aquatic with stems *floating* in water or *creeping* over mud, partly or completely submerged compound leaves, and *small white flowers.*

Flowers: ⅛" (4 mm) wide; petals 4.

Leaves: ¾–6" (2–15 cm) long, with 5–9 oval segments, terminal ones larger than side ones.

Fruit: Slightly up-curved pod, to 1" (2.5 cm) long.

Height: Aquatic; 4–10" (10–25 cm) above water.

Flowering: April–October.

Habitat: Brooks, streams, and springs.

Range: Throughout much of temperate North

America, except North Dakota,
Manitoba, Quebec, and far north.

Comments: Naturalized from Europe and often
cultivated there and in the Unites States,
this plant is highly prized for its pungent
leaves, which have a taste similar to that
of the garden Nasturtium *(Tropaeolum
majus).* High in vitamins A and C, the
plant was long used as a treatment for
scurvy. Our native watercress, the edible
Pennsylvania Bittercress *(Cardamine
pensylvanica),* is more erect.

BROMELIAD FAMILY
Bromeliaceae

Epiphytic (rarely terrestrial), scurfy herbs with generally
stiff long leaves, and flowers often in dense spikes or heads
with conspicuously colored bracts.

Flowers: Often bilaterally symmetrical. Sepals 3; petals 3;
stamens 6; all these parts attached at base or top of ovary.
Leaves: Often with spiny edges, bases sheathing stem.
Fruit: Berry or capsule, to which remains of calyx and
corolla adhere.

There are about 45 genera and 2,000 species, mostly
native of tropical America. Some have been introduced into
other warm regions and cultivated for use as ornamentals, as
fiber plants, or for their edible fruit, the best-known example of which is the pineapple *(Ananas comosus).* Bromeliaceae
has also been known as the pineapple family.

410 Giant Air Plant
Tillandsia fasciculata

Description: *An air plant* with inconspicuous flowers
in axils of *showy, usually red bracts.*
Flowers: 2" (5 cm) long; petals violet; stamens
and style protruding; in numerous
spikes to 6" (15 cm) long, on stalks
about as long as leaves; bracts about 1½"
(4 cm) long, ranging from yellow to red
to green.
Leaves: 12–20" (30–50 cm) long, *in rosettes,
grayish green with brown bases, stiff,*
lanceolate to linear.

Height: Epiphyte; to 26" (65 cm) in flower.
Flowering: January–August.
Habitat: Bald Cypress swamps and in sandy places, usually on cypress trees.
Range: Georgia and Florida.
Comments: This is the most common air plant (epiphyte), especially on Bald Cypress. Air plants get their nourishment from the air, the rain, and the minerals leached from the host tree. Among the 15 other erect species of *Tillandsia* that occur in Florida are Ball Moss (*T. recurvata*), with narrow leaves forming grayish, ball-like clusters on branches of deciduous trees, especially oaks; Needle-leaved Air Plant (*T. setacea*), with very narrow, needle-like leaves; Fuzzy-wuzzy Air Plant (*T. pruinosa*), with a distinctive coat of hoar scales; and the white-flowered Spreading Air Plant (*T. utriculata*), the largest species in the United States, with leaves reaching 2' (60 cm) in length and a flower stalk up to 6' (1.8 m) tall.

3 Spanish Moss
Tillandsia usneoides

Description: *Cascading* masses of slender *stems covered with gray scales*, with 1 inconspicuous flower in each leaf axil.
Flowers: ½–¾" (1.5–2 cm) long; petals 3, short, narrow, pale green fading to yellow; bracts short.
Leaves: 1–2" (2.5–5 cm) long, thread-like, covered with scales.
Height: Epiphyte; stems to 13' (4 m), occasionally to 26' (8 m).
Flowering: April–June.
Habitat: Hanging from branches of Live Oak and other trees and from telephone wires.
Range: Virginia south to Florida, primarily along coast, and west to Texas.
Comments: Spanish Moss is an air plant (epiphyte), not a parasite, because it photosynthesizes its own food. The scales help the plant absorb water and nutrients, most of which come from minerals leached from the foliage and bark of the host tree. The

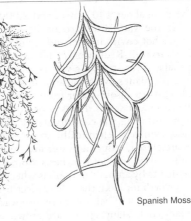

Spanish Moss

genus name recalls Elias Tillands (1640–1693), a Swede who allegedly was so seasick during an ocean voyage that he returned to Stockholm by walking more than 1,000 miles—his surname means "by land"; Linnaeus coined the genus name, thinking that air plants shared Tillands's dislike of water. The species name refers to the plant's similarity to *Usnea,* a genus of lichens.

CACTUS FAMILY
Cactaceae

Succulent, mostly leafless, commonly spiny, sometimes shrubby plants with often showy flowers and spherical, cylindrical, or flat, sometimes jointed stems.

Flowers: Radially symmetrical; borne singly on sides or near top of stem. Sepals many, separate, often petal-like; petals many, separate; bases of both sepals and petals may be fused into a long tube above ovary; stamens many; all these parts attached at top of ovary.

Leaves: Simple and obviously leaf-like in some tropical species, absent or very small and dropping early in most desert species.

Spines: Often developing in leaf axils (where leaves would be); needle-like or flat, in clusters, or absent; *Opuntia* species often also with minute bristles (glochids) in clusters.

Fruit: Berry-like, fleshy or dry, large or small, with many seeds.

There are about 140 genera and 2,000 species, nearly
found in the warm arid parts of the Americas. Most spec
favor dry hot environments and exhibit several adaptatio
aiding survival. Reduction of leaves, along with the cor
pact shape of the stem, is a water-conserving adaptation, r
ducing the plant's overall surface area. Shallow root syster
enable cacti to absorb water from brief showers and store
in the succulent stems. Pores (stomata) in the skin (epide
mis) open during the cool night, allowing entry of carbc
dioxide, which is chemically stored; during the day th
pores are closed, reducing water loss, and the stored carbc
dioxide is used in photosynthesis. Spines discourage eatir
of the plants by animals in regions where there is little oth
green growth for food; they also reflect light and heat, shac
ing the surface and helping to reduce water loss by keepin
the plant cool. Many species are grown as succulent nove
ties, and collecting cacti, a popular hobby, has brougl
some rarer species near extinction. Some are endangered an
have strong legal protection. The flattened stems, or pad
of certain *Opuntia* species are edible; when cut up, the piece
are called nopalitos, available canned or as a fresh vegetabl

---

263 Prickly Pear
Opuntia humifusa

Description: A clump-forming cactus bearing few
yellow flowers, often with reddish
centers and *flat, fleshy, green pads* covered
with clusters of minute, *reddish-brown,
barbed bristles.*

Flowers: 2–3" (5–7.5 cm) wide; sepals, petals,
and stamens numerous.

Leaves: Small, scale-like, dropping off.

Spines: 1–2, or *absent.*

Fruit: Green to dull purple, edible berry.

Height: To 1' (30 cm); clumps to 3' (90 cm)
wide.

Flowering: May–August.

Habitat: Sandy areas and open, rocky sites.

Range: Quebec, New York, and Massachusetts
south to Florida, west to Texas, and
north to South Dakota and Minnesota.

Comments: This showy native plant, the only cactus
widespread in the eastern United States,
is occasionally transplanted into
northern gardens. Care should be taken
in handling it, since the minute, tufted,
barbed bristles (glochids) at the base of

Prickly Pear

the spines can be more troublesome than
the spines typical of most cacti; they are
lined with backward-pointing hooks,
making them nearly impossible to
remove from the skin. Fragile Prickly
Pear *(O. fragilis),* also known as Brittle
Cactus, found from the Great Plains east
to Illinois and Michigan, and
Drummond's Prickly Pear *(O. pusilla),*
occurring in the southeastern United
States, have stems that are only slightly
flattened.

264 **Plains Prickly Pear**
Opuntia polyacantha

Description: A fleshy, sprawling, perennial cactus
bearing pale yellow flowers and *flat pads
with whitish spines.*

Flowers: 2–3″ (5–8 cm) wide, stalkless; sepals,
petals, and stamens numerous; stamens
much shorter than petals.

Leaves: Small, scale-like, dropping off.

Spines: 1″ (2.5 cm) long, with tufts of bristles
above; in groups of 5–12.

Fruit: Reddish, prickly, edible berry, 1″
(2.5 cm) long.

Height: 2–24″ (5–60 cm); sometimes forming
clumps 8–12′ (2.4–3.6 m) wide.

Flowering: May–June.

Habitat: Plains and dry soil.
Range: Saskatchewan south to Texas; also in much of West.
Comments: This plant spreads as a result of drough and overgrazing. Its seeds are also carried by rodents. It is one of several prickly pears with yellow or orange flowers found on plains and prairies in the western states and provinces. The large spines and finer bristles (glochids) are very painful and difficult to extract. With the skin and seeds removed, the fruits can be eaten raw or used to make cactus candy.

BELLFLOWER FAMILY
Campanulaceae

Usually herbs, rarely trees or shrubs, with blue, lavender, c white flowers borne singly or in clusters.

Flowers: Radially symmetrical, with tubular or bell-shaped 5-lobed corolla; or bilaterally symmetrical, with conspic uously 2-lipped corolla; calyx 5-parted; stamens 5; a these parts attached at top of ovary.
Leaves: Simple, sometimes deeply divided.
Fruit: Berry or capsule.

There are about 70 genera and 2,000 species, widely dis tributed in northern temperate and tropical regions. Specie in the tropics generally occur at higher elevations. Species o *Lobelia* and similar plants with usually 2-lipped corollas more common in temperate and tropical regions, are some times placed in their own family, the Lobeliaceae. Member of both groups contribute beautiful ornamentals to gardens An exception to the usual blue or lavender flower color i the scarlet Cardinal Flower *(Lobelia cardinalis).* Campanu laceae has also been known as the bluebell family.

622   Harebell; Bluebell
Campanula rotundifolia

Description: Radially symmetrical, *blue, bell-like flowers* borne singly or in clusters on *nodding, thread-like stalks.*
Flowers: Corolla ¾–1¼" (2–3 cm) long, 5-lobed; stigma 3-parted, not protruding beyond petals; stamens 5, lavender.

Leaves:	Those on stem to 3″ (7.5 cm) long, numerous, narrow; those at base, when present, broadly ovate.
Fruit:	Nodding capsule.
Height:	6–20″ (15–50 cm).
Flowering:	June–September.
Habitat:	Rocky banks and slopes, meadows, and shorelines.
Range:	Throughout much of North America, except southeastern United States.
Comments:	The characteristics of this perennial vary considerably, depending on habitat conditions. It also grows in northern Eurasia and the Arctic. The species name refers to the shape of the basal leaves. Among other common species are Southern Harebell *(C. divaricata),* typical of wet grassy meadows, with wider leaves and smaller, white or pale lavender flowers. The common garden Bellflower *(C. rapunculoides),* which frequently escapes from cultivation, has flowers usually borne on one side of the stems and lanceolate or heart-shaped leaves.

Harebell

627 Tall Bellflower
Campanulastrum americanum

Description: Radially symmetrical, *light blue to viole[t]*
flowers borne singly or in clusters in ax[il]
of upper leaves and forming an *elongate[d]*
spike-like cluster.

Flowers: Corolla ¾–1" (2–2.5 cm) wide, *flat, w[ith]*
5 deeply cleft lobes; style long, curving a[nd]
recurving, protruding; bracts beneath
lower flowers leaf-like, upper ones awl
shaped; cluster 1–2' (30–60 cm) long.

Leaves: 3–6" (7.5–15 cm) long, thin, ovate to
lanceolate, toothed.

Height: 2–6' (60–180 cm).

Flowering: June–August.

Habitat: Rich moist thickets and woods.

Range: Ontario and New York south to Florid[a,]
west to Louisiana and Oklahoma, and
north to South Dakota and Minnesota.

Comments: In spite of the common name and the
genus name, derived from the Latin
campana ("bell"), the flowers of this
species are usually flat, not bell-shaped
as are many others in this family. Tall
Bellflower was formerly included in th[e]
genus *Campanula.*

Tall Bellflower

413 Cardinal Flower; Scarlet Lobelia
Lobelia cardinalis

Description: Many *brilliant red, tubular, bilaterally symmetrical flowers* in an elongated cluster on an erect stalk.

Flowers: Corolla 1½" (4 cm) long, 2-lipped; upper corolla lip 2-lobed, split between lobes; lower corolla lip 3-lobed; *united stamens* forming a tube around style, extending beyond corolla; narrow leaf-like bracts beneath flower.

Leaves: To 6" (15 cm) long, lanceolate, toothed.

Fruit: Many-seeded capsule.

Height: 2–4′ (60–120 cm).

Flowering: July–September.

Habitat: Damp sites, especially along streams.

Range: Ontario east to New Brunswick, south to Florida, west to Texas, and north to Nebraska and Minnesota; also in California and southwestern United States.

Comments: One of our handsomest deep red wildflowers, this species is pollinated chiefly by hummingbirds, since most insects find it difficult to navigate the long, tubular flowers. Although the plant is relatively common, overpicking has resulted in its scarcity in some areas. The common name Cardinal Flower may allude to the bright red robes worn by Roman Catholic cardinals or possibly to the bright red bird of that name.

584 Indian Tobacco
Lobelia inflata

Description: Unbranched or branched, slightly hairy stems with several tiny, *lavender or blue-violet, bilaterally symmetrical flowers* in terminal, leafy, elongated clusters.

Flowers: Corolla ¼" (6 mm) long, 2-lipped; upper corolla lip 2-lobed, split between lobes; lower corolla lip 3-lobed, bearded; after flowering, *calyx becoming distinctly inflated and balloon-like,* to ⅜" (8 mm) wide.

Leaves:	1–2½" (2.5–6.5 cm) long, thin, light green, ovate, wavy-toothed.
Fruit:	Many-seeded capsule, enclosed in swollen calyx.
Height:	1–3' (30–90 cm).
Flowering:	June–October.
Habitat:	Fields, open woods, and roadsides.
Range:	Ontario east to Nova Scotia, south to Georgia, west to Louisiana and Oklahoma, and north to Nebraska and Minnesota.
Comments:	This acrid, poisonous annual is found in a variety of sites, often in poor soil. Native Americans were said to have smoked and chewed its leaves, hence the common name. Though once used as a emetic, the root should not be eaten, for if taken in quantity it can be fatal. Indian Tobacco contains lobeline, an alkaloid that was once used as an aid to help people stop smoking.

628 Great Lobelia
Lobelia siphilitica

Description:	Showy, bilaterally symmetrical, *bright blue flowers* in axils of leafy bracts and forming an elongated cluster on a leafy stem.
Flowers:	Corolla about 1" (2.5 cm) long, 2-lipped; upper corolla lip 2-lobed, split between lobes; lower corolla lip 3-lobed striped with white; calyx hairy, with 5 pointed lobes; stamens 5, forming a united tube around style.
Leaves:	2–6" (5–15 cm) long, oval to lanceolate untoothed or irregularly toothed.
Fruit:	Many-seeded capsule.
Height:	1–4' (30–120 cm).
Flowering:	August–September.
Habitat:	Rich lowland woods, meadows, and swamps.
Range:	Manitoba east to Nova Scotia; Vermont and New Hampshire south to Georgia, west to Texas, and north to North Dakota.
Comments:	This blue counterpart of Cardinal Flower (*L. cardinalis*) is a most desirable plant for wildflower gardens. The

species name is based on the fact that it was a supposed cure for syphilis. The root contains alkaloids that can cause vomiting.

582 Spiked Lobelia
Lobelia spicata

Description: Small, bilaterally symmetrical, *lavender to purplish-blue to bluish-white flowers* in an *elongated, slender, spike-like cluster;* stem leafy, often reddish and hairy at base, smooth above.

Flowers: Corolla ⅜–½" (8–13 mm) long, 2-lipped; upper corolla lip 2-lobed, split between lobes; lower corolla lip 3-lobed.

Leaves: Basal ones 1–3½" (2.5–9 cm) long, lanceolate to elliptical, light green, becoming smaller and stalkless up stem, reduced to bracts under flowers.

Fruit: Many-seeded capsule.

Height: 1–4' (30–120 cm).

Flowering: June–August.

Habitat: Fields, woodlands, and rich meadows.

Range: Alberta east to Nova Scotia, south to Georgia, west to Texas, and north to North Dakota.

Comments: This is a highly variable species with several varieties recognized by botanists.

610 Venus's Looking Glass
Triodanis perfoliata

Description: *Wheel-shaped, violet-blue,* radially symmetrical flowers borne singly in *axils of leaves clasping stem.*

Flowers: Corolla ¾" (2 cm) wide, 5-lobed.

Leaves: ¼–1" (6–25 mm) wide, *scallop-toothed, shell-shaped.*

Fruit: Many-seeded capsule.

Height: 6–18" (15–45 cm).

Flowering: May–August.

Habitat: Dry woods and fields and weedy sites, often in poor soil.

Range: Ontario east to New Brunswick, south to Florida, west to Texas, and north to North Dakota; also in much of West.

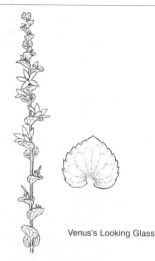

Venus's Looking Glass

Comments: This plant also occurs in Mexico. The flowers in the lower leaf axils do not open but nonetheless produce seeds. The genus name, from the Greek *treis* (three) and *odous* (tooth), alludes to the three lobes of the calyx in many of the non-opening flowers. This distinctive annual can appear in any open spot, even in cultivated flower gardens. The very similar Small Venus's Looking Glass (*T. biflora*) occurs from southeastern Virginia to Florida and west to the Pacific Coast; it has several flower clusters and a capsule opening near the top, whereas *T. perfoliata* has only 1–2 flower clusters and a capsule opening near or below the middle. Both species are sometimes placed in the genus *Specularia*.

HEMP FAMILY
Cannabaceae

Coarse, aromatic herbs with watery sap and clusters of small flowers in leaf axils.

Flowers: Male (staminate) flowers in long loose clusters, each with 5 sepals and 5 stamens; female (pistillate) flowers in dense clusters, each with 1 ovary.

Leaves: Simple or palmately compound, toothed.
Fruit: Small, seed-like.

There are only 2 genera and 4 species. The genus *Humulus,* widely distributed through the northern temperate region, is economically important as the source of hops (*Humulus lupulus*), used in beermaking. The genus *Cannabis,* from which marijuana and hemp fibers and oils are derived, is native to central Asia.

32 Marijuana; Hemp
Cannabis sativa

Description: *A coarse branching plant* with erect stems and clusters of small greenish flowers in leaf axils.

Flowers: To ⅛" (3 mm) wide; male and female flowers on separate plants.

Leaves: Hairy, *palmately divided,* with 5–7 long, *narrow, coarsely toothed, tapering leaflets,* each 2–6" (5–15 cm) long.

Height: 3–16′ (90–480 cm).

Flowering: June–October.

Habitat: Waste places and roadsides.

Range: Throughout temperate North America.

Comments: This annual, introduced from Asia, is the source of the narcotic marijuana. Its leaves and flowers are dried and smoked like tobacco for their euphoric effect. Hemp fiber, long used for rope and various woven items, is extracted from the stems; the seeds yield an oil used in cooking and for soaps and lotions. Hemp products are becoming increasingly popular; the raw materials for these must be imported because growing hemp is presently illegal in the United States.

HONEYSUCKLE FAMILY
Caprifoliaceae

Mostly shrubs, sometimes vines or herbs, commonly with showy flowers usually in a branched or forked cluster.

Flowers: Radially or bilaterally symmetrical. Calyx with 5 small sepals; corolla with 5 petals united into a slender

tube, flared into a trumpet-shaped end or forming a
upper and lower lip; stamens usually 5; all these parts at
tached at top of ovary.

Leaves: Opposite, simple or compound.
Fruit: Berry, drupe, or capsule.

There are about 15 genera and 400 species, found in th
northern temperate region and in tropical mountains
Snowberry *(Symphoricarpo albus)*, elderberries *(Sambucus)*
and various honeysuckles *(Lonicera)* are grown as ornamen
tals, and the fruits of elderberries are also eaten or made int
jelly and wine.

---

355   Southern Bush Honeysuckle
Diervilla sessilifolia

Description: *A low shrub with sulfur-yellow flowers* in
clusters of 3–7 atop stems and atop
small, nearly square branches.

Flowers: ¾" (2 cm) long; corolla tubular, with 5
lobes, 3 pointed forward, 2 backward.

Leaves: 2–5" (5–12.5 cm) long, opposite,
stalkless, ovate to lanceolate, toothed.

Height: 4–5' (1.2–1.5 m).

Flowering: June–August.

Habitat: Upland woods.

Range: Virginia south to Georgia and west to
Alabama and Tennessee.

Comments: A similar species, Northern Bush
Honeysuckle *(D. lonicera),* which grows
in central and northeastern United
States and adjacent Canada, has small
round branches, stalked leaves, and
clusters that are mostly made up of only
three flowers. The flowers of both
species turn partly dull red with age.

---

463   Twinflower
Linnaea borealis

Description: A low, delicate evergreen with hairy,
trailing stems with short upright
branches, each terminated by *2 pinkish-
white, nodding, bell-shaped flowers.*

Flowers: ½" (1.5 cm) long; corolla 5-lobed, hairy
inside.

Leaves: About ½" (1.5 cm) wide, ½–1"

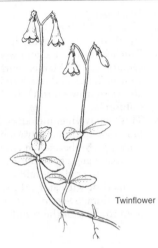

Twinflower

(1.5–2.5 cm) long, opposite, rounded, light green, with toothed edges; low on flower stalks.

Height: Creeper; flowering branches 3–6″ (7.5–15 cm).

Flowering: June–August.

Habitat: Cool woods and bogs.

Range: Alberta east to Newfoundland and south to Pennsylvania and West Virginia; Illinois and Wisconsin west to the Dakotas; also in much of western and northern North America.

Comments: A beautiful trailing plant of the north, this is the American variety of the European plant. The genus name honors Carolus Linnaeus (1707–1778), the father of modern botany, who was so fond of the species that he had his portrait painted with it.

94 Japanese Honeysuckle
Lonicera japonica

Description: A climbing or trailing vine with *white (yellowing with age), fragrant, tubular flowers* in pairs in leaf axils; twigs hairy.

Flowers: 1½″ (4 cm) long; corolla 2-lipped, 5-lobed; stamens long, curved, projecting.

Leaves: To 3″ (7.5 cm) long, opposite, ovate, *untoothed,* evergreen, hairy.

Fruit: Black berry.

Height: Vine; to 30′ (9 m) long.

Flowering: April–July, occasionally into fall.

Habitat: Thickets, roadsides, and woodlands.

Range: Ontario east to Maine, south to Florida, west to Texas, and north to Nebraska; also in southwestern United States and California.

Comments: This woody vine, introduced from Asia, has escaped from cultivation. A fast-growing climber, it can engulf a woodland and choke out trees. It is difficult to eradicate and is a serious competitor with and a threat to the native flora. Sweet nectar can be sucked from the base of the corolla.

433   Amur Honeysuckle
Lonicera maackii

Description: *An erect shrub with white to pink (yellowing with age), 2-lipped flowers rising in pairs in leaf axils; twigs hollow.*

Flowers: ½–1″ (1.5–2.5 cm) long; sepals 5, short; upper corolla lip 4-lobed, broader; lower corolla lip narrow, unlobed; stamens 5; stalks about ⅜″ (8 mm) long.

Amur Honeysuckle

Leaves: 1¼–6" (3–15 cm) long, opposite,
lanceolate to ovate, tapering to a slender
point, lightly hairy.

Fruit: Bright, translucent red, round to
ellipsoid berry, ⅛–⅜" (4–8 mm)
wide, paired, reminiscent of red
currants.

Height: 3–30' (90–900 cm).

Flowering: May–June, sporadically into September.

Habitat: Fencerows, thickets, woods, roadsides,
pastures, old fields, and lawns.

Range: Ontario east to Massachusetts, south to
Georgia, west to Texas, and north to
North Dakota.

Comments: Native to eastern Asia, Amur
Honeysuckle was deliberately
introduced into North America in 1896
for horticultural use. Since then it has
become one of the most impressively
invasive woody shrubs in parts of the
eastern United States. In places it is by
far the most common shrub, especially
showy in the fall when the bird-
dispersed red berries, borne in profusion
along the branches, can color entire
hillsides and woodland borders. In
forests the plant can adversely affect
populations of native members of the
community. It leafs out in the spring
before, and retains its leaves in the fall
after, most other woody plants found in
the same habitat.

418 Trumpet Honeysuckle
Lonicera sempervirens

Description: A vine with showy, *trumpet-shaped flowers
in several whorled clusters at stem ends;
flowers red outside, yellow inside.*

Flowers: 1–2" (2.5–5 cm) long; corolla 5-lobed.

Leaves: 1½–3" (4–7.5 cm) long, opposite,
oblong, deep green, with whitish bloom
beneath; uppermost pairs so united they
appear to be pierced by stem.

Fruit: Scarlet berry.

Height: Vine; to 16½' (5 m) long.

Flowering: April–August.

Habitat: Woods and thickets.

Range: Ontario east to Maine, south to
Florida, west to Texas, and north to
Kansas and Iowa; plants in the northern
part of the range may have escaped from
cultivation.

Comments: This beautiful, slender, climbing vine is
frequently visited by hummingbirds. It
is a desirable ornamental. The species
name, from the Latin *semper* ("always")
and *virens* ("green"), refers to the plant's
evergreen habit, especially in the
southern United States. Five additional
species also have united upper leaves;
they differ from *L. sempervirens* in having
wide spreading corolla lobes.

93, 435 **Tartarian Honeysuckle**
Lonicera tatarica

Description: A hollow-twigged, *erect shrub with pink
or white, paired, deeply lobed, 2-lipped
flowers* rising from leaf axils.

Flowers: ¾" (2 cm) long; corolla 5-lobed, hairy
inside; stalk ½–1" (1.5–2.5 cm) long.

Leaves: 1–2½" (2.5–6.5 cm) long, smooth,
ovate, opposite.

Fruit: Red berry.

Height: 4–10' (1.2–3 m).

Flowering: May–June.

Habitat: Thickets and field edges.

Range: Alberta east to Nova Scotia, south to
Virginia, west to Kansas, and north to
North Dakota; also in northern Rocky
Mountain states, California, and Alaska.

Comments: This shrub is an introduction from
Eurasia. It and other Eurasian
honeysuckles have escaped from
cultivation in eastern North America
and in the northern Plains states and
Prairie Provinces and pose a threat to
native vegetation. Standish Honeysuckle
(L. standishii) has solid twigs. Three
others have hollow twigs. Of these,
European Fly Honeysuckle *(L. xylosteum)*
has hairy filaments, and Morrow
Honeysuckle *(L. morrowii),* with white
hairy corollas turning yellow, has
smooth filaments.

166 Elderberry
Sambucus canadensis

Description: A smooth-stemmed shrub bearing *pinnately compound leaves, flat-topped clusters of tiny, white, fragrant flowers,* and twigs with large white pith and prominent pore-like structures (appearing as dots or short lines).

Flowers: ⅛" (4 mm) wide; corolla 5-lobed; cluster 2–10" (5–25 cm) wide.

Leaves: Opposite, with 5–11 elliptical to lanceolate, toothed leaflets, each 2–6" (5–15 cm) long.

Fruit: Purplish-black, berry-like, clustered drupes.

Height: 3–12' (90–360 cm).

Flowering: June–July.

Habitat: Low ground, wet areas, and borders of fields and thickets.

Range: Ontario east to Nova Scotia, south to Florida, west to Texas, and north to North Dakota; also in parts of West.

Comments: This woody species yields fruit that can be made into tasty jelly and wine. It is also an important food source for many songbirds and game birds. The genus name comes from the Greek *sambuca,* an ancient musical instrument, and refers to the soft pith, easily removed from the stems, which then can be made into flutes and whistles.

434 Redberry Elder
Sambucus pubens

Description: A shrub with downy twigs and leaves and concave or *pyramidal clusters of small white flowers.*

Flowers: ¼" (6 mm) wide; petals 5.

Leaves: Opposite, pinnately compound, with 5–7 oval or ovate-lanceolate, sharply toothed leaflets, each 2–5" (5–12.5 cm) long.

Fruit: *Bright red,* berry-like, clustered drupes.

Height: 2–10' (60–300 cm).

Flowering: April–July.

Habitat: Rich woods and clearings.

Range: Alberta east to Newfoundland, south to

Georgia, and northwest to Tennessee, Iowa, and North Dakota; also in much of western United States.

Comments: The fruit of this species has a disagreeab[le] bitter taste and is said to cause digestive upsets if eaten in quantity. However, it i[s] a favorite food of birds.

---

231   Common Snowberry
Symphoricarpos albus

Description: A hollow-stemmed shrub with *tiny, pinkish-white, bell-shaped flowers* in small clusters atop stems or in leaf axils.

Flowers: ¼" (6 mm) long; corolla 5-lobed.

Leaves: 1–2" (2.5–5 cm) long, opposite, oval, dull gray-green, usually hairy beneath.

Fruit: White, waxy, berry-like drupe, ½" (1.5 cm) wide, persisting into early winter.

Height: 1–4' (30–120 cm).

Flowering: May–July.

Habitat: Rocky banks and roadsides.

Range: Alberta east to Nova Scotia, south to North Carolina, west to Missouri and Nebraska, and north to North Dakota; also in much of West.

Comments: This plant is grown in old-fashioned dooryard gardens; the variety *laevigatus,* with leaves usually hairless on the lower surface, is also cultivated. Two other species are often encountered: Coralberr[y] *(S. orbiculatus),* with sessile, purplish-green flowers in leaf axils and showy clusters of pink berries, and Wolfberry *(S. occidentalis),* also known as Western Snowberry, a dry-prairie shrub with pale pink flowers, leathery, oval leaves, and greenish-white fruit.

---

424   Wild Coffee; Feverwort; Tinker's-weed
Triosteum perfoliatum

Description: A coarse plant with hairy, sticky stems and few-flowered clusters of small, *tubular, red to greenish flowers* in axils of upper leaves.

Flowers: ¾" (2 cm) long; *sepals 5, long;* corolla 5-lobed.

Leaves: 4–10" (10–25 cm) long, opposite, lanceolate to ovate, unstalked; *bases of paired leaves so united* they appear to be pierced by stem.

Fruit: Hairy, *yellow-orange berry* with persistent 5-lobed calyx and 3 seeds.

Height: 2–4' (60–120 cm).

Flowering: May–July.

Habitat: Open, rocky woods and thickets.

Range: Ontario and Quebec; New York and Massachusetts south to Georgia, west to Louisiana and Oklahoma, and north to Nebraska and Minnesota.

Comments: The fruit can be dried, roasted, ground, and used as a coffee substitute. The genus name refers to the fruit's trio of bony seeds. A closely related species with a similar range, Horse Gentian (*T. aurantiacum*), has a smooth stem. Narrow-leaved Horse Gentian (*T. augustifolium*) has yellow flowers and leaves to 2" (5 cm) long.

168 Maple-leaved Viburnum
Viburnum acerifolium

Description: A shrub with *maple-like leaves and small white flowers* of equal size in flat-topped clusters.

Flowers: ¼" (6 mm) wide; corolla 5-lobed; cluster 2–3" (5–7.5 cm) wide.

Leaves: 2–5" (5–12.5 cm) long, opposite, *3-lobed,* hairy, with minute black dots beneath.

Fruit: Purplish-black, berry-like drupe.

Height: 3–10' (90–300 cm).

Flowering: May–August.

Habitat: Shrub layer of moist, upland, hardwood forests.

Range: Ontario east to New Brunswick, south to Florida, west to Texas, and northeast to Arkansas, Illinois, and Wisconsin.

Comments: The distinctive, purplish-pink autumn foliage makes this one of our handsomest shrubs; plants may look like small maples when not in flower. Another

native with 3-lobed leaves, Highbush
Cranberry *(V. trilobum)*, has large, showy
white outer flowers in each cluster; in la
summer and fall it bears red fruit suitab
for jam. Few-flowered Cranberry Bush
(V. edule), with red fruit and slightly
lobed leaves, occurs at high elevations in
northeastern North America, extending
far north into Canada.

163   Wild Raisin; Witherod
Viburnum cassinoides

Description: A shrub with flat-topped, *stalked clusters
of small, white, fragrant flowers.*

Flowers: About ¼" (6 mm) wide; petals 5; cluste
about 4" (10 cm) wide.

Leaves: 2–4" (5–10 cm) long, opposite, thick,
dull green, oval to ovate, *edges usually
wavy* or toothed, occasionally untoothed
with brownish hairs beneath.

Fruit: Blue-black, raisin-like drupe with sweet
pulp.

Height: 3–12' (30–360 cm).

Flowering: May–early August.

Habitat: Wet thickets, swamps, clearings, and
woodland borders.

Range: Ontario east to Newfoundland, south to
Georgia, and west to Texas; Tennessee
north to Wisconsin.

Comments: This is one of several relatively similar
Viburnum species with edible fruit.
Blackhaw *(V. prunifolium)* is more tree-
like, growing to 20' (6 m) high, with
finely toothed, oval leaves and many
short twiggy branches borne at right
angles to the stem. Nannyberry *(V.
lentago)* is a shrub or tree growing to 30'
(9 m) high, with long, tapering leaf tips
and winged petioles.

162   Arrowwood
Viburnum dentatum

Description: A shrub with downy twigs, *coarsely
toothed leaves, and flat-topped clusters of
small white flowers.*

Flowers: ¼" (5 mm) wide; petals 5; cluster 2–3" (5–7.5 cm) wide.

Leaves: 1½–3" (4–7.5 cm) long, rounded or heart-shaped at base, opposite, ovate or egg-shaped, with *saw-like teeth.*

Fruit: Purplish-black or blue-gray, berry-like drupe.

Height: 3–15' (90–450 cm).

Flowering: May–August.

Habitat: Wet or dry thickets and woodland borders.

Range: Maine south to Florida, west to Texas, and northeast through Arkansas and Missouri to Iowa.

Comments: Some botanists recognize two separate species for this highly variable plant, the other being the smooth-twigged Northern Arrowwood *(V. recognitum).*

---

167 Hobblebush; Moosewood
Viburnum lantanoides

Description: A shrub with fragrant, *flat-topped clusters of small white flowers; outer flowers larger* than inner ones.

Flowers: Outer ones to 1" (2.5 cm) wide; petals 5, showy; stamens and pistils absent; cluster 2–6" (5–15 cm) wide.

Leaves: 3–8" (7.5–20 cm) wide, opposite, heart-shaped, prominently veined, *edges finely saw-toothed,* with star-like, rusty hairs beneath.

Fruit: Berry-like drupe, at first red, turning almost black.

Height: 3–10' (90–300 cm).

Flowering: May–June.

Habitat: Shrub layer of cooler forests in northern part of range; at higher elevations southward.

Range: Ontario east to Nova Scotia, south to North Carolina, and west to Tennessee, West Virginia, and Ohio.

Comments: This straggly shrub, formerly called *V. alnifolium,* has beautiful bronze-red or purple-pink autumn coloration and is used by wildlife for food and cover. Its branches may bend and take root, tripping or "hobbling" passersby. The fully ripe fruit is sweet.

CARNATION FAMILY
Caryophyllaceae

Herbs with swollen nodes on stems and flowers borne singl⟩ or in branched or forked clusters.

Flowers: Sepals 5, separate or united; petals 5, each ofte⟩ with a slender portion at base, fringed or toothed at en⟨ stamens 5 or 10; all these parts attached at base of ovar⟩
Leaves: Opposite, simple.
Fruit: Usually a capsule.

There are about 75 genera and 2,000 species, primarily i⟩ the Northern Hemisphere, especially in cool regions. Th⟩ family simultaneously soothes us with many beautiful addi⟩ tions to gardens, especially pinks and carnations (bot⟩ groups in *Dianthus*) and Sweet William *(Dianthus barbatus⟩* and harasses us by supplying many of the weeds foun⟨ there. Caryophyllaceae has also been known as the pin⟩ family.

---

449 Common Corn Cockle
Agrostemma githago

Description: A tall, *densely hairy plant with showy, pink⟩ or white flowers* at tips of long stalks.
Flowers: 2″ (5 cm) wide; calyx with 10 prominen⟩ ribs and 5 narrow sepals longer than petals; petals 5, wide.

Common Corn Cockle

Leaves:	To 4″ (10 cm) long, opposite, narrow, pale green.
Fruit:	Many-seeded capsule.
Height:	1–3′ (30–90 cm).
Flowering:	June–September.
Habitat:	Fields, roadsides, and waste places.
Range:	Throughout much of United States and southern Canada.
Comments:	This European introduction is especially bothersome in grain fields, because its seeds contain poisonous saponins like those of Bouncing Bet *(Saponaria officinalis).* Bread made from wheat contaminated with seeds of Corn Cockle can poison humans. The "corn" in the common name refers to wheat, "corn" being the name applied in Europe to various cereal grasses.

56 Mouse-ear Chickweed
Cerastium fontanum

Description:	A low, horizontally spreading perennial with *hairy, sticky stems, fuzzy leaves, and small white flowers* in clusters atop slender stalks.
Flowers:	¼″ (6 mm) wide; *petals 5, deeply notched.*
Leaves:	To ½″ (1.5 cm) long, paired, oblong, stalkless.
Fruit:	Small, cylindrical, many-seeded capsule.
Height:	6–12″ (15–30 cm).
Flowering:	May–September.
Habitat:	Waste places, fields, and roadsides.
Range:	Throughout much of temperate North America.
Comments:	This naturalized European plant takes its common name from the fuzzy leaves. Although it is a troublesome weed in gardens, its leaves can be boiled and eaten as greens. Nine additional species of *Cerastium,* mostly annuals, occur in our range; three are native, the rest introduced. The genus name, from the Greek for "horned," alludes to the shape of the capsule.

447 **Deptford Pink; Grass Pink**
Dianthus armeria

Description: *Deep pink flowers* in flat-topped clusters atop stiff erect stems.

Flowers: ½″ (1.5 cm) wide; petals 5, with jagged edges and *tiny white spots;* bracts below flowers leaf-like, lanceolate or awl-shaped.

Leaves: 1–4″ (2.5–10 cm) long, narrow, erect, light green.

Fruit: Many-seeded capsule.

Height: 6–24″ (15–60 cm).

Flowering: May–September.

Habitat: Dry fields and roadsides.

Range: Throughout East, except Prairie Provinces and Arctic; also in much of West.

Comments: This European introduction, closely related to Carnation *(D. caryophyllus),* somewhat resembles Sweet William *(D. barbatus).* The common name refers to Deptford, England (now part of London), where the flower was once abundant. A closely related species, Maiden Pink *(D. deltoides),* has larger, solitary flowers.

Deptford Pink

400 Maltese Cross
Lychnis chalcedonica

Description:	*Scarlet (rarely white) flowers with Y-shaped petals* in round clusters atop leafy, hairy stems.
Flowers:	About 1″ (2.5 cm) wide; petals 5, deeply notched.
Leaves:	2–4″ (5–10 cm) long, opposite, lanceolate to ovate, rounded or heart-shaped at base, often clasping stem.
Fruit:	Many-seeded capsule.
Height:	2–3′ (60–90 cm).
Flowering:	June–August.
Habitat:	Thickets, roadsides, and open woods.
Range:	Saskatchewan east to Nova Scotia, south to Pennsylvania, west to Illinois, and northwest to Minnesota.
Comments:	Introduced from Asia and planted in gardens, this species has escaped from cultivation. The common name reflects the similarity of the petal arrangement to the shape of the cross adopted by the Knights of Malta. The species name refers to Chalcedon, an ancient town on the Bosporus Strait, an area (now part of Turkey) where the species still occurs today.

502 Ragged Robin; Cuckoo Flower
Lychnis flos-cuculi

Description:	*Deep pink (sometimes white) flowers with deeply cut petals* in clusters at ends of thin branching stalks; stem slightly sticky toward top, downy below.
Flowers:	½″ (1.5 cm) wide; petals 5, each cut into 4 thin lobes, appearing ragged.
Leaves:	Opposite, lanceolate, lower ones 2–3″ (5–7.5 cm) long, decreasing in size up stem.
Fruit:	Many-seeded capsule.
Height:	1–3′ (30–90 cm).
Flowering:	May–July.
Habitat:	Moist fields, meadows, and waste places.
Range:	Ontario east to Newfoundland, south to Maryland, and west to Ohio.

Comments: This plant, introduced from Europe, |
become naturalized in the northeaster
United States. The genus name, deriv
from *lychnos* ("flame"), was originally
used by the ancient Greeks for some
flame-colored species. The species nam
means "cuckoo flower," another comm
name for this plant. The somewhat
similar Mullein Pink *(L. coronaria)* is a
densely woolly, white plant, which
sometimes escapes from gardens.

206 Mountain Sandwort
Minuartia groenlandica

Description: *A mat-forming plant with many small wh*
flowers at tips of slender stalks rising
from tufts of basal leaves.
Flowers: ½" (1.5 cm) wide, translucent; petals 5
separate, slightly notched.
Leaves: ½" (1.5 cm) long, opposite, narrow or
needle-like.
Fruit: Many-seeded capsule.
Height: 2–5" (5–12.5 cm).
Flowering: June–August.
Habitat: Granite crevices and gravelly sites, ofte
at high elevations in mountains.
Range: Northwest Territories and Greenland
south to Newfoundland, New York, an
Ontario; rare in Carolinas and Tennesse
Comments: This delicate plant with arctic affinitie
is often tucked into rock outcrops. On
Mount Washington in New Hampshir
it is called Mountain Daisy. It was
formerly placed in the genus *Arenaria,*
with the other sandworts.

208 Bouncing Bet; Soapwort
Saponaria officinalis

Description: A leafy, sparsely branched plant with
smooth stems, *swollen at nodes,* and
terminal *clusters of white or pinkish,*
fragrant flowers.
Flowers: About 1" (2.5 cm) wide; calyx 5-lobed,
tube often splitting in double-flowered

forms; petals 5, delicate, *scalloped,* with small appendages at center of flower, occasionally double or with extra petals.

Leaves: 2–3" (5–7.5 cm) long, opposite, oval, with 3–5 conspicuous veins.

Fruit: Many-seeded capsule.

Height: 1–2½' (30–75 cm).

Flowering: July–September.

Habitat: Roadsides and disturbed areas.

Range: Throughout North America, except far north.

Comments: This attractive, phlox-like perennial, introduced from Europe, spreads by underground stems and forms sizable colonies. The plant contains poisonous saponins (soap-like substances) that inspired the genus name (from the Latin *sapo,* meaning "soap") and the alternate common name Soapwort. Lather can be made from its crushed foliage. The common name Bouncing Bet is an old-fashioned nickname for a washerwoman.

448 Moss Campion; Moss Pink
Silene acaulis

Description: A dwarf plant, forming *dense tufts, with 1 pink to violet flower* at end of each short leafy branch.

Flowers: About ½" (1.5 cm) wide; petals 5, sometimes slightly notched.

Leaves: ⅜–½" (8–13 mm) long, crowded, small, overlapping, linear.

Fruit: Many-seeded capsule.

Height: 1–3" (2.5–7.5 cm).

Flowering: June–August.

Habitat: Alpine areas, barrens, and cliffs.

Range: Alaska east to Greenland and south to New Hampshire in East and to Arizona and New Mexico in West.

Comments: This beautiful little mountain-dwelling and arctic wildflower forms extensive flower-studded, moss-like carpets in the western mountains but appears only locally in the East, where Mount Washington in New Hampshire is its southern limit.

71 White Campion; Evening Lychnis; White Cockle
Silene latifolia

Description: A downy, much-branched plant with *white (occasionally pinkish), sweet-scented flowers.*

Flowers: 1″ (2.5 cm) wide; petals 5, deeply notched; female flower with 5 curved styles protruding from center and an *inflated calyx* with 20 veins and 5 sharp teeth; male flower with a slender, 10-veined calyx and 10 stamens.

Leaves: 1½–4″ (4–10 cm) long, opposite, hairy, ovate or lanceolate.

Fruit: Vase-shaped, many-seeded capsule.

Height: 1–3′ (30–90 cm).

Flowering: July–October.

Habitat: Fields, roadsides, and waste places.

Range: Throughout much of North America, except Gulf states and southwestern deserts.

Comments: This European introduction, which has male and female flowers on separate plants, blooms at night and attracts moths that pollinate the flowers. Until recently it was known as *Lychnis alba.* It is quite similar to Night-flowering Catchfly *(S. noctiflora),* another introduced species, which has sticky stems and white flowers with only three styles. Also very similar is the quite rare Red Campion *(S. dioica),* which has pink flowers.

73 Starry Campion
Silene stellata

Description: *Deeply fringed, 5-petaled, white flowers* clustered atop tall slender stalks and *leaves mostly in whorls of 4.*

Flowers: ¾″ (2 cm) wide; *sepals united, bell-shaped.*

Leaves: 1½–4″ (4–10 cm) long, lanceolate, smooth.

Fruit: Many-seeded capsule.

Height: 2–3′ (60–90 cm).

Flowering: June–September.

Habitat: Open woods.

Starry Campion

Range: Ontario southeast to New York and
Massachusetts, south to Georgia, west to
Texas, and north to South Dakota.

Comments: This delicate wildflower is pollinated by
butterflies and many kinds of moths. It
is sometimes grown in wildflower
gardens.

---

397 Fire Pink
Silene virginica

Description: *Bright red, long-stalked flowers* in loose
clusters atop slender, weak, or reclining
stems.

Flowers: 1½" (4 cm) wide; sepals united into a
long sticky tube; *petals 5, narrow,* often
deeply cleft.

Leaves: Basal leaves 1½–4" (4–10 cm) long,
lanceolate to spatulate; those on stem to
6" (15 cm) long, opposite, unstalked.

Fruit: Many-seeded capsule.

Height: 6–24" (15–60 cm).

Flowering: April–June.

Habitat: Open woods, thickets, and rocky and
sandy slopes.

Range: Minnesota east to New York, south to
Florida, west to Louisiana and
Oklahoma, and north to Iowa.

Comments: A common name for members of the
genus *Silene* is catchfly, which refers to
the insect-trapping, sticky hairs on the

stems. Another species with bright re
flowers, Royal Catchfly *(S. regia)*, is
found in midwestern prairies and dry
woods; it has short-stalked flowers, w
petals only slightly toothed or
untoothed, and thicker leaves.

72 Bladder Campion
Silene vulgaris

Description: Loose clusters of *white flowers with deep
notched petals and a balloon-like calyx.*
Flowers: 1″ (2.5 cm) wide; *calyx inflated,
prominently veined;* petals 5, each cut in
2 lobes; styles 3.
Leaves: 1½–4″ (4–10 cm) long, opposite,
lanceolate to oblong, often clasping
stem.
Fruit: Many-seeded capsule.
Height: 8–30″ (20–75 cm).
Flowering: April–August.
Habitat: Fields and roadsides.
Range: Throughout much of North America,
except far north; scattered in southern
United States.
Comments: The inflated calyx of this introduction
from Europe is distinctive; at the poin
where the flower stalk meets the calyx
a navel-like depression. Quite similar i
Balkan Catchfly *(S. cserei)*, although it
lacks the navel-like depression at the
base of the flower. Two related white-
flowered species found in our range are
Night-flowering Catchfly *(S. noctiflora*
which is hairy, sticky, and broader-
leaved than Bladder Campion, and
Forking Catchfly *(S. dichotoma)*, which
also hairy but has slender leaves and
stalkless flowers. These three species ar
also introductions from Eurasia.

209 Chickweed; Starwort
Stellaria media

Description: A weak-stemmed, much-branched, *low
plant* bearing small *white flowers with
deeply cleft petals* in terminal clusters or

solitary in leaf axils; stems with *a line of hairs* down one side.

Flowers: ¼" (6 mm) wide; sepals 5, green; petals 5, deeply divided and appearing to be 10.

Leaves: ½–1" (1.5–2.5 cm) long, relatively smooth, opposite, ovate; lower ones with petioles, upper without.

Fruit: Many-seeded capsule.

Height: 3–8" (7.5–20 cm); trailing stems to 16" (40 cm) long.

Flowering: February–December.

Habitat: Lawns and disturbed areas.

Range: Throughout most of North America, except Arctic islands.

Comments: This highly variable annual, introduced from Eurasia, is a cosmopolitan weed. It can be eaten as a salad green and is a favorite food of chickens and wild birds. There are a dozen or more chickweeds; those in *Stellaria* have three styles, while those in the closely related genus *Cerastium* have five. The petals of *Cerastium* species are deeply cleft.

210 Star Chickweed
Stellaria pubera

Description: *White flowers with deeply cleft petals* in clusters atop an erect stem and rising from leaf axils; stems with *2 lines of hairs, or more or less uniformly hairy.*

Flowers: ½" (1.5 cm) wide; *sepals shorter than petals;* petals 5, deeply divided and appearing to be 10.

Leaves: ¾–3" (2–7.5 cm) long, opposite, stalkless, elliptical.

Fruit: Many-seeded capsule.

Height: 6–16" (15–40 cm).

Flowering: March–May.

Habitat: Rich woods and rocky slopes.

Range: Illinois east to New York, south to Florida, west to Louisiana, and northeast to Kentucky; also in Nebraska and Minnesota.

Comments: With its beautiful star-like flowers, this is the showiest of the many chickweeds. Its stems are of two forms:

nonflowering and flowering, the form
usually taller and often with larger
leaves than the latter.

STAFF TREE FAMILY
Celastraceae

Trees or shrubs, sometimes vines, with small flowers, s[...]
tary or clustered, in leaf axils or at branch tips.

Flowers: Bisexual or occasionally unisexual, radially sy[...]
metrical. Calyx with 4–5 lobes; petals 4–5; stamens 4[...]
growing from edge of a conspicuous, fleshy disk at b[...]
of calyx; ovary embedded in disk or separate.
Leaves: Alternate or opposite, simple.
Fruit: Capsule, berry, or drupe.

There are about 50 genera and 800 species, fou[...]
throughout the world, except the Arctic.

---

431   **Climbing Bittersweet;**
       American Bittersweet
       Celastrus scandens

Description: A *twining, woody vine* with small green
               flowers and *bicolored fruit.*
    Flowers: ⅛" (4 mm) wide; petals 4–5; terminal
               cluster to 4" (10 cm) long.
     Leaves: To 2–4" (5–10 cm) long, ovate, pointe[...]
               finely toothed.
      Fruit: *Yellow-orange, opening at maturity and
               exposing a scarlet, berry-like interior*
               (actually fleshy seeds); in clusters at
               stem tips.
     Height: Vine; climbing sometimes to 56' (17 m[...]
  Flowering: May–June.
    Habitat: Thickets, woods, and riverbanks.
      Range: Saskatchewan east to New Brunswick,
               south to Georgia, west to Texas, and
               north to North Dakota.
  Comments: The fruit of Climbing Bittersweet is
               frequently used in winter bouquets. Th[...]
               native species is being replaced in the
               Northeast by the more aggressive
               Asiatic Bittersweet (*C. orbiculatus*),
               which has escaped from cultivation and
               can cover huge trees, much like Kudzu

(*Pueraria montana*) of the pea family
(Fabaceae). *C. orbiculatus* has flowers and
showy, yellow-orange and scarlet fruit
rising from the leaf axils.

GOOSEFOOT FAMILY
Chenopodiaceae

Herbs, rarely shrubs, sometimes succulent, with minute,
clustered, greenish flowers.

Flowers: Bisexual or unisexual, usually radially symmetrical.
Sepals 2–5, sometimes 1 or absent; petals absent; stamens
1–5; all these parts attached at base of ovary.
Leaves: Usually alternate, simple, toothed or lobed; often
with a grayish, mealy surface.
Fruit: Tiny, seed-like, 1-seeded.

There are about 100 genera and 1,500 species, many
found along seashores or in other saline places. Many members of the family are weeds, but some are grown as ornamentals. A number of garden vegetables are obtained from
Chenopodiaceae; beets and Swiss chard are obtained from
Beta vulgaris, and spinach from *Spinacia oleracea.*

21 Lamb's-quarters; Pigweed
Chenopodium album

Description: Clustered spikes of minute, *unstalked
flowers* on a branching plant often with
red-streaked stems.
Flowers: Less than ¹⁄₁₆″ (2 mm) wide, sessile;
calyx greenish; petals absent.
Leaves: 1–4″ (2.5–10 cm) long, *triangular or
diamond-shaped,* coarsely toothed, *mealy
white beneath.*
Height: 1–6′ (30–180 cm).
Flowering: June–October.
Habitat: Cultivated land, disturbed sites, and
roadsides.
Range: Throughout North America, except
Arctic islands.
Comments: The leaves of this European native are an
excellent source of greens, as tasty as
spinach but more bothersome to harvest.
Many of the introduced members of this
family are weeds with non-showy

flowers that invade lawns and gardens.
Eighteen more species of this genus
are found in our range, two of them
strongly aromatic: Mexican Tea or
Epazote *(C. ambrosioides),* an herb
used in Mexican cooking, has oblong
or lanceolate leaves with wavy-toothed
edges; Jerusalem Oak *(C. botrys)* has
oak-like leaves.

409   Slender Glasswort
Salicornia maritima

Description: *A fleshy, seemingly leafless,* opposite-
branched plant with green flower spike
turning reddish, and thick, cylindrical
stem joints longer than wide.

Flowers: Minute, green, borne in 3s in hollows
of upper stem joints; spike ⅛"
(3 mm) wide.

Leaves: Reduced to minute, opposite scales.

Height: 6–18" (15–45 cm).

Flowering: August–November.

Habitat: Coastal and inland salt marshes,
especially bare peat, and salt licks.

Range: Ontario east to Nova Scotia, south along
coast to Georgia, and west to Louisiana;
local in Michigan, Illinois, and Ohio;
also along Pacific Coast from Alaska
to California.

Comments: This succulent turns reddish in the
fall on northern tidal marshes. It is
very salty and can be pickled or added
raw to salads. Dwarf Glasswort
(S. bigelovii) is usually unbranched,
with joints wider than long; Woody
Glasswort *(S. virginica)* has creeping
stems that form extensive mats.

ROCKROSE FAMILY
Cistaceae

Herbs or shrubs with flowers borne singly or in branched
clusters.

Flowers: Radially symmetrical. Calyx usually with 3 large
sepals and 2 small ones, or small ones absent; petals 5,

sometimes fewer, separate, occasionally absent; stamens
usually many; all these parts attached at base of ovary.
Leaves: Alternate or opposite, simple.
Fruit: Leathery or woody capsule, with at least 3 chambers.

There are about 8 genera and 200 species, mostly in dry
sunny locations, often in chalky or sandy soil. The family is
found mostly in the northern temperate region, with a few
species in South America. Rockroses *(Cistus),* with vibrant
pink or bright white flowers, are popular ornamentals in
warmer parts of the West; a few others are also cultivated as
ornamentals.

240 Frostweed
Helianthemum canadense

Description:	1 (rarely 2) showy, yellow-petaled flower atop main stem; later in season clusters of inconspicuous, bud-like flowers without petals in leaf axils.
Flowers:	Showy flowers ¾–1½" (2–4 cm) wide; with 5 wedge-shaped petals and many stamens; inconspicuous flowers ⅛" (3 mm) wide, lacking petals, with 3–5 stamens.
Leaves:	About 1" (2.5 cm) long, narrow, dull green, underside hoary with white hairs.
Height:	8–18" (20–45 cm).
Flowering:	May–July.
Habitat:	Dry, sandy, or rocky, open woods and woodland openings.
Range:	Ontario east to Nova Scotia, south to Georgia, west to Alabama, Kentucky, and Missouri, and north to Minnesota.
Comments:	This perennial of dry open sites flowers only in the sunlight, a fact that explains the genus name, which is derived from the Greek *helios* ("the sun") and *anthemon* ("flower"). The common name refers to the ice crystals that form from sap exuding from cracks near the base of the stem in late fall. The flower lasts only one day and produces many seeds.

241 Beach Heath; False Heather; Poverty Grass
Hudsonia tomentosa

Description: A low, *matted, gray-green,* somewhat woody evergreen with numerous small, *sulfur-yellow flowers* atop short branches

Flowers: ¼″ (6 mm) wide; petals 5.

Leaves: *Tiny, scale-like, gray-woolly,* pressed close to stem.

Height: 3–8″ (7.5–20 cm).

Flowering: May–July.

Habitat: Sand dunes and sandy openings.

Range: Alberta east to Labrador, south to North Carolina, and northwest to Ohio, Illinois, Iowa, and North Dakota.

Comments: The flowers of this species open only in sunlight and last only one day. Golden Heather *(H. ericoides),* with greenish foliage and outward-spreading leaves, is found in dry pinelands or sands from Newfoundland and Nova Scotia south to Delaware and South Carolina.

CLETHRA FAMILY
Clethraceae

Shrubs or small trees with fragrant, white or pinkish flowers in terminal racemes or panicles.

Flowers: Calyx 5-lobed; corolla with 5 petals slightly united at base; stamens 10; all these parts attached at base of ovary.
Leaves: Simple, toothed.
Fruit: Capsule.

There is only 1 genus with about 65 species, found in tropical, subtropical, and temperate regions. The plants are often used as ornamentals. This family has also been known as the white alder family.

130 Sweet Pepperbush
Clethra alnifolia

Description: A tall, many-branched, leafy shrub with spike-like, *upright clusters of fragrant white flowers.*

Flowers: About ⅜″ (8 mm) wide; stamens 10; style protruding.

Leaves:	To 3″ (7.5 cm) long, wedge-shaped, sharply toothed above middle, untoothed at base, blunt or broadly pointed at tip.
Fruit:	Small, round, with a persistent style.
Height:	3–10′ (90–300 cm).
Flowering:	July–September.
Habitat:	Wetlands, swamps, and sandy woods.
Range:	Nova Scotia and Maine south to Florida and west to Texas.
Comments:	This shrub forms sizable patches. Its dry fruiting capsules remain long after flowering and help identify the plant in the winter. Mountain Pepperbush (*C. acuminata*) has tapering, pointed leaves and is found in southern mountains.

SPIDERWORT FAMILY
Commelinaceae

Herbs with more or less swollen nodes and clear, often sticky sap; flowers in clusters, sometimes enveloped in a boat-shaped bract (spathe).

Flowers: Radially symmetrical. Sepals 3; petals 3; stamens 6, filaments often with colored hairs; all these parts attached at base of ovary.
Leaves: Simple, base forming a tubular sheath around stem.
Fruit: 3-chambered capsule.

There are about 50 genera and 700 species, mostly in tropical and subtropical regions. Dayflowers (*Commelina*), Wandering Jew (*Zebrina pendula*), and Moses-in-a-boat (*Rhoeo discolor*) are cultivated as ornamentals.

626 Asiatic Dayflower; Mouse Flower
Commelina communis

Description:	Reclining stems with upright, leafy branches topped by *deep blue flowers* protruding from a heart-shaped, enfolding, leaf-like bract.
Flowers:	½″ (1.5 cm) wide; sepals 3, green; *2 rounded blue petals above 1 small white petal;* stamens 6.
Leaves:	3–5″ (8–13 cm) long, fleshy, oblong-lanceolate, tips pointed, rounded bases sheathing stem.

Height: Creeper; reclining stems 1–3′
(30–90 cm) long.

Flowering: June–October.

Habitat: Open, disturbed areas, roadsides,
and woodland borders.

Range: Throughout East, except Maritime
and Prairie Provinces.

Comments: This plant, introduced from Asia, has
flowers that open for only one day. It
often forms colonies by rooting from
the stem nodes, hence the species nam
The genus name refers to three Dutch
brothers named Commelin: Two
(represented by the two larger petals)
became well-known botanists; the thir
(represented by the small petal) died
without any achievements in botany.
Some call this plant Mouse Flower
because of the round, ear-like upper
petals. Of the five other species in our
range, the similar Slender Dayflower
(*C. erecta*) has an erect stem, and Virgin
Dayflower (*C. virginica*) has an erect
stem and three blue petals of equal size

---

600 Spiderwort
Tradescantia virginiana

Description: *Blue-violet (sometimes white) flowers with
showy, yellow stamens* in a terminal cluste
above a pair of long, narrow, leaf-like
bracts.

Flowers: 1–2″ (2.5–5 cm) wide; *sepals 3, hairy,
green;* petals 3; stamens 6, hairy.

Leaves: To 15″ (38 cm) long, linear, pointed,
folded lengthwise, forming a channel.

Height: 8–24″ (20–60 cm).

Flowering: April–July.

Habitat: Woodland borders, thickets, meadows,
and roadsides.

Range: Ontario; Maine south to Georgia, west
to Louisiana, and north to Missouri,
Illinois, and Wisconsin.

Comments: Spiderworts are so named because the
angular leaf arrangement suggests a
squatting spider. The flowers open only
in the morning; the petals then wilt and
turn to a jelly-like fluid. Each hair on th

stamens of this showy spiderwort consists of a chain of thin-walled cells; the hairs are a favorite subject for microscopic examination in biology classes because the flowing cytoplasm and nucleus can be seen easily. Other spiderworts with similar structure are Zigzag Spiderwort (*T. subaspera*), found from Virginia south to Florida and west to Missouri and Illinois, with blue flowers and a zigzag stem to 3' (90 cm) high; Ohio Spiderwort (*T. ohiensis*), occurring from Massachusetts to Florida and throughout the Midwest, with rose to blue flowers and whitish bloom on the hairless stem and leaves; and Hairy-stemmed Spiderwort (*T. hirsuticaulis*), a hairy plant with light blue flowers, found from North Carolina south to Florida and west to Texas.

MORNING GLORY FAMILY
Convolvulaceae

Trees, shrubs, vines, or herbs, some parasitic, commonly with handsome, funnel-shaped flowers.

Flowers: Radially symmetrical. Calyx with 5 sepals; corolla with 5 united petals, almost unlobed on rim; stamens 5; all these parts attached at base of ovary.
Leaves: Simple.
Fruit: Capsule, berry, or nut.

There are about 50 genera and 1,500 species, mostly in temperate and tropical regions. A number of species are considered noxious weeds, but some are cultivated for their handsome flowers. Sweet Potato (*Ipomoea batatas*) is grown for its edible, fleshy roots, and a cathartic is extracted from the roots of Jalap (*I. purga*). *Dichondra* species provide cool groundcover in shady areas.

461 **Hedge Bindweed**
    Calystegia sepium

Description: A smooth *twining vine* bearing funnel-shaped, *pinkish flowers with white stripes.*
    Flowers: 2–3" (5–7.5 cm) long; calyx 5-lobed, enclosed in 2 pale green bracts; petals 5, united.

Leaves: 2–4" (5–10 cm) long, *arrow-shaped or triangular.*

Height: Vine; 3–10' (90–300 cm) long.

Flowering: May–September.

Habitat: Moist soil along streams, thickets, roadsides, and waste places.

Range: Throughout North America, except far north.

Comments: Hedge Bindweed resembles morning glories *(Ipomoea)* but differs in having two rounded stigmas rather than one. It can be a pest, twining among and engulfing desirable ornamentals, and it is difficult to eradicate without removing the fleshy, creeping roots. The genus name is from the Greek words *calyc* ("calyx") and *steg* ("cover"), alluding to the bracts that enclose the calyx; the species name means "of hedges." The somewhat similar Erect Bindweed *(C. spithamaeus)* has oval leaves and may be trailing or erect but does not twine. The related Field Bindweed *(Convolvulus arvensis),* a perennial vine, is a troublesome weed; its calyx is not enclosed in bracts, and its flower stalks bear two small bracts.

221 Dodder; Love-tangle
Cuscuta gronovii

Description: *A climbing, parasitic vine* with dense clusters of *small, white, bell-shaped flowers on orange-yellow stems.*

Flowers: ⅛" (3 mm) wide; corolla 5-lobed.

Leaves: Reduced to few minute scales.

Height: Vine; forming a tangled mass on host plants.

Flowering: July–October.

Habitat: On a variety of plants in moist low ground.

Range: Alberta east to Nova Scotia, south to Florida, west to Texas, and north to North Dakota; also in parts of West.

Comments: Dodder seeds germinate in soil, but the roots eventually die as the plant twines around a host plant and sends out suckers that penetrate host tissues

and through which it obtains all its nourishment. The species name honors Dutch botanist Jan Fredrik Gronovius, teacher of Linnaeus. Other dodders grow exclusively on such plants as flax or clover and are significant agricultural weeds. At least 15 dodders, some from Europe, are found in our area, and all are difficult to distinguish from one another. The genus *Cuscuta* is often placed in its own family, the Cuscutaceae.

403 Small Red Morning Glory
Ipomoea coccinea

Description: A twining, annual vine with *small scarlet flowers,* each with a flaring tube flattening into 5 shallow lobes.

Flowers: About ¾" (2 cm) wide; *sepals 5, with bristle-like tips;* stamens and stigma protruding.

Leaves: 1½–4" (4–10 cm) long, heart-shaped, occasionally lobed.

Height: Vine; 3–9' (90–270 cm) long.

Flowering: July–October.

Habitat: Thickets, disturbed areas, and roadsides.

Range: Michigan east to Massachusetts, south to Florida, west to Texas, and north to Iowa and Illinois.

Comments: This showy vine, introduced as an ornamental from tropical America, has now escaped in many areas. The genus name derives from the Greek word for "worm-like" and refers to the plant's twining habit. The closely related Scarlet Cypress Vine *(I. quamoclit)* has leaves divided into very narrow segments, like teeth on a comb.

543 Ivy-leaved Morning Glory
Ipomoea hederacea

Description: A leafy, hairy, annual vine with *3-lobed leaves and blue, funnel-shaped flowers* (white inside) turning rose-purple late in the day.

Flowers: About 1½" (4 cm) wide; sepals 5, with long tips, narrow hairy base; corolla with 5 united petals.

Leaves: 2–5" (5–12.5 cm) long and wide, deep indented into 3 lobes, tapering to poin

Height: Vine; 3–6' (90–180 cm) long.

Flowering: July–October.

Habitat: Fields and disturbed areas.

Range: Ontario east to Maine, south to Florida west to Texas, and north to North Dako

Comments: Introduced from tropical America, this twining plant is often a troublesome weed. The species name refers to Engli Ivy *(Hedera helix)*, which has similar leaves.

460   Railroad Vine
Ipomoea pes-caprae

Description: A vine with a creeping stem and erect flower stalks with *purple or reddish-pink, funnel-shaped flowers.*

Flowers: About 2" (5 cm) long; corolla with 5 united petals.

Leaves: 1–4" (2.5–10 cm) long, round, bright green, usually *folded along midrib, notched at apex.*

Height: Vine; to 20' (6 m) long.

Flowering: Throughout year.

Habitat: Coastal sand dunes and beaches.

Range: South Carolina south to Florida and wes to Texas; also in Pennsylvania.

Comments: Introduced from the West Indies, this showy vine sometimes grows across beaches almost to the water's edge. It grows on beaches and dunes in warm areas worldwide. The species name, meaning "goat's foot," refers to the shape of the leaves.

459   Common Morning Glory
Ipomoea purpurea

Description: A twining, annual vine with hairy stems and *funnel-shaped, purple, pink, blue, or white flowers* in clusters of 1–5 rising from leaf axils.

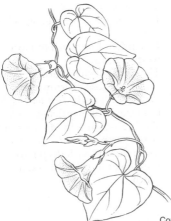

Common Morning Glory

Flowers:	2–3″ (5–7.5 cm) long; sepals narrow, pointed, hairy; corolla with 5 united petals.
Leaves:	2–5″ (5–12.5 cm) long, broad, *heart-shaped.*
Height:	Vine; to 10′ (3 m) long.
Flowering:	July–October.
Habitat:	Cultivated fields, roadsides, and disturbed areas.
Range:	Ontario east to Maine, south to Florida, west to Texas, and north to North Dakota; also in southwestern United States and California.
Comments:	Originally introduced from tropical America as an ornamental, this plant has escaped from gardens and become naturalized. Its broad, heart-shaped leaves are distinctive.

462 Saltmarsh Morning Glory
Ipomoea sagittata

Description:	A climbing vine with smooth stems and *pink or bright purple, funnel-shaped flowers* borne singly or in clusters of 2–3.
Flowers:	To 3″ (7.5 cm) long; corolla with 5 united petals.
Leaves:	1½–4″ (4–10 cm) long, *arrowhead-shaped,* with long, diverging, basal lobes.
Height:	Vine; to 8′ (2.5 m) long.

Flowering: Throughout year.

Habitat: Bogs, marshes, and wet areas between dunes.

Range: North Carolina south to Florida and west to Texas.

Comments: The leaves of this southern vine resemble those of arrowheads (*Sagittaria*), both with names derived from the Latin word *sagitta* ("arrow"). The high-climbing Manroot or Man-of-the-earth (*I. pandurata*), which has white flowers with deep purple throats, is frequent in the Midwest and in the South.

DOGWOOD FAMILY
Cornaceae

Mostly trees or shrubs, rarely herbs, commonly with tiny flowers surrounded by petal-like bracts and resembling large flower.

Flowers: Bisexual or unisexual, radially symmetrical. Sepals 4–5, small; petals 4–5; stamens 4–5; all these parts attached at top of ovary.
Leaves: Alternate or opposite, simple.
Fruit: Berry or berry-like drupe.

There are about 11 genera and 100 species, mostly in temperate regions. Many members of Cornaceae are grown as ornamentals.

45 Bunchberry
Cornus canadensis

Description: An erect herb growing from creeping roots and topped by *4 white, petal-like bracts* above a whorl of leaves.

Flowers: Tiny, yellowish-green; round cluster surrounded by set of bracts about 1½″ (4 cm) wide.

Leaves: 1½–3″ (4–7.5 cm) long, ovate, pointed, with veins curving into an arc; 1–2 pair of reduced, scale-like leaves on stem below whorled main leaves.

Fruit: Tight clusters of *bright red, berry-like drupes.*

Height: 3–8″ (7.5–20 cm).

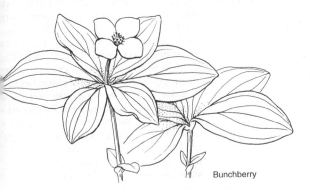

Bunchberry

Flowering: May–July.
Habitat: Cool woods and damp openings.
Range: Throughout North America south to Virginia, Iowa, New Mexico, and Oregon.
Comments: This showy wildflower and Northern Dwarf Cornel *(C. suecica),* also known as Dwarf Bog Bunchberry, found in northern forests, are the only herbs in the dogwood group, the other members being trees or shrubs. *C. suecica* occurs in Quebec, Newfoundland, New Brunswick, and Nova Scotia; it has small purple flowers surrounded by four white bracts.

165 Red Osier
Cornus stolonifera

Description: A shrub with small, *creamy white flowers in flat-topped clusters,* white fruit, and *deep red, smooth twigs with white pith.*
Flowers: Cluster 1–2″ (2.5–5 cm) wide; sepals 4, minute; petals 4.
Leaves: 2–4″ (5–10 cm) long, opposite, ovate, pale beneath, with curving veins.
Fruit: Clusters of white, berry-like drupes.
Height: 3–10′ (90–300 cm).
Flowering: May–August.
Habitat: Shorelines and thickets.
Range: Throughout North America, except southeastern United States and the far north.

Comments: This is the showiest of the red-twigged
dogwoods. The genus name comes from
the Latin *cornu* ("horn") and alludes to
the hardness of the wood. The common
name dogwood, derived from the Old
English word *dagge* ("dagger"), refers to
a European species that has long been
used for making butchers' skewers. A
closely related species, Silky Dogwood
(*C. amomum*), can be recognized by its
combination of slightly hairy red twigs,
tan pith, and blue fruit. At least eight
other species occur in the East, some
with blue fruit, some with white fruit.

STONECROP FAMILY
Crassulaceae

Succulent herbs or small shrubs, commonly with star-like
flowers in branched clusters.

Flowers: Sepals 4–5; petals 4–5, separate or united, with a
scale-like gland at base of each; stamens as many, or twice
as many, as petals; all these parts attached at base of 3 to
several pistils.
Leaves: Alternate or opposite, simple, fleshy.
Fruit: Usually a group of 4–5 tiny pods.

There are about 25 genera and 900 species. Many are cultivated as ornamentals or succulent novelties, including
Jade Tree (*Crassula arborescens*), air plants (*Kalanchoe*), and
stonecrops (*Sedum*). Vegetative reproduction is common in
the family; in some members, little plantlets grow along the
leaf edges, drop to the ground, and root. Crassulaceae has
also been known as the sedum family.

506 Live Forever
Sedum purpureum

Description: Small, *purplish-pink, star-like flowers* in
clusters at ends of *succulent stalks*.
Flowers: ⅜" (8 mm) wide; sepals short; petals 5.
Leaves: 1–2½" (2.5–6.5 cm) long, alternate,
smooth, fleshy, elliptical, coarsely toothed.
Height: 8–18" (20–45 cm).
Flowering: July–September.
Habitat: Disturbed areas, roadsides, and open
woods.

Range: Saskatchewan and Manitoba; Quebec east to Newfoundland, south to South Carolina, Alabama, and Mississippi, west to Missouri and Kansas, and north to Minnesota.

Comments: This coarse plant, a European introduction, frequently escapes from cultivation. It can regenerate from almost any fragment, hence the common name. Children like to separate outer leaf layers to form little "balloon purses." A native pink stonecrop, American Orpine *(S. telephioides),* found on cliffs and rocky outcroppings in Ontario and from Connecticut south to the Carolinas and west to Kentucky and Illinois, has pale pink flowers and oblong leaves covered with a bloom. Roseroot *(S. roseum)* inhabits rocky, coastal cliffs from Quebec and Newfoundland south to North Carolina; its 4-petaled (sometimes 5-petaled) flowers form terminal clusters, with purple pistillate flowers and yellow staminate ones on separate plants, and its leaves are fleshy, overlapping, and spirally arranged. A white-flowered, forest-dwelling species, Woods Stonecrop *(S. ternatum),* has its lower leaves in whorls of three or four.

CUCUMBER FAMILY
Cucurbitaceae

Herbs, often trailing or climbing by coiling tendrils.

Flowers: Radially symmetrical. Sepals 5; petals 5–6, united; male (staminate) flowers with usually 5 stamens and no ovary; female (pistillate) flowers lacking stamens and with an ovary to which all parts attach at top.
Leaves: Usually simple, varying from not lobed to deeply palmately lobed.
Fruit: Berry, with a leathery rind.

There are about 90 genera and 700 species, found in warm regions. Cucurbitaceae includes many economically important genera: *Cucumis* provides muskmelons and cucumbers, *Citrullus* provides watermelons, and *Cucurbita* provides squash and pumpkins.

113 Bur Cucumber; Wild Cucumber
Echinocystis lobata

Description:	*A climbing vine* with an angular stem an*greenish-white flowers;* flower stalks and 3-forked tendrils rising from leaf axils.
Flowers:	½–⅝" (13–16 mm) wide; *female and male flowers 6-petaled, on same vine;* fema*l* flowers usually solitary or in small clusters below a long stalk bearing numerous male flowers.
Leaves:	About 3" (7.5 cm) long, *maple-like,* toothed, with 3–7 mostly triangular lobes.
Fruit:	4-seeded, fleshy berry, to 2" (5 cm) long *covered with weak spines,* dry when mature, opening by pores at apex.
Height:	Vine; to 10' (30 m) long.
Flowering:	June–October.
Habitat:	Moist woods, streambanks, and fencerows.
Range:	British Columbia east to Nova Scotia, south to Georgia, west to Arizona, and north to Oregon; very rare in southeastern United States.
Comments:	As the common name suggests, the fruit looks like a cucumber, but it is inedible. A somewhat similar vine, Star Cucumbe*r* (*Sicyos angulatus*), also has maple-like leaves, but its flowers are 5-petaled and its 1-seeded fruit are in clusters, each fruit about ½" (1.5 cm) long.

SEDGE FAMILY
Cyperaceae

Often grass-like herbs of wet to dry sites, commonly witl 3-sided stems.

Flowers: Bisexual or unisexual, radially symmetrical; eacl nestled in axil of a bract, few to many aggregated intc small compact spikes or spikelets arranged in raceme-like or head-like, dense or openly branched clusters. Sepals and petals bristle-like or scale-like, or absent; stamens usually 3 or 6; all these parts attached at base of ovary.
Leaves: Long, narrow, with sheaths at base enclosing stem; leaf blade sometimes absent.
Fruit: Seed-like, lens-shaped or 3-sided.

There are about 70 genera and 4,000 species, found nearly throughout the world. Cotton grasses *(Eriophorum)*, bulrushes and tules (both groups in *Scirpus*), and Matai *(Eleocharis tuberosa),* a water chestnut, are members of Cyperaceae. Leaves of many species are woven into mats and baskets. Ancient Egyptians produced paper from the stems of Papyrus or Egyptian Paper Plant *(Cyperus papyrus).*

390 Tussock Sedge
Carex stricta

Description: Stems bearing *greenish or brownish spikes* of inconspicuous flowers above *dense tufts of grass-like leaves.*

Flowers: Spike narrow, with female spikelets below male spikelets.

Leaves: Linear, in 3 vertical rows along stem.

Fruit: Clustered, lens-shaped, seed-like, about ⅛" (3 mm) long, each within a sac-like structure.

Height: 2–3' (60–90 cm).

Flowering: May–August.

Habitat: Wet meadows, marshes, and open swamps.

Range: Ontario east to Nova Scotia, south to Georgia, west to Texas, and north to North Dakota.

Comments: The easiest way to recognize this sedge is by its distinctive, elevated tussocks (dense tufts) in open wet areas. It grows abundantly, often in seasonally flooded sites.

394 Shining Cyperus
Cyperus bipartitus

Description: *Umbels of spikelets with reddish-brown scales* enclosing tiny flowers atop a slender, triangular stem.

Flowers: Spikelet to ½" (1.5 cm) long, 3–10 per umbel; *scales lustrous;* sepals and petals absent; stamens 3; style 2-cleft; bracts beneath umbel 2–4, leaf-like.

Leaves: About ⅛" (3 mm) wide, shorter than stalk.

Fruit: Clustered, lens-shaped, seed-like, 1/16" (2 mm) long.

Height: 4–16″ (10–40 cm).
Flowering: July–October.
Habitat: Wet fields, ditches, marshes, and streambanks.
Range: Ontario east to New Brunswick, south to Georgia, west to Texas, and north to North Dakota; also in northwestern United States and California.
Comments: Although members of the sedge family resemble grasses, they are not good forage plants and are of little economic value, with the exception of those species used in making commercial mattings. Their seeds are eaten by some birds.

183, 392 **Tawny Cotton Grass**
Eriophorum virginicum

Description: *Spikelets in a dense, head-like, terminal cluster with tufts of tawny, copper-colored, or whitish, silky hairs* elongating greatly as seeds mature; stem triangular toward top, round below.
Flowers: Cluster about 1″ (2.5 cm) wide; spikelets about ¾″ (2 cm) long; sepals and petals absent; stamen 1; style 3-cleft; bracts beneath cluster 2–3, each 2–6″ (5–15 cm) long, spreading or downward-turning, leaf-like.
Leaves: About ⅛″ (4 mm) wide, flat, grass-like, upper ones often taller than stem.
Fruit: Clustered, seed-like, ⅛″ (4 mm) long, concealed among long hairs of spikelets.
Height: 1½–4′ (45–120 cm).
Flowering: June–September.
Habitat: Bogs and wet meadows.
Range: Manitoba east to Newfoundland, south to Georgia, and northwest to Tennessee, Iowa, and Minnesota.
Comments: There are numerous species of these mostly northern cotton grasses (actually sedges), most with white instead of tan bristles. They are especially showy in open northern bogs, which from a distance may appear to be covered with snow. The genus name is from the Greek *erion* ("cotton" or "wool") and *phoros*

("bearing") and refers to the cottony
nature of the fruiting head, as does the
common name cotton grass.

217 White-topped Sedge
Rhynchospora colorata

Description: *Spikelets in a round cluster* enclosed at base
by a set of 5–6 long, *drooping, white bracts
with green tips;* stem triangular.

Flowers: Cluster to ⅝″ (16 mm) wide; spikelet
about ¼″ (6 mm) long, with oblong,
whitish scales; sepals and petals absent;
stamens 6; style 2-cleft; bracts beneath
cluster widely spreading, unequal, to 3″
(7.5 cm) long.

Leaves: About ¹⁄₁₆″ (2 mm) wide, grass-like,
shorter than stalk.

Fruit: Clustered, seed-like, ¹⁄₁₆″ (1 mm) long.

Height: 8–24″ (20–60 cm).

Flowering: March–November.

Habitat: Swamps, marshes, and moist pinelands.

Range: Virginia south to Florida and west to
Texas.

Comments: The striking whitish bracts on this sedge
make it appear as if it has showy, daisy-
like flowers. These bracts attract insect
pollinators, which is unusual in this
primarily wind-pollinated family. The
genus name is from the Greek *rhynchos*
("beak") and *spora* ("seed") and alludes to
the beaked achenes. The showier Sand-
swamp White-topped Sedge (*R. latifolia*),
with at least seven longer, wider bracts, is
most conspicuous in wet pinelands and
savannas; it occurs on the coastal plain
from North Carolina to Florida and west
to Mississippi. Both species are sometimes
placed in the genus *Dichromena*.

383 Wool Grass
Scirpus cyperinus

Description: *Spikelets in a compound umbel* atop a
triangular or nearly round stem and
surrounded by *spreading, green, leaf-like
bracts; spikelets brown-woolly* in fruit.

Flowers: Spikelet about ¼" (6 mm) long, ovoid to cylindrical, with reddish to brownish ovate to lanceolate scales; sepals and petals represented by 6 protruding bristles; stamens 3; style 3-cleft; bracts beneath umbel unequal, drooping at tip.

Leaves: To 2' (60 cm) long, ½" (1.5 cm) wide, rough-edged.

Fruit: Clustered, seed-like, ¹⁄₁₆" (1 mm) long, concealed among long hairs of spikelets.

Height: 3–5' (90–150 cm).

Flowering: August–October.

Habitat: Swamps and wet meadows.

Range: Alberta; Manitoba east to Newfoundland, south to Florida, west to Texas, and north to Minnesota; also in Pacific Northwest.

Comments: This is one of several species of important wetland plants that provide food and cover for waterfowl and other wildlife. Nearly 30 species of *Scirpus* occur in our range.

393 Leafy Three-square; Saltmarsh Bulrush
Scirpus robustus

Description: Reddish-tan, ovoid to cylindrical *spikelets clustered closely against a sharply triangular stem.*

Flowers: Spikelet about 1½" (4 cm) long, ovoid to cylindrical, stalkless or stalked; scales hairy, ovate, overlapping, each with a stiff terminal bristle, enclosing inconspicuous flowers; stamens 3; style 3-cleft.

Leaves: 2–24" (5–60 cm) long, about ½" (1.5 cm) wide, dark green, smooth, in 3 vertical rows along stem.

Fruit: Clustered, seed-like, ⅛" (4 mm) long.

Height: 1–5' (30–150 cm).

Flowering: July–October.

Habitat: Brackish, coastal marshes.

Range: Maine and Nova Scotia south to Florida and west to Texas.

Comments: Three-squares are an important group of sedges for wildlife. Their seeds are among the most common food of ducks

and marsh birds. Their stems and roots are eaten by muskrats and geese, and they provide cover for many birds and animals. The larger marsh species Olney Three-square (*S. olneyi*) reaches a height of 10' (3 m); its small spikelets are all gathered along one side of the stalk near the top.

CYRILLA FAMILY
Cyrillaceae

Shrubs or small trees with small flowers in racemes.

Flowers: Radially symmetrical. Sepals 5; petals 5; stamens 5 or 10; all these parts attached at base of ovary.
Leaves: Simple.
Fruit: Capsule or berry-like drupe.

There are 3 genera and about 14 species, native to North and South America and the West Indies.

117 Titi; Leatherwood
Cyrilla racemiflora

Description: A shrub or small tree with terminal, *finger-like clusters of numerous small white flowers.*

Flowers: About ¼" (5 mm) wide; sepals 5, white; petals 5, pointed; cluster 2½–6" (6.5–15 cm) long.

Leaves: 2–5" (5–12.5 cm) long, shiny, elliptical, leathery.

Fruit: Brownish-yellow, berry-like drupe.

Height: To 25' (7.5 m).

Flowering: June–July.

Habitat: Swamps, low pinelands, and along watercourses.

Range: Virginia south to Florida and west to Texas.

Comments: This shrub of the Atlantic and Gulf coastal plains is particularly beautiful in the fall when its foliage turns scarlet or orange. The similar Buckwheat Tree or Black Titi (*Cliftonia monophylla*), which occurs in southern wetlands, has wider flower clusters and small, 4-winged fruit.

DIAPENSIA FAMILY
Diapensiaceae

Evergreen herbs or small tufted shrubs with pink or whit
flowers borne singly or in clusters.

Flowers: Radially symmetrical. Calyx and corolla each 5
   lobed; stamens 5, sometimes united into a tube; all thes
   parts attached at base of ovary.
Leaves: Alternate or opposite, simple.
Fruit: Capsule, with few to many seeds.

There are 6 genera and about 18 species, native to th
Northern Hemisphere. Members of this family are ofter
grown in alpine and rock gardens.

54 Diapensia; Pincushion Plant
Diapensia lapponica

Description: *A low-growing plant,* forming dense tufts,
   with *white, bell-shaped flowers borne singly*
   on short stalks.
Flowers: About ½" (1.5 cm) wide; corolla with 5
   spreading, roundish lobes; stamens 5,
   yellow, attached to corolla between petals.
Leaves: To ¾" (2 cm) long, leathery, evergreen,
   in tight basal rosettes.
Height: 1–3" (2.5–7.5 cm).
Flowering: June–July.
Habitat: Bare ledges, gravel patches, and
   mountain summits.
Range: Manitoba; Quebec and Newfoundland
   south to New York; also in much of far
   north.
Comments: This plant is strikingly showy when in
   flower. The low, mat-forming habit is
   typical of many plants in harsh arctic
   and alpine environments. Diapensia is
   especially common above the timberline
   on Mount Washington, New
   Hampshire. The species name refers to
   Lapland, where the plant also occurs.

128 Beetleweed; Galax
Galax urceolata

Description: *Small, milk-white flowers* in a spike-like
   cluster on a long *leafless flower stalk.*

Flowers:	About ⅛″ (4 mm) wide; petals 5, united at base.
Leaves:	2–5″ (5–12.5 cm) wide, *shiny, dark, evergreen, heart-shaped,* with rounded teeth, in basal tufts.
Height:	1–2½′ (30–75 cm).
Flowering:	May–July.
Habitat:	Open woods.
Range:	New York and Massachusetts south to Georgia and Alabama and north to Kentucky and Ohio.
Comments:	The long flower stalk rising from the roundish, evergreen leaves identifies this attractive southern wildflower. Its rare smaller relative Oconee Bells *(Shortia galacifolia)* is found only in the southern Appalachians. Planted in gardens as far north as Massachusetts, Beetleweed may escape from cultivation. The genus name is from the Greek word *gala* ("milk") and refers to the flower color.

53 Pyxie
Pyxidanthera barbulata

Description:	A moss-like, *trailing plant* with numerous *unstalked, white or pinkish, upright flowers* at ends of short leafy branches.
Flowers:	¼″ (6 mm) wide; petals 5, *wedge-shaped, spreading;* stamens 5, conspicuous, rising between petals.
Leaves:	To ⅜″ (8 mm) long, linear, sharp-pointed, hairy near base, crowded together toward branch ends.
Height:	Creeper; forming mats to 3½′ (1 m) wide.
Flowering:	March–May.
Habitat:	Sandy pine barrens.
Range:	New York and New Jersey; Virginia to South Carolina.
Comments:	This species, especially showy when in flower, is typical of dry sandy areas such as the Pine Barrens of New Jersey. The genus name, from the Greek *pyxis* ("small box") and the Latin *anthera* ("anther"), refers to the fact that the anthers open by means of a lid-like

structure. Shortleaf Pyxie *(P. brevifolia)* has leaves hairy over the entire surface; it grows in the Carolinas.

64 Oconee Bells
Shortia galacifolia

Description:	*1 white, bell-shaped flower* hanging from each erect, leafless stalk.
Flowers:	About 1" (2.5 cm) wide; sepals 5, longer than petals; *petals 5, with jagged edges.*
Leaves:	To 3" (7.5 cm) long, basal, evergreen, rounded, shiny, with scalloped edges.
Height:	2–8" (5–20 cm).
Flowering:	March–April.
Habitat:	Moist woods and streamsides.
Range:	Restricted to a few areas in mountains of Virginia and Tennessee south to Georgia.
Comments:	This species is of considerable interest to botanists. Extremely rare, it was not found again for almost a century after it initial discovery in 1788. It grows well in gardens. The species name suggests its resemblance to Beetleweed or Galax *(Galax urceolata),* but its scalloped leave are smaller, and the flowers are solitary, not in long spikes. The genus name honors a 19th-century Kentucky botanist, Dr. Charles Wilkins Short.

VENUS FLYTRAP FAMILY
Dionaeaceae

There is only 1 genus with 1 species, which is described below. It is usually included in the sundew family (Droser aceae).

207 Venus Flytrap
Dionaea muscipula

Description:	A carnivorous plant with a *cluster of whit flowers atop a leafless stalk* rising above a rosette of *bristly, folded, basal leaves.*

Venus Flytrap

Flowers: About 1″ (2.5 cm) wide; sepals and petals 5 each; stamens usually 15; all these parts attached at base of ovary.

Leaves: 1½–6″ (4–15 cm) long; blades folded lengthwise into 2 hinged lobes, green outside and often orange inside, fringed with long stout bristles to ⅜″ (8 mm) long; leafstalks long, winged.

Height: 4–12″ (10–30 cm).

Flowering: May–June.

Habitat: Moist sandy areas and pinelands.

Range: Coastal plain of North and South Carolina; also reported from New Jersey and Florida.

Comments: When insects or spiders disturb any two of the six tactile bristles on the upper surface of the folded leaves of this fascinating plant, the hinged halves of the leaf snap shut, trapping the prey. A chemical secreted by the prey stimulates the flow of the plant's digestive enzymes (this does not take place if the plant is stimulated by an inert object such as a pencil tip). Following digestion of the prey, the nutrients are absorbed and the leaf is reset. This plant is classified as an endangered species in both North and South Carolina and is protected by state law in the former. All the known locales are within a 50-mile radius of Wilmington, North Carolina.

TEASEL FAMILY
Dipsacaceae

Herbs with flowers clustered in dense heads.

Flowers: Bilaterally symmetrical; each associated with united bracts forming a calyx-like structure. Sepals 5 petals 5, united; stamens 4; all these parts attached at to of ovary.
Leaves: Opposite, simple or sometimes deeply divided.
Fruit: Seed-like.

There are about 10 genera and 270 species, native t Eurasia. Bluebutton *(Scabiosa caucasia)* and Pincushio Flower *(S. atropurpurea)* are grown as ornamentals, an the weedy teasels *(Dipsacus)* are used in dried flowe arrangements.

536 Teasel
Dipsacus fullonum

Description: A biennial with small, pink to lavender flowers clustered in an *egg-shaped, prickly head* on a *prickly stem.*

Flowers: Less than ½" (1.5 cm) long, tubular; calyx 5-lobed; corolla 4-lobed; cluster 1½–4" (4–10 cm) long, 1–2" (2.5–5 cm) wide; spiny bracts projecting between flowers and longer, horizontal or upward-curving spiny bracts surrounding base of flowering head.

Leaves: 4–16" (10–40 cm) long, lanceolate, toothed; upper ones with bases fused around stem.

Height: 2–6' (60–180 cm).

Flowering: July–October.

Habitat: Old fields and roadsides.

Range: Ontario and Quebec south to North Carolina, Alabama, and Mississippi, west to Oklahoma, and north to South Dakota; also in much of West.

Comments: This is the common weedy teasel introduced from Europe. Fuller's Teasel *(D. sativus),* occasionally found in the West, has small bracts with hooked tips; its dried flower heads were used by cloth cleaners to raise the nap of, or tease, fabric, hence the common name teasel. Cut-leaved Teasel *(D. laciniatus)* has

Teasel

coarsely lobed leaves that surround the stem and form a cup. The genus name is derived from the Greek *dipsa* ("thirst") and presumably refers to the water that can accumulate in the cup-like bases of these species' joined leaves. The progression of flowers opening on the head in all species of *Dipsacus* is unique; they start in a belt around the center, new ones opening daily in both directions, and in time forming two bands of flowers.

SUNDEW FAMILY
Droseraceae

Carnivorous herbs, mostly of acidic soil and bogs, with flowers in racemes or openly branched clusters.

Flowers: Radially symmetrical. Sepals 5, united; petals 4–8 (usually 5), separate; stamens 5; all these parts attached at base of ovary.

Leaves: Usually basal, simple; usually covered with sticky, glandular hairs that entrap insects and slowly position them for digestion.

Fruit: Many-seeded capsule.

There are 4 genera and about 100 species, generally growing in very poor soil. Extra nutrients obtained from digested insects and other small organisms may be devoted mostly to seed production. Some species are cultivated as curiosities.

474   Thread-leaved Sundew
Drosera filiformis

Description: A carnivorous plant with *lavender-rose flowers* in a 1-sided, elongated cluster on a leafless stalk, curved at tip, rising from *erect, thread-like, sticky, basal leaves.*

Flowers: About ½" (1.5 cm) wide; petals 5.

Leaves: To 1' (30 cm) long, *covered with glandular hairs* exuding sticky droplets.

Height: 4–12" (10–30 cm).

Flowering: June–September.

Habitat: Wet, sandy, coastal areas.

Range: Nova Scotia; New York and Massachusetts south to New Jersey and Pennsylvania; also in North Carolina and Florida.

Comments: This striking member of the sundew family is distinctive, with its stringy leaves covered with glistening droplets of sticky exudate. Insects trapped in the sticky hairs are digested by plant enzymes. Researchers have found that substantial quantities of protein from the insects end up in the storage roots, demonstrating the importance of this source of nutrients. The southern plants are larger than the northern and are considered by some to be the separate species *D. tracyi.* The genus name derives from the Greek *droseros* ("dewy") and refers to the sticky droplets on the leaves

74   Round-leaved Sundew
Drosera rotundifolia

Description: A carnivorous plant with *white flowers* in a 1-sided, elongated cluster on a leafless stalk rising from a rosette of *small, reddish, sticky, basal leaves.*

Flowers: About ¼" (6 mm) wide; petals 5, often pink-tinged.

Leaves: Blades about ½" (1.5 cm) long, *circular, covered with glandular hairs* exuding a sticky substance; stalk about 1½" (4 cm) long.

Height: 4–9" (10–22.5 cm).

Flowering: June–August.

Habitat: Bogs.
Range: Throughout North America south to
Florida, Mississippi, Iowa, Colorado,
Idaho, and California.
Comments: Sundews are able to survive on nutrient-
poor soils where other plants are at a
disadvantage. A similar species,
Spatulate-leaved Sundew *(D. leucantha),*
has oval or spoon-shaped leaves. The very
similar northern English Sundew *(D. anglica),* also known as Narrow-leaved
Sundew, has much narrower leaves; in
the East it grows only as far south as
northern Maine, Michigan, and
Wisconsin. Dwarf Sundew *(D. brevifolia),*
which has wedge-shaped leaves with
shorter stalks in a more compact rosette,
is a more southerly species, occurring in
damp areas from Virginia south to
Florida and west to Texas and Kansas.

HEATH FAMILY
Ericaceae

Usually shrubs or woody, perennial herbs, sometimes trees,
often with showy flowers borne singly or in clusters.

Flowers: Radially or bilaterally symmetrical. Sepals 4–5,
united; petals 4–5, usually united, often in shape of a
miniature lantern; stamens twice as many as petals, each
anther usually opening by a terminal pore; all these parts
attached either at base or top of ovary.
Leaves: Usually alternate, simple, often leathery.
Fruit: Capsule, berry, or drupe.

There are about 125 genera and 3,500 species, mostly in
acidic soil in temperate regions. Numerous handsome ornamentals, including spectacular species of *Rhododendron* and
Azalea, are cultivated as ornamentals. Ericaceae is also the
source of several edible fruits, such as blueberries, huckle-
berries, and cranberries, all members of the genus *Vaccinium.*

228 Bearberry; Kinnikinnick
Arctostaphylos uva-ursi

Description: A low, trailing, *evergreen shrub* with
terminal clusters of white or pale pink,
bell-shaped flowers.

Flowers:	About ¼" (5 mm) long; petals 5, fused
Leaves:	½–1½" (1.5–4 cm) long, *spatulate or wedge-shaped, smooth, leathery,* green on both sides.
Fruit:	Red, berry-like, dry.
Height:	Creeper; flowering branches 6–12" (15–30 cm).
Flowering:	May–July.
Habitat:	Exposed rocky and sandy sites.
Range:	Throughout much of North America south to Virginia, Illinois, South Dakota, New Mexico, and California.
Comments:	This trailing shrub has papery, reddish, exfoliating bark. It is frequently seen as a groundcover in sandy areas of other northeastern states, especially in the Pine Barrens of New Jersey. It is very common on Cape Cod, where it covers vast areas in open, sandy, pine-studded communities. It is a hardy shrub for landscaping rocky or sandy sites. An astringent tea (sometimes used as a laxative) can be made by steeping the dried leaves in boiling water. The fruit is edible but mealy and tasteless; it is much favored by birds, bears, and other wildlife. The genus name (from the Greek *arctos* meaning "bear" and *staphyle* meaning "bunch of grapes") and the species name (from the Latin *uva* meaning "grape" and *ursi* meaning "bear") both refer to the fruit. Alpine Bearberry *(A. alpina)* is found on New England mountaintops.

123 Leatherleaf
Chamaedaphne calyculata

Description:	A low, erect, many-branched, evergreen shrub with *white, bell- or urn-shaped flowers* hanging along *1-sided racemes.*
Flowers:	¼" (6 mm) long.
Leaves:	¾–2" (2–5 cm) long, *leathery,* elliptical, dull green; dotted with *round dry scales,* heaviest beneath; older leaves brownish bronze above, yellowish beneath.
Fruit:	Round capsule.
Height:	1–4' (30–120 cm).

Flowering: March–July.

Habitat: Peat bogs and pondsides.

Range: Alberta east to Newfoundland, south to South Carolina, and northwest to Illinois and Minnesota; also in Alaska and western Canadian provinces and territories, except Arctic islands.

Comments: One of the many evergreen members of the heath family, this species also occurs in Asia; it is typical of boggy wetlands and highly acidic sites. In Massachusetts, Leatherleaf colonies can expand radially at the rate of one foot per decade. The genus name is from the Greek *chamai* ("on the ground") and *daphne* ("laurel").

513 Trailing Arbutus
Epigaea repens

Description: A trailing, evergreen plant with *sweet-scented, pink or white flowers* in leaf axils and at ends of hairy stems.

Flowers: About ½" (1.5 cm) wide; corolla tubular, hairy within, flaring into 5 lobes, each as long as corolla tube.

Leaves: ¾–3" (2–7.5 cm) long, *leathery,* oval, with hairy edges.

Fruit: Fleshy capsule, inside whitish and pulpy.

Height: Creeper; stems to 16" (40 cm) long.

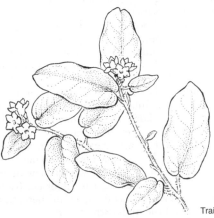

Trailing Arbutus

Flowering: February–May.
Habitat: Sandy or rocky woods, especially in acidic soil.
Range: Manitoba east to Newfoundland, south to Florida, west to Mississippi, and north to Illinois and Minnesota.
Comments: To find this favorite wildflower with an exquisite fragrance, one must search among the fallen leaves in early spring. It favors exposed sites where the plants are not smothered by leaf litter. It appears to be sensitive to abrupt environmental disturbances, such as lumbering and grazing, which may account for its present scarcity. It is difficult to cultivate.

69 Teaberry; Wintergreen
Gaultheria procumbens

Description: A low, evergreen shrub with creeping, underground stems with upright branches bearing *white, bell-shaped, nodding flowers,* singly or in groups of 2–3 in leaf axils.
Flowers: About ⅜" (8 mm) long; corolla with 5 lobes.
Leaves: 1–2" (2.5–5 cm) long, oval, slightly toothed.
Fruit: Bright red, pulpy, berry-like capsule.
Height: Creeper; branches 2–6" (5–15 cm).
Flowering: April–May.
Habitat: Oak woods or under evergreens, especially in sandy sites.
Range: Manitoba east to Newfoundland, south to Georgia and Alabama, and north to Illinois and Minnesota.
Comments: This leathery, semi-woody, aromatic perennial forms small colonies of plants. Its showy red fruit may persist through the winter. Both the fruit and leaves are edible and have a wintergreen flavor. Teaberry extract is used to flavor teas, candies, medicines, and chewing gum. The genus was named for Dr. Jean-François Gaultier, a Canadian physician of the mid-18th century.

512 Sheep Laurel; Lambkill
Kalmia angustifolia

Description: An evergreen shrub with small, *deep pink, saucer-shaped flowers in dense clusters around stem,* mostly below leaves.

Flowers: ⅜–½" (8–13 mm) wide; petals 5; stamens 10, with anthers tucked into pockets of corolla, popping out when touched.

Leaves: 1½–2" (4–5 cm) long, *in whorls of 3,* oblong, dark green above, pale beneath when mature.

Fruit: Round capsule, persisting through winter.

Height: 1–3' (30–90 cm).

Flowering: May–August.

Habitat: Old fields, bogs, and dry or wet, sandy or sterile soil.

Range: Ontario east to Newfoundland and south to Virginia; also in Michigan.

Comments: This small shrub is poisonous to livestock, hence one of its common names. Because of its colonial habit it can form sizable stands. The flowers are miniatures of the larger Mountain Laurel *(K. latifolia)*. Pale Laurel *(K. polifolia),* also known as Bog Laurel, has pink flowers in terminal clusters, 2-edged twigs, and opposite leaves with rolled edges, very white beneath; it is a northern bog plant and occurs only as far south as northern New Jersey and Pennsylvania. Two other species of

Sheep Laurel

Kalmia are found in the southern United States. The genus name honors Peter Kalm, a student of Linnaeus, who traveled and collected plants in the Americas in the 18th century.

203   Mountain Laurel
Kalmia latifolia

Description: A large, evergreen shrub with showy clusters of *deep pink buds and pinkish-white flowers on sticky stalks*.

Flowers: ¾–1″ (2–2.5 cm) wide; corolla with 5 united lobes, each with 2 pockets; 1 stamen tucked into each pocket.

Leaves: 2–4″ (5–10 cm) long, mostly alternate, ovate-lanceolate or elliptical, pointed at each end, leathery, shiny green with yellow-green petiole.

Fruit: Round capsule, persisting through winter.

Height: 3–15′ (90–450 cm).

Flowering: Late May–mid-July.

Habitat: Open forests and rocky places.

Range: Quebec and Maine south to Florida, west to Louisiana, and north to Indiana.

Comments: As the flowers mature, the stamens may pop out of the corolla pockets or they may be dislodged as an insect enters the flower, spraying the pollen onto the insect's back. Mountain Laurel is frequently used in ornamental plantings. Somewhat shade tolerant, it can be planted in open woods, where it lends an evergreen touch in winter and showy flowers in early summer. It is relatively tolerant of fire; when stem-killed to the ground, it grows back vigorously. It is long-lived; more than 100 annual rings have been reported on large plants.

170   Labrador Tea
Ledum groenlandicum

Description: A low, *evergreen* shrub with *densely hairy twigs* and rounded, terminal *clusters of white flowers*.

Flowers:	⅜–½" (8–13 mm) wide; petals 5, spreading.
Leaves:	1–2" (2.5–5 cm) long, evergreen, narrow, oblong, *rusty-woolly beneath,* with rolled edges, slightly fragrant when crushed.
Fruit:	Capsule on a recurved stalk, persisting through winter.
Height:	1–4' (30–120 cm).
Flowering:	June–August.
Habitat:	Peaty soil, especially bogs.
Range:	Alaska southeast to Newfoundland and south to Pennsylvania, Ohio, Michigan, Wisconsin, Minnesota, North Dakota, Idaho, and Oregon.
Comments:	This northern shrub, typical of acidic, boggy areas, can easily be recognized by the woolly brown undersurfaces of its leaves. A tea can be made from the leaves, as was done during the American Revolution. In northern Canada, the plant is known as Hudson's Bay Tea.

508 Sand Myrtle
Leiophyllum buxifolium

Description:	A low, upright, widely branching, evergreen shrub with crowded, leathery leaves and *small, pink or pinkish-white flowers in dense clusters.*
Flowers:	About ¼" (6 mm) wide; sepals and petals 5 each; stamens 10.
Leaves:	⅜–1" (8–25 mm) long, opposite or alternate, oval to oblong, *smooth, shiny.*

Sand Myrtle

Fruit: Capsule.
Height: 4–20″ (10–50 cm).
Flowering: April–June.
Habitat: Rocky or sandy woods and bluffs.
Range: New Jersey, North and South Carolina, Georgia, Tennessee, and perhaps Kentucky.
Comments: The genus name is from the Greek *leios* ("smooth") and *phyllon* ("leaf"). The species name also refers to the leaves, which are similar to those of boxes *(Buxus).*

511 **Alpine Azalea**
Loiseleuria procumbens

Description: A creeping, much-branched, *mat-forming, dwarf shrub* with 2–5 pink, bell-shaped flowers in terminal clusters and *evergreen leaves with rolled edges.*
Flowers: About ¼″ (6 mm) long and wide; petal 5, spreading.
Leaves: About ⅜″ (8 mm) long, leathery, elliptical, mostly opposite, on short stalks.
Fruit: Capsule.
Height: Creeper; branches to 4″ (10 cm).
Flowering: June–August.
Habitat: Peaty or rocky, exposed areas and mountain summits.
Range: Alaska and British Columbia east to Newfoundland and Greenland; also in Maine, New Hampshire, and New York.
Comments: In the Northeast this showy, prostrate shrub is especially common above the tree line on Mount Washington, New Hampshire. It is frequently found with Lapland Rosebay *(Rhododendron lapponicum)* or Diapensia *(Diapensia lapponica).*

120 **Maleberry**
Lyonia ligustrina

Description: A much-branched, deciduous shrub with terminal *clusters of round, white or pale rose flowers constricted at tips.*

Flowers: ⅛–¼" (3–5 mm) long.
Leaves: 1–3" (2.5–7.5 cm) long, oblong-oval, finely toothed.
Fruit: Capsule, persisting through winter.
Height: 3–12' (90–360 cm).
Flowering: May–July.
Habitat: Wet thickets and swamps.
Range: Maine south to Florida, west to Texas and Oklahoma, and north to Missouri and Kentucky.
Comments: At least three more species of *Lyonia* occur in our range: Staggerbush *(L. mariana)* has urn- or bell-shaped capsules; a southern evergreen species, Fetterbush *(L. lucida),* occurs from Virginia south to Florida and Louisiana and has white to pale pink flowers about ⅜" (1 cm) long, 3-angled branches, and dark green, lustrous leaves with a conspicuous vein next to the rolled edge; Rusty Staggerbush *(L. ferruginea),* another southern evergreen species, has white flowers and green leaves with scaly undersides. The genus name honors the early American botanist and explorer John Lyon, who died in 1818.

---

369 Flame Azalea
Rhododendron calendulaceum

Description: A deciduous shrub with terminal clusters of tubular, vase-shaped, *orange, red, or yellow flowers.*
Flowers: 1½–2" (4–5 cm) wide; corolla 5-lobed, *tube glandular and sticky;* style and 5 long stamens projecting beyond corolla; not fragrant.
Leaves: 2–4" (5–10 cm) long, ovate.
Fruit: Capsule, persisting through winter.
Height: To 15' (4.5 m).
Flowering: May–June.
Habitat: Dry open woods and treeless mountain areas.
Range: New York south to Georgia and Alabama, and north to Ohio.
Comments: This beautiful southern azalea forms striking displays on some of the treeless areas of the southern Appalachians.

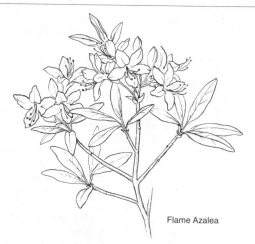

Flame Azalea

A wide variation of color forms occurs, from all shades of yellow to orange-yellow and scarlet. The flowers appear before or with the new leaves. This species is extensively planted as an ornamental. Like most members of the heath family, it does best in acidic soil.

---

517 Rhodora
Rhododendron canadense

Description: A deciduous shrub with *few-flowered, terminal clusters of pink to lavender flowers*

Flowers: ½–¾" (1.5–2 cm) long; corolla 2-lipped, upper lip 3-lobed, lower lip divided into 2 narrow segments, tube short; stamens 10.

Leaves: ¾–1½" (2–4 cm) long, oblong, gray-green beneath; edges hairy, rolled.

Fruit: Capsule, persisting through winter.

Height: 1–3′ (30–90 cm).

Flowering: March–July.

Habitat: Bogs, wet slopes, and rocky mountaintops.

Range: Ontario east to Newfoundland and south to New York, New Jersey, and Pennsylvania.

Comments: This small northern shrub has very showy flowers that open before or with its leaves.

516 Mountain Rosebay;
Catawba Rhododendron
Rhododendron catawbiense

Description: An evergreen shrub with clusters of large, *rose-pink or purple-lilac, funnel-shaped flowers.*

Flowers: 2–2½" (5–6.5 cm) wide; corolla 5-lobed.

Leaves: 2–6" (5–15 cm) long, thick, leathery, oblong, dark green above, lighter beneath, edges smooth, with *blunt base and tip.*

Fruit: Capsule, persisting through winter.

Height: 3–20' (90–600 cm).

Flowering: May–June.

Habitat: Rocky mountain summits and slopes, woods, and streambanks.

Range: Virginia south to Georgia, west to Alabama, and north to Kentucky and West Virginia.

Comments: This attractive flowering shrub forms dense thickets on mountain slopes. Frequently used as an ornamental, it has been hybridized with less hardy Himalayan species to produce some of our most spectacular, showy rhododendrons.

515 Lapland Rosebay
Rhododendron lapponicum

Description: *A low, aromatic, mat-forming, evergreen shrub* with scaly twigs and few-flowered clusters of *bell-shaped, pink to lavender flowers.*

Flowers: ⅝" (16 mm) wide; corolla deeply 5-lobed.

Leaves: About ⅝" (16 mm) long, leathery, elliptical to oblong, yellow-green, scaly beneath.

Fruit: Capsule, persisting through winter.

Height: 4–12" (10–30 cm).

Flowering: May–June.

Habitat: Mountain summits and sandstone cliffs.

Range: British Columbia east to Newfoundland and south to Maine, New Hampshire, and New York; also in Wisconsin and far north, including Arctic islands.

Comments: This little, mat-forming shrub is one of
the first showy alpine species to flower.
It is found on the peaks of higher New
England mountains such as Mount
Washington, New Hampshire, and the
Adirondack peaks of New York. It also
grows in the Wisconsin Dells.

204 Great Laurel
Rhododendron maximum

Description: A large, evergreen shrub with clusters *of
pinkish-white, cup-shaped flowers on sticky
glandular stalks.*

Flowers: 1½–2" (4–5 cm) wide; corolla with 5
blunt lobes.

Leaves: 4–8" (10–20 cm) long, leathery, smooth,
elliptical to oblong, *pointed at base and
tip,* dark green above, often paler and
closely hairy below.

Fruit: Capsule, persisting through winter.

Height: 5–35' (1.5–10.5 m).

Flowering: June–July.

Habitat: Damp woods and forested wetlands.

Range: Nova Scotia and Maine south to Georgia
and Alabama, and north to Ohio.

Comments: This tall straggly shrub often forms
impenetrable thickets on moist slopes or
in swamps. Due to its showy flowers and
handsome foliage, it is frequently used
as an ornamental. The leaves droop in

Great Laurel

frost and may curl under lengthwise; the colder the temperature, the tighter the roll. The hard wood is used for making tools and ornaments. Carolina Rhododendron *(R. minus)* has thinner leaves 2–5″ (5–12.5 cm) long, heavily dotted with brown beneath; it is found in the mountains of the Southeast.

518 Pinxter Flower; Pink Azalea
Rhododendron periclymenoides

Description:	A deciduous shrub with terminal clusters of *pink, tubular, vase-shaped, slightly fragrant flowers.*
Flowers:	1½–2″ (4–5 cm) wide; corolla 5-lobed; style and 5 long curved stamens projecting beyond corolla.
Leaves:	2–4″ (5–10 cm) long, thin, oblong, pointed at both ends, *hairy on midrib beneath;* in *whorl-like clusters* near ends of twigs.
Fruit:	Capsule, persisting through winter.
Height:	2–6′ (60–180 cm).
Flowering:	May–June.
Habitat:	Upland woods and thickets and borders of swamps and bogs.
Range:	New York and Massachusetts south to Georgia and Alabama, and north through Tennessee to Ohio; also in Illinois.
Comments:	This much-branched shrub is especially showy in flower. It is relatively tolerant of dry sites and can be transplanted into wild shrub gardens.

214 Swamp Honeysuckle; Clammy Azalea
Rhododendron viscosum

Description:	A deciduous shrub with *hairy twigs* and clusters of fragrant, *white, vase-shaped flowers.*
Flowers:	1½–2″ (4–5 cm) long; corolla 5-lobed, with *reddish, sticky hairs;* stamens 5, long, curved, projecting beyond corolla; style longer than stamens.

Leaves:	1–2½" (2.5–6.5 cm) long, obovate, *glossy above, often whitish with a hairy midrib beneath.*
Fruit:	Capsule, persisting through winter.
Height:	3–9' (90–270 cm).
Flowering:	June–August.
Habitat:	Swamps.
Range:	Maine south to Florida and west to Texas and Oklahoma.
Comments:	This wetland shrub is sometimes called Clammy Azalea because of its very sticky corolla. The species name means "sticky" in Latin. The flowers appear after the leaves. Another white wetland species of more southern distribution, Smooth Azalea *(R. arborescens),* has smooth twigs, hairless leaves, and red stamens. Dwarf Azalea *(R. atlanticum),* a shrub 3–4' (90–120 cm) tall with white or pink, fragrant flowers, is common in the Deep South and along the coastal plain from southern New Jersey to South Carolina.

227 Highbush Blueberry
Vaccinium corymbosum

Description:	A multi-stemmed shrub with *green or red twigs* and terminal clusters of *small, urn-shaped, white flowers.*
Flowers:	¼–½" (6–13 mm) long; corolla with 5 teeth.
Leaves:	1½–3" (4–7.5 cm) long, elliptical, untoothed, smooth above, usually somewhat hairy beneath.
Fruit:	*Blue berry,* with whitish bloom.
Height:	5–15' (1.5–4.5 m).
Flowering:	Flowers, May–June; fruit, June–August.
Habitat:	Swamps to dry upland woods.
Range:	Ontario east to Nova Scotia, south to Georgia, and west to Texas and Oklahoma; also from Tennessee north to Wisconsin.
Comments:	Our cultivated blueberries are derived from this tall-growing shrub. It is often found in wet areas but can also occur in dry sites. *Vaccinium* species are important to wildlife; their berries are relished by

Highbush Blueberry

songbirds, game birds, bears, and small mammals, and the twigs and foliage are eaten by deer and rabbits. Because of their food value and spectacular red foliage in the fall, these shrubs are excellent for naturalized landscaping.

70 **Cranberry**
Vaccinium macrocarpon

Description: An evergreen, trailing shrub with ascending branches bearing clusters of *nodding, pinkish-white flowers with 4 backward-pointing petals* in leaf axils.

Flowers: About ½″ (1.5 cm) long; stamens 8–10, with *anthers united into a long, projecting, pointed cone.*

Leaves: ¼–⅝″ (5–16 mm) long, oval, blunt, shiny above, slightly whitish beneath.

Fruit: *Dark red, round berry.*

Height: Creeper; branches to 8″ (20 cm).

Flowering: June–August.

Habitat: Open bogs, swamps, and lakesides.

Range: Ontario east to Newfoundland, south to North Carolina, west to Tennessee, and north to Illinois and Minnesota; also in British Columbia, Washington, and California.

Comments: Cultivated cranberry varieties developed from this native species are grown extensively on Cape Cod and in the Pine Barrens of New Jersey. Small Cranberry

(*V. oxycoccus*), a native of North America and Eurasia that occurs in mainland Canada and across the northern United States, has smaller leaves that are whiter beneath and have rolled edges. These two species were originally known as craneberries because of the resemblance of their petals and beaked anther to the head of those wading birds; they are sometimes placed in their own genus, *Oxycoceus*. Wild cranberries often form low dense masses over peaty, boggy areas. The berries are ready for picking in the fall.

465 Mountain Cranberry
Vaccinium vitis-idaea

Description: *A low, evergreen shrub* with creeping stems and upright branches bearing small, terminal clusters of *pink, nodding, bell-shaped flowers.*

Flowers: About ¼" (6 mm) long; corolla 4-lobed; stamens 8.

Leaves: About ⅝" (16 mm) long, elliptical, *with black dots beneath.*

Fruit: Dark red berry.

Height: Creeper; branches 3–8" (7.5–20 cm).

Flowering: June–July.

Habitat: Rocky places and bogs.

Range: Alaska; throughout Canada; Greenland; Maine south to Massachusetts; Wisconsin and Minnesota.

Comments: The acidic fruits, sometimes called lingonberries, are somewhat bitter but can be used as a substitute for regular cranberries when cooked. They often overwinter on the plant and become sweeter by the time the snow melts.

PIPEWORT FAMILY
Eriocaulaceae

Bog or aquatic herbs with a crowded, white to grayish head of tiny flowers on a long leafless stalk.

Flowers: Unisexual, usually radially symmetrical; nestled in a bract. Sepals and petals 2–3 each, similar; stamens as many

as, or fewer than, petals; all these parts attached at base of
ovary; entire flower head with conspicuous bracts at base.
Leaves: Basal, tufted, grass-like.
Fruit: Capsule.

There are about 13 genera and 1,200 species, widely distributed in warm tropical zones and extending into temperate regions.

---

179 Common Pipewort; Hatpins
Eriocaulon aquaticum

Description:	An emergent aquatic with a cottony, grayish-white, *knob-like flower head* atop a *7-sided, leafless stalk* above a submerged tuft of grass-like, basal leaves.
Flowers:	About ¹⁄₁₆″ (2 mm) long; petals 2, interspersed with bracts; head to ½″ (1.5 cm) wide, with bracts beneath.
Leaves:	1–4″ (2.5–10 cm) long.
Height:	Aquatic; flower heads to 6″ (15 cm) above water.
Flowering:	July–September.
Habitat:	Still water at edges of ponds and lakes.
Range:	Manitoba east to Nova Scotia, south to South Carolina, and north and northwest to Ohio, Indiana, Michigan, Wisconsin, and Minnesota.
Comments:	This striking wetland plant is the most common and widespread of several species of pipewort in the East. The plant's whitish roots have many conspicuous cross markings. The common name Hatpins aptly describes the plant's overall appearance. This species has also been called *E. septangulare.*

SPURGE FAMILY
Euphorbiaceae

Commonly herbs with milky sap; also shrubs or trees in
warmer areas and into the tropics.

Flowers: Unisexual, radially symmetrical. Calyx and corolla
each with 5 separate parts, attached at base of ovary in
female (pistillate) flowers; or corolla absent, or both calyx
and corolla absent; stamens 1–10 or more.

Leaves: Alternate or opposite, simple or compound.
Fruit: Round capsule, usually 3-lobed; usually divided into 3 sections, each with 1 seed.

There are about 300 genera and 7,500 species, mostly of warm or hot regions. Some species are grown as ornamentals in tropical areas, including *Croton* species, with their large, multicolored leaves, or as Christmas plants, such as Poinsettia *(Poinsettia pulcherrima)*. Most members of the family are poisonous; their milky sap will irritate the membranes of the eyes and mouth.

213   Tread Softly; Spurge Nettle
Cnidoscolus stimulosus

Description:	*White, trumpet-shaped flowers* in a few-flowered, terminal cluster on a *plant covered with stinging hairs.*
Flowers:	Male flowers about 1″ (2.5 cm) wide, usually in upper forks of cluster, calyx showy, with 5 spreading lobes, petals absent; female flowers in lower forks of cluster, petals and showy calyx absent.
Leaves:	2–9″ (5–22.5 cm) long, roundish, *deeply palmately lobed* into 3–5 segments, long-stalked, with fewer stinging hairs than on stem.
Fruit:	Oblong capsule, about ½″ (12 mm) long.
Height:	6–36″ (15–90 cm).
Flowering:	March–September.
Habitat:	Sandy woods and fields.
Range:	Virginia south to Florida, west to Louisiana, and north to Kentucky.
Comments:	The stinging hairs that cover this southern plant can produce a painful rash on contact; some people have a severe reaction. The sting is similar to that of certain northern nettles in the family Utricaceae.

191   Flowering Spurge
Euphorbia corollata

Description:	Minute flowers surrounded by 5 *white, round, petal-like bracts* attached to rim of a cup, all in a few- to much-branched, open cluster atop each stem; sap milky.

Flowers:	Cup ¹⁄₁₆″ (2 mm) long, ⅛–¼″ (4–6 mm) wide, *entire structure appearing as 1 flower;* 3-lobed ovary often extending beyond cup rim; cluster 1–10″ (2.5–25 cm) wide.
Leaves:	About 1½″ (4 cm) long, linear to oblong, mostly alternate, upper ones whorled.
Fruit:	Small, 3-seeded capsule.
Height:	10–36″ (25–90 cm).
Flowering:	June–October.
Habitat:	Dry open woods, fields, and roadsides.
Range:	Ontario; Maine south to Florida, west to Texas, and north to South Dakota and Minnesota.
Comments:	The often colored, petal-like bracts are typical of some spurges, as are the stems with milky juice; the flower-like cup-structure (cyathium) is a distinguishing feature of spurges. The common name spurge comes from the Latin *expurgare* ("to purge"). Flowering Spurge has been used as a laxative, but large doses can be poisonous. Snow-on-the-mountain *(E. marginata),* native to the Midwest, has upper leaves with white edges.

406 Wild Poinsettia
Euphorbia cyathophora

Description:	Minute flowers lacking petals within a 5-lobed, gland-rimmed cup, all in a cluster atop each leafy stem just above *partly red, white, or yellow leaves;* sap milky.
Flowers:	Cup about ¹⁄₁₆″ (2 mm) long and wide, jagged at top, *entire structure appearing as 1 flower; 3-lobed ovary projecting beyond cup rim;* cluster 1½″ (4 cm) wide.
Leaves:	About 3″ (7.5 cm) long, highly variable, narrow to ovate to fiddle-shaped.
Fruit:	Small, 3-seeded capsule.
Height:	2–3′ (60–90 cm).
Flowering:	August–September.
Habitat:	Open or wooded, disturbed areas, usually in sandy soil.
Range:	Georgia south to Florida, west to Texas, and north to South Dakota and

Minnesota; also in southwestern
United States and California.

Comments: This species, though a weedy
annual, recalls its relative,
Poinsettia *(Poinsettia pulcherrima)*,
which is popular at Christmas and
has large, red, pink, yellow, or
white leaves just below the flowering
cluster. Toothed Spurge *(E. dentata)*,
which occurs from Illinois east to
Pennsylvania and southward, has
hairier stems, opposite leaves, and leafy
bracts usually green or white at the base.

---

351 Cypress Spurge
Euphorbia cyparissias

Description: Minute flowers surrounded by *2 yellow
(turning orange or red with age), petal-like
bracts* attached to rim of a 4-lobed cup,
each lobe bearing a crescent-shaped,
yellow gland, all in a cluster atop each
stem covered with needle-like leaves; sap
milky.

Flowers: Cup $1/16$–$1/8''$ (2–3 mm) long, $1/16''$
(2 mm) wide, *entire structure appearing
as 1 flower;* 3-lobed ovary often
extending beyond cup rim; cluster
$3/4$–$4''$ (2–10 cm) wide.

Leaves: $1/2$–$1\frac{1}{2}''$ (1.5–4 cm) long, linear,
crowded, mostly alternate, upper ones
whorled; those among flower clusters
$3/8$–$5/8''$ (8–16 mm) wide, opposite,
heart-shaped.

Fruit: Small, 3-seeded capsule.

Height: 6–12″ (15–30 cm).

Flowering: March–June, sporadically to September.

Habitat: Roadsides, cemeteries, and disturbed
areas.

Range: Throughout much of North America,
except far north and the southwestern
deserts; less common in southern
United States.

Comments: This plant, introduced from Europe,
forms colonies by spreading from
horizontal roots; it frequently escapes
from cultivation. Although purgatives
have sometimes been made from its

roots, large doses can cause poisoning; animals can be poisoned by repeated feeding on hay containing this and other spurges. Contact with the milky juice can cause dermatitis. Many other species of *Euphorbia* occur in our area, all with wider leaves than Cypress Spurge.

PEA FAMILY
Fabaceae

Trees, shrubs, herbs, or vines with compound or occasionally simple leaves and flowers usually in clusters.

Flowers: 3 distinct types. Pea flower (most commonly described in this book) bilaterally symmetrical; calyx with 5 sepals more or less joined at base and forming a cup or tube; corolla with 1 broad upper petal (banner or standard), 2 lateral petals (wings), and 2 bottom petals (keel) joined by lower edges and shaped like prow of a boat; stamens usually 10, with 9 joined and 1 separate, surrounding ovary and hidden inside keel. Other 2 types: radially symmetrical, with conspicuous stamens (as in acacias); bilaterally symmetrical, without distinct banner and keel (as in sennas).

Leaves: Usually alternate, rarely opposite; pinnately or palmately compound, or sometimes simple.

Fruit: Usually a 1-chambered pod with 1 to many seeds, sometimes 2-chambered with several to many seeds; usually opening along 1–2 seams, sometimes not opening but separating into several 1-seeded segments.

Taken as a single family, there are about 640 genera and 17,000 species. This enormous family, also known as the bean family, includes many economically important genera: Peas belong to *Pisium;* beans to *Phaseolus;* soybeans to *Glycine;* peanuts to *Arachis;* lentils to *Lens;* and chickpeas (garbanzos) to *Cicer.* Alfalfa *(Medicago sativa)* and clover species *(Trifolium)* provide forage for domestic livestock, but many other species are poisonous range weeds. Exotic hardwoods and gum arabic are provided by tropical trees belonging to this family, and numerous members are cultivated as handsome ornamentals. The traditional family name, Leguminosae, reflects some of the family's importance (in Latin it refers to "plants with seedpods," and in French *légume* means "vegetable"). The family is sometimes split into three smaller families, each distinguished by one of the three flower types: the Fabaceae, Mimosaceae, and Caesalpiniaceae. The fruit, an important feature, is similar in all three.

437   **Rosary Pea; Crab's Eye**
Abrus precatorius

Description: A woody, somewhat hairy vine with clusters of *pink or lavender pea flowers* in leaf axils.

Flowers: ⅝″ (16 mm) long.

Leaves: Pinnately compound, with 10–32 oblong leaflets, each ½″ (1.5 cm) long.

Fruit: Rectangular or oblong pod, 1–1½″ (2.5–4 cm) long, with 3–5 *striking, shiny red seeds, each with a black spot.*

Height: Vine; to 10′ (3 m) long.

Flowering: May–September.

Habitat: Roadsides and thickets.

Range: Arkansas, Alabama, Georgia, and Florida.

Comments: The seeds of this plant are extremely poisonous. If a seed is swallowed without first being chewed, it is apparently less toxic, but if the seedcoat is crushed, even one seed can cause death. Because of their attractive red color the seeds are sometimes strung for necklaces or rosaries, but since children might be tempted to put these items in their mouths, such use is not recommended.

572   **Leadplant; False Indigo; Prairie Shoestring**
Amorpha canescens

Description: A *grayish shrub* with white-hairy stems, pinnately compound leaves, and many *small, purplish-blue flowers in spike-like clusters.*

Flowers: About ⅛″ (4 mm) long; only 1 petal; stamens 10, with bright orange anthers.

Leaves: 2–4″ (5–10 cm) long, densely covered with short hairs giving a grayish appearance, divided into 15–45 leaflets, each about ½″ (1.5 cm) long.

Fruit: Finely hairy pod, with 1–2 seeds.

Height: 1–3′ (30–90 cm).

Flowering: May–August.

Habitat: Dry prairies and hills.

Range: Saskatchewan east to Ontario, south to
Louisiana, west to New Mexico, and
north to Wyoming and North Dakota.
Comments: This is one of the most conspicuous and
characteristic shrubs of the upland
prairies. The common name Prairie
Shoestring probably refers to the laced-
shoestring look of the leaves and roots.
It has very deep roots, 4' (1.2 m) or
deeper. Native Americans used the
leaves for smoking and for making a tea.
The genus name, from the Greek
amorphos ("formless" or "deformed"),
alludes to the fact that the flower, with
only a single petal (the banner or
standard), is unlike the typical pea
flowers of the family.

571 Indigobush; False Indigo
Amorpha fruticosa

Description: A shrub with groups of erect *long racemes
of purple flowers.*
Flowers: ¼–⅜" (6–8 mm) long; only 1 petal,
wrapping around style and 10 orange
stamens.
Leaves: 4–12" (10–30 cm) long, long-stalked,
pinnately compound, with 13–25 dull
green *leaflets marked with resinous dots.*
Fruit: Pod, with 1–2 seeds, roughened with
resinous dots.
Height: 5–17' (1.5–5.1 m).
Flowering: May–June.
Habitat: Riverbanks, riverbeds, streambeds, and
moist thickets.
Range: Manitoba east to New Brunswick, south
to Florida, west to Texas, and north to
North Dakota; also in much of western
United States.
Comments: This shrub often forms thickets on
riverbanks and islands and is
occasionally cultivated. *A. canescens* is
also called False Indigo; yet another
species sharing this common name is *A.
herbacea,* which has whitish to blue-
violet flowers in fan-like masses on top
of the plant and gray-downy leaves with
up to 40 leaflets.

520 Hog Peanut
Amphicarpaea bracteata

Description: *A twining vine with 2 kinds of flowers.*
Flowers: Those on upper branches ½" (1.5 cm) long, *pale purple, pale pink, or lilac,* in clusters hanging from leaf axils; those on lower or creeping branches inconspicuous, lacking petals.
Leaves: Divided into *3 leaflets,* each ¾–3" (2–7.5 cm) long, ovate, pointed.
Fruit: Those of upper flowers flattened, oblong-linear, ½–1½" (1.5–4 cm) long, with 3–4 seeds; those of lower flowers fleshy, ovate or pear-shaped, often underground, 1-seeded.
Height: Vine; 4' (120 cm) long.
Flowering: August–September.
Habitat: Woodlands.
Range: Manitoba east to Nova Scotia, south to Florida, west to Texas, and north to North Dakota and Montana.
Comments: The genus name is from the Greek *amphi* ("of both kinds") and *carpos* ("fruit") and refers to the two kinds of fruit. The seeds of the upper fruit are inedible, but those from the underground fruit are edible when boiled. Birds feed on the seeds of both kinds of fruit. Hogs eat the seeds of the fruit below ground, hence the plant's common name.

Hog Peanut

426 Groundnut
Apios americana

Description: A climbing vine with *maroon or reddish-brown pea flowers in compact racemes* rising from leaf axils.

Flowers: ½" (1.5 cm) long; *keel scythe-shaped, upturned.*

Leaves: 4–8" (10–20 cm) long, pinnately compound, with 5–9 ovate to lanceolate leaflets.

Fruit: Several-seeded pod.

Height: Vine; to 10' (3 m) long.

Flowering: July–September.

Habitat: Moist low sites and thickets.

Range: Manitoba east to Nova Scotia, south to Florida, west to Texas, and north to North Dakota.

Comments: This legume has cord-like roots with edible tubers, which Native Americans gathered for food. The colonists relied on the tubers as a food source during their initial years in Massachusetts. The tubers can be used in soups and stews or fried like potatoes; the cooked seeds can also be eaten. The flowers are sufficiently beautiful to warrant cultivation, but the plant tends to be invasive. The genus name, from the Greek for "pear," alludes to the shape of the tubers. Price's Groundnut (*A. priceana*), a rare species with greenish-white, purple-tipped flowers, occurs in Kentucky, Tennessee, and southern Illinois.

144 Prairie False Indigo; White Wild Indigo
Baptisia alba

Description: A bushy perennial with smooth leaves and *white or cream-colored pea flowers in stiffly erect clusters;* stem covered with whitish bloom.

Flowers: To 1" (2.5 cm) long; cluster to 1' (30 cm) long.

Leaves: Compound, with 3 leaflets, each 1–2½" (2.5–6.5 cm) long.

Fruit:	Black, drooping, oblong, beaked pod.
Height:	2–5' (60–150 cm).
Flowering:	May–July.
Habitat:	Prairies, waste places, and open woods.
Range:	Ontario and New York south to Florida west to Texas, and north to Nebraska and Minnesota.
Comments:	This showy legume, long known as *B. leucantha,* often stands out above surrounding prairie grasses. Many species of this genus contain a blue dye that resembles indigo and becomes noticeable in autumn as the plants dry out and blacken. Large-bracted Wild Indigo *(B. leucophaea)* has two large stipules at the base of 3-parted leaves, giving the effect of five leaflets rather than three.

314 Wild Indigo
Baptisia tinctoria

Description:	A smooth, bushy perennial with numerous few-flowered, *elongated, terminal clusters of yellow pea flowers.*
Flowers:	½" (1.5 cm) long.
Leaves:	Compound, with 3 ovate to wedge-shaped leaflets, each ½–1½" (1.5–4 cm) long.
Fruit:	Short round pod, tipped with a style.
Height:	3' (90 cm).
Flowering:	May–September.
Habitat:	Dry fields.
Range:	Ontario; Maine south to Georgia and northwest to Tennessee, Indiana, Wisconsin, and Minnesota.
Comments:	Widely distributed, Wild Indigo often increases in burned fields. At least 15 other *Baptisia* are found in our range, including numerous yellow species in the southeastern United States as well as some white or creamy ones. Blue False Indigo *(B. australis),* which has upright racemes of blue flowers and sap that turns purple when exposed to air, has escaped from cultivation in the eastern United States north to New York and New Hampshire and in Ontario.

The genus name, from the Greek
baptizein ("to dye"), refers to the fact that
some species are used as an inferior
substitute for true indigo dye.

567 Spurred Butterfly Pea
Centrosema virginianum

Description:	A trailing or twining *vine with violet pea flowers,* solitary or in clusters of 2–4, in axils of compound leaves.
Flowers:	¾–1½" (2–4 cm) long; corolla reversed 180° from usual position in flowers of pea family; *standard broad, pointing toward ground; keel pointing upward,* with a *small spur* at base.
Leaves:	Divided into 3 ovate to lanceolate leaflets, each 1–2½" (2.5–6.5 cm) long.
Fruit:	Many-seeded pod, twisting into 2 spirals after opening.
Height:	Vine; 2–4' (60–120 cm) long.
Flowering:	July–August.
Habitat:	Acidic soil, sandy woodlands, and fields.
Range:	Maryland south to Florida, west to Texas and Oklahoma, and northeast to Missouri, Illinois, and Kentucky.
Comments:	This is a delicate, showy vine. The flowers of butterfly peas are recognized by their upside-down position. Sand Butterfly Pea (*C. arenicola*) has ovate leaflets indented at the base; Florida Butterfly Pea (*C. floridana*), with oval to lanceolate leaflets to 3" (7.5 cm) long, occurs in the pinewoods of Florida.

568 Butterfly Pea
Clitoria mariana

Description:	A twining (occasionally erect) vine with *large, showy, lavender to pink pea flowers,* usually solitary but occasionally 2–3, in axils of compound leaves.
Flowers:	2" (5 cm) long; corolla reversed 180° from usual position in flowers of pea family; *standard broad, pointing toward ground; keel pointing upward.*

Butterfly Pea

Leaves:	Divided into 3 ovate leaflets, each 1–2½" (2.5–6.5 cm) long.
Fruit:	Few-seeded pod, twisting into 2 spirals after opening.
Height:	1–3' (30–90 cm).
Flowering:	June–August.
Habitat:	Dry soil, open woods, and thickets.
Range:	Minnesota east to New York, south to Florida, west to Texas, and north to Nebraska.
Comments:	This plant is often confused with Spurred Butterfly Pea *(Centrosema virginianum),* which also has upside-down flowers. In Butterfly Pea the calyx tube is shorter than the calyx lobes; in Spurred Butterfly Pea the tube is longer than the lobes.

531 Crown Vetch; Axseed
Coronilla varia

Description:	*Pink-and-white pea flowers in head-like clusters rising from leaf axils on a sprawling or upward-curving stem.*
Flowers:	Standard pink; wings often whitish; cluster to 1" (2.5 cm) wide.
Leaves:	2–4" (5–10 cm) long, compound, pinnately divided into 15–25 leaflets, each ½–¾" (1.5–2 cm) long.

Fruit: 4-angled, linear pod, 1–2" (2.5–5 cm)
long.
Height: 1–2' (30–60 cm).
Flowering: June–August.
Habitat: Waste places, roadsides, and fields.
Range: Throughout much of North America,
except far north.
Comments: This European introduction is often
planted along roadsides as a stabilizing
perennial. It is now naturalized in many
areas; when in masses, as it often occurs,
it makes a striking groundcover. It adds
nitrogen to the soil, as do all members of
the pea family.

313 Showy Rattlebox
Crotalaria spectabilis

Description: *Yellow pea flowers* in elongated clusters
near top of an *erect plant* with dark
purplish stems.
Flowers: About 1" (2.5 cm) long; calyx bell-
shaped, purplish.
Leaves: 2–8" (5–20 cm) long, simple, ovate.
Fruit: Inflated pod, to 2" (5 cm) long.
Height: 2–3' (60–90 cm).
Flowering: August–October.
Habitat: Fields, roadsides, and waste places.
Range: Virginia and Tennessee south to Florida,
west to Texas and Oklahoma, and
northeast to Illinois.
Comments: The rattling of the dry seeds in
the pod accounts for both the
common and the genus names,
the latter from the Greek *crotalon*
("a rattle"). Rattlebox *(C. sagittalis),*
which occurs as far north as New
England and west to Texas and
Minnesota, has smaller flowers and
narrower leaves. Two other similar
species are Pursh's Rattlebox
(C. purshii) and Prostrate Rattlebox
(C. angulata). There are at least
four species of *Crotalaria* in our
range with larger flowers in
elongated clusters or leaves with
three leaflets.

573 Purple Prairie Clover
Dalea purpurea

Description: Tiny, *rose-purple flowers in cylindrical,
head-like clusters* at ends of upright, wiry
stems.

Flowers: About ⅛" (4 mm) long; calyx 5-parted,
hairy; corolla not pea-like, with *1 heart-
shaped petal* and 4 narrow, petal-like
stamens; stamens 5; cluster to 2" (5 cm)
long.

Leaves: Pinnately compound, with 3–7 (usually
5) narrow leaflets, each ½–¾" (1.5–2
cm) long.

Height: 1–3′ (30–90 cm).

Flowering: June–September.

Habitat: Prairies and dry hills.

Range: British Columbia east to Ontario, south
to New York, Kentucky, and Alabama,
west to Arizona, and north to Montana.

Comments: This is one of the most widespread of
the perennial prairie clovers, identified
by their cone-like flower heads. An
excellent range species, with high
protein content, Purple Prairie Clover
decreases in heavily grazed areas. A
midwestern white-flowering species,
White Prairie Clover *(D. candida),* has
elongated heads of white flowers and is

Purple Prairie Clover

2' (60 cm) tall. A white-flowering, southeastern coastal plain species, White Prairie Clover *(D. albida),* has conspicuous green bracts within the heads. Prairie clovers are sometimes included in the genus *Petalostemon.*

184 Prairie Mimosa
Desmanthus illinoensis

Description: An erect plant with *ball-like clusters of small, whitish or greenish flowers* on tall stalks rising in axils of compound leaves.
Flowers: Petals 5, each less than 1/16" (2 mm) long; stamens 5, projecting; cluster about 1/2" (1.5 cm) wide.
Leaves: 2–4" (5–10 cm) long, doubly pinnately divided into numerous small leaflets.
Fruit: Curved or twisted pod, to 1" (2.5 cm) long; in dense clusters of 20–30.
Height: 2–4' (60–120 cm).
Flowering: June–August.
Habitat: Plains, prairies, and riverbanks.
Range: Pennsylvania south to Florida, west to Texas, and north to North Dakota; also in parts of West.
Comments: The somewhat similar Prairie Acacia *(Acacia augustissima)* has fruit 1 1/2–3" (4–8 cm) long. Prairie Mimosa and Prairie Acacia are nutritious range plants, high in protein.

484 Showy Tick Trefoil
Desmodium canadense

Description: An erect, *bushy, hairy plant* with crowded, elongated, terminal clusters of *pink or rose-purple pea flowers.*
Flowers: 1/2" (1.5 cm) long, on stalk to 3/8" (8 mm) long.
Leaves: Pinnately compound, with 3 oblong, untoothed leaflets, each to 3" (7.5 cm) long; *lanceolate stipules at base of stalk.*
Fruit: Hairy, *jointed pod,* with 3–5 segments.
Height: 2–6' (60–180 cm).
Flowering: July–August.
Habitat: Moist open woods and edges of fields.

Showy Tick Trefoil

Range: Manitoba east to Nova Scotia,
         south to Virginia, west to Missouri
         and Texas, and north to North
         Dakota.

Comments: The showiest of the tick trefoils, this
            is one of some two dozen species of
            Desmodium distinguished by their leaf
            and fruit shape. The distinctively
            jointed fruits (loments) break into
            1-seeded segments that stick to clothes
            and animal fur, thus facilitating seed
            dispersal.

485 Illinois Tick Trefoil
Desmodium illinoense

Description: A tall, *spindly, hairy stem* topped
               with a slender, elongated cluster of
               *many white, purple, or lavender-pink
               pea flowers.*

Flowers: To ½" (1.5 cm) long, on stalks to ¾"
           (2 cm) long.

Leaves: Divided into 3 segments, terminal
          segment 2–3½" (5–9 cm) long, strongly
          veined beneath; *ovate stipules at base of
          stalks.*

Fruit: *Flattened, jointed pod,* with 3–7 segments.
Height: 2–5' (60–150 cm).
Flowering: July–August.
Habitat: Dry prairies.
Range: South Dakota east to Wisconsin and
         south to Arkansas and Oklahoma.

Illinois Tick Trefoil

Comments: A showy plant when in flower, this
species develops long fruits with
segments that separate and attach
themselves to clothing, thereby
promoting seed dispersal.

416 Coral Bean
Erythrina herbacea

Description: An erect, *prickly* plant with *leafy stems*
and *separate flowering stems* with *bright red
pea flowers.*
Flowers: Standard 1¼–2″ (3–5 cm) long,
projecting forward over other much
shorter petals.
Leaves: Compound, with 3 leaflets, each 1½–3″
(4–7.5 cm) long.
Fruit: Pod, ½″ (1.5 cm) long, with few to
many bright red seeds.
Height: 2–5′ (60–150 cm).
Flowering: March–July.
Habitat: Pinewoods, sandy places, and thickets.
Range: North Carolina south to Florida and
west to Texas and Oklahoma.
Comments: This is a showy member of a large
tropical genus with more than 100
species. The distinctive, flame-like
flower clusters appear before or with the
leaves. Its poisonous, hard, red seeds are
used as beads. This species is a woody
shrub in Florida but an herb in the rest
of its mainly coastal range.

526 Beach Pea
Lathyrus japonicus

Description: A *trailing vine* with a stout *angled stem*
and *pink-lavender pea flowers* in long-
stalked clusters.
Flowers: ¾" (2 cm) long.
Leaves: Pinnately compound, with 6–12 thic
fleshy, oval leaflets, each to 2½" (6.5 c
long, bristle-tipped; upper leaflets
modified into tendrils; *stipules large,
arrowhead-shaped,* each about 1¼" (3 c
long.
Fruit: Elongated, veiny pod, 2" (5 cm) long.
Height: Vine; 1–2' (30–60 cm) long.
Flowering: June–August.
Habitat: Beaches and gravelly areas.
Range: Manitoba east to Newfoundland, sout
to New Jersey, and west to Indiana an
Minnesota; also along Pacific Coast fr
Alaska south to California.
Comments: This widely distributed sweetpea-like
flower is also found in Chile and Japar
Marsh Pea *(L. palustris),* a similar spec
with purple flowers and lanceolate
stipules, is found in wet meadows and
marshes in the Northeast and Midwes
At least 10 species of *Lathyrus* occur
within our range.

525 Creeping Bush Clover
Lespedeza repens

Description: A *trailing plant* with stems bearing loo:
clusters of *pink to purple pea flowers and
clover-like leaves.*
Flowers: ¼" (6 mm) long.
Leaves: Compound, with 3 ovate leaflets, each
about ½" (1.5 cm) long.
Fruit: Small, *1-seeded pod.*
Height: Creeper; trailing stems 6–24" (15–60
cm) long.
Flowering: May–September.
Habitat: Open woods, clearings, and thickets.
Range: New York and Connecticut south to
Florida, west to Texas, and north to
Kansas and Wisconsin.
Comments: *Lespedeza* is a genus of large, somewhat

clover-like plants; considerable
hybridizing has made for much variation
in the 18 or more species found in our
region. They are useful plants for
improving the fertility of dry sites, and
their seeds are an important food source
for bobwhite quail, although they are
apparently not much used by songbirds.

480 Slender Bush Clover
Lespedeza virginica

Description: An upright stem with compound leaves
and *small crowded clusters of lavender to
pink pea flowers* in upper leaf axils.
Flowers: ¼" (6 mm) long.
Leaves: Divided into *3 narrow blunt leaflets,* each
about 1" (2.5 cm) long.
Fruit: *Small, 1-seeded pod.*
Height: 1–3' (30–90 cm).
Flowering: July–September.
Habitat: Dry open woods, thickets, and clearings.
Range: Ontario; New Hampshire and New
York south to Florida, west to Texas, and
north to Kansas and Minnesota.
Comments: Some cultivated *Lespedeza,* such as
Japanese Clover *(L. striata)* and Korean
Clover *(L. stipulacea),* frequently escape
from cultivation and occur wild from
Pennsylvania west to Kansas and
southward. Round-headed Bush Clover
(L. capitata) is a native species with
dense round flower clusters in the leaf
axils, a white and magenta-spotted
corolla concealed by long sepals, and
nearly stalkless, hairy leaves, each with
three oblong leaflets.

340 Birdsfoot Trefoil
Lotus corniculata

Description: A low plant, often with a reclining
stem, bearing *yellow pea flowers in flat-
topped, terminal umbels and clover-like
leaves.*
Flowers: ½" (1.5 cm) long.
Leaves: Compound, with 3 leaflets about ½"

Birdsfoot Trefoil

(1.5 cm) long and 2 leaflet-like stipule
at base of stalk, giving the impression
a leaf with 5 leaflets.

Fruit: Slender pod, about 1" (2.5 cm) long.
Height: 6–24" (15–60 cm).
Flowering: June–September.
Habitat: Fields and roadsides.
Range: Throughout much of temperate North
America, except far north; least comm
in southern United States.
Comments: This showy plant was introduced from
Europe. The pod arrangement suggest
a bird's foot, hence the common name.
The western Prairie Trefoil *(L. american*
has pink and yellowish flowers, as does
the southeastern Heller's Birdsfoot
Trefoil *(L. helleri).*

634 Wild Lupine
Lupinus perennis

Description: *Blue pea flowers* in an upright, elongate
terminal cluster on an erect stem with
palmately compound leaves.
Flowers: To ⅝" (16 mm) long.
Leaves: Palmately compound, with 7–11
leaflets, each to 2" (5 cm) long, radiatin
from a central point.
Fruit: Hairy pod, to 2" (5 cm) long.
Height: 8–24" (20–60 cm).

Flowering: April–July.
  Habitat: Dry open woods and fields.
    Range: Ontario and Newfoundland; New Hampshire south to Florida, west to Texas, and north to Kentucky, Illinois, and Minnesota.
Comments: Lupines were once thought to deplete or "wolf" the mineral content of the soil, hence the genus name, derived from the Latin *lupus* ("wolf"). Actually, plants in the pea family enhance soil fertility by fixing atmospheric nitrogen into a usable form. In the South this species has narrower leaflets and is often recognized as Nuttall's Lupine (*L. nuttallii*). Two southern species with undivided, elliptical leaves are Spreading Lupine (*L. diffusus*), with blue flowers and a whitish spot on the standard, and Hairy Lupine (*L. villosus*), a hairy plant with lavender-blue flowers and a red-purple spot on the standard. Both species are found from the Carolinas south to Florida and west to Louisiana. Blue-pod Lupine (*L. polyphyllus*) is becoming extremely abundant in the Northeast, particularly Maine and adjacent Canada; it was introduced from the Northwest.

143 White Sweet Clover
Melilotus alba

Description: Small *white pea flowers,* fragrant when crushed, *in long, slender, cylindrical, spike-like clusters* rising in leaf axils.
   Flowers: ¼" (6 mm) long; cluster to 8" (20 cm) long.
    Leaves: Compound, with 3 leaflets, each ½–1" (1.5–2.5 cm) long.
     Fruit: Small, ovoid, 1-seeded pod.
    Height: 3–8' (90–240 cm).
Flowering: May–October.
  Habitat: Roadsides and fields.
    Range: Throughout much of North America, except far north.
Comments: Native to Eurasia, this tall, introduced legume has a vanilla-like fragrance when

White Sweet Clover

crushed. Both this plant and Yellow
Sweet Clover (*M. officinalis*) are widely
used as pasture crops for nitrogen
enrichment of the soil. They are also
highly valued as honey plants, as
suggested by the genus name, which
derives from the Greek *meli,* meaning
"honey."

328 Yellow Sweet Clover
Melilotus officinalis

Description: A smooth, loosely branched plant with
*small yellow pea flowers in slender,
cylindrical, spike-like clusters* rising in leaf
axils.

Flowers: ¼" (6 mm) long; cluster to 6" (15 cm)
long.

Leaves: Compound, with 3 lanceolate to ovate,
toothed leaflets, each ½–1" (1.5–2.5 cm)
long.

Fruit: Small, ovoid, 1-seeded pod.

Height: 2–5' (60–150 cm).

Flowering: May–October.

Habitat: Waste places and fields.

Range: Throughout much of North America,
except far north.

Comments: The leaves of this native Eurasian plant,
like those of White Sweet Clover (*M.
alba*), have a vanilla-like fragrance when

crushed and can be used as a flavoring. The seeds are eaten by upland game birds such as grouse.

---

482 Purple Locoweed
Oxytropis lambertii

Description: Clusters of sweet-scented, *pink to lavender pea flowers* on leafless stalks rising above compound leaves emerging from soil at base of a hairy, deep-rooted plant.

Flowers: About ¾" (2 cm) long, *with pointed keel.*

Leaves: Pinnately compound, with 7–19 linear to oblong, hairy leaflets, each to 1" (2.5 cm) long.

Fruit: Erect, hairy, beaked pod.

Height: 8–12" (20–30 cm).

Flowering: May–July.

Habitat: Dry prairies and limestone sites.

Range: British Columbia, Saskatchewan, and Manitoba south to Texas and Arizona.

Comments: This is one of the most dangerous of the poisonous locoweeds that are widely distributed in mixed prairies. Its huge taproot can penetrate to a depth of 8' (2.4 m). Fortunately, the plant is unpalatable to livestock and is seldom eaten unless other forage is scarce. The pointed keels of *Oxytropis* distinguish the genus from *Astragalus,* which are blunt-keeled. Some members of both genera are given the name locoweed.

---

483 Showy Locoweed
Oxytropis splendens

Description: A tufted plant with *silvery, silky-hairy, leafless stems* rising from pinnately compound, basal leaves and topped by dense *spikes of rich pink to lavender pea flowers.*

Flowers: About ¾" (2 cm) long, with *pointed keel;* cluster 1½–7" (4–17.5 cm) long.

Leaves: To 9½" (24 cm) long, pinnately compound, with numerous leaflets often in groups of 3–4.

Showy Locoweed

Fruit: Ovoid, *hairy, short-beaked capsule,* to ⅝″ (16 mm) long.
Height: 4–12″ (10–30 cm).
Flowering: June–July.
Habitat: Prairies and plains.
Range: Alaska and British Columbia east to Ontario and south to Minnesota, North Dakota, and through Montana to New Mexico.
Comments: This is one of the poisonous locoweeds, similar to members of the genus *Astragalus* (whose flowers have a blunt keel), also known as locoweeds or poison vetches. There are nonpoisonous members of both genera as well; those of *Oxytropis* are known as point vetches.

570 Kudzu
Pueraria montana

Description: A *high-climbing vine* with a *hairy stem and violet-purple pea flowers* in dense clusters in leaf axils, flowering from base of cluster upward.
Flowers: 1″ (2.5 cm) long, fragrant; standard ovate, with a conspicuous, yellow patch at base.
Leaves: Compound, with 3 broadly ovate or rounded leaflets, each 4–6″ (10–15 cm) long, sometimes lobed.

Fruit:	Linear-oblong, flattened, brownish, *hairy pod,* to 2″ (5 cm) long.
Height:	Vine; to 60′ (18 m) long.
Flowering:	Late summer.
Habitat:	Borders of woods and fields.
Range:	New York and Massachusetts south to Florida, west to Texas, and north to Nebraska and Illinois.
Comments:	This species is native to Asia. An exceedingly aggressive vine, it forms a continuous blanket of foliage over trees and anything else in its path, often resulting in grotesque shapes. Although considered a pest, it is also planted to shade and feed livestock and for erosion control. Flowering is infrequent north of Virginia. The starchy, tuberous root is a food item in Japan.

357, 372 Wild Senna
Senna hebecarpa

Description:	*Clusters of light yellow to orange flowers* atop a sparsely branched perennial or in axils of compound leaves.
Flowers:	¾″ (2 cm) wide; petals 5, slightly unequal; stamens 10, prominent, unequal, with conspicuous, brown anthers opening by 2 pores.
Leaves:	6–8″ (15–20 cm) long, pinnately compound; leaflets oblong, blunt, each about 1″ (2.5 cm) long, in 5–9 pairs; *club-shaped gland* near base of stalk.
Fruit:	Flat, narrow, curved, segmented, *very hairy pod, with joints as long as broad.*
Height:	3–6′ (90–180 cm).
Flowering:	July–August.
Habitat:	Moist open woods and disturbed areas.
Range:	Ontario; Maine south to Georgia and northwest to Tennessee and Wisconsin.
Comments:	The flowers of this large plant are not typically pea-like. *S. marilandica,* also called Wild Senna, is a more southern species with fewer flowers and bigger leaflets. Two other species, Sicklepod *(S. obtusifolia)* and Coffee Senna *(S. occidentalis),* are also found in the East.

479 Goat's Rue; Devil's Shoestrings
Tephrosia virginiana

Description: *Bicolored pea flowers with pink wings and yellow standard* in crowded clusters atop a hairy stem.

Flowers: ¾" (2 cm) long; cluster to 3" (7.5 cm) long.

Leaves: Pinnately compound, with 9–31 elliptical to linear-oblong, *hoary leaflets* each ½–1½" (1.5–4 cm) long.

Fruit: Narrow, whitish-hairy pod, to 2" (5 cm) long.

Height: 1–2' (30–60 cm).

Flowering: May–August.

Habitat: Dry sandy woods and clearings.

Range: Ontario; New Hampshire south to Florida, west to Texas, and north to Nebraska and Minnesota.

Comments: At one time this species was fed to goats to increase their milk production, but since it is now known to contain rotenone (now used as an insecticide and fish poison), this practice has been discontinued. A distinctively silvery plant, Goat's Rue has long stringy roots to which the common name Devil's Shoestrings refers. Spiked Hoary Pea *(T. spicata)* and Scurfy Hoary Pea *(T. chrysophylla)* are among the several white-flowered species in the South with fewer flowers per cluster on the tips of long stalks; these flowers eventually turn pink, and the foliage is often distinctive because of brownish or golden hairs.

315 Bush Pea
Thermopsis mollis

Description: Finely hairy stems with *showy, yellow pea flowers* in terminal racemes.

Flowers: Calyx finely hairy, with triangular lobes sloping to a slender point; corolla ½" (1.5 cm) long, irregular, with petals of similar length.

Leaves: Compound, with 3 leaflets, each 1½–3" (4–7.5 cm) long, tapering at both ends; stipules broad, leaf-like.

Height:	1–4½' (30–135 cm).
Flowering:	May–June.
Habitat:	Dry woods, ridges, and mountain woods.
Range:	Virginia and Tennessee south to Georgia and Alabama.
Comments:	Because they are so attractive, plants of this genus are frequently cultivated. There are 20 species of *Thermopsis* in the United States and Asia.

535 Rabbit-foot Clover
Trifolium arvense

Description:	Erect, silky-hairy stems topped by *tiny pea flowers in fuzzy, soft pink or gray-pink, cylindrical heads* above leaves divided into 3 *narrow, elliptical leaflets.*
Flowers:	¼" (5 mm) long; sepals covered with long hairs obscuring small corolla; head about ¾" (2 cm) long.
Leaves:	Leaflets each ½–¾" (1.5–2 cm) long, toothed only at tips.
Fruit:	Pod, with 1–2 seeds.
Height:	6–18" (15–45 cm).
Flowering:	May–October.
Habitat:	Dry, sandy or gravelly areas and roadsides.
Range:	Ontario east to Newfoundland, south to Florida, west to Texas, and north to North Dakota; also in parts of West.
Comments:	Native to Europe, this attractive annual is well named, since its flower head is as furry as a rabbit's foot. It is frequently found in dry open sites, where it is especially showy in masses. The flowers make an interesting dried bouquet but tend to disintegrate quickly.

356 Hop Clover
Trifolium aureum

Description:	Erect, mostly smooth stems with small *yellow pea flowers in roundish-oblong heads* above leaves divided into 3 *wedge-shaped leaflets.*

Flowers: ¼" (6 mm) long; head ½–1" (1.5–2.5 cm) wide, with 20–40 flowers turning brown with age.

Leaves: Leaflets each ½–¾" (1.5–2 cm) long, lanceolate to oblong, stalkless.

Fruit: 1-seeded pod.

Height: 6–18" (15–45 cm).

Flowering: June–September.

Habitat: Fields, roadsides, and waste places.

Range: Alberta and Saskatchewan; Ontario east to Newfoundland, south to Georgia, and northwest to Missouri and Minnesota; also in parts of West.

Comments: This species is one of three annual yellow clovers in the eastern United States, all introduced from Europe. The are primarily low plants, often found in lawns, gardens, and waste places. Low Hop Clover (T. campestre) has sprawling hairy stems, and its terminal leaflet is stalked and notched. Least Hop Clover (T. dubium) is similar but has a very small flower head with only 3–15 flowers. A similar yellow group, the medicks (Medicago), are prostrate plants with distinctive, spiral-coiled fruit.

532 Red Clover
Trifolium pratense

Description: Dense, rounded *heads of magenta pea flowers* on an erect, hairy stem bearing leaves divided into *3 oval leaflets*.

Flowers: ½" (1.5 cm) long, turning brown and papery with age; standard folded over keel and wings; head about 1" (2.5 cm) long, ½–1" (1.5–2.5 cm) wide.

Leaves: Leaflets each ½–2" (1.5–5 cm) long, often with a *lighter, V-shaped pattern near middle*.

Fruit: 1-seeded pod.

Height: 6–24" (15–60 cm).

Flowering: May–September.

Habitat: Old fields, lawns, and roadsides.

Range: Throughout North America, except far north.

Comments: Introduced from Europe and extensively

planted here as a hay and pasture crop, this species is one of our most common perennial clovers. It stores nitrogen in its root nodules and is used in crop rotation to improve soil fertility. Alsike Clover *(T. hybridum),* with white-pink flower heads, lacks the chevron pattern on the leaves.

185 White Clover; Dutch Clover
Trifolium repens

Description: *Heads of white or pinkish pea flowers* and 3-parted leaves rising on *stalks from a creeping stem.*

Flowers: ¼–½″ (6–13 mm) long, turning brown and papery with age; head about ¾″ (2 cm) wide, long-stalked.

Leaves: Leaflets each ¾–1″ (2–2.5 cm) long, ovate.

Fruit: Pod, with 3–4 seeds.

Height: Creeper; stems 4–10″ (10–25 cm) long.

Flowering: May–October.

Habitat: Lawns, roadsides, and fields.

Range: Throughout much of North America, except far north.

Comments: This introduced perennial is common in lawns, where one may sometimes find a "four-leaf clover." White Clover is one of several species of the pea family that pass as "shamrocks." The similar Running Buffalo Clover *(T. stoloniferum)* has notched leaflets and a pair of leaves on an upright flowering stem; it is found in West Virginia, Ohio, and Kentucky and west to Missouri and eastern Kansas.

574 Cow Vetch; Blue Vetch
Vicia cracca

Description: A climbing vine with gray-green leaves and long, *1-sided, crowded spikes* of tubular, *lavender to blue pea flowers directed downward* on a long stalk.

Flowers: ½″ (1.5 cm) long.

Leaves: Pinnately compound, with *14–24 leaflets,* each 1″ (2.5 cm) long; pair of tendrils at end of each leaf.
Fruit: Few-seeded pod.
Height: Vine; to 4′ (1.2 m) long.
Flowering: May–August.
Habitat: Roadsides and fields.
Range: Alaska and British Columbia south and east across Canada to Newfoundland, south to Georgia and Alabama, northwest to South Dakota and Minnesota, and west and southwest to Washington and California.
Comments: This is one of 17 eastern vetches, all native to Eurasia. They are mostly climbing plants with compound leaves ending in tendrils. Used as cover crops they frequently escape from cultivation. American Vetch (*V. americana*) is a native species with toothed stipules and blue-purple flowers in loose clusters in leaf axils.

575 Hairy Vetch
Vicia villosa

Description: A climbing vine with *spreading hairs on stem* and long-stalked, *1-sided clusters of many violet and white pea flowers.*
Flowers: About ⅝″ (16 mm) long.
Leaves: Pinnately compound, with 10–20 leaflets, each ½–1″ (1.5–2.5 cm) long; tendrils at end of each leaf.
Fruit: Several-seeded pod.
Height: Vine; to 3′ (90 cm) long.
Flowering: May–October.
Habitat: Fields and thickets.
Range: Throughout North America, except Northwest Territories, Alberta, and Saskatchewan.
Comments: Introduced from Europe, Hairy Vetch is widely cultivated for fodder and often escapes from cultivation. It differs from the similar Cow Vetch (*V. cracca*) in the hairiness of its stem and in its larger flowers.

UMITORY FAMILY
amariaceae

afy herbs with succulent stems and flowers in racemes.

owers: Bilaterally symmetrical. Calyx with 2 small sepals
that drop off; corolla with 2 pairs of petals, 1 pair often
spurred or sac-like at base; stamens 4 and separate, or 6
and united into 2 groups of 3; all these parts attached at
base of ovary.
aves: Alternate or in rosettes, several times compound or
divided.
uit: Long, 1-chambered capsule; rarely hard, nut-like.

There are about 19 genera and 400 species, chiefly distrib-
ed in the northern temperate region of Eurasia. These plants
e sometimes placed in the poppy family (Papaveraceae).

---

524 Tall Corydalis
Corydalis sempervirens

Description: Drooping, sac-like, tubular, *pink and
yellow flowers* in clusters at ends of
branched stems bearing *intricately
divided leaves.*
Flowers: ½" (1.5 cm) long; petals 4, each of outer
2 often with a rounded spur protruding
upward; stamens 6; mouth and bottom
of flower golden yellow.
Leaves: 1–4" (2.5–10 cm) long, pale bluish
green, pinnately divided into mostly 3-
lobed leaflets, each about ½" (1.5 cm)
long.
Fruit: Smooth slender capsule.
Height: 5–24" (12.5–60 cm).
Flowering: May–September.
Habitat: Rocky clearings.
Range: Alberta east to Newfoundland, south to
Georgia, and northwest to Minnesota;
also in Alaska and far western Canada.
Comments: The delicate, dangling flowers and
bluish-green foliage distinguish this
corydalis. Five yellow-flowered species
occur in our area. Golden Corydalis *(C.
micrantha),* a winter annual or biennial
found in fields or along roadsides, has
long-spurred flowers about ½" (1.5 cm)
long and highly divided leaves. A

smaller species, Yellow Harlequin
(*C. flavula*), has flowers less than ½"
(1.5 cm) long and a very short spur.
Climbing Fumitory or Allegheny Vine
(*Adlumia fungosa*) is a closely related
woodland vine that climbs to 10' (3 m
it has similar foliage and pink flowers
very like those of Tall Corydalis and
occurs most frequently in the Alleghen
Mountains.

124 Dutchman's Breeches
Dicentra cucullaria

Description: Clusters of *white, pantaloon-shaped flowe*
on a leafless stalk above *much-divided,
feathery, basal leaves; tubers pinkish.*

Flowers: ¾" (2 cm) long; petals 4, outer 2 with
inflated *spurs forming a* V; not fragrant.

Leaves: 3–6" (7.5–15 cm) long, compound,
long-stalked, *grayish green* above, paler
beneath, with *deeply divided leaflets.*

Fruit: 2-parted capsule.

Height: 4–12" (10–30 cm).

Flowering: April–May.

Habitat: Rich woods.

Range: Manitoba east to Nova Scotia, south to
Georgia, west to Mississippi and
Oklahoma, and north to North Dakota
also in Washington, Idaho, and Oregon
also in Pacific Northwest.

Comments: The genus name of this delicate spring

Dutchman's Breeches

flower derives from the Greek for "two-spurred." The flowers are pollinated by early bumblebees, whose proboscises are long enough to tap the nectar. Honeybees, with shorter proboscises, gather the pollen with their front feet. Other bees with proboscises too short to reach the nectar the usual way simply snip a hole through the outside of the flower at the site of nectar accumulation; this allows the bees to rob the nectar. Such nectar-robbing does not bring about pollination. In some colonies of Dutchman's Breeches, it may be difficult to find unmutilated flowers. The closely related Squirrel Corn (*D. canadensis*), often found in the same habitats, has the same pollination story. Its flowers, however, are fragrant and heart-shaped. The yellow tubers' resemblance to corn kernels accounts for its common name. Both species are poisonous to grazing cattle.

523 Wild Bleeding Heart
Dicentra eximia

Description: Several *deep pink to red, drooping, heart-shaped flowers* along a leafless stem.
   Flowers: ¾" (2 cm) long; petals 4, rounded outer 2 forming a "heart," inner 2 forming a "drop of blood."

Wild Bleeding Heart

Leaves:	To 10″ (25 cm) long, all basal, pinnate compound, finely divided.
Fruit:	2-parted capsule.
Height:	10–18″ (25–45 cm).
Flowering:	May–August.
Habitat:	Rocky woods and cliffs.
Range:	Michigan east to Massachusetts, south to Georgia, and northwest to Tennessee and Illinois.
Comments:	This native perennial is common in the southern mountains. It resembles the more showy Asian Bleeding Heart (*D. spectabilis*), which is often cultivated in eastern gardens.

GENTIAN FAMILY
Gentianaceae

Leafy herbs, commonly with showy, bell- or trumpet shaped flowers in a branched cluster.

Flowers: Radially symmetrical. Sepals usually 4–5, separate or united; petals usually 4–5, united; stamens as many as petals; all these parts attached at base of ovary.
Leaves: Alternate, opposite, or whorled; simple.
Fruit: Usually a capsule, rarely a berry.

There are about 75 genera and 1,000 species, found in many different habitats in temperate and subtropical regions. Some species are cultivated as ornamentals.

601 Seaside Gentian; Catchfly Gentian
Eustoma exaltatum

Description:	Conspicuous *lavender, purple, or white, cup-shaped flowers,* solitary or in few-flowered terminal clusters.
Flowers:	About 1½″ (4 cm) wide; petals united at base into a short tube, flaring out into 5 long wide lobes.
Leaves:	To 3″ (7.5 cm) long, opposite, oblong, covered with whitish bloom, stalkless, clasping stem.
Height:	1–3′ (30–90 cm).
Flowering:	Throughout year, principally May–October.
Habitat:	Sandy, coastal areas and saline to freshwater marshes.

Range: Florida west to California and north in
the interior to Montana and South
Dakota.
Comments: Although it is most commonly known
as Seaside Gentian, this plant is not
restricted to coastal habitats; it also
grows in the Great Plains from Montana
to New Mexico. The genus name, from
the Greek *eu* ("good") and *stoma*
("mouth"), refers to the wide opening of
the corolla tube.

636 Closed Gentian; Bottle Gentian
Gentiana andrewsii

Description: Dark blue, *bottle-like, cylindrical flowers,
nearly closed at tips,* in tight clusters atop
stem and sometimes in axils of upper
leaves.
Flowers: 1–1½" (2.5–4 cm) long; corolla 5-lobed,
whitish at base, with fringed whitish
bands between lobes; bands slightly
longer than petals.
Leaves: To 4" (10 cm) long, ovate to lanceolate,
in a whorl below flower cluster, opposite
below.
Height: 1–2' (30–60 cm).
Flowering: August–October.
Habitat: Moist thickets and meadows.
Range: Saskatchewan east to Quebec, south to
Virginia, west to Missouri and
Nebraska, and north to North Dakota.
Comments: This is one of our most common
perennial gentians and the easiest to
grow in a moist wildflower garden.
Other bottle gentians include a
very similar species, Blind Gentian
(*G. clausa*), in which the bands are not
longer than the petals. Narrow-leaved
Gentian (*G. linearis*), which occurs
chiefly in the north and in the
mountains as far south as West Virginia,
has very narrow leaves and open flowers.
The flowers of Soapwort Gentian
(*G. saponaria*) are light blue and
slightly open at the tip; this midwestern
species has soapy juice. Stiff Gentian
(*Gentianella quinquefolia*), an annual, has

light blue or lilac, open flowers with bristle-pointed, fringeless lobes and a sided stem; it occurs from southwester Maine south to Florida and from southern Ontario to Missouri, Louisian and southern Tennessee.

609 Fringed Gentian
Gentianopsis crinita

Description: *1 blue fringed flower,* opening in sunlight and closing at night, at end of each erec stem of a branching plant.

Flowers: 2″ (5 cm) long, tubular; calyx with 4 unequal, pointed lobes, united below; *petals 4, flaring,* each tipped with fringe segments ¹⁄₁₆–¼″ (2–5 mm) long.

Leaves: 1–2″ (2.5–5 cm) long, typically ⅜–¾″ (1–2 cm) wide, opposite, ovate to lanceolate, rounded at base, pointed at tip.

Height: Usually 1′ (30 cm), sometimes to 3′ (90 cm).

Flowering: Late August–November.

Habitat: Wet thickets and meadows and seepage banks.

Range: Manitoba east to Quebec, south to Georgia, and northwest to Tennessee, Illinois, Iowa, and North Dakota.

Comments: One of the most beautiful of the gentians, with its delicately fringed petals and striking blue color, this species is becoming rare and must not be picked. It is a biennial and, along with other gentians, is among the last wildflowers to bloom in late summer and fall. Smaller Fringed Gentian (*G. procera*) is similar but has narrower leaves, a shorter fringe, and is 6–18″ (15–45 cm) tall; it occurs in midwestern boggy prairies and limestone sites. Both the common and genus names of this group come from that of King Gentius of Illyria, who, according to the ancient Roman naturalist Pliny, discovered the medicinal qualities of the roots of certain gentians for use as an emetic, cathartic, and tonic.

219 Pennywort
Obolaria virginica

Description: A low fleshy plant with *dull white or purplish flowers,* usually in groups of 3 *in axils of purplish, bract-like upper leaves* and atop stem.

Flowers: About ½" (1.5 cm) long; sepals 2, spatulate; petals 4, united to middle.

Leaves: Those under flowers ½" (1.5 cm) long, opposite, thick, round or wedge-shaped; lower leaves reduced to small scales.

Height: 3–8" (8–20 cm).

Flowering: March–May.

Habitat: Moist hardwoods and thickets.

Range: New Jersey and Pennsylvania south to Florida, west to Texas, and northeast to Arkansas, Missouri, and Illinois.

Comments: The genus name comes from the Greek *obolos* ("a small coin") and refers to the opposite, roundish leaves of this low, southern, woodland perennial. The common name also reflects the coin-like appearance of the leaves.

---

444 Saltmarsh Pink
Sabatia stellaris

Description: Stems with alternate braches, each terminated by wheel-shaped, *pink to white flowers with yellowish, red-edged, star-shaped centers.*

Flowers: ¾–1½" (2–4 cm) wide; sepals long, narrow, edged with red, *shorter than petals;* corolla lobes 4–7; stamens yellow; style twisted, divided to below middle.

Leaves: ¾–1½" (2–4 cm) long, light green, opposite, linear to narrowly lanceolate.

Height: 6–18" (15–45 cm).

Flowering: July–October.

Habitat: Saline or brackish coastal marshes and meadows.

Range: Along coast from New York and Massachusetts south to Florida and west to Louisiana.

Comments: The similar Slender Marsh Pink (*S. campanulata*), found on damp sands and peat in the coastal plain from

Massachusetts south to Florida and
Louisiana and in the southern
Appalachians, has alternate branches,
linear leaves and sepals, the latter as
long as the petals, and corollas with
4–7 lobes. Large Marsh Pink
(*S. dodecandra*), which occurs along
the coast from Connecticut to Florida
and Louisiana, has flowers 1½–2½"
(4–6.5 cm) wide and corollas with
8–13 lobes; it grows to a height of
1–2' (30–60 cm). A more southern
and midwestern species, Rose Pink
(*S. angularis*), has a 4-angled stem
and flowers on opposite branches.

GERANIUM FAMILY
Geraniaceae

Leafy herbs with white, pink, or purple, showy flowers in
clusters.

Flowers: Usually radially symmetrical. Sepals 5, separate or
slightly united at base; petals 5, separate; stamens 5, 10
or 15, with filaments sometimes united at base; all these
parts attached at base of ovary.
Leaves: Alternate or opposite; simple, pinnately or palmately
lobed, or compound.
Fruit: Developing from a long-beaked pistil with 5 united
chambers at base, each chamber 1-seeded, with a long
style attached to central core and coiling away from it at
maturity, thus lifting chambers of ovary upward and aiding in seed dispersal.

There are about 11 genera and 700 species, many frequent in the northern temperate region. Cultivated geraniums belong to *Pelargonium,* a tropical genus especially well
developed in South Africa.

454   Stork's Bill; Alfilaria; Filaree
Erodium cicutarium

Description: *Umbel-like clusters* of 6–9 small, *rose-
purple flowers* on long stalks rising
from axils of *fern-like, pinnately
compound leaves.*
Flowers: About ½" (1.5 cm) wide; petals 5;
fertile stamens 5; sterile stamens 5.

Leaves: Mostly in a basal, overwintering
rosette, doubly pinnately divided into
ovate or oblong leaflets, each to 1″
(2.5 cm) long.

Fruit: 5-parted, *beaked capsule,* each part of
beak separated from others and twisted
when dry.

Height: 6–12″ (15–30 cm).

Flowering: April–October.

Habitat: Disturbed areas, roadsides, and fields.

Range: Throughout much of North America,
except parts of far north.

Comments: This plant was introduced from the
Mediterranean region. It is quite
different from most of our species of
Geranium, which have palmately lobed
leaves; an important similarity is the
long, bill-like capsules, hence the
common name Stork's Bill. It is also
known as Clocks. The rarer Musk Stork's
Bill *(E. moschatum)* has also been
introduced from Europe; it has much
coarser foliage and the leaves are
pinnately lobed, not compound.

442 Wild Geranium; Crane's Bill
Geranium maculatum

Description: A perennial plant with *pink or white
flowers* in loose clusters of 2–5 at ends of
branches bearing a pair of *deeply 5-lobed
leaves.*

Flowers: 1–1½″ (2.5–4 cm) wide; sepals 5,
pointed, much shorter than petals;
petals 5, each ½–1″ (1.5–2.5 cm) long,
rounded, separate; stamens 10; pistil 1.

Leaves: 4–5″ (10–12.5 cm) wide, gray-green,
palmately divided into deeply toothed
lobes; basal leaves long-stalked.

Fruit: *Elongated, beaked capsule,* splitting into 5
upward-curving strips still united at
top.

Height: 1–2′ (30–60 cm).

Flowering: April–June.

Habitat: Woods, thickets, and meadows.

Range: Ontario; Maine south to Georgia, west
to Louisiana and Oklahoma, and north
to South Dakota and Minnesota.

Comments: Most of our geraniums are recognized
by their palmately lobed leaves and
distinctive capsules. An annual or
biennial, Bicknell's Crane's Bill
(*G. bicknellii*) has much smaller flowers,
notched petals, and more finely divided
leaves; it too is found in the Northeast
and Midwest. A more southern, annual
species, the closely related Carolina
Geranium (*G. carolinianum*), occurs
throughout our area and beyond; it
has a more compact flower cluster. The
common name Crane's Bill as well as the
genus name, from the Greek *geranos* ("a
crane"), refer to the beak-like capsule.
A number of species are naturalized
from Europe; a few are grown in
gardens.

548   Herb Robert
Geranium robertianum

Description: *Paired, pink to lavender flowers* on stalks
rising in axils of *intricately divided leaves*
on hairy, reddish, branching stems.
Flowers: ½" (1.5 cm) wide; petals 5.
Leaves: To 3" (7.5 cm) wide, palmately divided
into 3–5 lobed or toothed segments,
dark green or with a ruddy tinge.
Fruit: Long-beaked capsule.
Height: 1–2' (30–60 cm).
Flowering: May–October.
Habitat: Ravines and rocky woods.
Range: Ontario east to Newfoundland, south to
Virginia and Tennessee, west to
Missouri, and north to Wisconsin; also
from Alaska south to California.
Comments: This European introduction, naturalized
in North America, is an especially
attractive member of the geranium
family, but the leaves have an unpleasant
odor when crushed. It is variously
reported to have been named for Saint
Robert of Molesme, whose festival date
in April occurs at about the time the
flowers bloom in Europe, or for Robert
Goodfellow, who is known as Robin
Hood.

WITCH HAZEL FAMILY
Hamamelidaceae

Shrubs and trees with small flowers in head-like or spike-like clusters.

Flowers: Bisexual or unisexual, radially or bilaterally symmetrical. Tubular base bearing 4–5 sepals, 4–5 petals, and at least 4 stamens; ovary imbedded in base.
Leaves: Usually alternate, simple or palmately lobed, often toothed.
Fruit: Woody capsule, opening explosively and scattering seeds.

There are about 26 genera and 100 species, found in subtropical and warm temperate regions of North America, Asia, and South Africa. Members of this family are often planted as ornamentals.

354	**Witch Hazel**
	Hamamelis virginiana

Description:	A tall, autumn-flowering shrub or small tree with clusters of *spidery, yellow flowers* in leaf axils or on branches from which leaves have fallen; twigs smooth, zigzag.
Flowers:	About ¾" (2 cm) long; *petals 4,* very narrow, elongated, crumpled; buds hairy.
Leaves:	3–6" (7.5–15 cm) long, unequal at base, with wavy edges.
Height:	10–15' (3–4.5 m).
Flowering:	September–November.
Habitat:	Dry or moist woods.
Range:	Ontario east to Nova Scotia, south to Florida, west to Texas, and north to Missouri and Minnesota.
Comments:	The blooming of the yellow flowers in autumn makes this plant unique. The petals curl back into a bud when the temperature drops and expand again when it gets warmer. When the seed capsule opens, the seeds are expelled explosively for a distance of 15–20' (4.5–6 m). The bark and the leaves have long been used as a topical astringent, and the branches are sometimes used by dowsers for locating water. The similar

Vernal Witch Hazel *(H. vernalis)* flower in the late winter or early spring, from January to April; it has densely hairy twigs and coppery, fragrant flowers and is found on wet shorelines in the south-central United States.

WATERLEAF FAMILY
Hydrophyllaceae

Usually herbs, rarely shrubs, often bristly or glandular, with flowers often arranged along one side of branches or at stem tip in coils resembling fiddlenecks.

Flowers: Radially symmetrical. Calyx with 5 united sepals, corolla with 5 united petals, varying from nearly flat to bell- or funnel-shaped; stamens 5, often protruding; all these parts attached at base of ovary.
Leaves: Alternate or opposite, often in basal rosettes; simple or pinnately compound.
Fruit: Capsule, with 1 to many seeds.

There are about 20 genera and 250 species, nearly world-wide; the western United States is the main center of diversity. A few species are grown as ornamentals.

605 Virginia Waterleaf
Hydrophyllum virginianum

Description: Clusters of *white or dark violet flowers* on long stalks rising in leaf axils and extending above leaves; stem with minute hairs.
Flowers: ¼–½" (6–13 mm) long; corolla 5-lobed, *bell-shaped;* stamens 5, with *hairy filaments extending beyond petals.*
Leaves: 2–5" (5–12.5 cm) long, often *mottled, pinnately divided,* with 5–7 lanceolate or ovate, *sharply toothed leaflets.*
Height: 1–2½' (30–75 cm).
Flowering: May–August.
Habitat: Moist woods and clearings.
Range: Ontario, Quebec, and New England south to North Carolina, west to Oklahoma, and north to North Dakota.
Comments: The common name waterleaf alludes to the water-stained appearance of the leaves. This woodland perennial is one of

several in this genus with tubular flowers and protruding stamens. The similar Large-leaved Waterleaf *(H. macrophyllum),* a southern and midwestern species with pinnately divided leaves, is rough and hairy, the hairs 1/16–1/8" (1–3 mm) long. Broad-leaved Waterleaf *(H. canadense)* has flower stalks shorter than its palmately lobed, maple-like leaves and occurs from western New England to northern Alabama and Missouri. The flowers of both these species are white, but Appendaged Waterleaf *(H. appendiculatum),* also with palmately lobed leaves, has lavender flowers with small appendages alternating with the sepals; it is found from Ontario and Minnesota south to Pennsylvania, Tennessee, Missouri, and eastern Kansas.

201 Blue Ridge Phacelia
Phacelia fimbriata

Description: A branching plant with *1-sided, coiled clusters* of light blue, lavender, or white flowers with *deeply fringed corolla lobes.*

Flowers: 1/2" (1.5 cm) wide; corolla somewhat bell-shaped, with 5 *spreading lobes.*

Blue Ridge Phacelia

Leaves:	About 2" (5 cm) long, pinnately divided into 5–11 triangular-oblong lobes; upper leaves unstalked, lower ones stalked.
Height:	8–16" (20–40 cm).
Flowering:	May–June.
Habitat:	Upland woods.
Range:	Virginia and Tennessee south to Georgia and Alabama.
Comments:	The strikingly fringed petals, especially beautiful under a hand lens, characterize this spring wildflower of the Great Smoky Mountains, where it can occur in abundance. The similar Miami Mist *(P. purshii)* has the stem hairs closely pressed against the stem rather than spreading away from the stem as in Blue Ridge Phacelia.

ST. JOHN'S WORT FAMILY
Hypericaceae

Leafy herbs or shrubs with yellow to orange (sometimes pink) flowers in branched clusters and leaves usually covered with numerous often black or translucent dots.

Flowers: Bisexual, radially symmetrical. Sepals 4–5, separate; petals 4–5, separate; stamens numerous, usually united into several bunches by bases of filaments; all these parts attached at base of ovary.
Leaves: Opposite or whorled, simple.
Fruit: Usually a many-seeded capsule.

There are 8 genera and about 400 species, found in temperate and tropical regions. Some are grown as ornamentals. Many species have leaves with translucent dots; when held up to the light, these appear as tiny pinholes. This family is sometimes combined with the Clusiaceae (also known as Guttiferae), a tropical family of mostly trees and shrubs.

337   St. Peter's Wort
Hypericum crux-andreae

Description:	*An erect shrub with lemon yellow flowers* at branch tips.
Flowers:	1" (2.5 cm) wide; *sepals 4, unequal,* outer 2 larger and enclosing inner, much narrower 2; *petals 4;* stamens numerous; styles 3–4.

Leaves:	½–1½″ (1.5–4 cm) long, opposite, elliptical, partly clasping stem.
Height:	1–3′ (30–90 cm).
Flowering:	July–September.
Habitat:	Sandy sites and pine barrens.
Range:	New York south to Florida, west to Texas, and north to Oklahoma, Arkansas, and Kentucky.
Comments:	This shrubby member of the St. John's wort family has only four petals instead of the usual five, and the sepals are of very unequal sizes. The similar St. Andrew's Cross *(H. hypericoides),* with two styles, inner sepals minute or absent, and narrower leaves, is found on sandy sites from Massachusetts south to Florida, west to Texas, and north to Kansas; in the north it may form a mat on the ground. Low St. Andrew's Cross *(H. suffruticosum)* is only 2½–6″ (6.5–15 cm) tall, with usually only two sepals, the flowers eventually nodding; it is found in sandy sites in the coastal plain from South Carolina south to Florida and west to Louisiana.

256 Pineweed
Hypericum gentianoides

Description:	Small, *yellow, nearly sessile flowers on wiry, ascending branches* of a bushy plant.
Flowers:	⅛–¼″ (3–6 mm) wide; sepals 5; petals 5.
Leaves:	To ¼″ (5 mm) long, *scale-like,* pressed against stem.
Height:	4–20″ (10–50 cm).
Flowering:	July–October.
Habitat:	Open, sandy or rocky areas.
Range:	Ontario; Nova Scotia and Maine south to Florida, west to Texas, and north to Missouri and Minnesota.
Comments:	With its tiny flowers and scaly leaves on erect, wiry branches, this annual is unlike most St. John's worts. It is typical of sterile, bare, open sites, where its flowers open only in the sun. Its capsules are usually red. The similar Nits-and-lice *(H. drummondii)* has fewer branches,

Pineweed

a broad oval capsule, and larger leaves
½–1″ (1.5–2.5 cm) long; it occurs from
Maryland south to Florida, west to
Texas, and north to Iowa, southern
Illinois, and West Virginia.

336   Kalm's St. John's Wort
Hypericum kalmianum

Description: *A low shrub with bright yellow flowers* in
small clusters at ends of 4-sided
branches; bark papery, peeling when
older.

Flowers: ¾–1½″ (2–4 cm) wide; sepals 5; petals
5; stamens numerous; styles 5.

Leaves: About 2″ (5 cm) long, opposite, linear to
oblong, with translucent dots beneath;
clusters of tiny leaves in axils of larger leaves.

Height: 2–3′ (60–90 cm).

Flowering: July–August.

Habitat: Rocky or sandy soil.

Range: Ontario and Quebec south to New York,
Ohio, Indiana, Illinois, and Wisconsin.

Comments: The species and common names honor
Peter Kalm, a student of Linnaeus, who
discovered the plant in America around
1750. This is one of several shrubby St.
John's worts with yellow flowers and
small axillary clusters of leaves. Many
species of St. John's wort are found
throughout the South.

335 Common St. John's Wort
Hypericum perforatum

Description:	An herb with *bright yellow flowers* in broad, branched, terminal clusters; branches sharply ridged below each leaf.
Flowers:	¾–1″ (2–2.5 cm) wide; *petals 5, with black dots on edges;* stamens numerous, in 3s; styles 3, separate.
Leaves:	1–2″ (2.5–5 cm) long, opposite, elliptical, numerous, small, with *translucent dots.*
Height:	1–2½′ (30–75 cm).
Flowering:	June–September.
Habitat:	Fields, roadsides, and waste places.
Range:	Throughout much of North America, except far north, Prairie Provinces, Florida, Alabama, and most of southwestern United States.
Comments:	Introduced from Europe, this highly branched perennial is the most common St. John's wort. In many of the western states it is considered a noxious weed because it can cause photodermatitis in animals that graze on it. People who take Common St. John's Wort for medicinal purposes may develop increased sensitivity to sunlight. The common name of these species and of the family derives from the fact that the flowers are said to bloom on Saint John's Eve, June 24. A large-flowered member of this group is Great St. John's Wort *(H. ascyron)*, with showy flowers 1–2″ (2.5–5 cm) wide, five styles, and elliptical leaves; it is 2–6′ (60–180 cm) tall and is found in wet meadows and thickets from Ontario and Quebec south to Maryland and west to Kansas and Nebraska. Among the several smaller-flowered wetland species are Dwarf St. John's Wort *(H. mutilum)*, a diffusely branched plant with flowers ¼″ (5 mm) wide and oblong leaves, and Canada St. John's Wort *(H. canadense)*, with flowers ¼″ (5 mm) wide and linear leaves; both species are found throughout the East. Pale St. John's Wort *(H. ellipticum)* is a more northern species and occurs from southern Canada

as far south as Maryland and west to North Dakota; its flowers are ½" (1.5 cm) wide, borne on an unbranched stem and the leaves are oval-elliptical.

501   Marsh St. John's Wort
Triadenum virginicum

Description: A *marsh herb* with *pink flowers* clustered atop a leafy stem and in axils of opposite leaves.

Flowers: ½–¾" (1.5–2 cm) wide; sepals 5, often purple-red; petals 5; stamens 9, in 3s; conspicuous orange gland between each group of stamens.

Leaves: 1–2½" (2.5–6.5 cm) long, opposite, ovate, light green, stalkless, heart-shaped at base, with translucent dots.

Height: 8–24" (20–60 cm).

Flowering: July–August.

Habitat: Wet sandy areas, swamps, and bogs.

Range: Ontario, Quebec, and Nova Scotia; Maine south to Florida, west to Texas, and northeast to Indiana and Illinois.

Comments: This wetland perennial differs in flower color from most of the St. John's worts, which are yellow. The genus name derives from *tri* ("three") and *aden* ("gland") and refers to the three central glands among the stamens. The related *T. tubulosum,* also called Marsh St. John's Wort, is found only as far north as Maryland, Ohio, Indiana, and Missouri; the bases of its leaves are rounded or tapered, not heart-shaped.

IRIS FAMILY
Iridaceae

Herbs growing from rhizomes, bulbs, or swollen, underground stems, with narrow, basal leaves, sometimes arranged edge to edge in fan-shaped clusters, and showy flower clusters at tips of long stalks.

Flowers: Usually radially symmetrical. Sepals 3, petal-like; petals 3; stamens 3; all these parts attached at top of ovary.

Leaves: Simple, folded and overlapping one another at base, aligned in 2 rows.
Fruit: Many-seeded capsule.

There are about 80 genera and 1,500 species, found in temperate and tropical regions. Irises *(Iris)*, freesias *(Freesia)*, gladiolus *(Gladiolus)*, and montbretias *(Tritonia)* are popular ornamentals. Saffron dye is obtained from Saffron Crocus *(Crocus sativus)*, and "essence of violets," used in perfumes, is extracted from the rhizomes of irises.

368 Blackberry Lily
Belamcanda chinensis

Description: Leafless stalks with several *red-spotted, orange, lily-like flowers* growing from *narrow, flat, sword-like leaves* in fan-shaped clusters.
Flowers: 1½–2″ (4–5 cm) wide; petal-like parts 6, widely spreading; lasting only 1 day.
Leaves: 12–18″ (30–45 cm) long, about 1″ (2.5 cm) wide.
Fruit: Capsule, splitting open to reveal a blackberry-like cluster of shiny black seeds.
Height: 1½–4′ (45–120 cm).
Flowering: June–July.
Habitat: Roadsides and open woods.
Range: Minnesota east to Vermont, south to Florida, west to Texas, and north to South Dakota.
Comments: This handsome Chinese introduction has escaped from cultivation. Several flowers usually bloom at one time. The blackberry-like seed cluster, which is seen when the capsule breaks open, accounts for the common name.

550, 612 Crested Dwarf Iris
Iris cristata

Description: *1 (occasionally 2) violet-blue flower* with 6 spreading, petal-like parts, atop a short slender stalk.
Flowers: About 2½″ (6.5 cm) wide; sepals 3, broad, down-curved, petal-like, *crested* with crinkly, yellow or white ridges,

Crested Dwarf Iris

streaked with purple; petals 3, narrower, arching; styles 3, 2-lobed, curving over sepals; stamens 3, hidden under styles.

Leaves: 4–7″ (10–17.5 cm) long at flowering (longer later), ½–1″ (1.5–2.5 cm) wide, flat, lanceolate, sheathing stem.

Height: 4–9″ (10–22.5 cm).

Flowering: April–May.

Habitat: Wooded hillsides and ravines.

Range: Massachusetts; Pennsylvania south to Georgia, west to Mississippi, Arkansas, and Oklahoma, and northeast to Missouri and Illinois.

Comments: This is a low iris of southern and midwestern wooded uplands. Dwarf Iris *(I. verna)* has non-crested sepals, narrower leaves less than ½″ (1.5 cm) wide, and occurs in peaty soil and pine barrens from New York south to Florida, west to Arkansas, and northeast to Missouri, Kentucky, and Ohio.

---

374 Red Iris
Iris fulva

Description: Showy, *reddish-brown flowers with 6 widely spreading, petal-like parts* on a slender stalk taller than sword-like leaves.

Flowers: About 3″ (7.5 cm) wide; sepals 3, petal-like; petals 3, narrower, backward-

curving; stamens 3, hidden under 3
petal-like, arching styles.

Leaves: To 3' (90 cm) long, about ½" (1.5 cm)
wide, in a basal cluster.

Height: 2–5' (60–150 cm).

Flowering: May–June.

Habitat: Wet grasslands and swamp borders.

Range: Ohio south to Florida, west to Texas,
and northeast to Arkansas, Missouri,
and Illinois.

Comments: This beautiful southern iris of wet
sloughs and swampy woods has
distinctly flat-topped flowers compared
to other irises. It can be cultivated in
moist wildflower gardens.

270 Yellow Flag
Iris pseudacorus

Description: *1 to several yellow flowers* on a robust
stalk, often overtopped by long, stiff,
sword-like leaves; often in clumps.

Flowers: 3" (7.5 cm) wide; sepals 3, backward-
curving; petals 3, smaller, narrow,
upright; styles 3, arching over sepals,
with 3 stamens beneath.

Leaves: To 3' (90 cm) tall, rising from
basal cluster, often taller than flower
stalk.

Height: 2–3' (60–90 cm).

Flowering: June–August.

Habitat: Marshes and streamsides.

Range: Throughout much of East; also in much
of West.

Comments: This showy species was introduced from
Europe, escaped from cultivation, and is
spreading throughout our range.

611 Blue Flag
Iris versicolor

Description: Several violet-blue flowers with
intricately veined, *yellow-based sepals*
on a sturdy stalk among tall, sword-
like leaves rising from a basal cluster.

Flowers: 2½–4" (6.5–10 cm) wide; sepals 3;
petals 3, narrower, erect; styles 3,

2-lobed, arching over sepals; stamens 3, hidden under styles.

Leaves: 8–31" (20–80 cm) long, ½–1" (1.5–2.5 cm) wide, pale green to grayish.

Height: 2–3' (60–90 cm).

Flowering: May–August.

Habitat: Swamps, marshes, and wet shorelines.

Range: Saskatchewan east to Newfoundland, south to Virginia, and northwest to Ohio, Michigan, Wisconsin, and Minnesota.

Comments: This is a showy native iris of northeastern wetlands. Insects attracted to the sepals must crawl under the tip of a style and brush past a stigma and stamen, thus facilitating pollination. The rhizome is poisonous, but it was dried and used in small amounts as a cathartic and diuretic by Native Americans and colonists. A similar wetland species, occurring from Ontario and Quebec south to Florida and Texas, is Southern Blue Flag (*I. virginica*); it is a smaller plant, to 2' (60 cm) tall, with bright green leaves that often lie on the ground or float on water. A coastal, brackish-water species, Slender Blue Flag (*I. prismatica*), has extremely narrow, grass-like leaves less than ¼" (6 mm) wide; it occurs in Ontario and Nova Scotia and from Maine south to Georgia and Tennessee. The common name flag is from the Middle English *flagge*, meaning "rush" or "reed."

613 Blue-eyed Grass
Sisyrinchium angustifolium

Description: Small, *blue or violet-blue flowers with yellow centers* atop a long, flat, *twisted, usually branched stalk.*

Flowers: ½" (1.5 cm) wide; sepals 3, petal-like, each tipped with a point; petals 3.

Leaves: 4–20" (10–50 cm) long, less than ¼" (6 mm) wide, basal, linear, *grass-like,* may be shorter or longer than flower stalk.

Height: 4–20" (10–50 cm).

Flowering: May–July.

Habitat: Meadows, low woods, and shorelines.
Range: Ontario, Quebec, and Nova Scotia; Maine south to Florida, west to Texas, and north to Kansas, Iowa, and Minnesota.
Comments: Although the plant is small and has grass-like leaves, the flowers have all the features of the iris family. The various *Sisyrinchium* are all much alike; separation is based on such characteristics as branching pattern and leaf length.

RUSH FAMILY
Juncaceae

Herbs, rarely shrubs, with mostly grass-like leaves usually in basal tuft and small, greenish or brownish flowers in dense spikes or heads, sometimes in loose clusters or solitary.

Flowers: Sepals and petals 3 each, scale-like, papery, green to brown; stamens 3 or 6; all these parts attached at base of ovary.
Leaves: Narrow, cylindrical to flat, sometimes with cross partitions, with bases sheathing stem; blades sometimes absent.
Fruit: Small capsule, with at least 3 seeds.

There are about 8 genera and 300 species, found in temperate and cold regions, most abundant in the mountains of South America. The flower structure of members of this family closely resembles that of lilies (Liliaceae).

395 Soft Rush
Juncus effusus

Description: A seemingly leafless, strictly wetland plant with soft, grass-like stems in sometimes dense clumps, each bearing *very small, greenish-brown, scaly flowers in clusters* diverging from one point on side of stalk near top.
Flowers: About ¼" (4 mm) long; sepals and petals 3 each; stamens 3.
Leaves: Represented by basal sheaths to 6" (15 cm) long.
Height: 1½–4' (45–120 cm).
Flowering: July–September.

Habitat: Swamps and damp open ground.
Range: Throughout much of North America, except far north.
Comments: This common marsh plant forms large clumps. It is one of many rushes, most of which are found in wet soil or water. Muskrats feed on the roots, and birds find shelter among the stems.

---

396 Wood Rush
Luzula multiflora

Description: *Densely tufted stems* topped by 4–12 spike-like or head-like clusters of many *tiny, brownish flowers* enclosed in small shiny bracts, with leaf-like bracts beneath each cluster.
Flowers: About ⅛″ (3 mm) long; sepals and petals 3 each; stamens 6; pistil with 3 stigmas; cluster about ⅜″ (8 mm) long.
Leaves: 3–5″ (7.5–12.5 cm) long, mostly basal, grass-like, pale green, edges fringed with web-like hairs.
Height: 6–16″ (15–40 cm).
Flowering: April–July.
Habitat: Fields and open woods.
Range: Alaska and British Columbia south and east across Canada to Greenland and Newfoundland, south to South Carolina, west to Missouri, and north to South Dakota and Minnesota; also from Montana south to New Mexico and westward.
Comments: Most of the many wood rushes that grow in North America are rather difficult to tell apart. In spite of the resemblance of rushes and wood rushes to grasses or sedges, they have the same number and arrangement of flower parts as lilies.

MINT FAMILY
Lamiaceae

Aromatic herbs or shrubs, rarely trees or vines, usually with stems square in cross section, and flowers in long clusters, heads, or interrupted whorls on stem.

owers: Bilaterally symmetrical. Calyx with usually 5 united sepals, often each evident as a point on calyx, or sometimes calyx 2-lipped (or occasionally without points or lips); corolla with 5 united petals, usually forming an upper and lower lip, occasionally with 2 petals so well united corolla appears 4-lobed; stamens 2 or 4; all these parts attached at base of 4-lobed ovary.

eaves: Opposite or whorled, usually simple.

ruit: Nestled in persistent calyx, with 4 lobes, each lobe forming a hard, 1-seeded nutlet; rarely a drupe.

There are about 200 genera and 3,200 species, nearly orldwide. The Mediterranean region, the chief area of iversity, produces many spices and flavorings, such as regano and marjoram *(Origanum),* thyme *(Thymus),* sage *Salvia),* basil *(Ocimum),* and mints *(Mentha).* Catnip *(Nepeta ataria)* and Lavender *(Lavandula officinalis)* also belong to he family. Members of several genera, including *Coleus* and *alvia,* are popular ornamentals. The family's traditional ame, Labiatae, refers to the lip-like parts of the united petals.

---

596 Wild Basil
Clinopodium vulgare

Description:	*Rose-purple flowers, mingled with hairy bracts creating a woolly appearance,* in a dense rounded cluster atop a square hairy stem and in smaller clusters in upper leaf axils.
Flowers:	About ½″ (1.5 cm) long; calyx hairy; corolla 2-lipped; stamens 4.
Leaves:	¾–1½″ (2–4 cm) long, opposite, ovate, mostly untoothed.
Height:	8–20″ (20–50 cm).
Flowering:	June–September.
Habitat:	Roadsides, pastures, and thickets.
Range:	Manitoba east to Newfoundland, south to North Carolina, west to Arkansas and Kansas, and north to Minnesota; also scattered in western United States.
Comments:	This plant is native in the northern part of its North American range but may have been introduced from Europe, where it is widespread, into the southern part. The dried leaves can be used as a seasoning, although they are milder than those of the commercial basil, another member of the mint family.

318 Horse Balm
Collinsonia canadensis

Description: A stout square stem with *loose branching clusters of yellow flowers.*

Flowers: ⅜–½" (8–13 mm) long; corolla 2-lipped, lower lip long and *fringed; stamens 2, protruding with pistil beyond corolla tube.*

Leaves: Blades 4–8" (10–20 cm) long, opposite, ovate, sharply toothed.

Height: 2–4' (60–120 cm).

Flowering: July–September.

Habitat: Rich woods.

Range: Ontario and Quebec; New Hampshire south to Florida, west to Louisiana, and north to Missouri, Illinois, and Michigan.

Comments: This tall wildflower is typical of moist woodlands. Its foliage as well as its flowers have a citronella-like odor. Tea can be brewed from the leaves, and the rhizome was formerly used as a diuretic, tonic, and astringent.

597 Ground Ivy; Gill-over-the-ground; Creeping Charlie
Glechoma hederacea

Description: Ascending branches from a *creeping stem* with 3–7 *small, blue-violet flowers* whorled in axils of *scalloped leaves.*

Flowers: ½–¾" (1.5–2 cm) long; corolla 2-lipped, lower lip 3-lobed; stamens 4, not or only slightly protruding.

Leaves: Blade ½–1½" (1.5–4 cm) long, roundish, wavy-edged, opposite.

Height: Creeper; branches to 8" (20 cm), stems to 7' (2.1 m) long.

Flowering: March–July.

Habitat: Moist, shaded or sunny areas, roadsides, and lawns.

Range: Throughout much of North America, except the far north and the southwestern deserts.

Comments: This European introduction is considered a weed by some since it roots readily at the nodes and spreads rapidly. "Gill" in

the common name comes from the French *guiller* ("to ferment") because the leaves were once used to help ferment, or flavor, beer. This species is sometimes placed within the catnip genus *(Nepeta)* but differs in having the flowers in the axils of the leaves rather than at the ends of the stems and branches.

527 Henbit
Lamium amplexicaule

Description: *Lavender flowers* whorled around a square stem in axils of *horizontally held, stalkless, scalloped leaves.*

Flowers: ½–⅝" (13–16 mm) long, hairy; corolla 2-lipped, upper lip concave; stamens 4, protruding.

Leaves: ½–1½" (1.5–4 cm) long, roundish to ovate, opposite, upper ones stalkless, lower ones long-stalked.

Height: 4–16" (10–40 cm).

Flowering: March–November.

Habitat: Waste places, fields, and roadsides.

Range: Throughout North America, except Arctic.

Comments: This species was introduced from Europe. The genus name, from the Greek *lamios* ("thread"), refers to the straight corolla tube between the two lips. The species name is from the Latin for "clasping" or "embracing" and describes the leaves. The common name

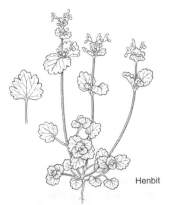

Henbit

implies that the seeds of the plant are eaten by chickens. Red Henbit *(L. purpureum),* also a widely distributed, weedy plant, has all of its leaves stalke~~d~~

---

595 Motherwort
Leonurus cardiaca

Description: *Small, pale lavender flowers clustered aroun~~d~~ a square stem* in axils of horizontally hel~~d~~ opposite, *lobed leaves;* several clusters together forming a long, interrupted, terminal spike.

Flowers: ½" (1.5 cm) long, ⅜" (8 mm) wide; calyx with 5 united sepals, 5-veined, tipped with sharp spines; corolla 2-lipped, 2-lobed upper lip *bearded* and arching, 3-lobed lower lip spreading; stamens 4; leafy bracts beneath cluster.

Leaves: Lower ones 2–4" (5–10 cm) long, *palmately cut into 3 lobes;* upper ones smaller, less deeply cut.

Height: 2–4' (60–120 cm).

Flowering: June–August.

Habitat: Waste places, roadsides, and disturbed areas.

Range: Throughout much of North America, except Florida, California, and far north~~.~~

Comments: Growing as a weed over much of temperate North America, this introduced European perennial with distinctly 3-lobed leaves has been used by herbalists as a stimulant (the species name means "for the heart") and traditionally for menstrual disorders, hence the common name referring to "mother." Siberian Motherwort *(L. sibiricus),* with a 10-veined calyx, is also naturalized from Europe and found in our range.

---

197 Water Horehound
Lycopus americanus

Description: *Tiny, white, tubular flowers* clustered in dense groups around a square stem in axils of opposite leaves.

Flowers:	About ¹⁄₁₆″ (2 mm) long; calyx with 5 sharply bristle-tipped lobes; corolla appearing 4-lobed; stamens 2.
Leaves:	1–3″ (2.5–7.5 cm) long, lanceolate, coarsely toothed or lobed, at least lower leaves *deeply toothed.*
Height:	6–24″ (15–60 cm).
Flowering:	June–September.
Habitat:	Moist sites, shorelines, and wetlands.
Range:	Throughout North America, except far north and Nevada.
Comments:	The members of this group are non-aromatic mints and are typical of wet sites. The various species are distinguished on the basis of technical details. They are sometimes called bugleweeds because of the resemblance of each flower to a bugle. Other species have less coarsely toothed leaves. The genus name is from the Greek *lycos* ("a wolf") and *pous* ("foot") and refers to the likeness of some species' leaves to a wolf's footprint. About 10 species of *Lycopus* occur in our area; most are very similar, making identification difficult.

507 Wild Mint; Field Mint
Mentha arvensis

Description:	*Tiny, bell-shaped, pale lilac, pink, or white flowers* clustered in circles around a square stem in axils of opposite leaves; stem angles hairy.
Flowers:	About ¼″ (6 mm) long, ⅛″ (3 mm) wide; corolla appearing 4-lobed; stamens 4.
Leaves:	2″ (5 cm) long, smaller toward top of plant, ovate to lanceolate, tapering at both ends, *strongly aromatic.*
Height:	6–24″ (15–60 cm).
Flowering:	July–September.
Habitat:	Damp to wet places.
Range:	Throughout North America, except from Florida west to Louisiana and Oklahoma, and Arctic.
Comments:	This aromatic perennial has glands containing essential oils; the leaves are

Wild Mint

used as flavoring in sauces, jellies, and beverages. Some mints are grown in gardens, where they can be highly invasive. The flowers of these so-called true mints appear 4-lobed and nearly radially symmetrical. At least 10 mint species occur in our range, but only Wild Mint is native.

534 Peppermint
Mentha piperita

Description: *Small, lavender to pink, whorled flowers* in terminal clusters *at first crowded and ovoid, eventually becoming cylindrical and looser.*

Flowers: About ¼" (5 mm) long; corolla appearing 4-lobed; cluster ½–¾" (1.5–2 cm) wide.

Leaves: 1–2½" (2.5–6.5 cm) long, opposite, lanceolate to oblong, soft, sharply toothed.

Height: 1–3' (30–90 cm).

Flowering: June–October.

Habitat: Marshes, ditches, brooksides, wet meadows, and lawns.

Range: Ontario east to Newfoundland, south to Florida, west to Texas, and north to

Nebraska and Minnesota; also in much of West.

Comments: This introduced mint is considered by some taxonomists to be a hybrid of Spearmint (*M. spicata*) and Water Mint (*M. aquatica*), both from Europe. Peppermint has stalked leaves; those of Spearmint are sessile or on stalks only to ⅛" (3 mm). Water Mint has a hairy calyx; the calyx of the Peppermint flower is hairy only on the teeth. Peppermint, with its strong odor and sharp taste, is used as a tea and as a flavoring.

419 Bee Balm; Oswego Tea
Monarda didyma

Description: A dense, rounded, terminal, *head-like cluster of bright red, tubular flowers* atop a square stem.

Flowers: About 1½" (4 cm) long; corolla 2-lipped, 5-lobed; stamens 2, projecting; stigma 2-parted; *reddish bracts* beneath cluster.

Leaves: 3–6" (7.5–15 cm) long, opposite, dark green, ovate to lanceolate, coarsely toothed.

Height: 2–5' (60–150 cm).

Flowering: June–August.

Habitat: Moist woods and thickets, especially along streams.

Range: Ontario east to Maine, south to Georgia, and northwest to Missouri and Minnesota; also in Oregon and Washington.

Comments: This species is coarser than true mints (*Mentha*) but is very showy and frequently cultivated in gardens. Hummingbirds are especially attracted to the red flowers. The common name Oswego Tea refers to the use of the leaves for a tea by the Oswegos of New York. Early colonists also used the plant for this purpose when regular tea was scarce. A white-flowered variant is sometimes grown in gardens.

528 Wild Bergamot
Monarda fistulosa

Description: A dense *rounded cluster* of *lavender to purplish-pink, tubular flowers* atop a square stem.

Flowers: 1″ (2.5 cm) long; corolla 2-lipped, hairy upper lip 2-lobed, broader lower lip 3-lobed; stamens 2, projecting; *bracts beneath cluster often pink-tinged.*

Leaves: About 2½″ (6.5 cm) long, gray-green, opposite, lanceolate, coarsely toothed.

Height: 2–4′ (60–120 cm).

Flowering: June–September.

Habitat: Dry fields, thickets, and borders; usually common in limestone regions.

Range: Throughout East, except Maritime Provinces, Newfoundland, and Florida; also in much of West.

Comments: This showy perennial, frequently cultivated, has aromatic leaves used to make mint tea. Oil from the leaves was formerly used to treat respiratory ailments.

Wild Bergamot

198 Catnip
Nepeta cataria

Description: A hairy plant bearing *clusters of pale white or whitish-lavender flowers with purplish spots* at ends of main stem and branches; *stem and leaves covered with grayish down.*

Flowers: ½″ (1.5 cm) long; calyx hairy; corolla 2-lipped, tubular; stamens 4.

Leaves:	To 2½" (6.5 cm) long, opposite, triangular, coarsely toothed.
Height:	1–3' (30–90 cm).
Flowering:	June–September.
Habitat:	Roadsides, waste places, pastures, and barnyards.
Range:	Throughout much of North America, except far north.
Comments:	Although introduced in North America from Europe, Catnip may have originated in Asia. This well-known, distinctly aromatic plant is often grown in gardens for the pleasure it gives cats. It contains a chemical that tends to repel insects and can therefore be used to protect other plants; it may be this chemical that affects the behavior of cats.

486 Obedient Plant; False Dragonhead
Physostegia virginiana

Description:	*Opposite, pinkish flowers in a spike-like cluster* along upper part of a square stem.
Flowers:	¾–1" (2–2.5 cm) long; calyx with 5 pointed teeth; corolla 2-lipped, *tubular, spotted with purple, enlarging outward;* stamens 4; cluster 4–8" (10–20 cm) long.
Leaves:	About 4" (10 cm) long, opposite, smaller toward top of plant, narrow, lanceolate, pointed, with sharp incurved teeth.
Height:	1–4' (30–120 cm).
Flowering:	June–September.
Habitat:	Damp thickets, swamps, and prairies.
Range:	Manitoba east to New Brunswick, south to Florida, west to Texas, and north to North Dakota.
Comments:	This attractive plant is snapdragon-like, but its square stem is typical of the mint family. If the flowers are bent, they tend to stay in the new position for a while, hence the common name Obedient Plant. Several garden forms occasionally escape to the wild.

638 Heal-all; Self-heal
Prunella vulgaris

Description: A square stem with *dense, cylindrical, terminal spikes of purple to blue flowers;* spikes elongate after flowering.

Flowers: ½" (1.5 cm) long; calyx 2-lipped, broa upper lip 3-toothed, lower lip deeply 2-lobed; corolla 2-lipped, upper lip arching, fringed lower lip drooping; stamens 4; greenish, hairy bracts beneath flowers.

Leaves: 1–3" (2.5–7.5 cm) long, variable, lanceolate to ovate, smooth or obscurel toothed, opposite.

Height: 6–12" (15–30 cm), sometimes sprawling

Flowering: May–September.

Habitat: Gardens, fields, and roadsides.

Range: Throughout much of North America, except far north.

Comments: This low, introduced perennial is easily recognized by its erect, many-flowered spikes and overlapping, hairy bracts. A form that flowers when only 2" (5 cm) tall is a common lawn weed. The common names are derived from the plant's wide use as an herbal remedy for throat ailments.

196 Hoary Mountain Mint
Pycnanthemum incanum

Description: *Small, white to lavender flowers in dense rounded clusters* in leaf axils or atop a hairy square stem and branches; *white bracts* beneath flowers.

Flowers: About ⅜" (8 mm) long; calyx hairy; corolla 2-lipped, lower lip spotted with purple; cluster to 1½" (4 cm) wide.

Leaves: 1½–4" (4–10 cm) long, opposite, lanceolate-ovate, toothed, *stalked, white beneath.*

Height: 1–3' (30–90 cm).

Flowering: July–September.

Habitat: Woods and thickets.

Range: Ontario; New Hampshire and Vermont south to Florida, west to Mississippi, and north to Illinois and Michigan.

Comments: The genus name derives from the Greek
for "dense" and "flower" and aptly
describes the crowded flower clusters.
The many species are closely related and
difficult to distinguish from one
another. These plants, particularly the
flower clusters, have a very strong odor
when crushed.

631 Blue Salvia
Salvia azurea

Description: A tall, delicate plant with *large, 2-lipped,
blue to violet flowers whorled around a
square stem and forming a terminal,
spike-like cluster.

Flowers: ½–1" (1.5–2.5 cm) long; corolla 2-
lipped, glandular and hairy outside,
lower lip much larger than upper lip;
stamens 2.

Leaves: To 4" (10 cm) long, linear to lanceolate,
opposite, basal leaves absent.

Height: 2–5' (60–150 cm).

Flowering: July–October.

Habitat: Dry, open or shaded prairies and
pastures and open pinelands.

Range: Wisconsin east to New York, south to
Florida, west to New Mexico and Utah,
and northeast to Nebraska and
Minnesota.

Comments: A widespread perennial of grasslands,
Blue Salvia also extends east to the
Carolinas. It begins to flower early and
may continue until the fall or into early
winter in Florida. A well-known
cultivated salvia is Garden Sage *(S.
officinalis),* used in cooking as a
flavoring.

414 Salvia; Blood Sage
Salvia coccinea

Description: Several whorls of *red flowers in an
interrupted spike* on a square stem.

Flowers: 1" (2.5 cm) long; corolla 2-lipped, lower
lip 3-lobed, smaller upper lip 2-lobed;
stamens 2.

Leaves:	About 2″ (5 cm) long, opposite, ovate, blunt, scalloped.
Height:	1–2′ (30–60 cm).
Flowering:	May–frost.
Habitat:	Sandy places.
Range:	South Carolina south to Florida and we to Texas; also in Ohio.
Comments:	This showy southern native is characterized by the loose, widely space flowering spike. It is found in the hot sands of the South. A flamboyant salvia Scarlet Sage *(S. splendens),* was introduced from Brazil for use as a garden ornamental.

581 Lyre-leaved Sage
Salvia lyrata

Description:	Whorls of 3–10 *lavender to blue flowers* surrounding a square stem in an interrupted, spike-like cluster.
Flowers:	About 1″ (2.5 cm) long; corolla 2-lipped, lower lip longer than upper lip; stamens 2.
Leaves:	Basal leaves to 8″ (20 cm) long, *deeply lobed* into rounded segments, stalked; stem leaves few, much smaller, short-stalked or unstalked.
Height:	1–2′ (30–60 cm).
Flowering:	April–June.

Lyre-leaved Sage

Habitat: Sandy, open woods, thickets, and weedy sites.

Range: Connecticut and Pennsylvania south to Florida, west to Texas, north to Kansas, and northeast to Ohio.

Comments: The exposed lower lip of salvias provides an excellent landing platform for bees. When a bee lands, the two stamens are tipped, and the insect is doused with pollen.

---

594 Hyssop Skullcap; Rough Skullcap
Scutellaria integrifolia

Description: *Bluish-lavender, 2-lipped flowers* clustered or solitary in axils of bract-like upper leaves, together forming an elongated cluster along a finely hairy, square stem.

Flowers: About 1″ (2.5 cm) long; *calyx with prominent hump* on upper side; corolla 2-lipped, lips about equal; stamens 4.

Leaves: ¾–2½″ (2–6.5 cm) long, opposite; upper ones elliptical to lanceolate, untoothed; lower ones broader, toothed, often dropping off early.

Height: 1–2½′ (30–75 cm).

Flowering: May–July.

Habitat: Clearings and open woods.

Range: New York south to Florida, west to Texas, and northeast to Missouri, Kentucky, and Ohio.

Comments: The many different skullcaps are recognized by the tiny yet prominent projection, somewhat resembling a tractor seat, on the top of the calyx surrounding the base of the flower.

---

481 Wood Sage; Germander
Teucrium canadense

Description: A rhizomatous perennial with a *terminal, spike-like cluster of lavender-pink flowers* on a downy square stem.

Flowers: ¾″ (2 cm) long; corolla seemingly 1-lipped, with 5 lobes, long lower lobe flattened, lateral and upper lobes short; stamens 4, projecting.

Wood Sage

Leaves: 2–4" (5–10 cm) long, opposite, lanceolate toothed, densely hairy beneath.
Height: 1–3' (30–90 cm).
Flowering: June–September.
Habitat: Thickets, woods, and shorelines.
Range: Saskatchewan east to Newfoundland, south to Florida, west to Texas, and north to North Dakota; also in all western states and British Columbia.
Comments: The most distinctive feature of *Teucrium* species is the seemingly 1-lipped corolla. The common name Germander was originally altered from a Greek name for ground oak, *chamaidrys.* Two smaller, bushier species have been introduced from Europe into our range: Wood Sage *(T. scorodonia),* with yellow flowers, and Cut-leaved Germander *(T. botrys),* an annual with purplish flowers.

614 **Eastern Blue Curls**
Trichostema dichotomum

Description: A small sticky plant with *2–3 blue, 2-lipped flowers* at tips of short branches rising from leaf axils.
Flowers: ½–¾" (1.5–2 cm) long; corolla 2-lipped, upper lip 4-lobed, lower lip with 1 backward-curved lobe; *stamens 4, long, protruding, distinctly curved.*

Leaves: ¾–2½" (2–6.5 cm) long, opposite, narrow, oblong to lanceolate, untoothed.

Fruit: 4 nutlets, conspicuous within calyx.

Height: 6–30" (15–75 cm).

Flowering: August–October.

Habitat: Dry, open, sandy, or sterile sites.

Range: Ontario; Maine south to Florida, west to Texas, and northeast to Iowa, Illinois, and Michigan.

Comments: The long curved stamens characterize this dainty plant. The southern Perennial Blue Curls (*T. suffrutescens*) has tiny, oblong leaves and may not be a distinct species. False Pennyroyal (*T. brachiatum*) has short stamens not protruding from the flowers; it occurs from Quebec south to Georgia, west to Texas, and north to Minnesota.

LAUREL FAMILY
Lauraceae

Aromatic plants, mainly trees and shrubs, with inconspicuous, yellow or green flowers.

Flowers: Bisexual or unisexual, radially symmetrical. Sepals 6; petals absent; stamens 3–12; all these parts usually attached at base of ovary.

Leaves: Simple; leathery and evergreen, or thin and deciduous.

Fruit: Drupe or berry.

There are about 40 genera and 2,000 species, mostly in tropical regions. Some species are grown as ornamentals. Avocados (*Persea americana*), bay leaves (*Laurus nobilis*), and cinnamon (*Cinnamomum*) are produced by this family. Sassafras (*Sassafras albidum*) is a well-known tree in our area.

346 Spicebush
Lindera benzoin

Description: A deciduous shrub with dense clusters of tiny, *pale yellow flowers blooming from round buds along twigs before leaves appear.*

Flowers: ⅛" (3 mm) wide; sepals 6, petal-like; male and female flowers on separate plants.

Leaves: 2–5½" (5–14 cm) long, dark green, oblong, smooth, untoothed; exuding an *aromatic, spicy fragrance* when crushed.

Spicebush

Fruit: Ovoid, shiny, red, berry-like drupe.
Height: 6–17' (1.8–5.1 m).
Flowering: March–April.
Habitat: Swamps and woods.
Range: Ontario; Maine south to Florida, west to Texas, and north to Kansas, Iowa, Illinois, and Michigan.
Comments: In the northern part of its range this plant is thought of as the "forsythia of the wilds" because its early spring flowering gives a subtle yellow tinge to many lowland woods where it is common. A tea can be made from the aromatic leaves and twigs, and the dried and powdered fruit can be used as a spice. Hairy Spicebush *(L. melissifolia),* with hairy twigs, is the only other species in our range, found from North Carolina south to Georgia and in Mississippi, Arkansas, and Missouri. Spicebush fruit is eaten by birds and particularly relished by wood thrushes and veeries.

BLADDERWORT FAMILY
Lentibulariaceae

Herbs of moist or aquatic habitats, usually carnivorous, with flowers borne singly or in racemes.

Flowers: Bilaterally symmetrical. Sepals 2–5, united; petals 5, united, forming an upper and lower lip, lower lip with a backward-projecting spur; stamens 2; all these parts attached at base of ovary.
Leaves: Alternate or in rosettes, simple or highly divided.
Fruit: 1-chambered, several-seeded capsule, with a central column to which seeds attach.

This small family has about 5 genera and 200 species, distributed throughout the world.

---

303 Yellow Butterwort
Pinguicula lutea

Description:	*1 yellow flower* atop a leafless, glandular stalk rising from a *basal rosette of yellow-green, sticky leaves.*
Flowers:	¾–1½" (2–4 cm) wide; corolla tubular, with 5 flattish lobes, lower lip tongue-like and spurred.
Leaves:	To 2½" (6.5 cm) long, lying flat against ground, ovate to oblong, with *rolled edges.*
Height:	5–18" (12.5–45 cm).
Flowering:	February–May.
Habitat:	Moist sandy sites.
Range:	North Carolina south to Florida and west to Louisiana.
Comments:	Insects trapped by the sticky leaves of butterworts are digested by enzymes secreted by the leaves, which then absorb the nutrients. The genus name derives from the Latin *pinguis* ("fat") and alludes to the greasy-feeling upper surface of the leaves.

---

565 Common Butterwort
Pinguicula vulgaris

Description:	*1 violet flower* atop a leafless stalk rising from a *basal rosette of sticky leaves.*
Flowers:	⅜" (8 mm) wide; corolla tubular, with 5 flattish lobes, lower lip spurred.
Leaves:	To 2" (5 cm) long, lying flat against ground, yellow-green, strap-shaped, with uprolled edges, shiny, sticky.
Height:	2–6" (5–15 cm).

Flowering: June–August.
Habitat: On wet rocks and in open moist soil in limestone areas.
Range: Alaska and British Columbia east to Newfoundland and Greenland, south to New York, and west to Minnesota.
Comments: The very similar Violet Butterwort (*P. caerulea*) is found in sandy moist pinelands, bogs, and ditches from North Carolina south to Florida and Louisiana. Dwarf Butterwort (*P. pumila*) found from North Carolina south to Florida and Texas, is smaller, with a pale lavender flower less than ½″ (1.5 cm) long on a stalk usually less than 4″ (10 cm) high. Southern Butterwort (*P. primuliflora*), found from Georgia and Florida west to Mississippi, usually growing in running water, has a violet flower with a white ring in the center and a yellow beard inside the lower lip.

342 Horned Bladderwort
Utricularia cornuta

Description: A terrestrial, carnivorous plant with few scale-like bracts and *1–5 yellowish, 2-lipped, spurred flowers* near top of a brownish stalk; leaves delicate, mostly underground.
Flowers: About ¾″ (2 cm) long; corolla 2-lipped, lower lip large, helmet-shaped, with a backward-projecting *spur*.
Leaves: Minute, thread-like, subterranean, bearing minute bladders; occasionally on ground, seldom seen.
Height: 2–12″ (5–30 cm).
Flowering: June–September.
Habitat: Bogs and wet, sandy, muddy, or peaty shorelines.
Range: Alberta east to Newfoundland, south to Florida, west to Texas, and north to Arkansas, Illinois, Wisconsin, and Minnesota.
Comments: This species differs from many other bladderworts in being terrestrial rather than aquatic, although it may occasionally be submerged. It is able to

suck in very small organisms through the bladders on the leaves and digest them.

341 Swollen Bladderwort
Utricularia inflata

Description: An aquatic, carnivorous plant with several *yellow flowers in a raceme* rising above *spoke-like, inflated leafstalks.*

Flowers: ⅝" (16 mm) wide; corolla 2-lipped; 6–17 flowers per raceme.

Leaves: Submerged leaves repeatedly divided into thread-like segments bearing bladders; floating leaves to 3" (8 cm) long, in a whorl of 3–8, basal portion unbranched and inflated, terminal portion much divided into thread-like segments.

Height: Aquatic; flower stalks 1½–8" (4–20 cm) above water.

Flowering: May–November.

Habitat: Ponds and ditches.

Range: New York; New Jersey south to Florida, west to Texas and Oklahoma, and northeast to Tennessee and Kentucky.

Comments: When swimming prey, such as minute crustaceans, touch the trigger hairs surrounding the mouth of one of the bladders, a trapdoor-like flap of tissue swings inward and the bladder quickly expands, sucking the organisms inside; enzymes are secreted to dissolve the prey into nutritional elements for the plant. This is true of all *Utricularia.* Among the 15 species that occur in our area, only two have spoke-like, inflated leafstalks; the other one is Little Floating Bladderwort (*U. radiata*), a somewhat smaller plant with six or fewer flowers per raceme or sometimes a single terminal flower. Reversed Bladderwort (*U. resupinata*) and Purple Bladderwort (*U. purpurea*), both of which grow in water, have purple flowers. Piedmont Bladderwort (*U. olivacea*) is the most delicate in the genus; the entire plant is no wider than

a dime, with a yellowish-white flower less than ⅛″ (3 mm) long on a stalk ⅛–⅜″ (3–8 mm) tall. Greater Bladderwort *(U. vulgaris)* is a common yellow-flowering species that lacks the inflated leafstalks; its racemes have usually 6–20 flowers on stalks that curv backward when in fruit.

LILY FAMILY
Liliaceae

Mostly perennial herbs (some rather woody and tree-like growing from rhizomes, bulbs, or swollen, undergroun stems, often with showy flowers borne singly or in some times branched clusters.

Flowers: Usually bisexual, radially symmetrical. Calyx wit
3 (rarely 2) separate sepals, green or colored like petals corolla with 3 (rarely 2) separate petals; or 6 (rarely 4 petal-like segments united below into a tube; stamen usually 6; all these parts attached at base of ovary.
Leaves: Alternate, whorled, or basal; simple, usually narrow
Fruit: 3-chambered capsule, with at least 3 seeds; or a berry with at least 1 seed.

This extremely complex family has about 280 genera and 4,000 species. Many botanists subdivide this family, but i has not yet been agreed how many families there are, o which species belong to certain families. Many species including tulips *(Tulipa)* and day lilies *(Hemerocallis),* are handsome ornamentals. Species of asparagus *(Asparagus,* and onion *(Allium),* as well as of the medicinally usefu genus *Aloe,* are members of this family. A few species are poisonous.

---

141   **Colicroot; Stargrass**
Aletris farinosa

Description: *A spike-like cluster of small, white, urn-shaped flowers atop a sturdy round stem.*
Flowers: ¼–½″ (6–13 mm) long; sepals and petals 3 each, fused to form a swollen-based, 6-lobed tube, *mealy* on outside, with small bracts beneath; stamens 6, showy orange.
Leaves: 2–7″ (5–17.5 cm) long, pale green, lanceolate, long-pointed, in a basal

cluster; stem leaves very small, bract-like.

Fruit: Capsule, enclosed by persisting sepals and petals.

Height: 1–3′ (30–90 cm).

Flowering: May–August.

Habitat: Dry or wet meadows, peaty bog edges, and open woods in acidic soil.

Range: Ontario; New Hampshire and New York south to Florida and west to Texas, Oklahoma, and Arkansas; inland from Tennessee to Wisconsin and Michigan.

Comments: Until the 19th century the roots of this plant were collected and used medicinally to treat colic, hence one of its common names. In the South, Blunt-leaved Colicroot *(A. obovata)* has round white flowers. Yellow Colicroot *(A. aurea)* has round yellow flowers ¼″ (6 mm) wide. Flowers of this group resemble ladies' tresses *(Spiranthes),* members of the orchid family.

503 Wild Garlic
Allium canadense

Description: *A dome-like umbel of star-shaped, pink or whitish flowers* atop a stem rising from narrow, grass-like leaves near base of stem; plant exudes a *strong, onion-like odor.*

Flowers: About ½″ (1.5 cm) wide; sepals 3, petal-like; petals 3; flowers often replaced by ovoid bulblets, with or without long tails; bracts 2–3, beneath umbel.

Leaves: 6–18″ (15–45 cm) long, linear, flat.

Fruit: 3-lobed, few-seeded capsule.

Height: 8–24″ (20–60 cm).

Flowering: May–July.

Habitat: Low woods, thickets, and meadows.

Range: Ontario east to New Brunswick, south to Florida, west to Texas, and north to North Dakota.

Comments: This native perennial's edible bulb has a brown fibrous skin and, despite its common name, tastes like onion. However, if Wild Garlic is eaten by

dairy cows, the milk and butter may have a garlic taste; wheat contaminated with Wild Garlic bulblets may yield garlic-flavored bread. Field Garlic *(A. vineale)* is similar but has a strong garlic taste, greenish or purplish flowers, small, long-tailed bulbs, one bract beneath the umbel, and hollow, cylindrical leaves; introduced from Europe, it has become a problem weed occurring from Ontario east to Maine, south to Florida, west to Louisiana, and north to Nebraska, Iowa, and Wisconsin. *A. ampeloprasum* (known as Wild Leek, but not to be confused with *A. tricoccum*), naturalized from Europe, is 3–4½' (90–135 cm) tall with long flat leaves 1–2' (30–60 cm) long and a lavender flower cluster 2–2½" (5–6.5 cm) wide; it is found from New York, Ohio, and Illinois south to Georgia and Texas.

505 Nodding Onion
Allium cernuum

Description: *Rose or white, bell-shaped flowers* clustered in a *nodding umbel* atop a leafless stem.

Flowers: ¼" (6 mm) long; sepals 3, petal-like; petals 3.

Nodding Onion

Leaves:	4–16" (10–40 cm) long, basal, flat, linear.
Fruit:	3-lobed, few-seeded capsule.
Height:	8–24" (20–60 cm).
Flowering:	July–August.
Habitat:	Open woods and rocky soil.
Range:	Alberta east to Ontario and New York, south to Georgia, west to Texas, and north to Arkansas, Missouri, Nebraska, South Dakota, and Minnesota; also in much of West.
Comments:	This plant is closely related to Autumn Wild Onion (*A. stellatum*) but differs in its nodding umbel and earlier flowering.

504 Autumn Wild Onion
Allium stellatum

Description:	An erect, *dome-like umbel of lavender to pink flowers* atop a leafless stem rising above flat, grass-like, basal leaves.
Flowers:	¼" (6 mm) long, 6-pointed; sepals and petals 3 each, colored alike; stamens 6; umbel about 2½" (6.5 cm) wide.
Leaves:	6–18" (15–45 cm) long, ½–¾" (1.5–2 cm) wide, rising from bulb, with potent onion scent and flavor.
Fruit:	3-lobed, few-seeded capsule.
Height:	1–2' (30–60 cm).
Flowering:	July–September.
Habitat:	Rocky slopes, prairies, and shorelines.
Range:	Saskatchewan east to Ontario; North Dakota east to Michigan, south through Indiana, Missouri, and Arkansas to Texas, and north to South Dakota.
Comments:	The bulbs of wild onions have a strong flavor but can be eaten raw or parboiled. Early explorers ate them, and they were also used by settlers to treat colds, coughs, and asthma, and to repel insects. Chives (*A. schoenoprasum*) has hollow leaves and long, narrow, sharply pointed, lavender petals; it was introduced from Europe in the northeastern United States and in Canada from Alberta to Newfoundland.

176 Wild Leek; Ramp
Allium tricoccum

Description: Tall leaves rising from an *onion-like bulb* and withering before flowers appear, leaving a naked stem topped by a *domed cluster of creamy-white flowers;* plant has a mild onion taste.

Flowers: ¼" (6 mm) long, cup-like; sepals and petals 3 each, colored alike; cluster about 1½" (4 cm) wide.

Leaves: 8–12" (20–30 cm) long, ¾–2" (2–5 cm) wide, lanceolate-elliptical.

Fruit: 3-lobed, few-seeded capsule.

Height: 6–20" (15–50 cm).

Flowering: June–July.

Habitat: Woods.

Range: Manitoba east to Nova Scotia, south to Georgia and Alabama, west to Oklahoma, and north to Missouri, Iowa, and the Dakotas.

Comments: In late April, before this species comes into flower, the people of the Great Smoky Mountains gather the plants for their annual Ramp Festival. The foliage and bulbs can be used in salads and soups. Native Americans treated stings with juice from the crushed bulbs.

Wild Leek

111 Fly Poison
Amianthium muscitoxicum

Description: *A cylindrical cluster of small white flowers,* turning greenish purple with age, atop a mostly leafless stem.

Flowers: ½" (1.5 cm) wide; sepals and petals 3 each, persisting as fruit matures.

Leaves: Basal ones at least 1' (30 cm) long, ¾" (2 cm) wide, *grass-like,* blunt-tipped; those on stem much reduced, bract-like.

Fruit: Few-seeded, 3-beaked capsule.

Height: 1–4' (30–120 cm).

Flowering: June–July.

Habitat: Bogs, open woods, and low sandy sites.

Range: Pennsylvania and New Jersey south to Florida, west to Louisiana and Oklahoma, and northeast to Missouri, Kentucky, and West Virginia.

Comments: This plant contains a very poisonous alkaloid that can kill livestock. Pulp from a crushed bulb, mixed with sugar, is used to poison flies, hence the species name, from the Latin *muscae* ("flies") and *toxicum* ("poison"). Bunchflower *(Melanthium virginicum)* has a somewhat similar white flower; its three petals and three sepals have narrow, stalk-like bases with two dark glands on each; there are several spikes in a cluster.

Fly Poison

587 Wild Hyacinth
Camassia scilloides

Description: A leafless stem with *lavender to blue flowers in an elongated, loose-flowered cluster* rising from an underground bulb.

Flowers: 1" (2.5 cm) wide, 6-pointed; sepals and petals 3 each, colored alike; long *green bracts* flaring out beneath flowers.

Leaves: 8–16" (20–40 cm) long, basal, linear, *keeled.*

Fruit: Several-seeded, triangular to spherical capsule.

Height: 6–24" (15–60 cm).

Flowering: May–June.

Habitat: Moist meadows and open woods.

Range: Ontario; Pennsylvania south to Georgia, west to Texas, and north to Kansas, Iowa, and Wisconsin.

Comments: The bulbs of this plant were used by Native Americans and early explorers for food. The flower somewhat resembles the cultivated Easter Hyacinth, in the genus *Hyacinthus.* Grape Hyacinth (*Muscari botryoides*), which occasionally escapes from cultivation, has blue, ball-like flower clusters resembling bunches of grapes.

103 Devil's Bit; Fairy Wand
Chamaelirium luteum

Description: A wand-like stem, often *drooping at tip,* rising from a basal cluster of leaves and bearing a *densely packed, elongated, terminal cluster of tiny white flowers.*

Flowers: About ⅛" (3 mm) long; sepals and petals 3 each, very narrow; male and female flowers on separate plants; female cluster shorter, more slender.

Leaves: Basal leaves 3–8" (7.5–20 cm) long, spatulate to ovate; those on stem smaller, narrower.

Fruit: Several-seeded, elliptical capsule.

Height: 1–4' (30–120 cm); male plant shorter.

Flowering: May–July.

Habitat: Wet meadows, rich woods, and thickets.

Devil's Bit

Range: Massachusetts and New York south to
Florida, west to Louisiana, and north to
Arkansas, Illinois, and Michigan.

Comments: Fairy Wand is a most descriptive name
for this interesting plant. On the plants
with all male flowers, yellow stamens
create the more creamy color of the male
flower spike. This species can be readily
cultivated.

226, 343 Bluebead Lily; Yellow Clintonia
Clintonia borealis

Description: A stalk rising from a basal set of shiny,
bright green, oblong leaves and topped
by 3–6 *greenish-yellow to whitish, drooping,
bell-like flowers.*

Flowers: ¾–1" (2–2.5 cm) long; sepals 3, petal-
like; petals 3; stamens 6.

Leaves: 5–8" (12.5–20 cm).

Fruit: Blue berry, ¼" (8 mm) wide, with
few to many seeds.

Height: 6–15" (15–38 cm).

Flowering: May–August.

Habitat: Moist woods in acidic soil.

Range: Manitoba east to Newfoundland,
south to North Carolina and
Tennessee, and northwest to Illinois
and Minnesota.

Bluebead Lily

Comments: The clusters of the beautiful but
somewhat poisonous fruit are notable for
their extraordinary true-blue color. The
genus name honors the former governor
of New York, DeWitt Clinton
(1769–1828). A less common species,
White Clintonia *(C. umbellulata),* found
from New York south to Georgia and
Tennessee, has numerous erect white
flowers and black, fewer-seeded berries.

225 Nodding Mandarin
Disporum maculatum

Description: *Creamy white or yellowish flowers, spotted
with purple, hanging singly or in pairs from
ends of usually forked stems, directly
opposite top leaf.*
Flowers: 1″ (2.5 cm) long; sepals and petals 3
each, separate; stamens projecting.
Leaves: 2–4″ (5–10 cm) long, stalkless,
elliptical, hairy beneath, conspicuously
parallel-veined.
Fruit: Few-seeded, red, *hairy berry.*
Height: 8–24″ (20–60 cm).
Flowering: April–May.
Habitat: Moist wooded slopes.

Range: Ohio and Virginia south to Georgia
and Alabama.
Comments: A similar yellow-flowered species,
Yellow Mandarin (*D. lanuginosum*),
found in Ontario and from New York
south to Georgia and Arkansas, has
yellow, unspotted flowers and smooth
red berries. These plants resemble
bellworts (*Uvularia*).

266 Trout Lily; Dogtooth Violet
Erythronium americanum

Description: A pair of *brownish-mottled leaves*
sheathing base of stalk bearing
*1 nodding flower, yellow inside, bronzy
outside.*
Flowers: 1" (2.5 cm) wide; petals and petal-like
sepals 3 each, *curving backward;* stamens
6, with brownish or yellow anthers.
Leaves: 2–8" (5–20 cm) long, elliptical.
Fruit: Many-seeded, ovoid capsule.
Height: 4–10" (10–25 cm).
Flowering: March–June.
Habitat: Rich woods and meadows.
Range: Ontario east to Nova Scotia, south to
Georgia, west to Mississippi and
Arkansas, and north to Minnesota.
Comments: Recognized by its brown-mottled leaves,
this is one of our most common spring

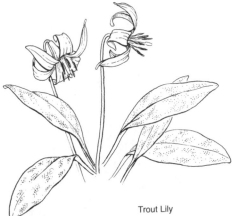

Trout Lily

wildflowers; it is found in sizable colonies. The common name Dogtooth Violet refers to the tooth-like shape of the white underground bulb. The name Trout Lily (a more suitable name, as the flower is not a violet) refers to the similarity between the leaf markings and those of Brown and Brook Trout. White Dogtooth Violet *(E. albidum)* has narrow, mottled leaves and white, bell-shaped flowers, often tinged with lavender on the outside; it is found from Ontario and New York south to Georgia, west to Texas, and north to South Dakota and Minnesota. Minnesota Adder's Tongue *(E. propullans),* found only in Minnesota, has pink flowers.

488 Swamp Pink
Helonias bullata

Description: A mostly leafless stem rising from a basal rosette of evergreen leaves and topped by a *dense cluster of small pink flowers.*

Flowers: About ½″ (1.5 cm) wide; cluster 1–3″ (2.5–7.5 cm) long; sepals and petals 3 each, pink; *stamens 6, blue-tipped.*

Swamp Pink

Leaves: Basal leaves 3–10" (7.5–25 cm) long, lanceolate; those on stem reduced to bracts.

Fruit: Several-seeded capsule.

Height: 1–3' (30–90 cm).

Flowering: April–May.

Habitat: Swamps and bogs.

Range: New Jersey south to Georgia.

Comments: This is a handsome and relatively rare wetland species. Its flowers should not be picked nor should the plants be removed from their natural habitat.

---

370 Day Lily
Hemerocallis fulva

Description: *A leafless stalk bearing several orange, funnel-shaped flowers and rising above sword-like, basal leaves.*

Flowers: 3½" (9 cm) wide; sepals 3, net-veined, *erect*; petals 3, *erect, with wavy edges;* stamens 6.

Leaves: 1–3' (30–90 cm) long, narrow, channeled.

Fruit: Many-seeded capsule.

Height: 2–4' (60–120 cm).

Flowering: May–July.

Habitat: Roadsides, meadows, and woodland borders.

Range: Throughout East, except Prairie Provinces and Newfoundland; scattered in West.

Comments: This native of Eurasia was introduced to our gardens and has escaped from cultivation. Apparently a hybrid, it does not set fertile seed but reproduces vegetatively from the roots. Each flower lasts only one day. In some areas, a doubled form, with more than the usual number of sepals and petals, is more common. Every part of the plant is mild and edible; the flower buds taste like green beans when cooked and served with butter. A smaller, yellow-flowered species, Yellow Day Lily (*H. lilioasphodelus*), has also escaped from cultivation; it, too, is edible.

361 Canada Lily; Meadow Lily; Wild Yellow Lily
Lilium canadense

Description:	1 to several long-stalked, *nodding flowers ranging in color from yellow to orange-red with dark spots,* atop a stem with *whorled leaves.*
Flowers:	2–3" (5–7.5 cm) wide; petals and *petal-like sepals* 3 each, *arching outward* but not backward; stamens 6, with brown anthers.
Leaves:	To 6" (15 cm) long, lanceolate, in whorls of 4–10, with veins beneath bearing minute prickles.
Fruit:	Many-seeded capsule.
Height:	2–5′ (60–150 cm).
Flowering:	June–August.
Habitat:	Wet meadows and woodland borders.
Range:	Ontario east to Nova Scotia, south to Georgia, west to Alabama, and north to Indiana; also in Arkansas, Kansas, and Nebraska.
Comments:	As many as 16–20 of these beautiful, stalked, nodding flowers may be borne on one plant, either rising from the axils of leafy bracts or in a group at the end of the flower stalk. The flower buds and roots were gathered and eaten by Native Americans. A similar midwestern species, Michigan Lily *(L. michiganense),* has petal-like segments that curve backward until they touch the flower tube; it is found from Ontario and Pennsylvania south to Alabama, west to Oklahoma, and north to South Dakota and Minnesota.

362 Wood Lily
Lilium philadelphicum

Description:	An erect stem bearing whorled leaves and 1–5 *upward-opening, orange flowers* with purplish-brown spots.
Flowers:	2" (5 cm) wide; petals and petal-like sepals 3 each, all tapering to a stalk-like base; stamens 6.

Wood Lily

Leaves: 1–4" (2.5–10 cm) long, lanceolate, at least upper ones in whorls of 3–8, or most leaves alternate.

Fruit: Many-seeded capsule.

Height: 1–3' (30–90 cm).

Flowering: June–August.

Habitat: Dry woods and thickets.

Range: British Columbia east to Quebec, south to Georgia, west to Arizona, and north to Montana.

Comments: This bulbous lily, one of our truly showy woodland species, is usually found in relatively dry sites. The bulbs were gathered for food by Native Americans. Among several southern species, Southern Red Lily (*L. catesbaei*), occurring in coastal states from Virginia to Louisiana, has alternate, lanceolate leaves pressed against the stem.

363 Turk's-cap Lily
Lilium superbum

Description: A tall stem bearing several somewhat *drooping, orange flowers* with reddish-brown spots and 6 *strongly curved-back, petal-like segments;* each segment with a green streak at base forming a *green star* at center of flower.

Flowers:	2½" (6.5 cm) long; stamens exposed, with dangling brown anthers.
Leaves:	2–6" (5–15 cm) long, lanceolate, alternate or whorled.
Fruit:	Many-seeded capsule.
Height:	3–7' (90–210 cm).
Flowering:	July–September.
Habitat:	Wet meadows, swamps, and woods.
Range:	New Hampshire and New York south t Florida, west to Mississippi and north t Arkansas, Illinois, and Ohio.
Comments:	This is the largest and most spectacular of our native lilies; up to 40 flowers have been recorded on a single plant. The recurved sepals and petals, which presumably resemble a type of cap worn by early Turks, and the showy, protruding stamens are distinctive features. Native Americans used the bulbs for soup. A somewhat smaller southern species, Carolina Lily *(L. michauxii),* found from Virginia and Kentucky south to Florida and Texas, also has strongly curved-back, petal-like segments, but it lacks the central star; its whorled leaves are thick and broadest toward the tip.

147 Canada Mayflower
Maianthemum canadense

Description:	A short, often zigzag stem topped by a small, dense cluster of *tiny, white, star-shaped flowers* and bearing 1–3 ovate leaves.
Flowers:	About ⅛" (4 mm) long; sepals 2, petal-like; petals 2; stamens 4.
Leaves:	1–3" (2.5–7.5 cm) long, *heart-shaped at base.*
Fruit:	Berry, with 1–2 seeds; initially green, turning a speckled, dull red in late summer and red in fall.
Height:	2–6" (5–15 cm).
Flowering:	May–June.
Habitat:	Upland woods and clearings.
Range:	Yukon and British Columbia east to Newfoundland, south to Georgia, and northwest through Tennessee, Iowa, and Nebraska to Montana.

Canada Mayflower

Comments: This common forest herb spreads by
rhizomes and frequently forms carpet-
like colonies. An unusual member of the
lily family, it has only two petals, two
sepals, and four stamens instead of the
usual 3–3–6 pattern. The somewhat
similar Three-leaved Solomon's Seal
(*Smilacina trifolia*) usually has three
elliptical leaves that taper at the base
and white flower parts in a 6-pointed,
star-like pattern; it is found in the East
in wet, boggy, or mossy areas from
Alberta east to Newfoundland and south
to Pennsylvania, Michigan, and
Minnesota.

1 **Indian Cucumber Root**
   Medeola virginiana

Description: Several *nodding, yellowish-green flowers*
emerging from center of a *whorl of 3
leaves* atop a slender, woolly, unbranched
stem; flower stalk sometimes bending
down below leaves.

Flowers: ½" (1.5 cm) long; sepals 3, petal-like,
curved-back; petals 3, curved-back;
stamens 6, reddish; ovary with *3 long,
brownish, curved-back stigmas.*

Leaves: Ovate to lanceolate, in 2 whorls; those
in whorl atop stem 1–3" (2.5–7.5 cm)

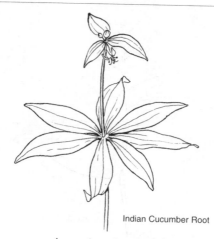

Indian Cucumber Root

long; those in whorl at midstem 2½–5″ (6.5–12.5 cm) long, 6–10 per whorl.

Fruit: Few-seeded, dark bluish-purple berry.
Height: 1–2½′ (30–75 cm).
Flowering: May–June.
Habitat: Moist woodlands.
Range: Ontario east to Nova Scotia, south to Florida, west to Louisiana, and north to Illinois and Minnesota.
Comments: The root, 2–3″ (5–7.5 cm) long, has a brittle texture and tastes and smells somewhat like cucumber. It was used by Native Americans for food, but digging it for such purposes today is not recommended because the plant is scarce. Birds are attracted to the fruit. At the time the berries turn bluish purple, the bases of the leaves whorled below them turn red.

4 Smooth Solomon's Seal
Polygonatum biflorum

Description: *2–10 pale green to whitish, bell-like flowers hanging* from leaf axils on an *arching stem.*
Flowers: ½–¾″ (1.5–2 cm) long, 6-lobed; stamens 6.
Leaves: 2–6″ (5–15 cm) long, stalkless, lanceolate to ovate, untoothed, light green, *smooth on both sides,* conspicuously parallel-veined.

Fruit: Few-seeded, blue-black berry.
Height: 8–84" (20–215 cm).
Flowering: May–June.
Habitat: Dry to moist woods and thickets.
Range: Saskatchewan east to New Brunswick, south to Florida, west to New Mexico, and north to Montana.
Comments: The graceful, arching stem, hanging flowers (often hidden under the leaves), and smooth leaves characterize this common plant. Hairy Solomon's Seal *(P. pubescens)* is distinguished by minute hairs along veins on the undersides of its leaves. The rhizome of these plants is jointed; the leafstalk breaks away from it, leaving a distinctive scar said to resemble the official seal of King Solomon. Native Americans and colonists used the starchy rhizome for food.

116 False Solomon's Seal
Smilacina racemosa

Description: An arching *stem tipped with a pyramidal panicle* of many small white flowers.
Flowers: ⅛" (3 mm) long; sepals 3, petal-like; petals 3; stamens 6.
Leaves: 3–6" (7.5–15 cm) long, alternate, elliptical, hairy beneath and along edges, conspicuously parallel-veined.
Fruit: Berry, with 1–2 seeds; initially green speckled with red, eventually translucent ruby red.

False Solomon's Seal

Height: 1–3' (30–90 cm).
Flowering: May–July.
Habitat: Woods and clearings.
Range: Throughout North America, except Arctic.
Comments: The feathery, creamy-white masses of flowers borne at the end of the stem distinguish this species from true Solomon's seals *(Polygonatum)*, which have hanging, bell-like flowers in the leaf axils. The rhizome lacks the seal-like scars of true Solomon's seals but exhibits circular stem scars. A smaller species, Star-flowered Solomon's Seal *(S. stellata)*, found throughout our area except for the coastal states from North Carolina to Texas, has a raceme of larger star-shaped flowers, ¼" (6 mm) long, leaves clasping the stem, and larger berries; at first the berries are striped with blackish red, eventually becoming completely blackish red. The Solomon's seals are sometimes included in the genus *Maianthemum*.

98 Featherbells
Stenanthium gramineum

Description: A large, narrow, pyramidal panicle of *small, white, nodding flowers* on a stem rising from a basal rosette of *folded, grass-like leaves*.
Flowers: About ½" (1.5 cm) wide; petals and petal-like sepals 3 each, sharp-pointed.
Leaves: 8–16" (20–40 cm) long, to ⅝" (16 mm) wide, narrow.
Fruit: Erect capsule.
Height: 3–5' (90–150 cm).
Flowering: June–September.
Habitat: Open, rocky woods and sandy bogs.
Range: Pennsylvania south to Florida, west to Texas, and northeast to Missouri and Michigan.
Comments: The genus name, from the Greek *stenos* ("narrow") and *anthos* ("flower"), refers to the narrow, pointed sepals and petals and to the shape of the panicle.

464 Rosy Twisted-stalk
Streptopus lanceolatus

Description: A branching plant with *zigzag stems and nodding, pink, bell-shaped flowers on short twisted stalks* rising near leaf axils.

Flowers: ⅜″ (8 mm) long; petal-like segments 6, pointed.

Leaves: 2½–6″ (6.5–15 cm) long, lanceolate, slightly clasping stem, conspicuously parallel-veined, edges fringed with hair or minute teeth.

Fruit: Many-seeded, red berry.

Height: 1–3′ (30–90 cm).

Flowering: April–July.

Habitat: Moist woods and thickets.

Range: Manitoba east to Newfoundland, south to Georgia, west to Tennessee, and north to Ohio, Michigan, Wisconsin, Minnesota, and Iowa; also from Alaska south through British Columbia to Oregon.

Comments: This plant is easily recognized by its branching habit and distinctly twisted flower stalks, reflected in the genus name, from the Greek *streptos* ("twisted") and *pous* ("foot" or "stalk"). The similar White Mandarin (*S. amplexifolius*) has greenish-white flowers and clasping leaves; it is found from Alberta to Newfoundland south to Virginia, North Carolina, and Tennessee, and in the north-central United States from Michigan to Minnesota.

---

38 Catesby's Trillium
Trillium catesbaei

Description: 1 somewhat nodding, *stalked, pink or white flower with strongly curved-back petals* and leaves in 3s.

Flowers: 2–3″ (5–7.5 cm) wide; sepals 3, *narrow;* petals 3; stamens 6, with yellow anthers.

Leaves: 1½–3″ (4–7.5 cm) long, elliptical, in a whorl of 3, stalked, usually with 3 or 5 main veins interconnected by cross-veins and a network of fine veins.

Fruit: Many-seeded berry.
Height: 8–20″ (20–50 cm).
Flowering: April–June.
Habitat: Woodlands.
Range: North Carolina south to Georgia and west to Alabama and Tennessee.
Comments: This beautiful pink trillium of the southeastern Piedmont and the adjacent Appalachian slopes may be confused with Large-flowered Trillium *(T. grandiflorum),* which has white flowers that turn pink with age. The flowers of Catesby's Trillium, however, face downward, and the sepals are narrower and more sickle-shaped than those of Large-flowered Trillium, which has upright flowers. The species name honors Mark Catesby (1679–1749), an English naturalist.

39 Nodding Trillium
Trillium cernuum

Description: *1 nodding white flower* on a short curved stalk *hanging beneath whorled leaves.*
Flowers: About 1½″ (4 cm) wide; sepals 3, green; petals 3, white (rarely pink), recurved; stamens 6, with pink anthers.
Leaves: 2½–4″ (6.5–10 cm) long, in a whorl of 3, diamond-shaped, barely stalked.
Fruit: Many-seeded berry.
Height: 6–24″ (15–60 cm).
Flowering: April–July.
Habitat: Moist, acidic woods and swamps.
Range: Saskatchewan east to Newfoundland, south to Virginia, west to Illinois, and north to the Dakotas.
Comments: The species name, from the Latin *cernuus* ("drooping" or "nodding"), refers to the stance of the flowers. Nodding Trillium is similar to Bent Trillium *(T. flexipes),* which has flowers with white rather than pink anthers.

405 Purple Trillium; Stinking Benjamin
Trillium erectum

Description:	*1 nodding flower, with an unpleasant odor,* rising on a stalk above a whorl of 3 broadly ovate, diamond-shaped leaves.
Flowers:	About 2½" (6.5 cm) wide; sepals 3, green; *petals 3, maroon or reddish brown;* stamens 6.
Leaves:	To 7" (17.5 cm) long, dark green, *net-veined,* sessile or nearly so.
Fruit:	Many-seeded berry.
Height:	8–16" (20–40 cm).
Flowering:	April–June.
Habitat:	Rich woods.
Range:	Manitoba east to Nova Scotia, south to Georgia and Alabama, and north to Illinois and Michigan.
Comments:	This common eastern trillium has foul-smelling flowers, which attract carrion flies that act as pollinators. Trilliums have net-veined leaves, rather than parallel-veined leaves, which are more typical of the lily family. As the genus name suggests, the flower parts and leaves of trilliums are arranged in multiples of 3, typical of the lily family. Vasey's Wake Robin *(T. vaseyi),* found in the southern Appalachians, is larger in all respects and has pleasant-smelling flowers.

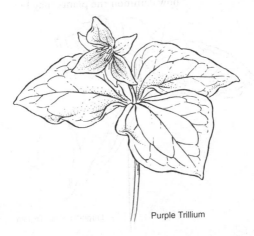

Purple Trillium

37 Large-flowered Trillium
Trillium grandiflorum

Description:	1 large, *waxy-white flower,* turning pink with age, on an *erect stalk* above a whorl of 3 broad leaves.
Flowers:	2–4" (5–10 cm) wide; sepals 3, green; petals 3, large, wavy-edged; stamens 6 with yellow anthers.
Leaves:	3–6" (7.5–15 cm) long, broadly ovate diamond-shaped, pointed, nearly stalkless.
Fruit:	Many-seeded berry.
Height:	8–18" (20–45 cm).
Flowering:	April–June.
Habitat:	Rich woods and thickets, usually in basic or neutral soil.
Range:	Ontario east to Nova Scotia, south to Georgia and Alabama, and north to Illinois and Minnesota.
Comments:	This largest and showiest trillium is frequently cultivated in wildflower gardens. The underground roots were gathered and chewed by Native Americans for a variety of medicinal purposes. The plants have also been picked and eaten as cooked greens or in salads. This practice may be fatal to the plant, since trilliums may die if the leaves are removed. No species of *Trillium* should be picked, no matter how common the plants may be.

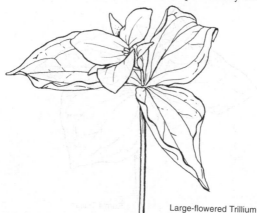

Large-flowered Trillium

375 Toadshade; Red Trillium
Trillium sessile

Description: *1 stalkless, carrion-scented flower, appearing closed,* directly above 3 whorled leaves.

Flowers: About 1½" (4 cm) long; sepals 3, green, spreading; petals 3, narrow, erect, reddish brown or maroon, rarely yellow; stamens 6.

Leaves: 1½–6" (4–15 cm) long, unstalked, ovate, *mottled with light and dark green.*

Fruit: Many-seeded berry.

Height: 4–12" (10–30 cm).

Flowering: April–June.

Habitat: Rich woods.

Range: New York south to North Carolina, Tennessee, and Alabama, west to Oklahoma, and north to Kansas, Illinois, and Michigan.

Comments: On warm days in places where this species is abundant, the woods can have the odor of decaying flesh as the aroma diffuses from the flowers. The flower somewhat resembles Purple Trillium *(T. erectum)* but is distinguished by its lack of stalk and closed appearance. There are several other species with stalkless flowers that appear closed: Sweet Betsy *(T. cuneatum),* an unpleasantly scented southeastern species with large flowers to 3" (7.5 cm) long and weakly mottled leaves; Yellow Trillium *(T. luteum),* found in southern and midwestern areas, with yellow, lemon-scented flowers and mottled leaves; Green Wake Robin *(T. viride),* also in southern and midwestern areas, with narrow, greenish, clawed petals to 2" (5 cm) long; and Prairie Trillium *(T. recurvatum),* a midwestern plant with erect, clawed, maroon petals, drooping sepals, and mottled, stalked leaves.

40 Painted Trillium
Trillium undulatum

Description: *1 erect stalked flower* with an *inverted, pink V* at base of each white, wavy-edged petal.

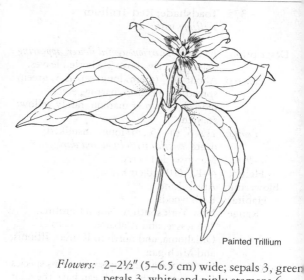

Painted Trillium

Flowers: 2–2½" (5–6.5 cm) wide; sepals 3, green; petals 3, white and pink; stamens 6, pink-tipped.
Leaves: 2½–5" (6.5–12.5 cm) long, in a whorl of 3, stalked, ovate, tapering to a point, bluish green, waxy.
Fruit: Many-seeded berry.
Height: 8–20" (20–50 cm).
Flowering: April–June.
Habitat: Moist, acidic woods and swamps.
Range: Ontario east to Nova Scotia, south to Georgia, and north to Tennessee, Ohio, and Michigan.
Comments: This is one of the most attractive woodland trilliums. It is easily recognized by the splash of pink in the center of the white flower.

78, 265 Sessile Bellwort
Uvularia sessilifolia

Description: *1–2 creamy yellow or whitish, drooping flowers atop an angled stem with sessile leaves.*
Flowers: About 1" (2.5 cm) long, narrowly bell-shaped; sepals 3, petal-like; petals 3; stamens 6.
Leaves: 1¾–3" (4.5–7.5 cm) long, oblong, light green above, whitish below.

Sessile Bellwort

Fruit: Several-seeded capsule.
Height: 6–12″ (15–30 cm).
Flowering: April–June.
Habitat: Woods and thickets.
Range: Manitoba east to Nova Scotia, south to Florida, west to Louisiana, and north to Oklahoma, Missouri, Iowa, and the Dakotas.
Comments: This common woodland wildflower has a near relative, Perfoliate Bellwort (*U. perfoliata*), whose stem appears to pierce the leaves; the interior surface of the flowers is roughened with small glands. A bigger version, Large-flowered Bellwort (*U. grandiflora*), has bright yellow flowers and leaves minutely hairy beneath; it reaches a height of 20″ (50 cm). Mountain Bellwort (*U. pudica*) has shiny leaves and stems in clumps and is similar to Sessile Bellwort, as is Florida Bellwort (*U. floridana*), which has a small, leaf-like bract on the flower stalk. At one time these plants were thought to be good for treating throat diseases because the drooping flowers resemble the uvula (the soft lobe hanging into the throat from the soft palate), hence the genus name.

16 False Hellebore; Indian Poke
Veratrum viride

Description: A stout plant with *greenish, star-shaped, hairy flowers* in a branching cluster and *large leaves* clasping stem.

Flowers: About ½" (1.5 cm) wide; sepals 3, petal-like; petals 3; stamens 6, curved.

Leaves: 6–12" (15–30 cm) long, 3–6" (8–15 cm) wide, large, *pleated, parallel-veined.*

Fruit: Capsule.

Height: 2–7' (60–210 cm).

Flowering: May–July.

Habitat: Swamps, wet woods, and wet meadows.

Range: Quebec east to Nova Scotia, south to Georgia and Alabama, and north to Tennessee, West Virginia, and Ohio; also from Alaska and Northwest Territories south to Wyoming, Oregon, and California.

Comments: The ribbed, yellow-green leaves of this wetland species are unmistakable in spring; the plant withers away before summer. The roots and the foliage are poisonous; the foliage can be lethal, but it has a burning taste and is usually avoided by animals. It is said that some Native American chiefs were selected only if they survived eating this plant. The two other false hellebores in our area have hairless flowers: Small-flowered False Hellebore (*V. parviflorum*), with leaves stalked and mostly basal, occurs in drier woods from Virginia and Kentucky south to Georgia and Alabama; Wood's False Hellebore (*V. woodii*), with greenish- to blackish-purple flowers, is found in dry woods from Iowa and Missouri east to Ohio and south to Florida, Alabama, Tennessee, and Oklahoma.

181 Turkey Beard
Xerophyllum asphodeloides

Description: *Small white flowers in a dense, elongated cluster* on a stem with short, bristle-like leaves toward top and many *long, grass-like leaves in a dense clump at base.*

Flowers: About ½" (1.5 cm) wide; petals and petal-like sepals 3 each, widely spreading.

Leaves: Those at base to 1½' (45 cm) long, ⅟₁₆" (2 mm) wide, rough-edged; those on stem gradually reduced to bracts.

Fruit: Capsule, with few to several seeds.

Height: 2–4' (60–120 cm).

Flowering: May–July.

Habitat: Dry sandy pinelands and mountain woods in strongly acidic soil.

Range: New Jersey, Maryland, and West Virginia south to Georgia and west to Alabama and Tennessee.

Comments: *Xerophyllum* has only two species, this and Bear Grass *(X. tenax)*, a similar plant of western North America. The genus name, from the Greek *xeros* ("dry") and *phyllon* ("leaf"), refers to the dry, wiry, basal leaves of this showy plant. It is difficult to cultivate and seldom blooms in gardens.

132 Camas
Zigadenus leimanthoides

Description: A tall smooth stem rising from a fibrous-coated bulb and bearing an elongated, branching cluster of small, *creamy or yellow, star-like flowers.*

Flowers: About ⅜" (8 mm) wide; sepals and petals 3 each, colored alike, with a small gland at base.

Leaves: Basal leaves to 2' (60 cm) long, about 3" (7.5 cm) wide, *grass-like;* upper ones much shorter, sharp-pointed.

Height: 1–4' (30–120 cm).

Flowering: June–August.

Habitat: Sandy pinelands and bogs.

Range: New Jersey south to Florida, west to Texas, and northeast to Tennessee, Kentucky, and West Virginia.

Comments: There are several species of *Zigadenus,* mostly in the South and West. The leaves, stems, flowers, and seeds of most species are poisonous and, particularly in the West, endanger livestock. Large-flowered Zigadenus *(Z. glaberrimus),*

3–5' (90–150 cm) high, has whitish-
yellow flowers with two glands at
the base of each sepal and petal; it is
found in wet pinelands and bogs
from Virginia south to Florida and
west to Texas.

131 Death Camas
Zigadenus nuttallii

Description: *Grass-like, basal leaves* and a leafless
stem rising from an onion-like bulb
and bearing a branching cluster of
numerous *greenish-white, star-like
flowers.*

Flowers: About ½" (1.5 cm) wide; sepals and
petals 3 each, similar, with a gland at
base.

Leaves: 8–24" (20–60 cm).

Fruit: Few-seeded capsule.

Height: 1–2½' (30–75 cm).

Flowering: April–May.

Habitat: Prairies and open woodlands.

Range: Kansas east to Missouri and Tennessee,
south to Louisiana, west to Texas, and
north to Oklahoma.

Comments: Livestock can be poisoned by grazing
on this plant or by feeding on hay
containing any part of it. The toxic
substance, also present in the bulb,
is an alkaloid that causes vomiting,
breathing difficulties, and coma in
humans. This species is similar to Camas
(*Z. leimanthoides*) but has a papery, not
fibrous, coat on the bulbous base.

FLAX FAMILY
Linaceae

Herbs, rarely shrubs or trees, with flowers in forked clusters.

Flowers: Radially symmetrical. Sepals 5, separate; petals 5,
separate, each with a narrow base, readily dropping off;
stamens 10, joined by bases of filaments; all these parts
attached at base of ovary.

Leaves: Alternate or opposite, simple.

Fruit: 5-chambered, several-seeded capsule; rarely a drupe.

There are about 6 genera and 220 species, found nearly throughout the world. Linseed oil and the fibers from which linen is woven are obtained from Common Flax *(Linum usitatissimum)*.

---

620 Wild Blue Flax
Linum lewisii

Description: *A tufted perennial with leafy stems* bearing loose, much-branched *clusters of blue flowers.*

Flowers: 1–1½" (2.5–4 cm) wide; sepals 5, with unfringed edges, much shorter than petals; petals 5.

Leaves: ½–¾" (1.5–2 cm) long, numerous, *linear.*

Height: 1–2' (30–60 cm).

Flowering: May–July.

Habitat: Prairies and plains.

Range: Throughout western North America, east through Northwest Territories to Ontario, and south to Michigan, Minnesota, South Dakota, Texas, Arkansas, and Louisiana.

Comments: This perennial is related to Common Flax *(L. usitatissimum),* an annual plant and source of the fiber from which linen is made and of the seeds from which linseed oil is derived. Common Flax escapes from cultivation to waste places; unlike Wild Blue Flax, at least some of its sepals have fringed edges.

LOGANIA FAMILY
Loganiaceae

Herbs, shrubs, or trees with flowers often clustered in spikes.

Flowers: Radially symmetrical. Calyx with 4–5 lobes; corolla tubular or bell-shaped, with 4–5 lobes; stamens 4–5; all these parts usually attached at base of ovary.
Leaves: Opposite, simple, with smooth or toothed edges.
Fruit: Berry, capsule, or drupe.

There are about 20 genera and 500 species, widely distributed in warm and tropical regions. Some are cultivated as ornamentals.

267 Yellow Jessamine
Gelsemium sempervirens

Description: A *woody vine* with short clusters of very *fragrant, yellow, trumpet-shaped flowers* in leaf axils.

Flowers: About 1" (2.5 cm) wide at flaring mouth, 1½" (4 cm) long; corolla 5-lobed.

Leaves: 1–4" (2.5–10 cm) long, evergreen, opposite, untoothed, lanceolate, edges rolled.

Fruit: Few-seeded capsule.

Height: Vine; stems to 17' (5.1 m) long.

Flowering: January–April.

Habitat: Thickets, dry woods, and sandy areas.

Range: Virginia and Tennessee south to Florida and west to Texas and Arkansas.

Comments: This high-climbing vine is very common in parts of the South; it is frequently found in abandoned fields. The flowers, leaves, and roots are poisonous and may be lethal to livestock. Rankin's Yellow Jessamine (*G. rankinii*), with odorless flowers, occurs in swamps from North Carolina south to Florida and Louisiana.

421 Indian Pink
Spigelia marilandica

Description: *Trumpet-shaped flowers, red outside and yellow inside,* in a narrow, 1-sided, curving, terminal cluster.

Flowers: 1" (2.5 cm) wide; corolla with a narrow tube and 5 sharp-pointed lobes; stamens 5, protruding.

Leaves: 2–4" (5–10 cm) long, opposite, ovate to lanceolate-ovate, stalkless.

Fruit: Few-seeded capsule.

Height: 1–2' (30–60 cm).

Flowering: March–June.

Habitat: Moist woods.

Range: Maryland, Virginia, and Kentucky south to Florida, west to Texas and Oklahoma, and northeast to Missouri and Indiana.

Comments: This plant does very well in gardens. It blooms from the bottom of the cluster

upward, and the flowering season can be prolonged by removing the flowers as they wither.

LOOSESTRIFE FAMILY
Lythraceae

Herbs, shrubs, or trees with flowers in racemes or branched clusters.

Flowers: Radially or bilaterally symmetrical. Sepals 4–6, joined at base to form a tube to which petals and stamens attach; petals as many as sepals, separate, often crumpled like crepe paper, or absent; stamens usually twice as many as sepals, in 2 series of different lengths; all these parts joined to tube attached at base of ovary.
Leaves: Usually opposite or whorled, simple.
Fruit: Many-seeded capsule, with 1–6 chambers.

There are about 24 genera and 500 species, distributed throughout the world except for very cold regions. A few species yield dyes, such as henna, derived from the leaves of Henna *(Lawsonia inermis);* some, including Crape Myrtle *(Lagerstroemia indica),* are grown as ornamentals.

529 Swamp Loosestrife; Water Willow
Decodon verticillatus

Description: *Arching stems* with showy, *deep pink flowers* in tufts in axils of upper, opposite or whorled, *willow-like leaves.*
Flowers: About ½" (1.5 cm) long, bell-shaped; petals 5, wedge-shaped; 5 short stamens, 5 long and protruding stamens.
Leaves: 2–6" (5–15 cm) long, lanceolate.
Fruit: Round capsule.
Height: Arching stems to 8' (2.4 m) long.
Flowering: July–August.
Habitat: Swamps, bogs, and edges of shallow water.
Range: Ontario east to Nova Scotia, south to Florida, west to Texas, and north through Arkansas to Minnesota.
Comments: The many intertwining, arching stems of this herb- to shrub-like plant may form sizable patches at the edges of lakes and sluggish streams or on floating bog mats. Wherever a stem is under the

water, air-filled, buoyant, spongy tissue
may develop. Despite the common name
and its willow-like leaves, the plant is
not related to willows.

569 Purple Loosestrife
Lythrum salicaria

Description: An erect stem with a *spike of purple-pink
flowers* above *opposite or whorled, unstalked
leaves.*

Flowers: ½–¾" (1.5–2 cm) wide; *petals 4–6,
wrinkled;* stamens as many or twice as
many as petals; flowers of 3 types, each
with different stamen and pistil lengths.

Leaves: 1½–4" (4–10 cm) long, lanceolate to
linear, rounded to heart-shaped at base,
stalkless.

Height: 2–4' (60–120 cm).

Flowering: June–September.

Habitat: Wet meadows, floodplains, and roadside
ditches.

Range: Throughout much of North America,
except parts of far north and parts of
southern United States.

Comments: This showy, magenta-flowered
perennial, a European introduction, may
cover acres of wetlands, providing a
truly spectacular sight. Classified as a
noxious weed in many states, it is an
aggressive species and tends to crowd
out native aquatics valuable to
waterfowl and other wildlife.

MALLOW FAMILY
Malvaceae

Herbs, shrubs, or rarely small trees, often velvety, with star-
like or branched hairs; flowers borne singly or in branched
clusters.

Flowers: Usually bisexual, radially symmetrical. Sepals 3–5,
partly united; petals 5, separate, bases often joined to base
of stamen tube; stamens many, joined by filaments into a
tube; all these parts attached at base of ovary.

Leaves: Simple, often palmately veined and lobed or deeply
divided, with stipules.

Fruit: At least 5 chambers, each with 1 to few seeds, separating from one another or forming a many-seeded capsule; rarely a berry.

There are about 75 genera and 1,500 species, many in
tropical America. Many species, such as Rose-of-Sharon
(*Hibiscus syriacus*) and Hollyhock (*Althaea rosea*), are grown
as ornamentals. The vegetable okra is the edible fruit of
Okra (*Hibiscus esculentus*). The hairs of seeds of *Gossypium*
provide the fiber cotton.

259 Velvetleaf; Pie-maker
Abutilon theophrasti

Description:	A tall plant with large, *heart-shaped, velvety leaves* and stalked *yellow flowers* in leaf axils.
Flowers:	1" (2.5 cm) wide; petals 5; stamens numerous, forming a tube.
Leaves:	To 8" (20 cm) long.
Fruit:	Many-seeded, flat-topped capsule.
Height:	1–6' (30–180 cm).
Flowering:	July–October.
Habitat:	Open, disturbed areas, roadsides, and fields.
Range:	Throughout North America, except Newfoundland and far north.
Comments:	A native of India, this tall plant has distinctively beaked fruit, the sides of which resemble the crimped edges of a piecrust, hence its common name Pie-maker. The fiber China jute, used especially in making rugs, can be obtained from the stem.

398 Hibiscus; Rose Mallow
Hibiscus coccineus

Description:	A large plant with *big, showy, crimson flowers* in upper leaf axils.
Flowers:	6–8" (15–20 cm) wide; petals 5; stamens many, yellow, forming a tube around style and red, disk-like stigmas; very narrow bracts beneath calyx.
Leaves:	*Palmately divided into narrow, pointed, toothed segments,* each 2–10" (5–25 cm) long.
Fruit:	Many-seeded capsule.

Height: 3–10' (90–300 cm).
Flowering: June–September.
Habitat: Swamps and freshwater and brackish marshes.
Range: Virginia south to Florida and west to Louisiana and Arkansas.
Comments: This very showy species, typical of the mallow family, is sometimes cultivated. It is certainly one of the loveliest of our native flowers.

440 Swamp Rose Mallow
Hibiscus moscheutos

Description: A tall coarse plant with *large, white or pink, 5-lobed, musky-smelling flowers*, often with a reddish or purple center, usually borne singly on short stalks from leaf axils.
Flowers: 4–7" (10–17.5 cm) wide; stamens numerous, forming a column around style, with anthers outside; 5 style branches and stigmas protruding from end of stamen column; narrow, green, leaf-like bracts beneath calyx.
Leaves: 4" (10 cm) long, yellow-green, ovate, toothed or lobed, pointed, white-downy beneath.
Fruit: Many-seeded capsule.
Height: 3–8' (90–240 cm).
Flowering: July–September.
Habitat: Tidal marshes and inland, freshwater marshes.
Range: Ontario; Massachusetts and Pennsylvania south to Florida, west through Kansas to New Mexico, and northeast to Kansas, Illinois, and Wisconsin.
Comments: This strikingly showy species is often found along edges of salt marshes but is more common in upper-valley wetlands. The lovely Flower-of-an-hour *(H. trionum)* is a weedy annual, 1–2' (30–60 cm) tall, with palmately divided leaves, a flower 2" (5 cm) wide, pale yellow with a purple band running up one side of each petal, and a dark-veined, inflated calyx enclosing the capsule; it occurs throughout the East, except Newfoundland.

441 Seashore Mallow
Kosteletzkya virginica

Description: A large plant bearing *pink stalked flowers,* with yellow stamens, *in leaf axils or atop stems.*

Flowers: 1½–2½" (4–6.5 cm) wide; petals 5; stamens numerous, forming a tubular column around style, with anthers outside.

Leaves: 2–5" (5–12.5 cm) long, gray-green, ovate, slightly hairy or rough, with *divergent, basal lobes.*

Fruit: *Flat ring of 1-seeded sections.*

Height: 1–3' (30–90 cm).

Flowering: May–October.

Habitat: Brackish to nearly freshwater marshes.

Range: New Jersey and Pennsylvania south to Florida and west to Texas.

Comments: This mallow is especially abundant in southern Louisiana. It is distinguished from *Hibiscus* by the flat ring of fruit segments. Some authorities divide this species into several varieties.

439 Musk Mallow
Malva moschata

Description: *Pink (sometimes white or lavender), musk-scented flowers* in scattered groups at branch ends.

Flowers: 1½" (4 cm) wide; petals 5; stamens with anthers fused into a column around style.

Leaves: 3–4" (7.5–10 cm) wide, *palmately divided into very narrow, toothed lobes.*

Fruit: *Hairy ring of 1-seeded sections.*

Height: 8–24" (20–60 cm).

Flowering: June–October.

Habitat: Disturbed areas.

Range: Manitoba east to Newfoundland, south to North Carolina, west to Missouri, and north to Illinois and Wisconsin; also from British Columbia southeast to Wyoming, and in California.

Comments: A native of Europe, this beautiful perennial is now widely naturalized in North America in fields and old gardens and along roadsides. The highly divided

leaves and the hairy ring of fruit segments are distinctive. Vervain Mallow (*M. alcea*), a European introduction, differs only in having little, star-like clusters of hairs on the stems; it is naturalized from Saskatchewan east to Nova Scotia, south to New Jersey, and west to Illinois and Wisconsin.

63 Cheeses
Malva neglecta

Description: A *low trailing plant* with small, *whitish-lavender flowers* in leaf axils.

Flowers: ½–¾" (1.5–2 cm) wide; petals 5, notched at tips; stamens united in a column around style.

Leaves: About 1½" (4 cm) wide, *round, scallop-edged,* prominently veined.

Fruit: Ring of 1-seeded, round, flattish sections.

Height: Creeper; stems to 2' (60 cm) long.

Flowering: April–October.

Habitat: Disturbed areas.

Range: Throughout North America, except far north and parts of southeastern United States.

Comments: This low-growing mallow is considered a weed of barnyards and waste places, but the foliage and flowers are attractive. The flowers are somewhat like hollyhocks (*Alcea*) of the mallow family (Malvaceae) but much smaller. The fruit is distinctive, consisting of many round, flattish sections forming a ring, which, as the common name implies, resembles a wheel of cheese. The related and very similar Low Mallow (*M. rotundifolia*) has white flowers about ¼" (6 mm) wide.

402 Carolina Mallow
Modiola caroliniana

Description: A *low creeping perennial with reddish-orange to purple-red flowers* on slender stalks in leaf axils.

Flowers: To ½" (1.5 cm) wide; petals 5; stamens united to form a tube around style; 3 bracts beneath calyx.

Leaves: ¾–2¾" (2–7 cm) long, palmately divided into 6–7 coarsely toothed lobes.

Fruit: *Ring of 1-seeded sections.*

Height: Creeper; stems to 3' (90 cm) long.

Flowering: February–June.

Habitat: Lawns, gardens, disturbed sites, and wet areas.

Range: New Jersey and Pennsylvania south to Florida and west to Texas and Oklahoma; also in Oregon, California, and Arizona.

Comments: This widely distributed species, abundant in the South, is often a lawn weed. It has many branches, and roots at the nodes.

MEADOW BEAUTY FAMILY
Melastomataceae

Herbs, trees, or shrubs in tropical regions, with flowers generally in clusters.

Flowers: Radially symmetrical. Calyx tubular, with usually 4–5 lobes; corolla with 4–5 petals; stamens twice as many as petals; all these parts usually attached at top of ovary.

Leaves: Usually opposite, simple, edges smooth or toothed; often with 3 main veins and ladder-like, connecting veins.

Fruit: Capsule or berry.

There are about 200 genera and 4,000 species, mostly in tropical regions, particularly South America. Plants in the genus *Rhexia* are the only members of the family that occur in the northeastern United States and adjacent Canada. Melastomataceae has also been known as the melastome family.

453 Virginia Meadow Beauty
Rhexia virginica

Description: Several *pink flowers* in broad, terminal clusters on a sturdy, *slightly winged, 4-sided stem* with sides nearly equal in width.

Flowers: 1–1½" (2.5–4 cm) wide; petals 4;

Virginia Meadow Beauty

stamens 8, prominent, with anthers
opening by pores.

Leaves: ¾–2½" (2–6.5 cm) long, opposite, ovate
to elliptical, toothed, rounded at base,
with 3 prominent veins.

Fruit: *Urn-shaped,* 4-pointed capsule.

Height: 1–2' (30–60 cm).

Flowering: July–September.

Habitat: Moist open places.

Range: Ontario and Newfoundland south to
Florida, west to Texas, and north to
Oklahoma, Missouri, and Wisconsin.

Comments: Members of this genus have a distinctive
urn-shaped fruit that Thoreau once
compared to a little cream pitcher.
Although the family is mostly tropical,
at least 10 species are native to the
United States. Awn-sepal Meadow
Beauty *(R. aristosa)* is similar to Virginia
Meadow Beauty but has very narrow
leaves and sharp-pointed sepals; it is
found in pine barrens from New Jersey
south to Alabama. Maryland Meadow
Beauty *(R. mariana)* has four lop-sided,
pink to white petals and a 4-sided stem
with two opposite sides narrower than
the other two; it is found in moist open
places from Massachusetts south to
Florida, west to Texas, and north to
Kansas, Missouri, and Wisconsin.

MOONSEED FAMILY
Menispermaceae

Woody vines, occasionally herbaceous, with clusters of inconspicuous flowers.

Flowers: Unisexual, radially symmetrical. Sepals variable in number, petal-like, larger than petals, those in male (staminate) flowers in 2–4 whorls; petals commonly 6–9, separate; stamens 3 or 6 or numerous; all these parts attached at base of ovary.
Leaves: Sometimes alternate, usually simple, lobed or 3-parted.
Fruit: Berry-like drupe.

There are about 70 genera and 400 species, mostly tropical, with a few extending into temperate regions. Some species are grown as ornamentals.

118 Common Moonseed
Menispermum canadense

Description: *A climbing vine with small, greenish-white flowers* in small loose clusters in axils of *large leaves;* each leafstalk attached just inside leaf's edge.

Flowers: About ⅛" (4 mm) wide; sepals 4–8; petals 4–8, shorter than sepals; stamens 12–24, longer than sepals.

Leaves: 4–7" (10–17.5 cm) wide, ovate to shield-shaped, sometimes shallowly lobed.

Fruit: Black, 1-seeded, berry-like drupe.

Height: Vine; stems to 12' (3.6 m) long.

Flowering: June–July.

Habitat: Woodland edges, thickets, and streambanks.

Range: Manitoba east to Quebec, south through Vermont and New Hampshire to Florida, west to Texas, and north to North Dakota.

Comments: Poisonous when eaten in large quantities, the fruit of this plant ripens in September and resembles whitish-powdered grapes.

BUCKBEAN FAMILY
Menyanthaceae

Perennial herbs of freshwater ponds or marshes with flower in showy clusters.

Flowers: Radially symmetrical. Calyx with usually 5 unite sepals; corolla with usually 5 united petals; stamens usu ally 5; all these parts attached at base of ovary.
Leaves: Simple or with 3 leaflets.
Fruit: 1-celled, many-seeded capsule.

There are 5 genera and 30 species, found in temperat regions and tropical Asia. Indigenous people have made us of the leaves of some species for medicinal purposes Menyanthaceae is sometimes included in the gentian family (Gentianaceae).

---

212 Buckbean; Bogbean
Menyanthes trifoliata

Description:	Large, long-stalked leaves and racemes or narrow clusters of *white or purple-tinged, star-like flowers* atop stout stalks, about as high as leaves.
Flowers:	Corolla about ½″ (1.5 cm) wide, forming a tube ¼–⅜″ (6–9 mm) long (about twice as long as calyx), with 5–6 pointed lobes covered with short hairs.
Leaves:	4–12″ (10–30 cm) long; leaflets 3, each 1½–5″ (4–12.5 cm) long, broadly lanceolate.
Fruit:	Capsule, with many small, hard, smooth, shiny seeds.
Height:	Aquatic; leaves and flower stalks 4–12″ (10–30 cm) above water.
Flowering:	May–August.
Habitat:	Bogs and shallow lakes.
Range:	Alaska east to Greenland and Newfoundland, south to North Carolina, west to Ohio, Missouri, and Nebraska, and north to Minnesota and North Dakota; widely distributed in West.
Comments:	This easily recognized species also occurs in Eurasia. In at least some localities, its flowers are of two kinds: those with

short styles and long stamens and
those with long styles and short
stamens. The common name Bogbean
alludes to the plant's habitat and to
its small, bean-like seeds; these durable
seeds have been found deeply buried in
bogs. The leaves were sometimes used
in Europe as a substitute for hops in
beer brewing, and various medicinal
applications of this species have been
recorded.

205 Floating Heart
Nymphoides aquatica

Description: A water lily–like plant with *floating,
heart-shaped, long-stalked leaves* and a flat-
topped cluster of *small white flowers*
rising just above leaves.

Flowers: ½–¾" (1.5–2 cm) wide; petals 5, nearly
separate.

Leaves: 2–8" (5–20 cm) long, thick, green
above, very veiny beneath.

Fruit: Capsule, maturing underwater, with
many rough seeds.

Height: Aquatic; flowers just above water.

Flowering: July–September.

Habitat: Ponds and slow streams.

Range: Along coastal plain from Maryland
and Delaware south to Florida and
west to Texas.

Comments: The genus name refers to the plant's
resemblance to *Nymphaea* water lilies.
However, its clusters of small white
flowers with only five petals make it
quite different from the single, many-
petaled water lilies. *N. cordata*, also
called Floating Heart, has smaller
green leaves mottled with purple above
and smooth beneath; it occurs from
Ontario and Newfoundland south to
Pennsylvania and Florida, and west to
Louisiana. Yellow Floating Heart
(*N. peltata*), a yellow-flowered species
from Europe with fringed corolla lobes,
is established in Quebec and from New
England southwest to Texas.

INDIAN PIPE FAMILY
Monotropaceae

Saprophytic, perennial herbs, usually somewhat fleshy ar
white, yellow, brown, pink, or red, lacking chlorophyll.

Flowers: Radially symmetrical; borne singly or in raceme
or heads. Sepals usually 4–5, occasionally joined at bas
or absent, when sepals absent bracts on upper stem ma
be sepal-like; petals usually 4–5, separate or unitec
stamens usually twice as many as petals, with anthe.
opening by slits or terminal pores; all these parts attache
at base of ovary.
Leaves: Simple, reduced to scales.
Fruit: Usually a 5-chambered capsule, sometimes a berry.

There are about 10 genera and 12 species, mostly in th
temperate regions of the Northern Hemisphere. The root
of these plants grow in a close association with fungi, fror
which they receive all their nutrition and water; the fung
also form an association with the roots of trees, making
Monotropaceae indirect parasites. Classification is equivo
cal: Some botanists place the species in a family o
their own, as is done here; other botanists include them i
the heath family (Ericaceae) or in the wintergreen family
(Pyrolaceae).

423 Pinesap; False Beechdrops
Monotropa hypopithys

Description: A saprophytic, *red, pink, lavender, or
yellow plant with several vase-like, nodding
flowers* on a downy, scaly stem; stem and
flowers colored alike.
Flowers: About ½" (1.5 cm) long; 4 petals on
lateral flowers, 5 on terminal one.
Leaves: Reduced to scales to ½" (1.5 cm) long,
clasping stem, more numerous toward
base of plant.
Fruit: Erect, ovoid capsule.
Height: 4–16" (10–40 cm).
Flowering: June–November.
Habitat: Upland woods, usually in acidic soil.
Range: Alberta east to Newfoundland, south to
Florida, west to Texas, and north to
Nebraska and Minnesota; widely
distributed in West.
Comments: The plant in the photograph is an
autumn-flowering one, characterized by

Pinesap

the red color. Early-flowering forms are
yellow. Like its single-flowered relative,
Indian Pipe *(M. uniflora)*, Pinesap does
not carry on photosynthesis but obtains
its nourishment from fungi associated
with roots, often those of oaks and pines.
The closely related, similar Sweet
Pinesap *(Monotropsis odorata)* has united
petals; it occurs in Maryland, Virginia,
and Kentucky south to Florida and
Alabama. Sweet Pinesap has two
flowering periods: February to April,
when the flowers produced are faded
rose colored and very fragrant, and
September and October, when the
flowers are lavender and odorless.

77 Indian Pipe
Monotropa uniflora

Description: A saprophytic, *white to red (rarely pink)*
plant with a thick, *translucent stem*
covered with scaly bracts and terminated
by *1 nodding flower.*

Flowers: ½–1" (1.5–2.5 cm) long, white or
salmon-pink; petals 4–5; stamens
10–12; pistil 1.

Leaves: Reduced to scales.

Fruit: Ovoid capsule, becoming enlarged and
erect as seeds mature.

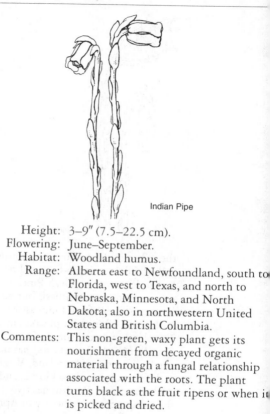

Indian Pipe

Height: 3–9″ (7.5–22.5 cm).
Flowering: June–September.
Habitat: Woodland humus.
Range: Alberta east to Newfoundland, south to
            Florida, west to Texas, and north to
            Nebraska, Minnesota, and North
            Dakota; also in northwestern United
            States and British Columbia.
Comments: This non-green, waxy plant gets its
            nourishment from decayed organic
            material through a fungal relationship
            associated with the roots. The plant
            turns black as the fruit ripens or when it
            is picked and dried.

LOTUS FAMILY
Nelumbonaceae

Aquatic plants with large leaves, floating or held above
water, and showy, long-stalked, solitary flowers.

Flowers: Radially symmetrical. Sepals and petals many, similar in shape, outer ones greenish; stamens many; pistils
many, each buried in a cavity in a top-shaped receptacle.
Leaves: Round, with a centrally attached leafstalk; flat when
floating, somewhat bowl-shaped or resembling an inside-
out umbrella when above water.
Fruit: Acorn-like nut.

There is only 1 genus with 2 species, one North American, one Asian. Both species are used as ornamental water
plants.

260 **American Lotus;
Water Chinaquin**
Nelumbo lutea

Description: An aquatic with fragrant, *pale yellow
flowers* on stalks above water and *long-
stalked leaves above water or floating on
surface.*

Flowers: 6–10" (15–25 cm) wide, fragrant;
petals and petal-like sepals numerous,
intergrading into one another; stamens
many; center of flower a large, upside-
down, cone-shaped receptacle 3–4"
(7.5–10 cm) wide, with *numerous
cavities,* each containing a pistil.

Leaves: 1–2' (30–60 cm) wide, leafstalk
centrally attached; bowl-shaped when
held above water, flat and disk-like
when floating.

Height: Aquatic; leaves to 3' (90 cm) above
water.

Flowering: July–September.

Habitat: Ponds and quiet streams.

Range: Ontario; Maine south to Florida,
west to Texas, and north to Nebraska,
Iowa, and Minnesota.

Comments: This member of the lotus family is
recognized by its large round leaves
attached at their middle (umbrella
fashion) to the leafstalk; by its
yellow, many-petaled flowers;
and by the upside-down, cone-
shaped, seed-bearing receptacle
in the center of the flower. It covers
extensive areas along the Mississippi
River and elsewhere. The pink-
flowered Sacred Lotus *(N. nucifera),*
introduced from Asia, is naturalized
in places, mostly in the southeastern
United States; it is notable for its
long-lived seeds, which can retain
their ability to germinate even after
hundreds of years. The kernel of the
nut-like fruit of both species, while
still green, can be boiled for a few
minutes, salted and buttered, and
eaten, tasting like roasted sweet corn.

WATER LILY FAMILY
Nymphaeaceae

Perennial, aquatic herbs, usually with round or heart-shaped, often floating leaves and large flowers either floating or held above water on long stalks.

Flowers: Radially symmetrical. Sepals 3–14, often intergrading into many petals; stamens many; pistil narrowing beneath a broad stigma.
Leaves: Simple, with very long stalks.
Fruit: Each pistil opening on one side or forming a nutlet, or all pistils growing together as a leathery berry.

There are about 5 genera and 50 species, found in aquatic habitats throughout temperate and tropical regions. Several are cultivated as pond ornamentals.

262 Yellow Pond Lily; Bullhead Lily
Nuphar variegata

Description: An aquatic with *yellow, cup-like flowers.*
Flowers: 1½–2½″ (4–6.5 cm) wide; sepals 6, showy, petal-like; petals numerous, small, stamen-like; stamens numerous, in several rows; pistil greenish, with 6–25 lines radiating from center.
Leaves: 3–15″ (7.5–38 cm) long, *floating or raised above water surface,* heart-shaped, with V-shaped notch at base.
Fruit: Many-seeded, more or less egg-shaped berry.
Height: Aquatic; flowers and leaves sometimes to 1′ (30 cm) above water.
Flowering: May–September.
Habitat: Pondsides and quiet streams.
Range: Yukon south and east across Canada to Newfoundland, south to Maryland and Pennsylvania, west to Illinois, Iowa, and Kansas, and northwest to Idaho.
Comments: This is the most familiar yellow pond lily in the Northeast. Common Spatterdock *(N. advena)* is very similar; it occurs in the southern United States and as far north as New England, New York, Ohio, Michigan, and Wisconsin.

Small Pond Lily *(N. microphylla)* has leaves only 2–4″ (5–10 cm) long, flowers 1″ (2.5 cm) wide, and a stigmatic disk with only 6–10 rays; it occurs in Canada and only as far south as New Jersey. Arrowleaf Pond Lily *(N. sagittifolia),* found from Virginia to northeastern South Carolina, has leaves three times as long as wide. The leaves and long, stem-like petioles and flower stalks of water lilies and pond lilies die back each year and contribute to the organic buildup in lakes and marshes.

261 **Yellow Water Lily;**
Mexican Water Lily;
Banana Water Lily
Nymphaea mexicana

Description: An aquatic with *bright yellow flowers and floating leaves.*

Flowers: 4–5″ (10–12.5 cm) wide; sepals 4, green; petals and stamens numerous; pistil 1, many-seeded.

Leaves: 3–5″ (7.5–12.5 cm) wide, ovate, dark green with brown blotches above, reddish brown with dark dots below.

Height: Aquatic; flowers about 4″ (10 cm) above water.

Flowering: Spring–summer.

Habitat: Quiet water of ditches and ponds.

Range: North Carolina south to Florida and west to Texas and Oklahoma; sparingly introduced in West.

Comments: The lovely flowers are open from midday to late afternoon. When the plants are crowded, the leaves may rise above the water. The plant was first discovered in Mexico, which accounts for the species name and one of its common names. The common name Banana Water Lily refers to the plant's clusters of twining roots, which resemble tiny bananas. This species is considered a noxious weed in California.

61 Fragrant Water Lily
Nymphaea odorata

Description: An aquatic with *fragrant, white or pink flowers* and flat *floating leaves.*

Flowers: 3–5″ (7.5–12.5 cm) wide; sepals 4, green; petals many, narrowing in width toward center, intergrading with numerous yellow stamens; pistil 1, many-seeded.

Leaves: 4–12″ (10–30 cm) wide, shiny green above, purplish red beneath.

Height: Aquatic.

Flowering: June–September.

Habitat: Quiet water of ditches and ponds.

Range: Saskatchewan east to Newfoundland, south to Florida, west to Texas, and north to Nebraska and Minnesota; widely distributed in West.

Comments: This is one of the most common white water lilies; its flowers and leaves float on the water. The flowers usually open only from early morning until noon. The stomata, tiny openings on the leaf surface through which carbon dioxide and other gases pass into the plant, are on the upper, shiny, water-repellent leaf surface rather than on the lower surface, as is the case for most dryland plants. The leafstalk is soft and spongy and can be used as a drinking "straw"; it has four main air channels for the movement of gases, especially oxygen, from the leaves to the large rhizomes buried in the muck, which are frequently eaten by muskrats.

EVENING PRIMROSE FAMILY
Onagraceae

Usually herbs, rarely shrubs or trees, with often showy flowers borne singly or in racemes, spikes, or branched clusters.

Flowers: Usually radially symmetrical. Sepals usually 4, mostly separate; petals 4, mostly separate; sepals and petals united into a long, short, or barely discernible tube at base; stamens usually 4 or 8; all these parts attached at top of ovary.

leaves: Alternate or opposite, simple.
ruit: Usually a 4-chambered, many-seeded capsule; sometimes a berry or a hard, nut-like structure.

There are about 17 genera and 675 species, found world-
vide but especially abundant in temperate regions of
vestern North and South America. Evening primroses
Oenothera), fuchsias *(Fuchsia),* and lopezias *(Lopezia)* are pop-
ılar ornamentals. The name primrose is derived from a Latin
vord meaning "first"; true primroses (Primulaceae), unre-
ated to this family, are among the first flowers to bloom in
he spring. Apparently, in the early 1600s when an eastern
J.S. species of *Oenothera* was being described, its sweet scent
eminded the botanist of the wild primroses of Europe; he
ıamed these plants accordingly, and the name stuck. The
ıame Onagraceae refers to *Oenothera,* the flowers of which
ppen late in the afternoon or evening; other genera have
lowers that bloom early in the morning. In some, flowers
ast only one day, but in others they may last several days.

473 Fireweed
Chamerion angustifolium

Description: A terminal, spike-like cluster of *deep
pink (occasionally white) flowers* and
alternate, narrow, *willow-like leaves* on a
tall stem.

Flowers: 1" (2.5 cm) wide; petals 4, spreading;
stamens 8; style hairy at base, longer
than stamens, with a 4-parted stigma
at end.

Fireweed

Leaves: To 8" (20 cm) long, lanceolate to linear.
Fruit: Many-seeded capsule, each seed with a tuft of white hairs aiding in seed dispersal by wind.
Height: 2–6' (60–180 cm).
Flowering: July–September.
Habitat: Recently cleared woodlands, especially burned-over areas.
Range: Alberta east to Newfoundland, south to North Carolina, west to Tennessee, and northwest to Illinois, Iowa, and North Dakota; also in much of West.
Comments: This is a showy, post-fire invader and a spectacular sight in mass. The seeds are dispersed far and wide by their long, white, silky hairs. The plant spreads rapidly in wildflower gardens. Bees value it as a source of nectar, and the very young shoots and leaves can be eaten as cooked greens. A similar, lower plant, River Beauty *(C. latifolium),* is a northern and western species occurring in our area from Alberta to Newfoundland; its style is hairless and much shorter than the stamens. Recent work at the genetic level has shown that *Chamerion,* recognized by its alternate leaves, is distinct from *Epilobium* (with leaves opposite, at least near base), the genus in which Fireweed was formerly placed.

193 Enchanter's Nightshade
Circaea lutetiana

Description: *Small white flowers* in elongated, terminal clusters.
Flowers: Less than ¼" (6 mm) wide; sepals 2, curving back; *petals 2, deeply cleft,* appearing as 4; *stamens 2;* cluster to 8" (20 cm) long.
Leaves: 2½–5" (6.5–12.5 cm) long, dark green, opposite, thin, ovate, pointed, slightly toothed, decreasing in size toward flower cluster.
Fruit: Nut-like, with 1–2 seeds, *covered with hooked bristles,* oblong to ovoid, bending downward at maturity.
Height: 1–3' (30–90 cm).

Flowering: June–August.
Habitat: Shady rich woods.
Range: Manitoba east to Nova Scotia, south to Georgia, west to Louisiana, and northwest to Oklahoma, Wyoming, and North Dakota.
Comments: This is one of the few 2-petaled flowers; it is considered to be a subspecies, *canadensis,* of a Eurasian plant. The hooked bristles of the fruit are an adaptation for dispersal by animals. A smaller species of more northern distribution, Smaller Enchanter's Nightshade *(C. alpina),* has smaller leaves that are more coarsely toothed. Both the genus and common names derive from the mythological enchantress Circe, who is said to have used a poisonous member of this genus in her sorcery.

500 Hairy Willow Herb
Epilobium hirsutum

Description: Branching, *hairy stems topped with rose-pink to purple flowers* in upper leaf axils.
Flowers: About 1″ (2.5 cm) wide; petals 4, *notched;* stigma 4-cleft, forming a cross in center of flower.
Leaves: 1½–4″ (4–10 cm) long, mostly opposite, lanceolate or oblong, sharply toothed, hairy on both sides, unstalked.
Fruit: Many-seeded capsule, each seed with a tuft of white hairs aiding in seed dispersal by wind.
Height: 2–5′ (60–150 cm).
Flowering: July–September.
Habitat: Waste places, roadsides, and meadows.
Range: Ontario east to Nova Scotia, south to Maryland, west to Illinois, and north to Wisconsin; also from British Columbia south to Oregon.
Comments: This plant, naturalized from Europe, is similar to Fireweed *(Chamerion angustifolium)* but differs in the hairiness of the leaves, reflected in the species name, and in having notched petals. Several other much smaller-flowered willow herbs occur in the East.

519 Southern Gaura; Morning Honeysuckle
Gaura angustifolia

Description: Small, *pink or white flowers in wand-like, branched clusters* at ends of rather straggl[y] branches.

Flowers: ¼" (6 mm) wide; calyx cylindrical, with 3–4 lobes; petals 3–4; stamens 6–8, protruding; style with a 4-cleft stigma.

Leaves: 1½–3" (4–7.5 cm) long, narrowly lanceolate, sharply toothed, progressively smaller toward top, frequently clustered.

Fruit: Nut-like.

Height: 2–5' (60–150 cm).

Flowering: May–September.

Habitat: Open woods, sandy fields, roadsides, an[d] dunes.

Range: North Carolina south to Florida and west to Mississippi.

Comments: The rather inconspicuous flowers, which open near sunset and fade the next day, are at first white but soon turn pink. The fruit is distinctive in that it does not split open when mature.

238 Seedbox
Ludwigia alternifolia

Description: A many-branched, smooth-stemmed plant with *1 short-stalked, yellow flower* in each upper leaf axil.

Flowers: About ½" (1.5 cm) wide; *sepals 4, broad, green, of unequal length;* petals 4.

Leaves: 2–4" (5–10 cm) long, lanceolate, pointed at both ends, untoothed.

Fruit: Stalked, many-seeded, nearly *cubical capsule,* opening by pores at top.

Height: 2–3' (60–90 cm).

Flowering: June–September.

Habitat: Swamps and wet soil.

Range: Ontario; Massachusetts and New York south to Florida, west to Texas, and north to Nebraska, Iowa, and Wisconsin.

Comments: The few other species of seedboxes in our area have sessile leaves. Seedboxes

are mostly wetland plants and bear distinctive, box-like fruit, square on top and filled with many seeds. Other members of the genus do not have such fruit.

338 Evening Primrose
Oenothera biennis

Description:	*Lemon-scented, large, yellow flowers* atop a leafy stalk; stem hairy, often purple-tinged.
Flowers:	1–2" (2.5–5 cm) wide; sepals 4, reflexed, rising from top of long tube; petals 4; stamens 8, prominent; stigma cross-shaped.
Leaves:	4–8" (10–20 cm) long, slightly toothed, lanceolate.
Fruit:	Many-seeded capsule.
Height:	2–5' (60–150 cm).
Flowering:	June–September.
Habitat:	Fields and roadsides.
Range:	Alberta east to Newfoundland, south to Florida, west to Texas, and north to North Dakota; also in much of West.
Comments:	The flowers of this night-blooming biennial open in the evening and close by noon or earlier. Those of some plants open fully in about 15 minutes. The plant takes two years to complete its life cycle, with basal leaves becoming established the first year and flowering occurring the second. The first-year roots are edible, and the seeds are important as bird feed. Hawk moths are among the pollinators of this plant.

443 Showy Evening Primrose
Oenothera speciosa

Description:	*Nodding buds, opening into pink or white flowers,* in upper leaf axils on slender, downy stems.
Flowers:	2½–3" (6–7.5 cm) wide; petals 4, broad, sometimes white with pink stripes.
Leaves:	2–3" (5–7.5 cm) long, wavy-edged or pinnately cleft, linear to lanceolate.

Showy Evening Primrose

Fruit: Many-seeded capsule.
Height: 8–24″ (20–60 cm).
Flowering: May–July.
Habitat: Prairies, plains, and roadsides.
Range: Connecticut and Pennsylvania south to Florida, west to Texas, and north to Nebraska and Iowa; also in southwestern United States.
Comments: This hardy, drought-resistant species can form colonies of considerable size. The flowers may be as small as 1″ (2.5 cm) wide under drought conditions. The plant is frequently grown in gardens and escapes from cultivation.

ORCHID FAMILY
Orchidaceae

Perennial herbs with complicated, unusual, often beautiful flowers borne singly or in spikes, racemes, or branched clusters.

Flowers: Usually bisexual, bilaterally symmetrical; usually twisting one-half turn during development, the bottom of flower becoming the top. Sepals 3, separate, often petal-like; petals 3, separate, lower petal usually different from upper 2 and modified into an elaborate lip, often bearing a backward-projecting spur or sac; stamens 1–2, united with style and stigma, forming a complex structure (column); all these parts attached at top of ovary.

aves: Usually alternate, simple.
uit: Usually a 1-chambered, rarely 3-chambered, many-seeded capsule.

There are 1,000 genera and about 20,000 species, most undant in the tropics, where they frequently grow on her plants (elsewhere they are usually terrestrial), but me species grow even in the Arctic. This is possibly the rgest family of flowering plants in number of species, but is rarely, if ever, dominant. Vanilla is obtained from the uit of the tropical genus *Vanilla.* Many species are grown beautiful greenhouse novelties. Certain species and hy-rids, once very rare and difficult to acquire, are now repro-uced in great numbers by cloning. Others are being driven extinction by habitat destruction. The elaborate flower as highly specialized relationships with pollinators. Pollen usually held together in masses and in many cases must e properly positioned on the insect for pollination of an-her flower to occur. Natural pollination is so precise that ese plants have not evolved other ways of preventing hy-ridization, making possible the production of many hy-rids, even between unrelated species, by artificial ollination.

472 Swamp Pink; Dragon's Mouth
Arethusa bulbosa

Description: A smooth stalk bearing 1–3 long, tubular, sheathing, nearly bladeless leaves and topped by *1 bright pink, fragrant flower.*

Flowers: About 2″ (5 cm) long; lip petal *showy, spotted with darker pink, crested* with 3 rows of yellow or whitish hairs; upper petals 2, arching over lip; sepals 3, erect.

Leaves: Absent when plant is in flower; growing to 9″ (22.5 cm) as fruit matures.

Height: 5–10″ (12.5–25 cm).

Flowering: May (in southern part of range)–August (in northern part).

Habitat: Bogs, swamps, and wet meadows.

Range: Saskatchewan east to Newfoundland, south to South Carolina, and north and northwest to Ohio, Illinois, and Minnesota.

Comments: This genus was named for Arethusa, the

fountain nymph. The flower suggests an animal's open mouth; its unusual lip petal serves as a platform for insects, especially bumblebees, to enter the flower for nectar and pick up the powdery pollen masses as they leave.

476 Grass Pink
Calopogon tuberosus

Description: *2–10 fragrant pink flowers in a spike-like cluster,* opening sequentially up a leafless stalk.

Flowers: 1½" (4 cm) long; *lip petal yellow-bearded,* standing erect over 3 sepals and 2 similar upper petals spreading forward and laterally; column incurved, somewhat petal-like.

Leaves: To 1' (30 cm) long, solitary, *basal, grass-like.*

Height: 6–20" (15–50 cm).

Flowering: Principally March–August; throughout year in Florida.

Habitat: Bogs and bog meadows and acidic, sandy or gravelly sites.

Range: Manitoba east to Newfoundland, south to Florida, west to Texas, and north to Kansas, Missouri, Illinois, and Minnesota.

Comments: This delicate, sweet-smelling orchid often springs from peat moss and is easily recognized by the bearded lip petal and solitary, grass-like leaf. Its genus name is derived from the Greek for "beautiful beard," and the species name is Latin for "tuberous." Bearded Grass Pink *(C. barbatus),* found from North Carolina southward, has pink flowers that all open together, whereas the flowers of *C. tuberosus* open successively. Pale Grass Pink *(C. pallidus),* found from North Carolina south to Florida and west to Louisiana, has pale pink to whitish flowers and is smaller in all respects than *C. tuberosus.*

468 Calypso; Fairy Slipper
Calypso bulbosa

Description:	1 showy, nodding flower with an *inflated, slipper-like lip petal.*
Flowers:	1½–2″ (4–5 cm) long; lip petal white, blotched with purple, bearded with yellow hairs, with 2 horn-like points at "toe"; 3 sepals and 2 similar upper petals purplish pink, narrow, above lip.
Leaves:	About 3″ (7.5 cm) long, *solitary, basal,* ovate, edges wavy; withering after plant flowers, replaced by an overwintering leaf.
Height:	3–8″ (7.5–20 cm).
Flowering:	May–July.
Habitat:	Cool, damp, mossy, mainly coniferous woods.
Range:	Alaska south and east across Canada to Newfoundland, south to Vermont, and from Michigan west to South Dakota; also in much of West.
Comments:	This short perennial rises from a small tuber; it is the only species in this genus found in northern latitudes. It was named for the sea nymph Calypso, of Homer's *Odyssey,* who detained the willing Odysseus on his return to Troy; like Calypso, the plant is beautiful and prefers secluded haunts.

Calypso

471 Rosebud Orchid
Cleistes divaricata

Description: A long stalk topped by *1 flower with very long, narrow, spreading, brownish or purplish-green sepals and pink petals.*

Flowers: About 2" (5 cm) long; upper petals and lip petal forming a cylindrical tube; 1 narrow, leaf-like bract just below flower to 4" (10 cm) long.

Leaves: To 8" (20 cm) long, solitary, basal, oblong-lanceolate, above midstem.

Height: 1–2' (30–60 cm).

Flowering: April–July.

Habitat: Wet to dry grasslands, pine barrens, and thickets.

Range: North Carolina (rarely southern New Jersey) south to Florida.

Comments: This orchid, the only species in this genus, is related to the genus *Pogonia.* Although it can occupy either wet or dry sites, it apparently requires a habitat with very acidic soil.

380 Spotted Coral Root
Corallorhiza maculata

Description: A saprophytic orchid with 10–30 *purplish-brown to yellowish flowers along a yellowish or brownish, leafless flower stalk* bearing several sheaths toward base.

Flowers: About ¾" (2 cm) long; lip petal white, squarish, spotted with crimson; 3 short, petal-like sepals above and 2 longer upper petals embracing upper part of lip.

Leaves: Reduced to tubular sheaths to 3" (7.5 cm) long.

Height: 6–20" (15–50 cm).

Flowering: July–September.

Habitat: Moist to dry, upland, deciduous or coniferous forests.

Range: Alberta east to Newfoundland, south to Georgia, and north and west to Tennessee, Illinois, Iowa, Nebraska, and North Dakota; Texas; also throughout West.

Comments: This northern orchid is the most common and largest coral root. It lacks chlorophyll and gets its nourishment from fungi in

its coral-like underground stem. Several smaller species differ in color and in the nature of the lip petal. Five species of *Corallorhiza* occur in our area, among them Wister's Coral Root *(C. wisteriana),* which flowers from March to May, before any of the others, and Late Coral Root *(C. odontorhiza),* also known as Autumn Coral Root, with flowers less than ¼" (5 mm) long; *C. odontorhiza* is the last of these species to flower, appearing from late August to October.

379 Striped Coral Root
Corallorhiza striata

Description: A saprophytic orchid with 10–20 *purplish- or brownish-red flowers in an elongated cluster* along a purplish stalk bearing 3–4 tubular sheaths.
Flowers: About 1¼" (3 cm) long; lip petal tongue-shaped, white, striped with purplish red, or all purple; 3 sepals and 2 upper petals curving forward, hood-like.
Leaves: Reduced to tubular sheaths.
Height: 8–20" (20–50 cm).
Flowering: May–August.
Habitat: Rich woods.
Range: Alberta east to Quebec, south to New York, west to the Dakotas and Nebraska; Texas; also throughout West.
Comments: The most attractive of several coral roots, this orchid can withstand cold but not heat and thus cannot be successfully cultivated south of its natural range. Coral roots lack chlorophyll and get their nourishment from organic material absorbed from the coral-like, much-branched underground stem.

469 Pink Lady's Slipper;
Pink Moccasin-flower
Cypripedium acaule

Description: A leafless stalk bearing 1–2 (usually 1) flowers with a *distinctive pink, inflated,*

slipper-like lip petal, veined with red and with a fissure down front.

Flowers: Lip petal about 2½" (6.5 cm) long; 3 sepals and 2 upper petals greenish brown, spreading; upper petals lanceolate, narrower than sepals.

Leaves: 1 basal pair, each to 8" (20 cm) long, oval, ribbed, dark green above, silvery-hairy beneath.

Height: 6–15" (15–38 cm).

Flowering: April–July.

Habitat: Dry to moist forests, especially pinewoods; often in humus mats covering rock outcrops.

Range: Northwest Territories and Alberta east to Newfoundland, south to Georgia, west to Alabama, and northwest through Illinois to Minnesota.

Comments: One of the largest native orchids, this species is found both in low sandy woods and in higher, rocky, mountain woods. Several hundred of these striking flowers can sometimes be counted within a small area. Nevertheless, like other woodland wildflowers, it should not be picked. Nor should it be dug up for transplanting, as lady's slippers reproduce poorly and are very difficult to grow in wildflower gardens. The genus name derives from the Latin for "Venus's foot."

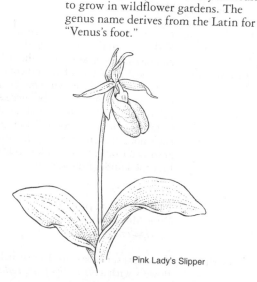

Pink Lady's Slipper

306 Large Yellow Lady's Slipper
Cypripedium calceolus

Description: A leafy stalk topped by 1–2 fragrant flowers with an *inflated, yellow, pouch-shaped lip petal.*

Flowers: Lip petal about 2" (5 cm) long; upper petals 2, spirally twisted, greenish yellow to brownish purple; sepals seemingly 2, greenish yellow, lanceolate, 1 above and 1 below lip, lower sepal actually 2 united sepals.

Leaves: To 8" (20 cm) long, usually 3–5, oval to elliptical, conspicuously parallel-veined.

Height: 8–28" (20–70 cm).

Flowering: April–August.

Habitat: Bogs, swamps, and rich woods.

Range: Alberta east to Newfoundland, south to Georgia, west to Mississippi, Arkansas, and Oklahoma, and north to North Dakota; also in most of West.

Comments: The species name derives from Latin and means "a little shoe." Native Americans made a preparation from the roots, which was drunk as a treatment for worms. Large Yellow Lady's Slipper is recognized as the variety *pubescens.* Another variety is known as Small Yellow Lady's Slipper (variety *parviflorum*), which reaches a height of about 22" (55 cm) and has very fragrant

Large Yellow Lady's Slipper

flowers, a lip petal only ¾–1½" (2–4 cm) long, and brownish upper petals; it is found mostly in limestone wetlands from Kansas and Nebraska east to Vermont and south to Georgia. Southern Lady's Slipper *(C. kentuckiense),* a rare species known from only about 150 populations, is found in Texas and Oklahoma east to Alabama, Kentucky, and Virginia; its lip petal, cream-colored rather than yellow, is 2–2½" (5–6 cm) long.

467 Showy Lady's Slipper
Cypripedium reginae

Description: A stout, hairy, often twisted, *leafy stalk* bearing 1–3 large flowers with a *white and pink, pouch-like lip petal.*

Flowers: Lip petal 1–2" (2.5–5 cm) long, white, rose-pink in front, often veined with purple or deep pink, with many shallow, vertical furrows; 3 sepals and 2 upper petals waxy-white, ovate-lanceolate, spreading.

Leaves: To 10" (25 cm) long, usually 3–7, ribbed, elliptical.

Height: 1–3' (30–90 cm).

Flowering: May–August.

Habitat: Swamps and moist woods, especially limestone sites.

Range: Saskatchewan east to Newfoundland, south to North Carolina, west to Arkansas, and north to Minnesota and North Dakota.

Comments: This plant, the tallest and most beautiful of our northern native orchids, is especially common in the Great Lakes region. It has been overpicked and should be protected from further exploitation. The glandular hairs of the foliage may cause a rash similar to that caused by Poison Ivy *(Toxicodendron radicans).* Small White Lady's Slipper *(C. candidum),* a smaller plant, has a little flower with a white lip petal; it occurs in limestone soil and boggy places from Saskatchewan east to

Ontario and New York, south to
Virginia and Alabama, west to
Missouri, and north to Nebraska
and the Dakotas.

7 Greenfly Orchid
Epidendrum conopseum

Description: *An epiphytic orchid* with numerous
grayish-green flowers, sometimes tinged
with purple, in a terminal cluster.

Flowers: About ⅜" (8 mm) wide; lip petal
spreading, 3-lobed; 3 sepals and 2 upper
petals narrow, blunt, colored alike.

Leaves: 1–3" (2.5–7.5 cm) long, 1–3, elliptical,
smooth, often purplish.

Height: 2½–16" (6.5–40 cm).

Flowering: Throughout year, mainly
January–August.

Habitat: On live oaks, magnolias, and other trees
in cypress swamps and sandy places.

Range: North Carolina south to Florida and
west to Louisiana.

Comments: This orchid is often found in association
with, and hidden by, the epiphytic
Resurrection Fern *(Polypodium
polypodioides).* It is one of the hardiest
and most widespread of the epiphytic
orchids and the only one found north of
Florida. Its common and species names
(the latter from a Greek word meaning
"gnat-like") refer to the insect-like
appearance of the rather inconspicuous
flowers. Its genus name is derived from
Greek words for "upon" and "tree,"
alluding to the plant's habitat.

477 Showy Orchis
Galearis spectabilis

Description: A short stalk rising between *2 large,
glossy, green leaves* and topped by 2–15
white and pink to deep lavender flowers.

Flowers: 1" (2.5 cm) long; 3 sepals and 2 upper
petals fused together, forming a *purple or
pink hood over a white, spurred lip petal;*
flowers borne in bract axils.

Showy Orchis

Leaves: 2½–8″ (6.5–20 cm) long, ovate or elliptical, with base sheathing stem.
Height: 5–12″ (12.5–30 cm).
Flowering: April–June.
Habitat: Rich damp woods and swamp edges.
Range: Ontario east to New Brunswick, south to Georgia, west to Louisiana and Oklahoma, and north to Nebraska and Minnesota.
Comments: Within the long spur of this beautiful, fragrant, woodland orchid is a syrup very rich in sugar. A rare northern species, Small Round-leaved Orchis (*Amerorchis rotundifolia*), has a solitary leaf and a white lip petal with purple spots and occurs mostly in the moss of limestone swamps from Alberta to Newfoundland and in Maine, Michigan, Wisconsin, and Minnesota, ranging north and west of our area; its genus name, from the word "America" and the Greek *orchis* ("testicle"), refers to the shape of the roundish, fleshy tubers.

140 **Rattlesnake Plantain;**
Rattlesnake Orchid
Goodyera pubescens

Description: A cylindrical cluster of many *small, white, round flowers* atop a leafless, *woolly stalk* rising from a rosette of *dark blue-green, white-veined leaves.*

Flowers:	¼" (6 mm) long; upper sepal and 2 united upper petals forming a hood over a cupped lip petal; 2 side sepals ovate, concave; sepals and petals colored alike.
Leaves:	1–3½" (2.5–9 cm) long, ovate to oblong; short, scale-like bracts on stalk.
Height:	To 18" (45 cm).
Flowering:	May–September.
Habitat:	Dry or moist, deciduous or coniferous woods and well-drained wooded slopes.
Range:	Ontario east to New Brunswick, south to Florida, west to Louisiana and Oklahoma, and north through Missouri to Minnesota.
Comments:	The highly decorative leaves of this plant are most unusual and often collected for terraria, a practice to be discouraged. A smaller species, Dwarf Rattlesnake Plantain *(G. repens)*, has flowers less than ¼" (6 mm) long on only one side of the flowering stalk. Two species found in Canada and the northern states are Checkered Rattlesnake Plantain *(G. tesselata)*, which has dull green leaves mottled with paler lines, and Green-leaved Rattlesnake Plantain *(G. oblongifolia)*, which has leaves usually with only one main white vein. The common names refer to the mottled leaves, which resemble a snake's skin, a similarity that once suggested their use as a snakebite remedy.

6 Small Whorled Pogonia
Isotria medeoloides

Description:	*1–2 yellowish-green flowers* atop a greenish stem just above a *whorl of 5–6 leaves.*
Flowers:	About ¾" (2 cm) long; lip petal white, 3-lobed, crested with pale green; upper petals 2, yellowish green; sepals 3, yellowish green, side 2 shorter than arching upper sepal.
Leaves:	To 3" (7.5 cm) long, pale dusty green, elliptical, drooping.
Height:	4–10" (10–25 cm).
Flowering:	May–July.

Habitat: Dry woodlands.

Range: Ontario; Maine south to Georgia, west to Tennessee, and north to Illinois and Michigan.

Comments: This is an extremely rare orchid with a very long resting period of at least 10 years between bloomings, during which time it remains dormant underground. The species name apparently refers to the similarity of the leaf structure to that of Indian Cucumber Root *(Medeola virginiana)* of the lily family (Liliaceae).

8 Large Twayblade
Liparis liliifolia

Description: An angled stalk rising between 2 large, oval, *shiny, basal leaves* and bearing several *brown to maroon to green flowers.*

Flowers: Lip petal ½" (1.5 cm) long, *translucent, brown with purple veins,* rounded, with a point at bottom center; *2 upper petals thread-like,* spreading; sepals 3, narrow, green.

Leaves: 2–7" (5–17.5 cm) long, sheathing lower stem.

Height: 4–10" (10–25 cm).

Flowering: May–July.

Habitat: Rich or sandy woods and clearings and on moss along streambanks.

Range: Ontario east to Vermont, south to Georgia, west to Oklahoma, and north through Missouri to Minnesota.

Comments: Three features characterize this small woodland orchid: its brownish-purple flowers, filamentous upper petals, and greasy-looking leaves (from which comes its genus name, derived from the Greek *liparos,* meaning "fat" or "shining"). An inconspicuous plant, it may be easily overlooked. Our other species of *Liparis,* Fen Orchid *(L. loeselii),* has a small green lip petal and occurs from Saskatchewan east to Newfoundland, south to North Carolina, Tennessee, and Alabama, west to Arkansas, and north to Missouri, Nebraska, and the Dakotas.

135 White Fringed Orchid
Platanthera blephariglottis

Description: A leafy stalk topped by an elongated, dense or sparse cluster of *pure white flowers with a deeply fringed lip petal.*

Flowers: About 1½″ (4 cm) long; upper sepal and 2 narrow upper petals forming hood over lip petal; 2 side sepals oblong-elliptical; sepals and petals colored alike; long narrow spur projecting behind flower.

Leaves: Lower ones to 14″ (35 cm) long, ovate-lanceolate to linear-lanceolate; upper ones reduced to bracts.

Height: 1–2′ (30–60 cm).

Flowering: June–September.

Habitat: Wet meadows, marshes, and bogs.

Range: Ontario east to Newfoundland, south to Florida, and west to Texas; also in Ohio, Michigan, and Illinois.

Comments: The appropriate species name derives from Greek and means "fringe-tongued." Other white *Platanthera* species include Small Woodland Orchid *(P. clavellata),* found throughout our range, with a short blunt lip petal and a solitary clasping leaf on the flower stalk; Round-leaved Orchid *(P. orbiculata),* with greenish-white flowers and two roundish, basal leaves, found in Canada and the northern United States and in the mountains of the South; Prairie White Fringed Orchid *(P. leucophaea),* with a 3-parted, deeply fringed lip petal, found on wet prairies of the Midwest; and Snowy Orchid *(P. nivea),* which has an unfringed lip petal.

316 Yellow Fringed Orchid
Platanthera ciliaris

Description: A leafy stem topped by a large, many-flowered cluster of *deep orange to bright yellow flowers with a drooping, deeply fringed lip petal.*

Flowers: Lip petal ¾″ (2 cm) long, with a long slender spur projecting downward and

backward to 1½" (4 cm) long; upper
sepal and 2 upper petals erect; 2 side
sepals broadly ovate, spreading.

Leaves: Lower ones 3–10" (7.5–25 cm) long,
lanceolate, sheathing stem; upper ones
smaller.

Height: 1–2½' (30–75 cm).

Flowering: July–September.

Habitat: Peaty or wet, sandy woods, thickets, and
dry meadows and slopes.

Range: New York east to Rhode Island, south to
Florida, west to Texas, and northeast to
Michigan.

Comments: This is a very showy orchid of meadows
and open woods. A more southern
species, Orange Fringed Orchid *(P.
cristata),* has a flower ⅜" (9 mm) wide
and a spur ½" (1.5 cm) long, shorter
than the fringed lip petal. Yellow
Fringeless Orchid *(P. integra),* found in
southern New Jersey and from eastern
North Carolina south to Florida and
Texas and east to Tennessee, has orange-
yellow flowers with unfringed lip
petals. Yellow Fringed Orchid and
White Fringed Orchid *(P. blephariglottis)*
frequently hybridize when they grow
together; similarly, Yellow Fringed
Orchid hybridizes with Orange Fringed
Orchid.

586 Large Purple Fringed Orchid
Platanthera grandiflora

Description: *Deeply fringed, fragrant, lavender flowers* in
many-flowered, elongated clusters on a
leafy stem.

Flowers: 1" (2.5 cm) long; lip petal with 3 fan-
shaped, fringed lobes and a backward-
pointing spur; upper sepal and 2 upper
petals erect; 2 side sepals ovate,
spreading; sepals and petals colored
alike.

Leaves: Lower ones to 8" (20 cm) long, ovate to
lanceolate, sheathing stem; upper ones
small, lanceolate.

Height: 2–4' (60–120 cm).

Flowering: June–August.

Habitat: Cool moist woods, wet meadows, and swamp edges.

Range: Ontario east to Newfoundland, south to Georgia, and north to Tennessee, West Virginia, Ohio, and Michigan.

Comments: A close-up of the individual flowers reveals the striking beauty of the fringed orchids. The method of pollination by moths is interesting. The pollen masses (pollinia) bear a sticky disk that protrudes below the anther. As the moth extends its tongue into the spur of the lip petal and then out again, it pulls the pollen mass from the anther and carries it to another flower where cross-pollination occurs. Small Purple Fringed Orchid *(P. psycodes)*, occurring from Manitoba east to Newfoundland, south to Georgia, and northwest to Tennessee, Missouri, and Minnesota, has smaller flowers. Purple Fringeless Orchid *(P. peramoena)* has an unfringed lip petal; it grows from Pennsylvania and New Jersey south to Georgia, west to Arkansas, and north to Missouri and Illinois.

137 Ragged Fringed Orchid
Platanthera lacera

Description: Spike-like clusters of *whitish-green or creamy-yellow flowers with a highly lacerated, 3-parted lip petal.*

Flowers: ½" (1.5 cm) long; lip petal deeply 3-parted, with deeply cut lateral divisions, a coarsely fringed middle division, and a curved slender spur ½" (1.5 cm) long; upper sepal and 2 narrow upper petals erect; 2 side sepals ovate, spreading; sepals and petals colored alike.

Leaves: Lower ones to 8" (20 cm) long, lanceolate, sheathing stem; upper ones smaller.

Height: 1–2' (30–60 cm).

Flowering: June–September.

Habitat: Bogs, wet woods, and dry to wet meadows and fields.

Range: Manitoba east to Newfoundland, south to Georgia, west to Texas, and north to Kansas, Iowa, and Minnesota.

Comments: This orchid is one of the more common and widespread members of the genus. The genus name is from the Greek *platys* ("broad") and *anthera* ("anther"), alluding to the anther that, for an orchid, is unusually broad. At least 10 other greenish-flowered species of *Platanthera* occur in our range, none with the lip petal so fringed. In the Nova Scotia area this species hybridizes freely with Large Purple Fringed Orchid (*P. grandiflora*).

470 Rose Pogonia
Pogonia ophioglossoides

Description: A slender, greenish stem with *1 leaf at about midstem* and usually *1 rose-pink (rarely white) flower at top.*

Flowers: About 1¾" (4.5 cm) long; lip petal spatulate, fringed, bearded in center with short, yellowish bristles; upper petals 2, ovate, arching over lip; sepals 3, linear-lanceolate, upper sepal erect; sepals and petals colored alike; 1 leaf-like bract just beneath flower to 1" (2.5 cm) long.

Leaves: To 4½" (12 cm) long, solitary, ovate to broadly lanceolate.

Height: 3–24" (7.5–60 cm).

Flowering: May–August.

Habitat: Wet open woods, meadows, swamps, and peat bogs.

Range: Manitoba east to Newfoundland, south to Florida, west to Texas, and north to Oklahoma, Missouri, Illinois, and Minnesota.

Comments: This orchid is found in places in the eastern United States where soil conditions rather than temperature are the controlling factors. The flowers smell like raspberries.

139 Nodding Ladies' Tresses
Spiranthes cernua

Description: A spike of small, *cream-white, fragrant, nodding flowers in 3–4 spiral rows.*

Flowers: ½" (1.5 cm) long; 2 upper petals and upper sepal united to form a hood over wavy-edged lip petal.

Leaves: Basal ones to 10" (25 cm) long, lanceolate; those on upper stem reduced to scales.

Height: 6–24" (15–60 cm).

Flowering: August (in northern part of range)–November (in southern part).

Habitat: Fields, damp meadows, moist thickets, and grassy swamps.

Range: Ontario east to Nova Scotia, south to Georgia, west to Texas, and north to Nebraska and Minnesota.

Comments: A dozen or more species of ladies' tresses are known in the eastern United States. Among those with flowers in pronounced spirals are Slender Ladies' Tresses (*S. lacera*), with ovate leaves and a green spot on the lip petal; Short-lipped Ladies' Tresses (*S. brevilabris*), with a downy flower spike; and Little Ladies' Tresses (*S. grayi*), with tiny flowers. Fragrant Ladies' Tresses (*S. odorata*) reaches a height of 2–3' (60–90 cm) in southern marshes and swamps and has spirally arranged clusters of fragrant flowers.

218 Three-birds Orchid; Little Bird Orchid
Triphora trianthophora

Description: Small, ovate, *clasping leaves* scattered along a fragile stem and *1 pink or white, nodding flower* rising from each axil of uppermost 1–6 (usually 3) leaves.

Flowers: About ¾" (2 cm) long; *lip petal rounded, with crinkled edges* and a purplish-green crest; 2 upper petals forming a hood over lip; sepals and petals similar.

Leaves:	To ¾" (2 cm) long, spreading away from stem, often tinged with purple.
Height:	3–12" (7.5–30 cm).
Flowering:	July–October.
Habitat:	Rich woods, swamp edges, and floodplains.
Range:	Ontario; Maine south to Florida, west to Texas, and north to Nebraska, Iowa, and Wisconsin.
Comments:	As the common names imply, each flower resembles a small bird in flight. The plant may remain dormant for long periods, with the underground tuber giving rise to a new stem after several years; when the flowers bloom, they last only one day. Five species of this genus are known in the United States; the four others grow in Florida. Of these, the most common is Rickett's Three-birds Orchid *(T. rickettii)*, with leaves spreading away from the stem, both leaf surfaces green, and 1–8 erect flowers.

134 Lawn Orchid
Zeuxine strateumatica

Description:	A slender, leafy plant with *small, white or yellowish flowers in dense spikes.*
Flowers:	About ¼" (6 mm) long; lip petal yellow, fleshy, broadest near end; upper sepal and 2 upper petals united to form a hood over column; 2 side sepals ovate-oblong.
Leaves:	¾–3½" (2–9 cm) long, *grass-like, overlapping,* tinged with purplish brown.
Height:	2–7" (5–17.5 cm).
Flowering:	Throughout year; mainly January–February.
Habitat:	Lawns, wet fields, sandy places, and roadside ditches.
Range:	Georgia, Florida, Louisiana, and Texas.
Comments:	Native to Asia and Africa, this species was introduced to Florida, probably around 1917, and has spread. It is often common in lawns and waste places.

BROOMRAPE FAMILY
Orobanchaceae

Herbaceous root parasites, annual or perennial, usually somewhat fleshy and some shade of yellow, brown, violet, or red, lacking chlorophyll.

Flowers: Bilaterally symmetrical; in racemes, spikes, or borne singly atop a slender stem. Sepals 2–5, united; petals 5, united, forming an upper and lower lip; stamens 4; all these parts attached at base of ovary.
Leaves: Simple, reduced to scales.
Fruit: 1-chambered capsule.

There are about 17 genera and 150 species, primarily in the northern temperate region, especially the warmer parts of Europe. The common name of the family alludes to the parasitism of various species of *Orobanche* on shrubs in the pea family (Fabaceae) known as brooms *(Cytisus)*. Other Orobanchaceae may parasitize various families of plants, some becoming serious agricultural pests. This family is very closely related to the figwort family (Scrophulariaceae).

329 Squawroot
Conopholis americana

Description: A parasitic plant with *yellowish to cream-colored flowers* emerging among lanceolate or ovate, pointed, *yellow-tan scales* on upper part of a fleshy stalk.
Flowers: ½" (1.5 cm) long; upper corolla lip forming a narrow hood over a 3-lobed, spreading lower lip; stamens 4.
Leaves: Reduced to scales.
Fruit: Capsule.
Height: 3–10" (7.5–25 cm).
Flowering: May–June.
Habitat: Woods, under oaks.
Range: Manitoba east to Nova Scotia, south to Florida, west to Mississippi, and north to Illinois, Iowa, and Wisconsin.
Comments: This plant resembles a pinecone as it becomes dry and brown with age. A parasite, it gets its nourishment from the roots of oaks, its host trees. A closely related species, Alpine Squawroot *(C. alpina),* occurs in the southwestern United States.

378 Beechdrops
Epifagus virginiana

Description: A parasitic plant with *unbranched to many-branched, brownish-tan stems and buff-brown or dull magenta flowers* in axils of scattered dry scales.

Flowers: Upper flowers ½" (1.5 cm) long, tubular; lower flowers ¼" (5 mm) long, bud-like, never opening, self-pollinated producing seeds abundantly.

Leaves: Reduced to scales.

Fruit: Small, brown, many-seeded capsule, ¼" (6 mm) long, opening like a clamshell at top; seeds dislodged by raindrops.

Height: 6–18" (15–45 cm).

Flowering: August–October.

Habitat: Woods, under beech trees.

Range: Ontario east to Nova Scotia, south to Florida, west to Texas, and north to Missouri, Illinois, and Wisconsin.

Comments: As the genus name, from the Greek *epi* ("upon") and *phagos* ("beech") implies, this annual plant is found under beech trees, where it grows on and receives nourishment from the roots The flowers are delicately marked and worth a close-up look with a hand lens. Dried stalks often persist all winter under the trees.

95 Naked Broomrape; Cancer Root
Orobanche uniflora

Description: A parasitic plant with mostly 1–3 erect, slender, leafless stalks rising from a short underground stem, each stalk topped by *1 white to whitish-lavender, fragrant flower* with a yellow center.

Flowers: ¾" (2 cm) long; corolla finely hairy, with fused petals flaring out into 5 lobes, lower 3 lobes with yellow stripes.

Leaves: Reduced to overlapping brown scales near base.

Fruit: Capsule.

Height: 3–10" (7.5–25 cm).

Flowering: April–June.

Habitat: Damp woods and thickets.

Range: Alberta and Saskatchewan; Ontario east
to Newfoundland, south to Florida, west
to Texas, and north to South Dakota;
also in much of West.

Comments: This parasitic plant obtains its
nourishment from the roots of various
other plants. Its underground stem is
quite short, usually 1–1½″ (2.5–4 cm)
long. Clustered Broomrape (*O.
fasciculata*), also known as Yellow
Broomrape, has mostly 5–10 long,
slender, 1-flowered stalks rising from a
short, trunk-like stem usually 2–6″
(5–15 cm) long; it occurs in the
midwestern and Plains states. Louisiana
Broomrape (*O. ludoviciana*), also found
in the Midwest and on the plains, has
flowers in dense, spike-like clusters.
Both of these species are parasitic,
especially on members of the aster
family (Asteraceae). Lesser Broomrape
(*O. minor*), with purple-tinged flowers in
dense spikes, is parasitic mostly on the
roots of clovers (*Trifolium*), of the pea
family (Fabaceae); it was naturalized
from Europe and now occurs from New
York to Florida.

WOOD SORREL FAMILY
Oxalidaceae

Herbs, shrubs, rarely trees, with alternate or basal, usually
compound leaves and flowers usually borne singly or in an
umbel; sap often sour.

Flowers: Radially symmetrical. Sepals 5, separate; petals 5,
separate or united at base; stamens 10, joined by filaments; all these parts attached at base of ovary with 5
styles.
Leaves: Usually palmately compound and clover-like, with
usually 3 leaflets; or pinnately compound.
Fruit: 5-chambered capsule, rarely a berry.

There are about 8 genera and 900 species, primarily in
tropical and subtropical regions. Several are cultivated as ornamentals, and the greens of a few are used in salads or as
potherbs. The tree-like tropical species Carambola (*Averrhoa
carambola*) produces the 5-angled starfruit increasingly seen
in grocery stores and fresh-food markets.

446 Common Wood Sorrel
Oxalis montana

Description: A low-growing plant with *clover-like leaves and 1 white or pink flower on each of several stalks.*

Flowers: ¾" (2 cm) wide; petals 5, notched, with *deep pink veins;* stamens 10; pistil 1.

Leaves: Basal, divided into 3 heart-shaped leaflets, each about ½" (1.5 cm) wide; closing at night.

Fruit: Capsule.

Height: 3–6" (7.5–15 cm).

Flowering: May–July.

Habitat: Rich damp woods.

Range: Ontario east to Newfoundland, south to Georgia, and northwest to Tennessee, Indiana, and Minnesota.

Comments: This dainty flower of the mountains and cool, moist, woodland glens is especially common in New England and westward to the Great Lakes. It is difficult to grow in gardens. Non-opening but seed-producing flowers are produced at the base of the plant on curved stems. With their clover-like, heart-shaped leaflets, wood sorrels are easy to recognize. The sour taste of the fruit and leaves (due to oxalic acid) is distinctive, and the leaves may be used sparingly in salads. The genus name comes from the Greek *oxys* ("sour").

Common Wood Sorrel

242 Yellow Wood Sorrel; Sour Grass
Oxalis stricta

Description: A low spreading plant with *clover-like, sour-tasting leaves and 1 to several yellow flowers.*

Flowers: ½" (1.5 cm) wide; petals 5; stamens 10; pistil erect, pencil-like.

Leaves: Palmately divided into 3 heart-shaped leaflets, each ½–¾" (1.5–2 cm) wide; closing at night.

Fruit: Capsule, on a straight or ascending stalk.

Height: 6–15" (15–38 cm).

Flowering: May–October.

Habitat: Waste places, roadsides, and fields.

Range: Saskatchewan east to Newfoundland, south to Florida, west to Texas, and north to Minnesota; also in West.

Comments: This plant is a cosmopolitan weed, perhaps originally native to North America. It is especially common as a garden weed. The very similar Upright Yellow Wood Sorrel *(O. dillenii),* also a European introduction, has seed capsules on reflexed stalks. Large Yellow Wood Sorrel *(O. grandis)* has flowers to 1" (2.5 cm) wide and leaves often with purple edges; it is native and grows from Indiana east to Pennsylvania and south to Georgia and Louisiana.

495 Violet Wood Sorrel
Oxalis violacea

Description: A fragile plant with several *rose-purple flowers* on each stalk rising above *clover-like leaves.*

Flowers: ¾" (2 cm) wide; sepals green, with orange tips; petals 5, flaring; stamens 10.

Leaves: Palmately divided into 3 heart-shaped leaflets, each about ¾" (2 cm) wide, reddish or purple beneath; closing at night.

Fruit: Capsule.

Height: 4–8" (10–20 cm).

Flowering: April–June, sometimes again in fall.

Habitat: Open woods, banks, rocky ground, and prairies.

Range: North Dakota east to Massachusetts, south to Florida, west to Arizona, and north to Wyoming.

Comments: This common, native, woodland and moist prairie species is occasionally cultivated in the north. It spreads rapidly by runners from its bulbs and often flowers again in the fall after the leaves have died.

POPPY FAMILY
Papaveraceae

Annual or perennial herbs, occasionally shrubs, rarely small trees, often with clear, white, or colored sap.

Flowers: Radially symmetrical; mostly borne singly. Sepals 2–3, separate or united into a cone (calyptra), quickly dropping off; petals 4–6, separate, showy, often crumpled in bud; stamens numerous; all these parts attached at base of ovary.

Leaves: Usually alternate, sometimes opposite or basal; simple or deeply divided.

Fruit: Usually a capsule, varying from long and slender to more or less urn-shaped, sometimes with a cap-like structure at top, opening by slits or well-defined pores near top (when cap present, pores are just beneath rim).

There are about 25 genera and 200 species, mostly in temperate and subtropical regions. Several genera are well developed in western North America. Several species are grown as ornamentals. Poppy seeds used in baking are obtained from species of *Papaver*. Opium is extracted from the sap of Opium Poppy (*Papaver somniferum*). The seeds of some Papaveraceae have a white, oily appendage attractive to ants as food; the insects carry the seeds about, aiding in dispersal.

65 White Prickly Poppy
Argemone albiflora

Description: A *cupped white flower* atop a tall *bristly stem;* plant has *white sap* turning yellow after drying.

Flowers: About 3″ (7.5 cm) wide; petals 4–6; stamens numerous, yellow, surrounding 1 pistil; stigma with 4–6 lobes.

Leaves:	3–8" (7.5–20 cm) long, alternate, lobed, *spiny-edged,* often mottled.
Fruit:	Spiny capsule.
Height:	1–3' (30–90 cm).
Flowering:	April–August.
Habitat:	Waste places and roadsides.
Range:	Wisconsin east to Massachusetts, south to Florida, west to Texas, and north through Arkansas to Iowa.
Comments:	A similar thistle-leaved species, a native of tropical America, is Yellow Prickly Poppy *(A. mexicana),* which has yellow flowers; it occurs from Virginia and Tennessee south to Florida and west to Texas, and has escaped from cultivation northward.

243 Celandine
Chelidonium majus

Description:	*Deep yellow flowers* in small loose clusters; plant has *saffron-colored sap.*
Flowers:	⅝" (16 mm) wide; sepals 2, dropping off as flower opens; petals 4, more in double-flowered forms.
Leaves:	4–8" (10–20 cm) long, alternate, light green, divided into several *intricately lobed segments.*
Fruit:	Smooth slender capsule.
Height:	1–2' (30–60 cm).
Flowering:	April–August.
Habitat:	Moist soil of roadsides, woodland edges, and around dwellings.
Range:	Ontario northeast to Newfoundland, south to Georgia, northwest to Nebraska, and northeast to Minnesota; also in parts of West.
Comments:	This European introduction is attractive but aggressive and poisonous to chickens. Since its sap resembles bile, it was at one time used for liver disorders; it was also used for removing warts and freckles. The plant called Lesser Celandine *(Ranunculus ficaria),* of the buttercup family (Ranunculaceae), is similar but not closely related.

60 Bloodroot
Sanguinaria canadensis

Description: *1 lobed basal leaf* often curling around a smooth flower stalk bearing *1 white flower* with a golden-orange center; *roots and stem have acrid, red-orange sap.*

Flowers: To 1½" (4 cm) wide; sepals 2, dropping off as flower opens; petals 8–10, separate, alternate ones slightly narrower; stamens numerous, golden, surrounding 1 pistil.

Leaves: 4–7" (10–17.5 cm) long, bluish green, *palmately scalloped into 5–9 lobes.*

Fruit: 2-parted capsule, pointed at both ends.

Height: To 10" (25 cm).

Flowering: March–May.

Habitat: Rich woodlands and along streams.

Range: Manitoba east to Newfoundland, south to Florida, west to Texas, and north to North Dakota.

Comments: This fragile spring flower opens in full sunlight and closes at night. Like the flowers of most members of the poppy family, it lasts for a relatively short time. The red sap from the underground stem was used by Native Americans as a dye for baskets, clothing, and war paint, as well as for insect repellent. The genus name, from the Latin *sanguinarius,* means "bleeding."

Bloodroot

244 Wood Poppy; Celandine Poppy
Stylophorum diphyllum

Description: A plant with *yellow sap and yellow flowers,* solitary or in small clusters, atop a stem bearing *a pair of deeply lobed leaves;* other leaves basal.

Flowers: 1½–2" (4–5 cm) wide; petals 4; stamens numerous; pistil 1.

Leaves: 4–10" (10–25 cm) long, opposite or basal, pinnately divided into lobed or toothed segments.

Fruit: Hairy, 2-parted capsule.

Height: 1–1½' (30–45 cm).

Flowering: March–May.

Habitat: Rich woods and bluffs.

Range: Ontario, Michigan, and Pennsylvania south to Georgia, west to Arkansas, and north to Illinois.

Comments: This is a fine species to grow in wildflower gardens. The species name, Greek for "two-leaved," refers to the pair of opposite leaves below the flower.

PASSIONFLOWER FAMILY
Passifloraceae

Herbaceous or woody vines, climbing by tendrils borne in leaf axils, less often shrubs or trees, with bizarre, elaborate flowers usually in pairs in leaf axils.

Flowers: Radially symmetrical. Sepals usually 5, often petal-like, usually separate, sometimes united at base; petals 5, separate, or sometimes absent; numerous thread-like structures forming a crown (corona) at base of corolla; stamens 3–5, or 10; ovary with 3–5 styles, often raised on a stalk also bearing stamens.
Leaves: Simple, often deeply lobed.
Fruit: Capsule or berry.

There are about 16 genera and 650 species in this mostly tropical American family. Several species are cultivated for their unusual and often gaudy flowers; a few *Passiflora* produce edible fruit, known as passion fruit.

551 **Purple Passionflower**
Passiflora incarnata

Description: A climbing or trailing vine with large, *strikingly fringed flowers.*

Flowers: 1½–2½" (4–6.5 cm) wide; sepals and petals 5 each, forming a whitish or bluish-purple, wheel-like backdrop behind a fringed corona with 2–3 circle of *purple and pinkish, thread-like segments;* stamens 5, drooping, suspended around 3-styled pistil.

Leaves: 3–5" (7.5–12.5 cm) wide, palmately divided into 3 lobes, with 2 conspicuou glands on stalk near blade; tendrils present.

Fruit: Green to yellow, many-seeded berry, 2–3" (5–7.5 cm) long, with edible pulp around each seed.

Height: Vine; to 6½' (2 m) long.

Flowering: June–September.

Habitat: Sandy thickets and open areas.

Range: Kansas northeast to Pennsylvania, south to Florida, west to Texas, and north to Oklahoma.

Comments: This unusual plant is widely distributed in the South, especially from Florida to Texas. Its fruit is sometimes called maypop. The common name passionflower relates to the resemblance of the flower parts to aspects of the Crucifixion story: The 10 petal-like

Purple Passionflower

parts represent the disciples, excluding Peter and Judas; the 5 stamens, the wounds Jesus received; the knob-like stigmas, the nails; and the fringed corona, the crown of thorns. Yellow Passionflower *(P. lutea),* with greenish-yellow flowers ½–1" (1.5–2.5 cm) wide and purple to black fruit, occurs in much the same area as Purple Passionflower.

POKEWEED FAMILY
Phytolaccaceae

Herbs, shrubs, or trees, with racemes of flowers at stem ends or in leaf axils.

Flowers: Bisexual or unisexual, radially symmetrical. Sepals 4–5, separate; petals absent; stamens as many as sepals; all these parts attached at base of ovary.
Leaves: Simple.
Fruit: Berry, capsule, or winged and seed-like.

There are about 18 genera and 125 species, mostly in tropical or subtropical regions. Members of this family are infrequently cultivated.

119   Pokeweed
Phytolacca americana

Description: A tall, large-leaved, branching plant with *reddish stems and long racemes of small white flowers.*
  Flowers: About ¼" (6 mm) wide; sepals 5, white, petal-like.
  Leaves: 5–12" (12.5–30 cm) long, elliptical-lanceolate, tapering at both ends.
  Fruit: Drooping clusters of *dark purple-black berries,* each ¼" (6 mm) wide.
  Height: To 10' (3 m).
  Flowering: July–September.
  Habitat: Open woods, damp thickets, clearings, and roadsides.
  Range: Ontario east to New Brunswick, south to Florida, west to Texas, and north to Nebraska and Minnesota; also from Oregon south to California and east to New Mexico.

Comments: This frequently troublesome weed has poisonous berries and roots; however, emerging young shoots can be gathered before the pink color appears, boiled in at least two changes of water, and eaten as greens. The berry sap was used as a dye by the early colonists and has also been used to color cheap wine.

PLANTAIN FAMILY
Plantaginaceae

Herbs mostly with basal leaves and inconspicuous flowers in spikes or heads.

Flowers: Radially symmetrical. Calyx with 4 united, membranous sepals; corolla with 4 united, papery petals; stamens 4, protruding; all these parts attached at base of ovary.

Leaves: Often basal, simple, with major veins mostly parallel or curved from base to tip.

Fruit: Seeded capsule, with top lifting free; or a small nut.

There are 3 genera and about 250 species, found nearly throughout the world. Some are unwelcome weeds. The seeds of certain species become sticky when wet; those of Psyllium (*Plantago afra*) and related species are used in making natural laxatives.

106 English Plantain
Plantago lanceolata

Description: A *round to cylindrical head* of tiny, crowded, spirally arranged, greenish-white flowers atop a long leafless stalk rising from a basal rosette of long, *narrow, strongly veined leaves.*

Flowers: About ⅛″ (3 mm) long; corolla 4-lobed, papery; stamens 4, white, protruding; bracts beneath flowers.

Leaves: 4–16″ (10–40 cm) long, about one-sixth as wide, narrowly elliptical or lanceolate.

Fruit: 2-seeded capsule, opening around middle.

Height: 6–20″ (15–50 cm).

Flowering: May–October.

Habitat: Waste places and lawns.

Range: Alberta east to Newfoundland, south to

English Plantain

Florida, west to Texas, and north to North Dakota; also throughout West.

Comments: This narrow-leaved plantain, naturalized from Europe, is often a troublesome weed in lawns and gardens. The seeds are often eaten by songbirds and are used for feeding caged birds. The leaves are a favorite food of rabbits. At least five other narrow-leaved plantains occur in our range, but they have elongated flower spikes.

104 Common Plantain
Plantago major

Description: Small flowers massed in a *narrow, cylindrical, greenish-white spike* rising from a rosette of *broad, strongly ribbed, basal leaves.*

Flowers: 1/16" (2 mm) long; corolla 4-lobed, papery; stamens 4; pistil 1; bracts beneath flowers.

Leaves: To 6" (15 cm) long, 4" (10 cm) wide, ovate to elliptical.

Fruit: Capsule, with 12–18 seeds, splitting open around middle.

Height: 6–18" (15–45 cm).

Flowering: June–October.

Habitat: Waste places, fields, roadsides, and lawns.

Range: Throughout North America, except parts of far north.

Comments: This broad-leaved plantain, naturalized from Europe, is considered a weed in lawns and gardens. The equally common but native Pale Plantain (*P. rugelii*) can usually be distinguished from Common Plantain by its more elongated fruit capsule that splits open closer to the base and often has fewer seeds. The rare Heart-leaved Plantain (*P. cordata*), also known as Water Plantain, another broad-leaved but native species, occurs in streams from Ontario and New York south to Florida, west to Louisiana, and north to Missouri, Illinois, and Michigan; it can be distinguished from the other eastern plantains by the hollow stalk of its flower cluster and its seed capsule that opens while still alive and green.

LEADWORT FAMILY
Plumbaginaceae

Herbs or shrubs with leaves often in basal rosettes and small flowers in heads, modified racemes, or branched clusters.

Flowers: Radially symmetrical. Sepals 5, united, often pleated, showy, stiff and membranous; petals 5, united corolla often deeply lobed and seeming to have separate petals; stamens 5, each opposite a corolla lobe; all these parts attached at base of ovary.

Leaves: Alternate or in a basal rosette.

Fruit: 1-chambered, 1-seeded, often leathery; not opening, or opening very late.

There are about 12 genera and 400 species, found predominantly in dry parts of the Mediterranean region and in central Asia. A few species are cultivated as ornamentals.

602   Sea Lavender
Limonium carolinianum

Description: A smooth saltmarsh plant with *small, pale purple flowers along one side of stems* and forming a loose branching cluster.

Flowers: About ⅛" (3 mm) wide; calyx 5-

toothed, with 10 faint ribs, persistent; corolla funnel-shaped, with 5 spatulate lobes.

Leaves: 2–10″ (5–25 cm) long, basal, lanceolate, with broadest part toward tip, edges smooth or slightly wavy.

Fruit: Seed-like, 1-seeded.

Height: 1–2′ (30–60 cm).

Flowering: July–October.

Habitat: Salt marshes.

Range: Quebec east to Newfoundland, south to Florida, and west to Texas.

Comments: A strikingly showy perennial in late summer on tidal marshes, this species is often associated with other broad-leaved marsh plants that occur in masses or are scattered among marsh grasses. Individual plants may vary greatly in size and vigor depending upon growing conditions.

GRASS FAMILY
Poaceae

Herbs, rarely woody, with cylindrical, jointed flowering stems (culms), hollow or solid between joints, leaves mostly long and narrow, and tiny flowers aggregated into highly modified clusters.

Flowers: Bisexual or unisexual. Sepals and petals absent; stamens usually 3, seldom 1–2, rarely 6; pistil with 2 feathery stigmas; all these parts attached at base of ovary. Individual flowers enclosed in overlapping, scale-like bracts grouped in spikelets; spikelets in a conspicuous flower cluster (usually a spike, head, tassel, or openly branched panicle).

Leaves: Alternate, in 2 rows, one on each side of stem; base forming sheath around stem, usually with a hairy or membranous ring (ligule) at junction of sheath and blade.

Fruit: Grain.

There are about 500 genera and 8,000 species, found throughout the world in almost every habitat. The greatest diversity of species is found in the tropics, and the greatest abundance in tropical and temperate regions with semi-arid climates, where the plants form extensive grasslands. This agriculturally and economically significant family provides much of the food used by humans; rice is obtained from the genus *Oryza*, wheat from *Triticum,* corn from *Zea,* barley

from *Hordeum,* and millets from *Panicum* (among other genera). The family is also important as a source of fodder for livestock. Poaceae has also been known as Gramineae.

---

387 Sweet Vernal Grass
Anthoxanthum odoratum

Description: Tufted, slender stems bearing compact, *spike-like clusters* of narrow, greenish- or yellowish-brown *spikelets with projecting bristles.*

Flowers: Enclosed in scales grouped in spikelets 3/8" (8 mm) long; cluster to 3" (7.5 cm) long.

Leaves: Blades to 6" (15 cm) long, to 1/4" (6 mm) wide, flat, rough above, sheathing stem at base; long projection at base of blade present.

Fruit: Yellowish grain.

Height: 12–28" (30–70 cm).

Flowering: April–August.

Habitat: Fields, roadsides, and waste places.

Range: Ontario east to Newfoundland, south to Georgia, west to Texas, and north through Arkansas to Wisconsin; also in parts of West.

Comments: When this species is in flower, the projecting, long-stalked anthers are conspicuous. Naturalized from Europe, Sweet Vernal Grass is very fragrant when dried. The genus name is from the Greek *anthos* ("flower") and *xanthos* ("yellow") and refers to the color of the spikelets.

---

385 Grama Grass; Mesquite Grass
Bouteloua gracilis

Description: Numerous *greenish- to reddish-brown spikelets along one side of often curved stalks* in 1–3 spikes borne on a stem rising above a curly mass of *very thin leaves.*

Flowers: Enclosed in scales grouped in spikelets about 1/4" (6 mm) long; spike to 2" (5 cm) long.

Leaves: 3–6" (7.5–15 cm) long, 1/16" (2 mm) wide, smooth.

Fruit: Small grain.

Height: 6–20″ (15–50 cm).
Flowering: July–September.
Habitat: Prairies.
Range: British Columbia east to Manitoba, south to Minnesota and Texas, and westward throughout West; adventive in northeastern United States.
Comments: This is an important, drought-resistant, short grass in the mixed prairies and throughout the Great Plains and the Southwest. It can be confused with another grass in its range, Hairy Grama Grass *(B. hirsuta),* which is distinguished by a sharp point extending beyond the tip of the spikes. A somewhat similar but shorter species in about the same range, the sod-forming Buffalo Grass *(Buchloe dactyloides),* is usually less than 6″ (15 cm) high and is typical of dry, short-grass plains; it has male and female flowers on separate plants.

27 Smooth Brome; Hungarian Brome
Bromus inermis

Description: A rhizomatous, clump-forming, perennial grass bearing many light green (sometimes purple- or bronze-tinged), *narrow, usually hairless spikelets* in a loose, much-branched terminal cluster.
Flowers: Enclosed in 5–12 scales sometimes tipped with short bristles to about ¹⁄₁₆″ (2 mm) long; spikelets ¾–1½″ (2–4 cm) long, ⅛–¼″ (3–5 mm) wide, on thread-like, flexible stalks mostly shorter than spikelets; cluster 4–12″ (10–30 cm) long.
Leaves: Blades 6–15″ (15–40 cm) long, ¼–⅝″ (5–16 mm) wide, smooth or slightly rough, rising from long-tubular sheaths surrounding stem; often with a crimp forming a more or less distinct W or U at blade midsection.
Fruit: Small grain.
Height: 16–46″ (40–120 cm).
Flowering: May–July, sporadically to September.

Habitat:	Roadsides, fields, pastures, nursery plots, and waste places.
Range:	Throughout much of North America, except parts of far north; least common in southeastern United States.
Comments:	This drought-resistant Eurasian species was deliberately introduced into the United States around 1880 as a hay and pasture grass and for reseeding western ranges. It has since gone wild throughout the United States and much of Canada (except the far north) and is now one of our most common weedy grasses; in some areas it is considered an undesirable plant because of its aggressiveness. However, its deep roots make it an excellent soil binder, protecting against erosion. Relished by all kinds of livestock, it is a fine forage. The species name means "unarmed," alluding to the spikelets, which do not have the long bristles characteristic of some of Smooth Brome's relatives. A rare variant has hairy spikelets.

28 Downy Brome; Downy Chess
Bromus tectorum

Description:	An annual grass bearing many *finely hairy, drooping, yellowish-green, bristly spikelets* in a loose, much-branched, terminal cluster.
Flowers:	Enclosed in 3–8 scales mostly tipped with bristles ¼–¾" (5–18 mm) long; spikelets ¾–1½" (2–3.5 cm) long, on thread-like, flexible stalks mostly shorter than spikelets; cluster 2–10" (5–25 cm) long.
Leaves:	Blades 6–15" (15–40 cm) long, ¼–⅝" (5–16 mm) wide, finely hairy, rising from long-tubular, hairy sheaths surrounding stem.
Fruit:	Small grain.
Height:	8–30" (20–76 cm).
Flowering:	April–June, sporadically later in wet summers.
Habitat:	Roadsides, fields, pastures, and waste places.

Range: Throughout North America, except
Northwest Territories and
Newfoundland.

Comments: This Eurasian grass was unintentionally
introduced into North America in the
mid-1800s and has spread rapidly over
much of the continent except the far
north. It is one of our common grasses of
roadsides and waste places, sometimes
lining roads and railways for long
distances; in some areas, as in the
sagebrush and range country of the
western United States, it is considered a
troublesome weed. The plants, sometimes
with a purplish or reddish hue, eventually
turn brown. At maturity the spikelets
break apart; the sharp-pointed, bristly
sections can injure grazing animals,
working into the nose, ears, mouth, or
eyes. Hikers call this grass sometimes
unprintable names as they try to remove
the shattered spikelets that cling
tenaciously to their clothing. The species
name means "of roofs," alluding to thatch,
which is a habitat of the plant in Europe.

389 Barnyard Grass
Echinochloa crusgalli

Description: A coarse grass with *ovate, brown,
1-flowered, prickly spikelets* crowded on
one side of ascending or divergent spikes
arranged in an open cluster.

Flowers: Enclosed in scales, 1 scale tipped with a
long slender bristle, all scales covered
with short bristles; spikelets ⅛" (4 mm)
long; spikes 2–6" (5–15 cm) long, in
clusters 4–12" (10–30 cm) long.

Leaves: Blades 6–24" (15–60 cm) long, about
½" (1.5 cm) wide, sheathing stem at
base, edges rough; ligule absent.

Fruit: Grain.

Height: 6–48" (15–120 cm).

Flowering: July–September.

Habitat: Low ground, marshes, wet places, and
roadsides.

Range: Throughout North America, except far
north.

Comments: Barnyard Grass is naturalized from
Eurasia. There are several very closely
related species of *Echinochloa*. All are
weeds of moist fertile places, where they
may encroach upon gardens and are
serious competitors of more desirable
forage crops. Otherwise, they decorate
our roadsides.

24 Eastern Bottlebrush Grass
Elymus hystrix

Description: Greenish-brown, *bristly spikelets* in
several to many clusters along a *terminal
spike* atop an erect smooth stem.

Flowers: Enclosed in scales tipped with long
slender bristles; spikelets at first erect
against stem, later divergent; cluster 10″
(25 cm) long.

Leaves: 4–12″ (10–30 cm) long, to ⅝″ (16 mm)
wide, rough, diverging, sheaths smooth.

Fruit: Grain.

Height: 2–5′ (60–150 cm).

Flowering: June–August.

Habitat: Woods.

Range: Manitoba east to Nova Scotia, south to
Georgia, west to Oklahoma, and north
to North Dakota.

Comments: Together, the groups of spikelets
resemble a bottlebrush, hence the
common name. The species name,
from the Greek *hystrix* ("hedgehog"),
aptly describes the bristly spikelets.
This grass is sometimes known as
Hystrix patula.

26 Little Barley
Hordeum pusillum

Description: An annual grass with each stem bearing
an unbranched, *erect, flattened, bristly
spike of narrow, crowded, greenish-brown
spikelets.*

Flowers: Enclosed in scales tipped with bristles to
½″ (12 mm) long; spikelets ¾–3″ (2–7.5
cm) long, ¼–½″ (6–13 mm) wide,
stalkless, hairy.

Leaves: ⅜–4″ (1–10 cm) long, rough to densely hairy.
Fruit: Small grain.
Height: 4–20″ (10–50 cm).
Flowering: May–June.
Habitat: Roadsides, fields, and waste places, often in alkaline soil.
Range: Throughout United States; also in Ontario and far western provinces.
Comments: Although now widespread in the United States, this relative of the cultivated Barley *(H. vulgare)* was probably originally native only in the southern states. In some areas it is extremely abundant, becoming especially conspicuous when the plants mature, which they do quickly, and turn brown; at that stage the spikes break up into short sections.

25 Timothy
Phleum pratense

Description: A *narrow, compact spike* of several hundred small, green, flattened, 1-flowered spikelets on an *erect, stiff, unbranched stem with a distinctly swollen base.*
Flowers: Enclosed in scales tipped with bristles about 1/16″ (2 mm) long; spike to 8″ (20 cm) long, ⅜″ (8 mm) wide.
Leaves: 4–10″ (10–25 cm) long, ¼″ (6 mm) wide, tapering to a point.
Fruit: Grain.
Height: 1½–3′ (45–90 cm).
Flowering: June–August.
Habitat: Fields, roadsides, and clearings.
Range: Throughout North America, except parts of far north.
Comments: This common old-field or pasture grass, naturalized from Europe, is easily recognized by the somewhat bristly spike, especially fuzzy when in flower, with projecting stamens. It is an excellent hay plant, and songbirds enjoy the seeds. Native to our mountaintops is the much

smaller Mountain Timothy *(P. alpinum)*, also known as Foxtail, with shorter spikes.

386 Giant Reed
Phragmites australis

Description: A *tall, thick-stemmed grass* bearing flat, sharp-pointed, blue-green leaves and *spikelets in large, initially reddish then silver, plume-like, terminal clusters* becoming increasingly downy and purplish gray with maturity.

Flowers: Enclosed in scales about ¼" (6 mm) long; spikelets with many silky hairs among scales; cluster to 1' (30 cm) long.

Leaves: Blades to 20" (50 cm) long, 2" (5 cm) wide, rough-edged, sheathing stem at base.

Fruit: Grain (rarely produced).

Height: 5–15' (1.5–4.5 m).

Flowering: August–September.

Habitat: Freshwater and brackish marshes, ditches, and waste places.

Range: Throughout North America, except much of far north.

Comments: Native to all continents except Antarctica, this tall striking plant rarely produces seed but spreads vigorously by rhizomes that often trail over the surface of the ground for up to 15' (4.6 m), sometimes to 35' (10.5 m). It can form dense stands that exclude all other wetland species. It is the dominant vegetation of the still extant Hackensack Meadows of New Jersey, where it filters pollutants from the greater New York–New Jersey metropolitan area, thus serving a vital role. In New England, tidal gates across estuaries have restricted tidal flow and created heavily brackish conditions on tidal marshes, with the result that Giant Reed has replaced extensive areas of tidal marsh grasses. The stems of this species are used as thatching material for roofs. This grass was formerly called *P. communis.*

592 Kentucky Bluegrass
Poa pratensis

Description: A rhizomatous, sod-forming grass with smooth erect stems topped by *pyramidal clusters of ovoid, green or purplish spikelets borne on thread-like, spreading or ascending branches.*

Flowers: Enclosed in scales grouped in spikelets at branch ends; spikelets and branches forming a cluster to 6″ (15 cm) long.

Leaves: To 8″ (20 cm) long, ¼″ (6 mm) wide, basal and on lower part of stem, with tips shaped like prow of a canoe.

Fruit: Small grain.

Height: 1–3′ (30–90 cm).

Flowering: May–August.

Habitat: Moist or dry soil, meadows, fields, and lawns.

Range: Throughout much of North America.

Comments: Whether this grass is an introduction from Europe or a native, at least in northern North America, has long been a matter of debate. Often cultivated as a lawn or pasture grass, it gives Kentucky the nickname Bluegrass State; the Bluegrass region near Lexington is noted for the famous racehorses that graze on the grasses. The many species of *Poa* in our area are mostly difficult to distinguish from one another.

366 Little Bluestem
Schizachyrium scoparium

Description: An erect, *tufted grass,* orangish tan in fall, with *spikelets in narrow, terminal, spike-like clusters* on slender stems intermingling with leaves.

Flowers: Enclosed in scales tipped with long slender bristles; spikelets to ⅜″ (8 mm) long; cluster to 2½″ (6.5 cm) long.

Leaves: Blades to 10″ (25 cm) long, 1½″ (4 cm) wide, slightly folded, sheathing stem at base.

Fruit: Purplish or yellow grain.

Height: 1½–4½′ (45–135 cm).

Flowering: August–October.

Habitat: Old fields, prairies, and open woods.

Range: Throughout North America, except Oregon, Nevada, and far north.

Comments: This mid-prairie species gets its name from the bluish color of the stem bases in the spring, but most striking is the plant's orangish-tan color in the fall, which persists through winter snows. In the winter the fragments of the spikelets that contain the seeds are a valuable food source for small birds. This grass is sometimes classified as *Andropogon scoparius*. A related species, Big Bluestem or Turkeyfoot *(Andropogon gerardii),* with finger-like seed heads that somewhat resemble a turkey's foot, reaches a height of 12' (3.6 m) in favorable bottomland sites; it is one of the East's important native prairie grasses and grows throughout our area except Newfoundland and the Maritime Provinces.

388   Indian Grass
Sorghastrum nutans

Description: A loosely tufted grass with *spikelets in shiny, golden-brown, plume-like clusters* on tall stems; individual flowers tiny, with *prominent, yellow, protruding anthers.*

Flowers: Enclosed in hairy scales tipped with long, slender, twisted bristles; spikelets to ⅜" (8 mm) long; cluster to 10" (25 cm) long.

Leaves: Blades to 2' (60 cm) long, ½" (1.5 cm) wide, projecting from stem at a 45° angle.

Fruit: Small grain.

Height: 3–8' (90–240 cm).

Flowering: August–September.

Habitat: Prairies, dry fields, and roadsides.

Range: Saskatchewan south to Arizona and eastward throughout East.

Comments: This is a beautiful grass with a somewhat metallic, golden sheen to its flowering parts. It is an important associate in the tall-grass prairies and is relished by livestock. It appears to be

favored by occasional flooding and
repeated burning and sometimes forms
nearly pure stands in lowlands.

384 Sea Oats
Uniola paniculata

Description: *Flat, oval, scaly, brownish, drooping*
spikelets in a crowded, curving, branched
cluster on a tall smooth stem.

Flowers: Enclosed in rough scales to ½" (1.5 cm)
long; spikelets to 1½" (4 cm) long, on
ascending stalks; cluster 8–16" (20–40
cm) long.

Leaves: Blades to 16" (40 cm) long, less than ½"
(1.5 cm) wide, smooth.

Fruit: Compressed grain.

Height: 3–7' (90–210 cm).

Flowering: June–July.

Habitat: Coastal sands.

Range: Maryland south to Florida and west to
Texas.

Comments: It is illegal to damage or disturb this
spectacular grass, often used for erosion
control along beaches. A similar but
smaller and more delicate species,
Inland Sea Oats *(Chasmanthium
latifolium),* also has nodding spikelets
but does not exceed 3½' (1 m) tall; it is
sometimes planted as an ornamental and
collected for dried bouquets.

PHLOX FAMILY
Polemoniaceae

Usually leafy herbs, rarely small shrubs, commonly with
showy flowers in open or dense clusters branched in a forked
manner.

Flowers: Radially symmetrical or slightly bilaterally symmetrical. Calyx with 5 united sepals; corolla with 5
united petals, sometimes dish-like, more often forming a
slender tube with an abruptly expanded top; stamens 5;
style 3-branched; all these parts attached at base of ovary.

Leaves: Alternate or opposite, simple or pinnately compound.

Fruit: 3-chambered capsule.

There are about 18 genera and 300 species in this chiefl[y]
North American family. It is especially well developed i[n]
the western United States. Some species are grown as orna[-]
mentals.

417   Scarlet Gilia; Standing Cypress
Ipomopsis rubra

Description:	*Red, tubular flowers* in a long, slender, branching cluster on a leafy stem.
Flowers:	About 1″ (2.5 cm) long; corolla with 5 somewhat spreading lobes, marked inside with *red spots against a yellow background*.
Leaves:	Pinnately divided into numerous linear or thread-like, bristle-tipped segments, each ¼–1¼″ (5–31 mm) long.
Fruit:	Capsule.
Height:	2–6′ (60–180 cm).
Flowering:	May–September.
Habitat:	Riverbanks and sandy open places.
Range:	Ontario east to Massachusetts, south to Florida, west to Texas, and north to Kansas, Iowa, and Wisconsin.
Comments:	This southern biennial is often cultivated in northern gardens. It is closely related to the showy genus *Gilia* (in fact, some authorities now place it in *Gilia*), a large group of western plants also in the phlox family. It grows in Florida's orange groves, where it is often called Spanish Larkspur.

616   Wild Blue Phlox; Wild Sweet William
Phlox divaricata

Description:	A loose cluster of slightly fragrant, *light blue flowers* atop a somewhat *sticky stem* with leafy, *creeping shoots at base*.
Flowers:	¾–1½″ (2–4 cm) wide; corolla with 5 united petals, trumpet-shaped; stamens 5, short, hidden inside corolla tube; pistil 1, with 3 stigmas.
Leaves:	1–2″ (2.5–5 cm) long, opposite, ovate to lanceolate, unstalked.

Fruit: Capsule.
Height: 10–20" (25–50 cm).
Flowering: April–June.
Habitat: Rich woods and fields.
Range: Ontario, Quebec, and Vermont south to Florida, west to Texas, and north to Nebraska and Minnesota.
Comments: This beautiful species is most common in midwestern woods and fields. The common name Wild Sweet William is also given to *P. maculata.* The mature plants in the eastern part of the range have notched petals; those in the western part do not. The runners of the lovely Creeping Phlox (*P. stolonifera*) form large patches; its stamens and styles reach the end of the corolla tube; it occurs from Quebec south to Georgia and Alabama.

497 Annual Phlox; Drummond Phlox
Phlox drummondii

Description: A much-branched, *sticky-glandular annual with bright rose-red, pink, or white flowers* in tight clusters at stem ends.
Flowers: 1" (2.5 cm) wide; corolla trumpet-shaped, with 5 spreading lobes; stamens 5, short.
Leaves: 1–3" (2.5–7.5 cm) long, alternate, ovate to lanceolate.
Fruit: Capsule.
Height: 8–18" (20–45 cm).
Flowering: April–July.
Habitat: Waste places and fields.
Range: Maryland south to Florida and west to Texas and Oklahoma; escaped from gardens farther north to Minnesota, Ontario, Quebec, and New Brunswick.
Comments: This southern plant escapes from cultivation to roadsides and fields. It differs from most *Phlox* in that its leaves are alternate rather than opposite. The species is named for Thomas Drummond, who sent seeds from Texas to England in 1835.

498 Garden Phlox; Fall Phlox
Phlox paniculata

Description: A *pyramidal cluster of white to pink or lavender flowers* atop a stout, *smooth, erect stem.*

Flowers: 1" (2.5 cm) wide; corolla trumpet-shaped, with 5 spreading lobes, tube hairy; stamens 5, short; pistil 1, with 3 stigmas.

Leaves: 3–5" (7.5–12.5 cm) long, opposite, ovate-lanceolate, bristly edged, with *prominent side veins;* usually 15–40 pairs below flower cluster.

Fruit: Capsule.

Height: 2–6' (60–180 cm).

Flowering: July–October.

Habitat: Open woods and thickets.

Range: Ontario east to Nova Scotia, south to Georgia, west to Louisiana and Oklahoma, and north to Nebraska and Minnesota.

Comments: If found in the wilds beyond its natural range, this species has probably escaped from cultivation. The plant has been widely used as a medicinal herb; the leaf extract is used as a laxative and for treating boils. Many color forms are found in gardens. The very similar Large-leaved Phlox *(P. amplifolia)* has a hairy stem, only 6–15 leaf pairs below the flower cluster, and a hairless corolla tube; it is found in the southern Appalachian Mountains.

450 Moss Phlox; Moss Pink
Phlox subulata

Description: A low plant, forming *moss-like mats, with pink to lavender (rarely white) flowers* in clusters at stem ends, collectively forming a continuous carpet of flowers.

Flowers: ¾" (2 cm) wide; corolla tubular, with 5 notched spreading lobes; stamens 5, slightly protruding.

Leaves: To ½" (1.5 cm) long, opposite, *closely set, needle-like.*

Fruit: Capsule.
Height: Creeper; flowering branches 2–5″
(5–12.5 cm).
Flowering: April–May.
Habitat: Dry sandy places, rocky slopes, and
pine or oak barrens.
Range: Ontario east to Nova Scotia,
south to North Carolina, Tennessee,
and Louisiana, and north to
Minnesota.
Comments: Various color forms of this species
are cultivated, especially in rock
gardens. Those growing wild in
New England have escaped from
cultivation. Trailing Phlox *(P. nivalis)*,
found in sandy pine or oak barrens
from Virginia south to Florida and
west to Texas, has unnotched petals.
Sand Phlox *(P. bifida)* occurs in
sandy habitats in the Midwest
and has petals with notches at
least ⅛″ (3 mm) deep.

599 Greek Valerian
Polemonium reptans

Description: A smooth, weak-stemmed plant with
light blue to purple, bell-shaped flowers in
loose clusters.
Flowers: ½″ (1.5 cm) wide; corolla with 5
spreading lobes as long as tube; stamens
5, about equal with corolla; stigma 3-
lobed, protruding.
Leaves: *Pinnately compound,* with 5–21 ovate to
lanceolate leaflets, each about 1½″ (4
cm) long.
Fruit: Capsule.
Height: 1–1½′ (30–45 cm).
Flowering: April–June.
Habitat: Rich woods.
Range: Ontario and Quebec south to Georgia,
west to Mississippi and Kansas, and
north to Iowa, South Dakota, and
Minnesota.
Comments: This attractive wildflower, with its
delicate, compound leaves, is sometimes
cultivated in eastern gardens.

598   Jacob's Ladder
Polemonium van-bruntiae

Description: An erect stem, leafy to top, bearing few-flowered clusters of *bell-shaped, bluish-purple flowers with long, protruding stamens.*

Flowers: ¾" (2 cm) wide; corolla with 5 flaring lobes; stamens 5, white-tipped, protruding.

Leaves: Pinnately divided into 15–21 ovate to lanceolate, sharp-pointed, paired leaflets, each ½–1½" (1.5–4 cm) long.

Fruit: Capsule.

Height: 1½–3' (45–90 cm).

Flowering: June–July.

Habitat: Swamps, bogs, and mountain openings.

Range: Quebec and New Brunswick south to Maryland and West Virginia.

Comments: The paired leaflets seem to form a ladder up the stem and account for the common name, which alludes to the ladder to heaven seen by Jacob in a dream, as told in the Old Testament. This species is rare throughout its range.

MILKWORT FAMILY
Polygalaceae

Herbs, shrubs, or small trees with oddly shaped flowers in spikes, racemes, or branched clusters.

Flowers: Bilaterally symmetrical. Sepals usually 5, separate, inner 2 larger and petal-like; petals 3, often fringed; stamens usually 8, united; all these parts attached at base of ovary.
Leaves: Simple.
Fruit: Usually a 2-chambered capsule.

There are about 12 genera and 750 species, found nearly throughout the world. A few species are grown as ornamentals. The flower superficially resembles the pea flower of the pea family (Fabaceae) and is often confused with it by those unfamiliar with milkworts. It was once thought that nursing mothers and cows that consumed milkworts would produce more milk.

371 Orange Milkwort
Polygala lutea

Description: Compact, head-like, terminal clusters of *brilliant orange flowers* on leafy, unbranched or branched stems.

Flowers: ¼" (6 mm) long; sepals 5, inner 2 forming petal-like wings; petals 3, united into a tube; cluster about 1" (2.5 cm) long, ¾" (2 cm) wide.

Leaves: Those on stem to 1¾" (4.5 cm) long, lanceolate to spatulate; those at base broader, in a rosette.

Fruit: Capsule.

Height: 6–12" (15–30 cm).

Flowering: June–October.

Habitat: Damp, sandy or peaty soil.

Range: New York south to Florida and west to Louisiana.

Comments: Orange Milkwort is typical of the wet sandy soil and bogs of pine barrens. The species name, Latin for "yellow," refers to the flower's distinctive color when dried; when fresh, the flower is bright orange, whereas most milkworts are pinkish, yellow, or white. Tall Milkwort *(P. cymosa),* found from Maryland south to Florida and west to Louisiana, is very similar but taller. Candyroot *(P. nana),* another southeastern species, has lemon yellow flowers on stems to only 6" (15 cm) tall.

564 Fringed Polygala; Gaywings
Polygala paucifolia

Description: A low plant, growing from prostrate, underground stems and roots, with *pink (rarely white), purple-tinged, or all purple flowers* in axils of *clustered upper leaves.*

Flowers: ¾" (2 cm) long; sepals 5, inner 2 forming wings; petals 3, forming a tube with a delicate, finely fringed, yellow or pink crest.

Leaves: Upper ones ¾–1½" (2–4 cm) long, oval, crowded at top of stem; lower ones reduced to bracts.

Fruit: Capsule.

Fringed Polygala

Height: 3–7" (7.5–17.5 cm).
Flowering: May–June.
Habitat: Rich moist woods.
Range: Alberta east to New Brunswick, south to Georgia, and northwest to Tennessee, Illinois, and Minnesota.
Comments: This exquisite, orchid-like wildflower resembles a tiny airplane without a tail.

---

344   Yellow Milkwort
Polygala ramosa

Description: *Very small, yellow flowers* in a branched, *flat-topped cluster;* roots exude a spicy fragrance.
Flowers: About ⅛" (3 mm) long; sepals 5, inner 2 petal-like, other 3 minute; petals 3, united into a short tube with tiny lobes; stamens 8, filaments united into a tube; cluster 5–6" (12.5–15 cm) wide.
Leaves: Basal ones to 1" (2.5 cm) long, progressively smaller up stem, ovate or narrowly elliptical.
Fruit: Capsule.
Height: 5–16" (12.5–40 cm).
Flowering: June–August.
Habitat: Marshes, pine-barren swamps, and low ground.
Range: Maryland south to Florida and west to Texas.

Comments: Other species of milkwort with flat-topped clusters include Tall Milkwort *(P. cymosa)*, a larger plant to 4' (1.2 m) tall with yellow flowers and narrow, mostly basal leaves, and Baldwin's Milkwort *(P. balduinii)*, also known as White Bachelor's Button, with white flowers; both species are found in the southeastern United States.

533 Field Milkwort; Purple Milkwort
Polygala sanguinea

Description: *Tiny, pink to rose or greenish flowers in a dense, cylindrical, head-like cluster* above bracts persisting on stem after flowers drop off; root exudes a wintergreen odor when crushed.

Flowers: About ¼" (6 mm) long; sepals 5, green or pink, inner 2 forming wings; petals 3; cluster about ½–¾" (1.5–2 cm) long.

Leaves: ½–1½" (1.5–4 cm) long, narrow, scattered.

Fruit: Capsule.

Height: 5–15" (13–38 cm).

Flowering: June–October.

Habitat: Fields, meadows, and open woods.

Range: Ontario east to Nova Scotia, south to Georgia, west to New Mexico, and northeast to South Dakota and Minnesota.

Comments: There are at least a dozen species of milkworts with pink or white flowers. A somewhat similar, pink-flowered species of the eastern United States, Ontario, and Quebec is Sandfield Milkwort *(P. polygama)*, a perennial with a less dense flower cluster; in addition to flowers that open, this species also produces non-opening flowers on whitish, subterranean, horizontal branches. The white-flowered Seneca Snakeroot *(P. senega)*, also found in much of the eastern United States and from Alberta to New Brunswick, has elongated clusters of tiny white flowers and lanceolate to ovate leaves. These species are typical of dry, often sandy or rocky woods.

BUCKWHEAT FAMILY
Polygonaceae

Mostly herbs, sometimes shrubs or vines, rarely trees, with small flowers in racemes, spike-like clusters, or heads and stems commonly with swollen nodes.

Flowers: Usually bisexual, radially symmetrical. Sepals 3–6, separate, petal-like, sometimes in 2 series of 3, outer series differing somewhat from inner; petals absent; stamens 3–9; all these parts attached at base of ovary.
Leaves: Usually alternate, simple; stipules commonly fused into a papery sheath around stem at each node.
Fruit: Small, hard, seed-like, generally 3-sided or lens-shaped.

There are about 30 genera and 1,000 species, primarily in the northern temperate region. Rhubarb (*Rheum rhabarbarum*) and Buckwheat (*Fagopyrum esculentum*) are sources of food and a few species are cultivated as ornamentals. The name Polygonaceae, derived from Greek words meaning "many knees," refers to the stems' swollen nodes. This family has also been known as the knotweed family.

---

494 Swamp Smartweed
Polygonum amphibium

Description:	A terrestrial or aquatic plant with *tiny, deep pink flowers in slender, elongated or narrowly egg-shaped, terminal, spike-like clusters.*
Flowers:	About ⅛" (4 mm) long; calyx 5-parted; petals absent; cluster 1½–7" (4–17.5 cm) long.
Leaves:	Those of terrestrial plants to 8" (20 cm) long, lanceolate, tapering at both ends, with encircling sheath at axil (young shoots usually very hairy); those of aquatic plants to 6" (15 cm) long, floating, thin, lanceolate-ovate, with a rounded or heart-shaped base (young shoots smooth).
Fruit:	Seed-like, dark brown or black, lens-shaped.
Height:	Terrestrial plants 2–3' (60–90 cm); aquatic plants with stems to 4' (1.2 m) long, flower clusters to 3" (7 cm) above water.

Flowering: July–September.
Habitat: Shorelines, wet prairies, swamps, ponds, and quiet streams.
Range: Throughout North America, except Georgia, Alabama, Florida, and Arctic.
Comments: This aquatic or wetland plant is rather showy when growing in colonies. The genus name is from the Greek *poly* ("many") and *gona* ("knee" or "joint"), as is the family name, and refers to the thickened joints of the stem where a sheath often surrounds the stem at the leaf axil. The genus includes the smartweeds, with tiny flowers in terminal spikes, and the knotweeds, with flower clusters in the leaf axils.

492 Long-bristled Smartweed
Polygonum caespitosum

Description: Narrow, spike-like, terminal *clusters of tiny pink flowers* atop stems with *long bristles rising from encircling sheaths* at nodes.
Flowers: About ⅛″ (3 mm) long; calyx 5-parted; petals absent; cluster ¾–1½″ (2–4 cm) long.
Leaves: To 3″ (7.5 cm) long, elliptical to lanceolate; bristles of encircling sheath at leaf axil to ½″ (1.5 cm) long.
Fruit: Seed-like, black, 3-sided.
Height: 1–3′ (30–90 cm).
Flowering: June–October.
Habitat: Waste places, dry streambeds, and cultivated sites.
Range: Ontario east to New Brunswick, south to Florida, west to New Mexico, and northeast to Nebraska, Iowa, and Minnesota.
Comments: This slender, loosely branched annual, a weedy species naturalized from eastern Asia, is distinguished from our many other smartweeds by long bristles on the leaf sheath, equal to or longer than the sheath itself.

97   Japanese Bamboo; Japanese Knotweed
Polygonum cuspidatum

Description: A large bushy plant with spreading *clusters of greenish-white flowers on large, hollow, jointed, mottled stems* in leaf axils; male and female flowers on separate plants.

Flowers: About ⅛″ (3 mm) long; sepals mostly 5; petals absent; cluster 2–3″ (5–7.5 cm) long.

Leaves: 4–6″ (10–15 cm) long, rounded or ovate, tapering to a point, straight across at base.

Fruit: Seed-like, black, smooth, 3-sided.

Height: 3–7′ (90–210 cm).

Flowering: August–September.

Habitat: Waste places and roadsides.

Range: Manitoba east to Newfoundland, south to Georgia, west to Louisiana and Oklahoma, and north to Nebraska and Minnesota; also in parts of West.

Comments: This introduction from Asia is recognizable by the stout, bushy, branched, jointed, bamboo-like stems. Once established it can rapidly take over a given area and is quite difficult to eradicate. In the Pacific coastal states and Virginia it is considered a noxious weed. Its young shoots can be cooked and eaten like asparagus, and the seeds are eaten by ground-feeding songbirds. The similar, robust Giant Knotweed *(P. sachalinense)* has leaves that are heart-shaped at the base; also from Asia, it is naturalized in some places in the East.

491   Pennsylvania Smartweed; Pink Knotweed
Polygonum pensylvanicum

Description: Dense, erect, terminal, spike-like clusters of small, *bright pink flowers on sticky-hairy stalks.*

Flowers: About ⅛″ (3 mm) long; sepals 4–6, petal-like, showy, colorful; petals absent; stamens 3–9; cluster ½–2½″ (1.5–6.5 cm) long.

Leaves:	4–6" (10–15 cm) long, narrow, lanceolate; *bases forming a distinctive cylindrical sheath* where stalk joins stem.
Fruit:	Lens-shaped, 2-sided, concave, smooth.
Height:	1–4' (30–120 cm).
Flowering:	May–October.
Habitat:	Moist waste places and fields.
Range:	Throughout East, except Prairie Provinces; also in parts of West.
Comments:	About 35 species of smartweed occur in our area and are identified by technical features and leaves. The closely related Pale Smartweed *(P. lapathifolium)* has white or pale rose, arching flower spikes and usually smooth stems. Both species are found in gardens as well as in damp waste places. The seeds are eaten by songbirds and waterfowl. There are also climbing smartweeds.

493 Lady's Thumb
Polygonum persicaria

Description:	Dense, erect, oblong or cylindrical *spikes of small, pink or purplish flowers* atop unbranched or branching, *pinkish stems.*
Flowers:	About ⅛" (4 mm) long; sepals 4–6; petals absent; cluster ½–2" (1.5–5 cm) long.
Leaves:	2–6" (5–15 cm) long, narrowly or broadly lanceolate, with a *dark green triangle in center; cylindrical sheath, fringed with short bristles,* where leaf bases join stem.
Fruit:	Seed-like, glossy black, 3-sided.
Height:	8–31" (20–80 cm).
Flowering:	June–October.
Habitat:	Roadsides, damp clearings, and cultivated sites.
Range:	Throughout much of North America, except Northwest Territories.
Comments:	Naturalized from Europe, this is an abundant weed, common in North America, the British Isles, and Europe. The dark green splotch in the center of the leaf was apparently thought to resemble a lady's thumbprint.

412 Sheep Sorrel; Common Sorrel
Rumex acetosella

Description: A *sour-tasting weed* bearing distinctive *arrowhead-shaped leaves with outward-curving, basal lobes* and long, spike-like clusters of tiny, reddish or greenish flowers; male and female flowers on separate plants.

Flowers: About 1/16" (2 mm) long; calyx 6-parted, petals absent; male flowers nodding on short jointed stalks; female flowers with calyx and fruit about same length, calyx eventually dropping off; cluster to half as long as stem.

Leaves: 3/4–2" (2–5 cm) long.

Fruit: Seed-like, shiny, golden brown, 3-sided.

Height: 6–12" (15–30 cm).

Flowering: June–October.

Habitat: Open sites, especially in acidic soil.

Range: Throughout much of North America, except Northwest Territories.

Comments: Naturalized from Europe, this vigorous, rhizomatous, perennial weed is especially favored by soil low in nutrients. In pure stands the flowers are sufficiently showy to be attractive, and bees and small butterflies serve as pollinators. The seeds are eaten by ground-feeding songbirds and the leaves, or even whole plants, by rabbits and deer. Two other species in our area have unisexual flowers. Engelman's Sorrel (*R. hastatulus*) lacks rhizomes and its calyx is longer than the fruit; its leaves also have outward-curving, basal lobes. Green Sorrel (*R. acetosa*) has leaves 4–6" (10–15 cm) long, with basal lobes that do not curve outward; it is grown in gardens as a salad plant.

411 Curly Dock
Rumex crispus

Description: A stout plant with small, *reddish or greenish, bisexual flowers in a long, slender, branching cluster* atop a stem bearing *leaves with very wavy edges.*

Flowers:	About ⅛" (4 mm) long; sepals in 2 series of 3; petals absent.
Leaves:	6–10" (15–25 cm) long, oblong to lanceolate.
Fruit:	Seed-like, brown, 3-sided; enclosed by 3-winged calyx with smooth edges.
Height:	2–4' (60–120 cm).
Flowering:	June–September.
Habitat:	Old fields and waste places.
Range:	Throughout much of North America, except Northwest Territories.
Comments:	The somewhat similar Bitter Dock (*R. obtusifolius*) has heart-shaped leaves with reddish veins, calyx lobes with toothed edges, and flower stalks longer than the flowers. Both species, naturalized from Europe, are common pasture, meadow, garden, or roadside weeds. The young leaves of these plants have a pleasantly bitter, lemony flavor and can be used with other greens in salads.

PICKERELWEED FAMILY
Pontederiaceae

Erect or floating aquatics with flowers commonly clustered in spikes or sometimes solitary.

Flowers: More or less bilaterally symmetrical. Petal-like parts 6, often united at base; stamens 3 or 6; all these parts attached at base of ovary.
Leaves: Long-stalked, floating or emergent, sometimes absent in submerged plants.
Fruit: Capsule or seed-like.

There are 9 genera and about 30 species, found in shallow fresh water in warm and temperate regions of America, Asia, and Africa.

633 Water Hyacinth
Eichhornia crassipes

Description:	*A floating aquatic with a spike of showy, bluish-purple or lavender, funnel-shaped flowers.*
Flowers:	About 2" (5 cm) wide and long, 6-lobed; upper lobe larger, with a conspicuous yellow spot; stamens 6.

Leaves: 1–5" (2.5–12.5 cm) wide, roundish or kidney-shaped, bright green, shiny; stalks usually with *inflated bulbs* filled with spongy, air-filled tissue acting as floats.

Fruit: Capsule.

Height: Aquatic; flower stalks to 16" (40 cm) above water.

Flowering: June–September; throughout year in Deep South.

Habitat: Swamps, freshwater marshes, streams, lakes, and ditches.

Range: Virginia south to Florida and west to Texas, Arkansas, and Missouri; adventive farther north and west, but not persistent, from discarded aquarium plants.

Comments: Naturalized from South America, this attractive tropical species spreads rapidly, clogging waterways in the southern states and in warm regions worldwide. This plant has been called the world's worst aquatic weed, but it may have some potential for removing excessive nutrients from overly enriched aquatic systems. If the plants are harvested periodically, the nutrient load in the water can be reduced; they can also remove heavy metals and other toxins from polluted water.

588 Pickerelweed
Pontederia cordata

Description: An aquatic herb with a creeping, submerged rhizome and *violet-blue flower spikes extending above water.*

Flowers: ⅜" (8 mm) long, funnel-shaped; upper lip 3-lobed, middle lobe with 2 yellow spots; 3 lower flower parts separate; 3 long stamens and 3 short stamens, often dropping off; 2 bracts beneath flower spike, lower bract resembling basal leaves, upper bract a sheath.

Leaves: 4–10" (10–25 cm) long, basal, heart-shaped, indented at base, tapering to a point, *extending above water.*

Fruit: Seed-like.

Height:	Aquatic; flower stalks 1–2' (30–60 cm) above water.
Flowering:	June–November.
Habitat:	Freshwater marshes and edges of ponds, lakes, and streams.
Range:	Ontario east to Nova Scotia, south to Florida, west to Texas, and north to Kansas, Missouri, and Minnesota.
Comments:	This emergent aquatic, with its leaves and flowers above water and portions of the stem under water, is found typically in shallow, quiet water. The seeds can be eaten like nuts and the young leaves cooked as greens. Deer also feed on these plants. The common name suggests that this plant and the fish known as pickerel occupy the same habitat.

PURSLANE FAMILY
Portulacaceae

Herbs, often succulent, with delicate flowers borne singly or in branched clusters.

Flowers: Radially symmetrical. Sepals usually 2, united or separate; petals at least 4–6, separate or united at base; stamens many, or 1 opposite each petal; all these parts attached at base of ovary.

Leaves: Alternate, opposite, or in a dense basal rosette; simple.

Fruit: Usually a capsule, opening lengthwise or top coming off like a lid.

There are about 20 genera and 500 species, found throughout the world, many in the Americas. A few are grown as ornamentals, and some are used as potherbs.

445 Spring Beauty
Claytonia virginica

Description:	A low plant with loose clusters of *pink or whitish flowers, striped with dark pink.*
Flowers:	½–¾" (1.5–2 cm) wide; sepals 2; petals 5, veiny; stamens 5, with pink anthers, each stamen opposite a petal.
Leaves:	2–8" (5–20 cm) long, *usually 1 pair at midstem,* opposite, dark green, linear, tapering at both ends.

Spring Beauty

Fruit: Small capsule, enclosed by calyx.

Height: 6–12″ (15–30 cm).

Flowering: March–May.

Habitat: Moist woods, thickets, clearings, and lawns.

Range: Ontario east to Nova Scotia, south to Georgia, west to Texas, and north to Nebraska and Minnesota.

Comments: This attractive spring perennial is spectacular in large patches, as sometimes seen on lawns; it is one of the first plants to flower in the spring. The plant grows from an underground tuber like a small potato; the tuber has a sweet, chestnut-like flavor. Native Americans and colonists used the tubers for food, as do those interested in edible wild plants today. A similar species of much the same range, Carolina Spring Beauty *(C. caroliniana),* has broader, oval to oblong leaves.

257 Common Purslane; Pusley
Portulaca oleracea

Description: A *sprawling plant* with *smooth, thick, fleshy, reddish stems* and small, pale to often dark or deep yellow flowers, solitary or in small rounded clusters.

Flowers: About ¼″ (6 mm) wide; sepals 2; petals usually 5; stamens at least 8.

Leaves:	½–1½″ (1.5–4 cm) long, alternate or occasionally opposite, *fleshy,* flat, spatulate to ovate, rounded at tip.
Fruit:	Small round capsule.
Height:	Creeper; prostrate branches to 1′ (30 cm) long.
Flowering:	June–November.
Habitat:	Cultivated and waste sites.
Range:	Throughout much of North America, except far north.
Comments:	This European introduction is a widespread and well-known weed that can become quite a pest in gardens during hot weather, but it is easily pulled out. It has long been valued as a salad plant and potherb and even cultivated because of its exceptionally high iron content. The flowers open only in sunlight.

451 Rose Moss; Rose Purslane
Portulaca pilosa

Description:	*A prostrate, fleshy, branching plant with small, pink or purplish flowers* at branch ends and *tufts of whitish hairs in leaf axils.*
Flowers:	About ⅝″ (16 mm) wide; sepals 2; petals usually 5, large; stamens many.
Leaves:	About 1″ (2.5 cm) long, fleshy; spatulate, linear, or lanceolate.
Fruit:	Dry capsule; top coming off like a lid near middle, exposing smooth red seeds.
Height:	2–8″ (5–20 cm).
Flowering:	June–October.
Habitat:	Dry sandy soil and disturbed areas.
Range:	North Carolina south to Florida, west to Texas, and north to Kansas, Missouri, and Tennessee; also in southwestern United States.
Comments:	This low, sprawling native plant is similar to Garden Portulaca (*P. grandiflora*), which also has tufts of hair in the leaf axils, but its larger flowers are to 2″ (5 cm) wide; introduced from South America, it is a popular garden annual that sometimes escapes from cultivation.

PRIMROSE FAMILY
Primulaceae

Leafy herbs, usually with showy flowers borne singly or clusters.

Flowers: Radially symmetrical. Calyx with 5 sepals oft united at base; corolla with usually 5 united or separa petals, or absent; stamens usually 5, each opposite a pet or corolla lobe, or alternate with sepals if corolla absen all these parts usually attached at base of ovary.
Leaves: Alternate, opposite, whorled, or basal; usually simpl
Fruit: 1-chambered capsule, with few to many seeds.

There are about 30 genera and 1,000 species, mostly i the northern temperate region. In the United States th family is most diverse in the eastern region. Primrose (*Primula*), cyclamens (*Cyclamen*), and several others ar grown as ornamentals.

399, 619 Scarlet Pimpernel; Poor Man's Weatherglass
Anagallis arvensis

Description: A sprawling, low-branched plant with *1 long-stalked, nodding, star-like flower* rising from each leaf axil; fruit on thread-like, recurved stalks.

Flowers: ¼" (6 mm) wide; petals 5, commonly *orange to scarlet,* sometimes white or blue *fringed with minute teeth;* stamens 5, with bearded filaments.

Leaves: ¼–1¼" (6–31 mm) long, opposite, ovate, unstalked.

Fruit: Many-seeded capsule; top coming off like a lid.

Height: 4–12" (10–30 cm).

Flowering: June–August.

Habitat: Sandy soil, waste places, and roadsides.

Range: Ontario east to Greenland and Newfoundland, south to Florida, west to Texas, and north to South Dakota and Minnesota; also in much of West.

Comments: Naturalized from Europe, this attractive little annual often shows up in flower beds or in other open soil sites. The flowers close in late afternoon; it is sometimes called Poor Man's

Weatherglass because it closes its flowers in cloudy or bad weather. It was at one time used in a treatment for melancholy. The leaves may cause a severe dermatitis.

224 Shooting Star
Dodecatheon meadia

Description:	Nodding flowers with *strongly backward-pointing petals* in flat-topped umbels.
Flowers:	1" (2.5 cm) long; petals 5, *rose, lilac, or white;* stamens 5, yellow, protruding.
Leaves:	To 6" (15 cm) long, basal, dark green, lanceolate, with reddish bases.
Fruit:	Many-seeded capsule, opening lengthwise.
Height:	8–20" (20–50 cm).
Flowering:	April–June.
Habitat:	Open woods, meadows, and prairies.
Range:	Manitoba and Minnesota east to Pennsylvania, south to Florida, west to Texas, and north to Kansas and Iowa.
Comments:	Shooting Star is often cultivated. Bees, the chief pollinators, must force their tongues between the united stamens to reach the nectar. The plant was far more abundant during the days of the prairie settlers, who called it Prairie Pointers. Amethyst Shooting Star

Shooting Star

(*D. amethystinum*), with reddish-purple
flowers and usually green leaf bases,
occurs from Minnesota and Wisconsin
south to Illinois and Missouri, and also
in Pennsylvania and West Virginia.

57 Sea Milkwort
Glaux maritima

Description: A low, fleshy, saltmarsh plant with
opposite, oval leaves and *tiny, white,
pink, lavender, or crimson flowers* rising
from leaf axils.

Flowers: ⅛–¼" (3–5 mm) wide; sepals 5, petal-
like, united into a tube; petals absent.

Leaves: About ½" (1.5 cm) long, opposite,
narrow or oblong.

Fruit: Few-seeded capsule.

Height: 2–12" (5–30 cm).

Flowering: June–July.

Habitat: Seashores and borders of salt marshes.

Range: Alberta east to Newfoundland and south
to Massachusetts; also in Virginia,
Nebraska, North Dakota, Minnesota,
and throughout West.

Comments: This low, often spreading plant is
associated with salt marshes. Although
its stalkless flowers are not very showy,
its habit and opposite, succulent leaves
help identify the species. It is much
more widely distributed in western
North America, from Alaska to northern
Canada and south to California and
Colorado.

125 Featherfoil
Hottonia inflata

Description: An aquatic with several thick, *hollow,
inflated, upright stalks* emerging from
water and bearing *tiny, greenish-white
flowers* in terminal clusters and in circles
at stalk joints.

Flowers: ⅜" (8 mm) long; sepals 5, larger than
petals, green, linear; petals 5, white,
inconspicuous.

Leaves: ¾–2½" (2–6.5 cm) long, crowded at

base of plant, alternate, opposite, or whorled, *pinnately divided into narrow segments.*

Fruit: Many-seeded capsule, opening lengthwise.

Height: Aquatic; stems 3–8″ (7.5–20 cm) above water.

Flowering: April–June.

Habitat: Pools, ditches, swamps, and stagnant ponds; usually in more than 1′ (30 cm) of water.

Range: Maine south to Georgia, west to Texas, and north to Missouri, Illinois, Indiana, and Ohio.

Comments: The unusual appearance of this floating aquatic plant is due to the ½″ (1.5 cm) thick, inflated flower stalks that are constricted at the joints and essentially leafless. Plants appear in great abundance for a season and then completely vanish for as many as seven or eight years before appearing again.

---

247 **Fringed Loosestrife**
Lysimachia ciliata

Description: An erect stem, unbranched or branched, bearing *yellow flowers* rising on stalks in axils of opposite leaves; *leafstalks fringed with spreading hairs.*

Flowers: ¾″ (2 cm) wide, usually pointing outward, sometimes downward; petals 5, minutely toothed, coming to a sharp point; fertile stamens 5, separate; sterile stamens 5, rudimentary.

Leaves: 2½–5″ (6.5–12.5 cm) long, lanceolate to ovate.

Fruit: Capsule.

Height: 1–4′ (30–120 cm).

Flowering: June–August.

Habitat: Damp woods, thickets, and floodplains.

Range: Alberta east to Nova Scotia, south to Florida, west to Mississippi and Oklahoma, and north to North Dakota; also in much of West.

Comments: The species name emphasizes the hairy leafstalks of this wetland plant, which is sometimes placed in the genus

Steironema. Southern Loosestrife
(L. tonsa) has smooth leafstalks, grows
only to 3' (90 cm) tall, and occurs
from Kentucky and Virginia south to
Georgia and west to Texas. Lance-leaved
Loosestrife *(L. lanceolata)* has narrow
leaves tapering to the base and occurs
in a range similar to that of Fringed
Loosestrife but not in Canada or
the northern Plains states. Trailing
Loosestrife *(L. radicans)* has very weak
stems, virtually trailing on the ground,
and occurs in the south-central United
States east to Florida and Virginia.

248 Moneywort
Lysimachia nummularia

Description: A trailing plant with *opposite, nearly
round leaves and showy, yellow flowers* on
slender stalks rising from leaf axils.

Flowers: 1" (2.5 cm) wide; petals usually 5,
dotted with dark red; stamens 5, erect.

Leaves: ½–1" (1.5–2.5 cm) long.

Fruit: Capsule.

Height: Creeper; stems 6–20" (15–50 cm) long.

Flowering: June–August.

Habitat: Damp roadsides, shorelines, and
grasslands, often in shade.

Range: Ontario east to Newfoundland, south to
Georgia, west to Louisiana, Arkansas,
and Kansas, and north to Nebraska and
Minnesota; also in far west.

Comments: This species, naturalized from Europe,
takes well to cultivation, especially in
rock gardens or in hanging baskets. The
species name is from the Latin *nummus*
("a coin") and refers to the shape of the
leaves, as does the common name.

246 Garden Loosestrife
Lysimachia punctata

Description: *Crowded, yellow flowers* in axils of usually
whorled leaves on a hairy stem.

Flowers: ¾" (2 cm) wide; petals 5, minutely
hairy.

Leaves: 2–4″ (5–10 cm) long, whorled or occasionally opposite, lanceolate.

Fruit: Capsule.

Height: 2–3′ (60–90 cm).

Flowering: June–September.

Habitat: Waste places and roadsides.

Range: Ontario east to Newfoundland, south to North Carolina, west to Ohio, Illinois, and Nebraska, and north to Wisconsin.

Comments: This plant, a native of Eurasia, has escaped from gardens and become a minor weed, especially in the Northeast. Plants in the family Lythraceae are also called loosestrifes, which demonstrates the confusion often caused by the use of common names.

245 Whorled Loosestrife
Lysimachia quadrifolia

Description: An erect plant with *delicate, yellow, stalked, star-like flowers* rising from axils of *whorled leaves.*

Flowers: About ½″ (1.5 cm) wide; petals 5, each *marked with red at base,* often with streaks extending to tip; stamens 5; pistil 1, protruding beyond stamens.

Leaves: 2–4″ (5–10 cm) long, in whorls of 3–6 (usually 4), light green, lanceolate.

Fruit: Capsule.

Height: 1–3′ (30–90 cm).

Flowering: June–August.

Habitat: Dry or moist, open woods, thickets, and fields.

Range: Ontario east to New Brunswick, south to Georgia, west to Alabama, and north to Illinois and Minnesota.

Comments: The whorled leaves and dark-streaked petals are the characteristic features of this rapidly spreading species. The genus name honors Lysimachus, a king in ancient Sicily who purportedly used a member of the genus to pacify a maddened bull. Colonists are said to have fed the plant to oxen as calmatives so that they would work together peacefully.

317   Swamp Candles; Bog Loosestrife
Lysimachia terrestris

Description: An erect stem bearing a *terminal, spike-like cluster of yellow flowers* with 2 red spots at base of each petal.

Flowers: ½" (1.5 cm) wide; petals 5; stamens 5.

Leaves: 1½–4" (4–10 cm) long, lanceolate, opposite, sharp-pointed at both ends; *small reddish bulblets* often present in leaf axils after flowering.

Fruit: Capsule.

Height: 1–3' (30–90 cm).

Flowering: June–August.

Habitat: Marshes, moist thickets, and low ground.

Range: Manitoba east to Newfoundland, south to Georgia, and northwest to Illinois, Iowa, and Minnesota; also in Oklahoma and from British Columbia south to Oregon and Idaho.

Comments: In a wetland garden this showy species will spread rapidly by underground stems. Loomis's Loosestrife *(L. loomisii),* with candle-like clusters of yellow flowers and whorled, very narrow leaves 1" (2.5 cm) long, occurs from North Carolina south to Georgia. Tufted Loosestrife *(L. thyrsiflora)* looks very different, with flowers in dense stalked clusters borne in the lower leaf axils; it is found in swamps and bogs in much of Canada south to New Jersey and west to West Virginia, Missouri, Colorado, and California. Swamp Candles freely hybridizes with Whorled Loosestrife *(L. quadrifolia),* producing lovely intermediates, and with Tufted Loosestrife, producing plants with flower clusters both at stalk ends and in leaf axils.

43   Starflower
Trientalis borealis

Description: *Fragile white flowers* on delicate stalks rising from a *whorl of 5–9 leaves.*

Flowers: About ½" (1.5 cm) wide; petals usually

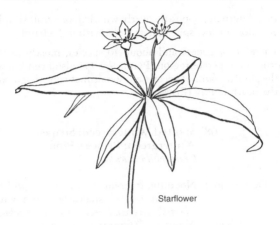
Starflower

7; stamens usually 7, with golden anthers.

Leaves: 1¾–4″ (4.5–10 cm) long, lanceolate; small, scale-like leaf present near midstem below whorled leaves.

Fruit: Capsule, splitting open along seams into 5 parts.

Height: 4–8″ (10–20 cm).

Flowering: May–August.

Habitat: Cool woodlands and peaty slopes, ascending to subalpine regions.

Range: Alberta east to Newfoundland, south to Georgia, and northwest to Illinois, Wisconsin, and Minnesota; also in far west.

Comments: The background of shiny green leaves accentuates the flowers' star-like appearance. The genus name is from a Latin word meaning "one-third of a foot" and refers to the height of the plant.

WINTERGREEN FAMILY
Pyrolaceae

Perennial herbs, with or without leaves; flowers often dish-shaped, borne singly, in racemes, or in branched clusters.

Flowers: Radially symmetrical. Sepals 4–5, separate or slightly united; petals 4–5, separate; stamens usually 10, with anthers opening by terminal pores; all these parts attached at base of ovary.

Leaves: Alternate, opposite, nearly whorled, or basal; simple.
Fruit: More or less spherical capsule, with 4–5 chambers.

There are 4 genera and about 40 species, mostly in the northern temperate region. Pyrolaceae has also been known as the shinleaf family; species are sometimes considered part of the heath family (Ericaceae).

---

68   **Spotted Wintergreen; Striped Wintergreen; Prince's Pine**
Chimaphila maculata

Description: Nodding, fragrant, *waxy, white or pinkish flowers* in small clusters atop a stem with *whorled, evergreen leaves mottled with white.*

Flowers: About ⅝″ (16 mm) wide; petals 5; stamens 10; pistil 1, knobby.

Leaves: ¾–2¾″ (2–7 cm) long, lanceolate, striped with white along midvein.

Fruit: Brown capsule, persisting through winter.

Height: 3–9″ (7.5–22.5 cm).

Flowering: June–August.

Habitat: Dry woods.

Range: Ontario, Quebec, and Maine south to Florida, west to Mississippi, and north to Illinois and Michigan.

Comments: This is a conspicuous plant in both the winter and summer because of its white and green mottled leaves. The genus name is from the Greek *cheima* ("winter") and *philein* ("to love"). This species appears to increase both vegetatively and by seedling reproduction following light wildfires. A slightly taller relative, Pipsissewa *(C. umbellata),* has shiny, dark green leaves that lack the mottling; it is found from Alberta east to Newfoundland and south to Georgia, and from Ohio west to Nebraska and north to Minnesota.

---

122   **Shinleaf**
Pyrola elliptica

Description: *Greenish-white, waxy, fragrant flowers* in an elongated cluster on a stalk rising above evergreen, basal leaves.

Shinleaf

Flowers: About ⅝″ (16 mm) wide; petals 5, thin, encircling 10 stamens with yellow anthers; pistil 1, with distinctly curved, protruding style.

Leaves: To 2¾″ (7 cm) long, dark olive green, broadly elliptical or oblong; stalk red.

Fruit: 5-chambered capsule.

Height: 5–10″ (12.5–25 cm).

Flowering: June–August.

Habitat: Dry to moist woods.

Range: Alberta east to Newfoundland, south to Virginia, and west to Illinois and South Dakota; also in parts of West.

Comments: *Pyrola* species contain a drug closely related to aspirin; the leaves have been used on bruises and wounds to reduce pain. Such a leaf plaster has been referred to as a shinplaster, which accounts for the common name. Shinleaf is one of the most common species of *Pyrola*. Round-leaved Pyrola (*P. americana*) has leathery, roundish leaves. One-sided Pyrola (*Orthilia secunda*) has flowers arranged along one side of the stem, and One-flowered Pyrola (*Moneses uniflora*) has a single flower atop a stem 1¼–4″ (3–10 cm) tall and is found from Alberta east to Newfoundland, south to Connecticut, and west through Ohio and Michigan to South Dakota; both of these species were formerly in the genus *Pyrola*.

BUTTERCUP FAMILY
Ranunculaceae

Usually leafy herbs, sometimes woody vines or shrub-like, with flowers borne singly, in racemes, or in branched clusters.

Flowers: Usually bisexual, radially or sometimes bilaterally symmetrical. Sepals and petals variable in number, separate, or petals absent and sepals petal-like; stamens usually many; pistils 1 to many.

Leaves: Alternate or rarely opposite; commonly shallowly to deeply palmately lobed, sometimes palmately compound, or pinnately lobed or compound, or simple and not lobed.

Fruit: Small, hard, seed-like; or a small pod or a berry.

There are about 50 genera and 2,000 species, primarily in cool regions of the Northern Hemisphere. Several are grown as ornamentals. Some species are used medicinally, and some are poisonous. The family is most likely to be confused with the rose family (Rosaceae), from which it is distinguished by the absence of a cup-like flower base (hypanthium) and by the absence of stipules.

---

593 Monkshood
Aconitum uncinatum

Description:	Several *hooded, violet-blue flowers* in loose clusters atop a *weak stem.*
Flowers:	¾" (2 cm) long; sepals 5, violet, petal-like, upper sepal enlarged and helmet-shaped; petals 2–5, inconspicuous; stamens numerous; pistils several.
Leaves:	To 6" (15 cm) long and wide, palmately divided into 3–5 lobes, toothed.
Fruit:	Pod, splitting open along one side.
Height:	2–4' (60–120 cm); often leaning on other plants.
Flowering:	August–October.
Habitat:	Low woods and damp slopes.
Range:	Missouri northeast to Pennsylvania, south to Georgia, west to Alabama, and north to Tennessee.
Comments:	The roots and seeds of this plant contain alkaloids that are particularly poisonous just before the plant flowers. A drug made from the plant has been used to treat neuralgia and sciatica. A white-flowered southern Appalachian species,

Trailing Wolfsbane *(A. reclinatum)*,
has a trailing or sometimes erect stem.
New York Monkshood *(A. noveboracense)*,
a very similar, violet-blue-flowered
species, occurs from New York west to
Ohio, Wisconsin, and Iowa.

---

112 White Baneberry; Doll's Eyes
Actaea pachypoda

Description: An erect stem bearing large, highly
divided leaves and topped with a dense
oblong cluster of many small white flowers.

Flowers: About ¼" (6 mm) wide; petals 4–10,
narrow; stamens numerous; pistil 1.

Leaves: Leaflets to 4" (10 cm) long, toothed,
ovate.

Fruit: Clustered, *shiny, white berries,* each with a
black dot, on *thick red stalks.*

Height: 1–2' (30–60 cm).

Flowering: May–June.

Habitat: Rich woods and thickets.

Range: Ontario east to Nova Scotia, south to
Florida, west to Louisiana and
Oklahoma, and north to Nebraska and
Minnesota.

Comments: This plant is sometimes called Doll's
Eyes because the shiny white berries
resemble the china eyes once used in
dolls. A red-fruited form of this species

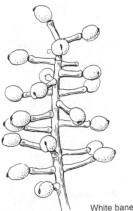

White baneberry

is distinguished from the otherwise
similar Red Baneberry *(A. rubra)* by its
thick fruit stalk. The berries of both are
very poisonous.

114 Red Baneberry
Actaea rubra

Description: A bushy plant with large, highly
divided leaves and a *short, thick, rounded
cluster of small white flowers.*

Flowers: About ¼" (6 mm) wide; petals dropping
off as flower opens, leaving numerous
stamens.

Leaves: 9–27 ovate, sharply toothed leaflets,
each about 2½" (6.5 cm) long.

Fruit: Clustered red berries, on slender stalks.

Height: 1–2' (30–60 cm).

Flowering: May–July.

Habitat: Rich woods and thickets.

Range: Alberta east to Newfoundland, south to
Pennsylvania, west to Illinois, Iowa, and
Kansas, and north to North Dakota; also
throughout West.

Comments: In flower, the stamens give each cluster a
feathery appearance. The showy red
berries are poisonous, as are those of the
similar but white-fruited species White
Baneberry *(A. pachypoda).*

Red Baneberry

452 Round-lobed Hepatica
Anemone americana

Description: A low plant with *round-lobed, basal leaves* and several hairy stalks, each bearing *1 pinkish, lavender-blue, or white flower.*

Flowers: ½–1" (1.5–2.5 cm) wide; sepals 5–9, petal-like; petals absent; stamens numerous; pistils several; 3 green, *sepal-like, broadly oval to elliptical bracts* surrounding flower.

Leaves: 2–2½" (5–6.5 cm) wide, basal, with 3 rounded lobes.

Fruit: Hairy, seed-like, 1-seeded.

Height: 4–6" (10–15 cm).

Flowering: March–June.

Habitat: Dry rocky woods.

Range: Manitoba east to Nova Scotia, south to Florida, west to Louisiana and Arkansas, and north to Minnesota.

Comments: This is an early spring wildflower, usually with lavender flowers and 3-lobed leaves that persist throughout the winter. Sharp-lobed Hepatica *(A. acutiloba)*, with nearly the same range as Round-lobed Hepatica, has more pointed leaf lobes and bracts. These two hepaticas are closely related to the European *A. nobilis* and are considered by some botanists to be varieties of that

Round-lobed Hepatica

species. The word hepatica, derived from the Latin word meaning "liver," refers to the supposed resemblance of the 3-lobed leaves to the liver. This resemblance led early herbalists to assume these plants to be effective in treating liver ailments.

---

46 Wood Anemone
Anemone quinquefolia

Description: A low, delicate plant with 1 long-stalked, basal leaf, *a whorl of 3 stalked, deeply cut leaves, and 1 stalked white flower.*

Flowers: 1" (2.5 cm) wide; sepals 4–9, white, often pink on reverse side, petal-like; petals absent; pistils and stamens numerous.

Leaves: Palmately divided into 5 (sometimes 3) sharply toothed segments, each about 1¼" (3 cm) long; basal leaf similar.

Fruit: Seed-like, hairy; in round clusters.

Height: 4–8" (10–20 cm).

Flowering: April–June.

Habitat: Open woods, clearings, and thickets.

Range: Alberta east to Nova Scotia, south to Georgia, west to Mississippi and Arkansas, and north to Iowa, Minnesota, and the Dakotas.

Wood Anemone

Comments: This is an early spring wildflower that often forms sizable stands on woodland borders. Since the flowers of anemones are usually slender-stalked and tremble in the breeze, they have been called wind flowers; the genus name derives from the Greek *anemos* ("wind").

---

48 Thimbleweed
Anemone virginiana

Description: *A tall hairy plant with 3–9 greenish-white (sometimes pure white) flowers* on a stem with few long-stalked, basal leaves and several paired or whorled, stalked, deeply cut stem leaves.

Flowers: About 1″ (2.5 cm) wide; sepals 4–9 (usually 5), petal-like; petals absent; stamens and pistils numerous.

Leaves: To 3″ (7.5 cm) long, basal and stem leaves similar, palmately divided into pointed, wedge-shaped to oblong, toothed, lobed segments.

Fruit: Mature, seed-like pistils; in *thimble-like clusters* about 1″ (2.5 cm) long.

Height: 2–3′ (60–90 cm).

Flowering: June–August.

Habitat: Dry or rocky, open woods and thickets.

Range: Alberta east to Newfoundland, south to Georgia, west to Louisiana and Oklahoma, and north to the Dakotas.

Comments: The distinctive, thimble-shaped group of pistils accounts for the common name. Long-headed Thimbleweed (*A. cylindrica*) has narrower leaf segments and fruit in a long, cylindrical cone 1½″ (4 cm) long; it is found from Alberta east to Quebec and south to New Jersey and Kansas.

---

404 Wild Columbine
Aquilegia canadensis

Description: *A nodding, red and yellow flower with upward-spurred petals* alternating with spreading, colored sepals and numerous yellow stamens hanging below petals.

Wild Columbine

Flowers: 1–2" (2.5–5 cm) long; sepals 5, red; petals 5, each yellow, with a hollow, long, red spur; stamens forming a column.

Leaves: 4–6" (10–15 cm) wide, long-stalked, compound; divided into 9–27 light green, 3-lobed leaflets.

Fruit: Beaked, many-seeded pod, splitting open along inner side.

Height: 1–2' (30–60 cm).

Flowering: April–July.

Habitat: Rocky, wooded, or open slopes.

Range: Saskatchewan east to Nova Scotia, south to Florida, west to Arkansas and Texas, and north to North Dakota.

Comments: This beautiful woodland wildflower has showy, drooping, bell-like flowers bearing distinctly backward-pointing, tubular spurs, similar to those of garden columbines (also in the genus *Aquilegia*). These spurs contain nectar that attracts hummingbirds and long-tongued insects especially adapted for reaching the sweet secretion. European Columbine (*A. vulgaris*), a garden plant with blue, violet, pink, or white, short-spurred flowers, was introduced from Europe and has now become established in many parts of our range.

251 Marsh Marigold; Cowslip
Caltha palustris

Description:	A succulent plant with glossy, heart- or kidney-shaped leaves and a *thick, hollow, branching stem* with bright, *shiny, yellow flowers.*
Flowers:	1–1½" (2.5–4 cm) wide; sepals 5–9, petal-like; petals absent; stamens and pistils numerous.
Leaves:	Basal ones 2–7" (5–17.5 cm) wide, stalked, dark green, shallowly toothed; upper ones stalkless.
Fruit:	Pod, opening along one side.
Height:	1–2' (30–60 cm).
Flowering:	April–June.
Habitat:	Swamps, marshes, wet meadows, and along streams and brooks.
Range:	Alberta east to Newfoundland, south to North Carolina, west to Illinois and Nebraska, and north to North Dakota; also in parts of West.
Comments:	The flowers of this showy spring plant resemble those of large buttercups rather than true marigolds *(Tagetes),* of the aster family (Asteraceae). The leaves are sometimes used as potherbs but require several short boilings with changes of water between; they should not be eaten raw. A smaller species, Floating Marsh Marigold *(C. natans),* found from Alberta to Ontario and in Minnesota and Wisconsin, has small, white or pinkish flowers, kidney-shaped leaves, and stems that often float. Marsh Marigold is often confused with Lesser Celandine *(Ranunculus ficaria),* which has flowers with yellow petals and green sepals and seed-like fruit.

127 Black Cohosh; Bugbane
Cimicifuga racemosa

Description:	A large plant with *small white flowers in several long narrow clusters* on a leafy stalk; plant has an *unpleasant odor.*
Flowers:	½" (1.5 cm) wide; sepals 4–5, frequently dropping off as flower opens; petals

absent; stamens numerous, in a tuft;
pistil 1.

Leaves: Large, bilaterally compound (twice
divided into 3s), sharply toothed, each
leaflet to 4″ (10 cm) long.

Fruit: Pod, opening along one side.

Height: 3–8′ (90–240 cm).

Flowering: June–September.

Habitat: Rich woods.

Range: Ontario; Michigan east to Maine, south
to Georgia, west to Mississippi and
Arkansas, and north to Missouri and
Illinois.

Comments: The bad odor of this plant is repellent to
bugs, accounting for the common name
Bugbane and the genus name, which
derives from the Latin *cimex* ("a bug")
and *fugere* ("to drive away"). The root
was used in the 1800s to treat various
conditions, ranging from snakebite and
lung inflammations to the pains of
childbirth. American Bugbane *(C.
podocarpa),* also called Mountain
Bugbane, is slightly smaller, 2–6′
(60–180 cm) high, lacks the unpleasant
odor, and has flowers with several pistils;
it is found mostly from Pennsylvania
south in the Appalachian Mountains to
Georgia. Both these species are
sometimes placed in the genus *Actaea*.

---

466 Dwarf Clematis; Pine Hyacinth
Clematis baldwinii

Description: An erect plant with 1 *nodding, pink to
bluish-lavender, bell-shaped flower* on a
stalk taller than leaves.

Flowers: 1–2″ (2.5–5 cm) long; sepals 4, petal-
like, thick, leathery; petals absent;
stamens and pistils many; each flower on
a stalk 4–12″ (10–30 cm) high.

Leaves: 1–4″ (2.5–10 cm) long, simple, opposite,
variable in shape, lower ones unlobed,
upper ones lobed.

Fruit: Seed-like, each tipped by a *long style* to
4″ (10 cm) long; in *feathery heads.*

Height: 1–2′ (30–60 cm).

Flowering: Throughout year.

Habitat: Wet areas and pinewoods.
Range: Peninsular Florida.
Comments: The long stalks elevating the flowers
well above the simple leaves of this
species are distinctive. Dwarf Clematis is
the only simple-leaved clematis known
from Florida, the only state in which it
occurs.

211 Virgin's Bower
Clematis virginiana

Description: *A climbing vine with white flowers* in many
clusters rising from leaf axils.
Flowers: About 1″ (2.5 cm) wide; sepals 4–5,
petal-like; petals absent; *male and female
flowers on separate plants;* male flowers
with numerous stamens; female flowers
with sterile stamens and numerous
pistils.
Leaves: Compound, with 3 *sharply-toothed
(sometimes lobed), ovate leaflets,* each about
2″ (5 cm) long.
Fruit: 1-seeded, with plume-like tails; in
round heads.
Height: Vine; stems 6–10′ (1.8–3 m) long.
Flowering: July–September.
Habitat: Borders of woods, thickets, and moist
places.
Range: Manitoba east to Nova Scotia, south to
Florida, west to Texas, and north to
North Dakota.
Comments: A beautiful, common, and sometimes
cultivated clematis, this species trails
over fences and other shrubs along moist
roadsides and riverbanks. The female
flowers, with their feathery tails or
plumes, give the plant a hoary
appearance and are especially showy in
late summer. Lacking tendrils, the vine
supports itself by means of twining
leafstalks, which wrap around other
plants. A few susceptible people may
acquire a dermatitis from handling the
leaves of this plant. Yam-leaved
Clematis *(C. terniflora),* a Japanese
species naturalized and spreading in the
United States, may be mistaken for

Virgin's Bower; it differs in having leaves with five leaflets rather than three.

58   Goldthread; Canker Root
Coptis trifolia

Description: A small plant with *1 white flower* and lustrous, *evergreen, basal leaves* rising from a *thread-like, yellow, underground stem.*

Flowers: ½" (1.5 cm) wide; sepals 5–7, white, petal-like; petals very small, club-like; stamens numerous; pistils several.

Leaves: 1–2" (2.5–5 cm) wide, basal, palmately divided into 3 leaflets with scalloped, toothed edges.

Fruit: Several-seeded pod, opening along one side.

Height: 3–6" (7.5–15 cm).

Flowering: May–July.

Habitat: Cool woods, swamps, and bogs.

Range: Alberta east to Newfoundland, south to North Carolina, and northwest to West Virginia, Ohio, Indiana, Wisconsin, and Minnesota.

Comments: The common name Goldthread refers to the golden yellow underground stem; Native Americans and colonists chewed the stem to treat mouth sores, hence the common name Canker Root. This species frequently grows with various mosses.

138   Prairie Larkspur; Plains Larkspur; White Larkspur
Delphinium carolinianum

Description: *White to pale blue, spurred flowers* in a narrow cluster on a finely downy stalk.

Flowers: About 1" (2.5 cm) long; sepals 5, petal-like, upper sepal extending into a spur at least ½" (1.5 cm) long; petals 4, inconspicuous, upper pair extending into calyx spur, each of lower pair narrowing to a stalk-like base.

Leaves: Palmately divided, with narrow leaf segments, each about ¼" (6 mm) wide.

Prairie Larkspur

Fruit: At least 3 many-seeded pods, each
opening along one side.

Height: 1–3′ (30–90 cm).

Flowering: May–July.

Habitat: Prairies and dry open woods.

Range: Saskatchewan; Minnesota southeast to
Illinois, Kentucky, South Carolina, and
Florida, west to Texas, and north to
North Dakota.

Comments: When in flower, this midwestern species
can carpet acres of prairie before the
grasses take over. The showy sepals
range from white to pale blue to
greenish.

583 Spring Larkspur; Dwarf Larkspur
Delphinium tricorne

Description: An open cluster of *blue or violet, spurred
flowers* atop an unbranched, fleshy stem
with deeply cleft leaves.

Flowers: ¾″ (2 cm) wide; sepals 5, petal-like,
upper one extending into a slightly
bent, backward-projecting spur about
½″ (1.5 cm) long; petals 4, very small,
upper ones enclosed in calyx spur;
pistils 3.

Leaves: 2–4″ (5–10 cm) wide, deeply palmately
cut into narrow lobes.

Spring Larkspur

Fruit: 3 (sometimes fewer) widely diverging, horn-like, several-seeded pods, each opening along one side.

Height: 4–24" (10–60 cm).

Flowering: April–May.

Habitat: Rich woods.

Range: Minnesota southeast to Illinois and Pennsylvania, south to Georgia, west to Oklahoma, and north to Nebraska and Iowa.

Comments: The species name refers to the three horn-like fruit pods. The flower structure is similar to that of Rocket Larkspur (*Consolida ajacis*), which is often cultivated in gardens and may escape to roadsides and waste places; it has only one pistil. Spring Larkspur is the most frequently seen species of *Delphinium* east of the Plains states. Tall Larkspur (*D. exaltatum*) reaches a height of 6' (1.8 m) and is leafier, with more flowers; it occurs from Ohio and Pennsylvania south to North Carolina and Tennessee, and in Missouri. Larkspurs contain a harmful alkaloid that frequently poisons grazing cattle.

49 **False Rue Anemone**
Enemion biternatum

Description: *White, anemone-like flowers* in small clusters at ends of stems or on stalks rising in axils of alternate leaves.

Flowers:	½" (1.5 cm) wide; sepals mostly 5, petal-like; petals absent; stamens numerous; pistils several.
Leaves:	Compound, with 9 broadly ovate, 3-lobed leaflets, each about ½" (1.5 cm) long.
Fruit:	2–4 dry, curved pods; each pod with 2–6 seeds and a tapering beak, splitting open along one side.
Height:	4–16" (10–40 cm).
Flowering:	April–May.
Habitat:	Rich limestone woods and thickets.
Range:	Ontario southeast to Virginia and Florida, west to Louisiana and Oklahoma, and north to Kansas and Minnesota.
Comments:	This small, herbaceous perennial grows from thick, tuberous, fibrous roots. Long known as *Isopyrum biternatum,* it is found mostly in the southern and western part of our range, extending to the eastern part of the Black Hills of South Dakota, where it is rare. It may be confused with Rue Anemone *(Thalictrum thalictroides),* which has opposite or whorled stem leaves just below the flowers, 5–10 petal-like sepals, and fruit with one seed.

62 Goldenseal
Hydrastis canadensis

Description:	*1 large, wrinkled, basal leaf* and a hairy stalk bearing 1 flower above a pair of 5-lobed stem leaves, all rising from a yellow, underground stem.
Flowers:	½" (1.5 cm) wide; sepals 3, greenish white, dropping off early, leaving many *prominent, whitish stamens;* petals absent; pistils numerous.
Leaves:	To 4" (10 cm) wide at flowering, to 10" (25 cm) wide later, toothed, prominently veined; basal leaf similar to stem leaves but long-stalked.
Fruit:	Red berry.
Height:	12–15" (30–38 cm).
Flowering:	April–May.
Habitat:	Rich woods.

Range: Ontario east to Vermont, south to
Georgia, west to Mississippi, northwest
to Arkansas and Kansas, and north to
Iowa and Minnesota.

Comments: Lacking petals and losing the sepals
early, the flowers of this species owe
their color to the many whitish stamens.
The plant was used medicinally by
Native Americans and colonists, and is
still in use today, ranking with
American Ginseng *(Panax quinquefolius)*
of the ginseng family (Araliaceae), as one
of the most-collected of eastern North
American medicinal herbs. Its current
rarity is due at least in part to
overcollection.

621 Pasque Flower
Pulsatilla patens

Description: *A silky-hairy stalk bearing 1 blue to
purple or white flower* above *a circle of 3
unstalked leaves* with linear segments,
all rising from a cluster of deeply cut,
basal leaves.

Flowers: About 2½" (6.5 cm) wide; sepals 5–7,
each about 1" (2.5 cm) long, petal-like;
petals absent; stamens numerous; pistils
numerous, with long styles.

Leaves: Basal ones to 3" (7.5 cm) long, hairy,
palmately divided into segments cut
again into narrow divisions; ones
beneath flowers hairy, divided into
linear lobes.

Fruit: Seed-like, each tipped by a *long style;
in feathery heads.*

Height: 6–16" (15–40 cm).

Flowering: April–June.

Habitat: Grasslands.

Range: Alberta east to Ontario; North Dakota
east to Michigan, south to Illinois, Iowa,
and Texas, and north to South Dakota;
also in parts of West.

Comments: The feathery, silky fruiting head is the
distinctive feature of this grassland
species. The common name, derived
from the French *Pâques* ("Easter"), refers
to the plant's Eastertime flowering

throughout much of its range. Pasque
flowers are often included in the genus
Anemone.

---

252 Kidneyleaf Buttercup; Small-flowered Buttercup
Ranunculus abortivus

Description: A branching plant bearing *kidney-shaped, basal leaves* and inconspicuous, *yellow flowers with drooping sepals.*

Flowers: To ¼" (6 mm) wide; sepals 5, reflexed; petals shorter and narrower than sepals; stamens and pistils numerous.

Leaves: Basal ones ½–1½" (1.5–4 cm) wide, stalked, with scalloped edges; those on stem unstalked, divided into 3–5 lobes, distinctly unlike basal leaves.

Fruit: Dry, 1-seeded; in *round heads.*

Height: 6–24" (15–60 cm).

Flowering: April–August.

Habitat: Fields, open woods, and waste places.

Range: Alberta east to Newfoundland, south to Florida, west to Texas, and north to North Dakota; also in parts of West.

Comments: With its small petals, this species does not look much like a buttercup, but its many separate stamens and pistils are typical of the genus. The species name refers to the reduced petals. At least 10 similarly small-flowered species occur in our range.

Kidneyleaf Buttercup

250 Common Buttercup
Ranunculus acris

Description: A tall, erect, hairy, branching plant with *glossy, yellow flowers.*

Flowers: 1" (2.5 cm) wide; sepals 5, spreading, greenish; petals 5, longer than sepals; stamens and pistils numerous.

Leaves: Basal ones 1–4" (2.5–10 cm) wide, long-stalked, *blades deeply and palmately cut into unstalked segments;* upper ones smaller.

Fruit: Dry, seed-like; in round clusters.

Height: 2–3' (60–90 cm).

Flowering: May–September.

Habitat: Old fields, meadows, and disturbed areas.

Range: Throughout North America, except Louisiana, Texas, Arkansas, Oklahoma, Nebraska, Colorado, and Arizona.

Comments: This European introduction is one of our tallest and most common buttercups. It thrives in moist sites. As the species name implies, the sap from the stems and leaves is acrid, discouraging animals from browsing this somewhat poisonous plant. The distinctive, shiny, waxy texture of buttercup petals is caused by a special layer of cells just beneath the surface cells.

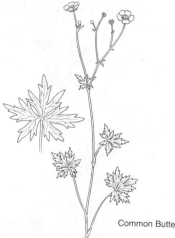

Common Buttercup

254 Bulbous Buttercup
Ranunculus bulbosus

Description:	A hairy plant with a *bulbous base* and bearing *golden yellow flowers*.
Flowers:	1″ (2.5 cm) wide; *sepals 5, downward-pointing;* petals 5, longer than sepals; stamens and pistils numerous.
Leaves:	Basal ones 1–4″ (2.5–10 cm) wide, stalked, cut into 3 lobed and cleft parts, *terminal lobe stalked* and about 1″ (2.5 cm) long; those on stem smaller.
Fruit:	Dry, seed-like; in round clusters.
Height:	1–2′ (30–60 cm).
Flowering:	April–June.
Habitat:	Old fields, roadsides, lawns, and cultivated sites.
Range:	Ontario east to Newfoundland, south to Georgia, west to Louisiana, Arkansas, and Kansas, and northeast to Illinois and Michigan; also from British Columbia south to California.
Comments:	This buttercup is naturalized from Europe. Buttercups have at the base of each petal a distinctive scale under which the nectar is hidden. Most of the common species of buttercup are somewhat poisonous and will affect animals if eaten fresh but not when dried and eaten in hay. Milk produced by cows that have eaten the plants may have an unpleasant flavor or reddish color.

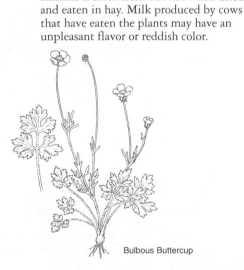

Bulbous Buttercup

302 Lesser Celandine; Pilewort
Ranunculus ficaria

Description:	A smooth, perennial herb with long-stalked leaves, *1 yellow flower, and round clusters of hairy, seed-like fruit.*
Flowers:	1–1½" (2.5–4 cm) wide, bilaterally symmetrical; sepals 3–4, dropping off soon after flower opens; petals 8–10, yellow, often fading to whitish; stamens and pistils many.
Leaves:	Simple, *heart-shaped, glossy,* blades longer than stalks, smooth-edged or scalloped; often clustered at base of plant.
Fruit:	About ⅛" (3 mm) long.
Height:	5–10" (12.5–25 cm).
Flowering:	March–May.
Habitat:	Lawns, shaded areas, streamsides, and moist disturbed places.
Range:	Ontario east to Newfoundland; Vermont south to Virginia, west to Missouri, and north to Wisconsin.
Comments:	The small, bud-like bulblets often produced at the leaf axils are easily detached; they are dispersed by rain and readily grow into new plants. The common name Lesser Celandine serves to distinguish this plant from Celandine *(Chelidonium majus),* a similar but taller species in the poppy family (Papaveraceae). The common name Pilewort alludes to the folk medicinal use of the astringent root to treat hemorrhoids (piles). The roots often produce tubers to 1" (2.5 cm) long. The plant has been implicated in the poisoning of livestock that grazed on it.

249 Swamp Buttercup; Marsh Buttercup
Ranunculus septentrionalis

Description:	*Arching or reclining, hollow stems* bearing bright, *glossy, yellow flowers.*
Flowers:	1" (2.5 cm) wide; sepals 5; petals 5, showy; stamens and pistils numerous.
Leaves:	Divided into 3-lobed segments, each 1½–4" (4–10 cm) long, on *short stalks.*

Swamp Buttercup

Fruit:	Dry, seed-like, with winged edges and a bird-like beak; in round clusters.
Height:	1–3′ (30–90 cm).
Flowering:	April–July.
Habitat:	Moist woods, thickets, and meadows.
Range:	Manitoba east to New Brunswick, south to Florida, west to Texas, and north to North Dakota.
Comments:	A native, weak-stemmed, highly variable species, this buttercup is typical of swamps and marshes. Some botanists divide it into three or four species or varieties. Between 20 and 30 *Ranunculus* species are found in a variety of habitats; all are pollinated by flies and bees.

222 Early Meadow Rue
Thalictrum dioicum

Description:	*Drooping, greenish-white flowers* in long-stalked clusters atop a smooth leafy stem and in leaf axils.
Flowers:	About ¼″ (6 mm) long; petals absent; *male and female flowers on separate plants;* male flowers with numerous long, pale yellow, *showy stamens* protruding from 4–5 petal-like sepals; female flowers with few elongated, purplish pistils.

Leaves:	*Long-stalked,* divided into 3–4 roundish lobed segments, each ½–2″ (1.5–5 cm) wide, pale beneath.
Fruit:	Seed-like, 1-seeded, strongly ribbed.
Height:	8–30″ (20–75 cm).
Flowering:	April–May.
Habitat:	Rich moist woods and ravines.
Range:	Ontario east to Maine, south to Georgia, west to Mississippi and Arkansas, and northwest to Nebraska and the Dakotas.
Comments:	This species blooms in the early spring, just as the trees are leafing out, which accounts for its common name. The species name, derived from the Greek word meaning "two households," alludes to the fact that the male and female flowers are on separate plants.

164 Tall Meadow Rue
Thalictrum pubescens

Description:	A tall plant with *plume-like clusters of white flowers.*
Flowers:	About ⅜″ (8 mm) wide; sepals greenish white, dropping off early; petals absent; male and female flowers on same plant (or partially unisexual); female flowers with several pistils and usually some stamens; male flowers with *many erect, thread-like stamens.*
Leaves:	Compound, bluish to olive green, divided into roundish, 3-lobed leaflets, each about 1″ (2.5 cm) long; upper stem leaf sessile.
Fruit:	Seed-like; in rounded clusters, lower clusters bent backward.
Height:	2–8′ (60–240 cm).
Flowering:	June–August.
Habitat:	Swamps, meadows, and streamsides.
Range:	Ontario east to Newfoundland, south to Georgia, west to Mississippi, and north to Illinois and Michigan.
Comments:	This summer-blooming plant is popular with bees and butterflies. At least 10 other species of *Thalictrum* are found in our range.

47 **Rue Anemone**
Thalictrum thalictroides

Description: A delicate plant with several stalked, *white or pinkish-tinged flowers* rising above a pair or whorl of compound leaves with *3 round-lobed leaflets.*

Flowers: 1″ (2.5 cm) wide; sepals 5–10, petal-like; petals absent; stamens and pistils numerous.

Leaves: Basal and stem leaflets to 1″ (2.5 cm) wide, ovate.

Fruit: Seed-like, 1-seeded.

Height: 4–8″ (10–20 cm).

Flowering: April–June.

Habitat: Open woods.

Range: Ontario; Maine south to Florida, west to Arkansas and Oklahoma, and north to Kansas, Iowa, and Minnesota.

Comments: This slender, spring-blooming plant is easily cultivated in wildflower gardens. It is sometimes confused with False Rue Anemone *(Enemion biternatum),* which has alternate stem leaves, mostly five petal-like sepals, and fruit with 2–6 seeds. It is also similar to Wood Anemone *(Anemone quinquefolia),* except for the numerous flowers and rounded leaflets. The leaves of Rue Anemone are similar to those of meadow rues (also in *Thalictrum*), which accounts for both the common and species names. Some botanists include Rue Anemone in the genus *Anemonella.*

253 **Yellow Globeflower**
Trollius laxus

Description: *1 greenish-yellow flower* atop a leafy stem surrounded by *stalkless upper leaves.*

Flowers: 1–1½″ (2.5–4 cm) wide; sepals 5–7, petal-like; petals numerous, shorter than stamens; stamens many; pistils usually 5–12.

Leaves: 2–4″ (5–10 cm) wide, smooth, palmately divided into 5–7 toothed or cleft lobes.

Fruit:	Pod, opening along one side.
Height:	12–20″ (30–50 cm).
Flowering:	April–June.
Habitat:	Moist meadows and swamps.
Range:	New York and Connecticut south to New Jersey, Pennsylvania, and Ohio; also in parts of West.
Comments:	This is a rare species and should not be picked or disturbed. It is listed as an endangered species in eight eastern states. White Globeflower *(T. laxus* subsp. *albiflorus),* with white sepals, is found in the West.

BUCKTHORN FAMILY
Rhamnaceae

Shrubs, trees, or vines, usually with small flowers in clusters.

Flowers: Radially symmetrical. Sepals 5, rarely 4, separate; petals often 5, sometimes 4, separate, or absent; 1 stamen opposite each petal, or alternate with sepals if petals absent; all these parts attached near edge of a conspicuous disk surrounding ovary.
Leaves: Alternate or opposite, simple, unlobed.
Fruit: Capsule, with 2–3 chambers, or berry-like.

There are about 55 genera and 900 species, throughout the world. Edible fruits are obtained from the tropical Jujube *(Ziziphus jujube),* and the bark of Cascara *(Rhamnus purshiana)* is collected for its purgative properties. Several species are grown as ornamentals.

172   New Jersey Tea
Ceanothus americanus

Description:	*A low shrub with tiny white flowers* in oval clusters rising from leaf axils on current year's shoots.
Flowers:	About ¼″ (5 mm) wide; petals 5, each narrowing to a stalk-like base; stamens 5, protruding.
Leaves:	1–3″ (2.5–7.5 cm) long, 3-veined, toothed, ovate, sharp-pointed.
Fruit:	Capsule, splitting into 3 parts, each 1-sided.

Height: 3–4' (90–120 cm).
Flowering: May–July.
Habitat: Open woods and roadside clearings.
Range: Ontario east to Maine, south to Florida, west to Texas, and north to Nebraska and Minnesota.
Comments: The dried leaves of this shrub make an excellent tea that was very popular during the Revolutionary War period. Smaller Redroot *(C. herbaceus)*, with flowers in a round cluster and narrower leaves, is found from Manitoba east to Quebec, south to North Carolina, Tennessee, and Louisiana, west to Texas, and north to North Dakota. Small-leaved Redroot *(C. microphyllus)* has tiny leaves less than ½" (1.5 cm) long and occurs in sandy pine or oak woods in Georgia, Florida, and Alabama.

ROSE FAMILY
Rosaceae

Herbs, shrubs, or trees, often with prickly stems.

Flowers: Usually bisexual, radially symmetrical. Sepals 5; petals 5, separate, or sometimes absent; stamens usually numerous; all these parts attached at edge of a cup-like flower base (hypanthium) or at top of ovary; pistils 1 to many.
Leaves: Simple or compound; usually with small, leaf-like structures (stipules) at base of leafstalk.
Fruit: Dry or fleshy, sometimes opening at maturity; hip of *Rosa* species a fleshy receptacle enclosing numerous achenes.

There are about 100 genera and 3,000 species in this worldwide family. Several genera provide important fruits: apples and crab apples are from *Malus;* pears are from *Pyrus;* quinces are from *Cydonia;* cherries, plums, peaches, nectarines, and apricots are from *Prunus;* loquats are from *Eriobotrya;* blackberries and raspberries are from *Rubus;* and strawberries are from *Fragaria.* Roses *(Rosa)*, cotoneasters *(Cotoneaster)*, firethorns *(Pyracantha)*, mountain ash *(Sorbus)*, spiraeas *(Spiraea)*, and hawthorns *(Crataegus)* are common ornamentals. It is estimated that there are 2,000 named varieties of apples and 5,000 of roses.

319 Agrimony
Agrimonia gryposepala

Description: *An erect, wand-like cluster of small yellow flowers* extending above pinnately compound leaves; *stem exudes spicy odor when crushed.*

Flowers: About ¼" (6 mm) wide; petals 5; stamens several; pistils 2.

Leaves: 5–9, each with leaflets 2–4" (5–10 cm) long, bright green, many-veined, coarsely toothed, with *tiny leaflets* present between larger leaflets.

Fruit: Seed-like, *top-shaped, with hooked bristles.*

Height: 1–6' (30–180 cm), usually 4–5' (1.2–1.5 m).

Flowering: July–August.

Habitat: Thickets and woods.

Range: Ontario east to Nova Scotia, south to Georgia, west to Louisiana, and north to Kansas and North Dakota; also in parts of West.

Comments: The species name means "having hooked sepals." The similar Southern Agrimony (*A. parviflora*) has leaves with 11–23 leaflets; it occurs from Ontario east to Massachusetts, south to Florida, west to Texas, and north to South Dakota. Five other very similar *Agrimonia* species occur in our range.

Agrimony

99 Goatsbeard
Aruncus dioicus

Description: Small, *whitish-cream flowers in narrow, elongated, spike-like clusters* branching off a tall flower stalk.

Flowers: About ⅛" (4 mm) wide; sepals and petals 5 each; *male and female flowers on separate plants;* male flowers with numerous stamens, female flowers with usually 3 pistils.

Leaves: To 15" (38 cm) long, compound, divided 2–3 times into toothed leaflets 2–5" (5–12.5 cm) long.

Fruit: Pod, opening along one side.

Height: 3–6' (90–180 cm).

Flowering: May–July.

Habitat: Rich woods and ravines.

Range: Ontario and Quebec south to Georgia, west to Arkansas and Oklahoma, and north to Iowa and Wisconsin; also in parts of West.

Comments: The showy, finger-like flower clusters form feathery masses of all male or all female flowers. The common name refers to the appearance of the white flower cluster. The very similar False Goatsbeard *(Astilbe biternata),* of the saxifrage family (Saxifragaceae), has a lobed terminal leaflet on each leaf and two pistils.

52 False Violet; Robin-run-away
Dalibarda repens

Description: A low creeping plant with *1 white flower* on each reddish, *leafless stalk.*

Flowers: About ½" (1.5 cm) wide; petals 5; stamens numerous; also non-opening flowers, producing seeds, on short recurved stalks.

Leaves: 1–2" (2.5–5 cm) long, *dark green, heart-shaped,* downy, scallop-toothed.

Fruit: Seed-like.

Height: Creeper; flower stalks 2–5" (5–12.5 cm).

Flowering: June–August.

Habitat: Woods and boggy areas.

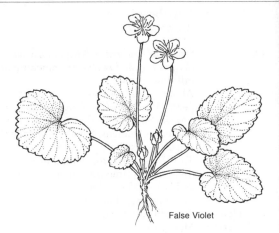

False Violet

Range: Ontario east to Nova Scotia, south to
North Carolina, and northwest to Ohio,
Michigan, and Minnesota.

Comments: This northern species, found in cool
woods and boggy areas, will grow in wet
bog gardens. Its violet-like appearance
accounts for the common name. Violets
(Viola), though, have bilaterally
symmetrical flowers, whereas members
of the rose family have radially
symmetrical flowers.

237, 436 Indian Strawberry
Duchesnea indica

Description: A strawberry-like, *trailing plant with
yellow flowers,* each rising from axil of a
leaf with 3 leaflets.

Flowers: ¾″ (2 cm) wide; sepals and petals 5 each;
stamens numerous; *5 leaf-like, 3-toothed
bracts,* longer than sepals and petals,
behind flower.

Leaves: Leaflets ¾–3″ (2–7.5 cm) long, ovate to
elliptical, toothed.

Fruit: Strawberry-like, but tasteless.

Height: Creeper; flower stalks to 3″ (7.5 cm).

Flowering: April–June.

Habitat: Waste places, disturbed areas, and
lawns.

Range: Ontario and Michigan east to
Connecticut, south to Florida, west to

Texas, and north to Nebraska, Iowa, and Illinois; also in far west.

Comments: This plant is naturalized from India, which accounts for the species and common names. The genus name honors Antoine Nicolas Duchesne, a 17th- and early 18th-century botanist who wrote a study on *Fragaria,* the genus to which the true strawberry belongs. Indian Strawberry may be confused with Common Cinquefoil *(Potentilla simplex),* which has five leaflets.

458 Queen-of-the-prairie
Filipendula rubra

Description: Large, *feathery clusters* of small, fragrant, *pink flowers.*
Flowers: ⅜–½" (8–13 mm) wide; sepals and petals 5 each; stamens numerous, protruding; pistils 5–7.
Leaves: Pinnately compound, divided into deeply lobed and toothed leaflets, terminal leaflet to 8" (20 cm) wide and long.
Fruit: Seed-like, 1-seeded.
Height: 3–6' (90–180 cm).
Flowering: June–August.
Habitat: Prairies, meadows, and thickets.
Range: Ontario east to Newfoundland, south to North Carolina and West Virginia, west

Queen-of-the-prairie

to Illinois and Missouri, and north to
Iowa and Wisconsin.

Comments: A showy species, this coarse-leaved
perennial flourishes in wildflower
gardens. Meadow Queen *(F. ulmaria),* a
shorter European introduction with
white or greenish-white flowers, is also
found in our range.

---

51   Common Strawberry
Fragaria virginiana

Description: A low perennial forming runners and
bearing several *small white flowers and
long-stalked, 3-parted, basal leaves.*

Flowers: ¾" (2 cm) wide; sepals 5; petals 5,
roundish; stamens many; pistils many,
on a *dome-like structure.*

Leaves: Leaflets 1–1½" (2.5–4 cm) long,
toothed, with hairy stalks.

Fruit: Dry, seed-like; *each in a depression on
surface of a greatly enlarged receptacle (the
"strawberry").*

Height: Creeper; flower stalks 3–6" (7.5–15 cm).

Flowering: April–June.

Habitat: Open fields and edges of woods.

Range: Throughout North America, except
Arctic islands and Greenland.

Comments: Found in patches in fields and dry
openings, this plant produces the finest,
sweetest wild strawberries. The edible
portion of a strawberry is actually the
central portion of the flower (receptacle),
which enlarges greatly with maturity
and is covered with sunken, seed-like
fruits. Cultivated strawberries are
hybrids developed from this native
species and a South American one.

---

552   Prairie Smoke; Prairie Avens; Old
Man's Whiskers
Geum triflorum

Description: A softly hairy plant with *brownish-purple
or pinkish flowers,* often in groups of 3,
atop a stalk rising from *fern-like, basal
leaves.*

Prairie Smoke

Flowers: To ¾" (2 cm) long; calyx 5-lobed; petals 5; narrow bracts alternate with sepals.

Leaves: 4–9" (10–22.5 cm) long, pinnately divided into wedge-shaped to oblong, toothed or lobed leaflets; stem leaves few, small.

Fruit: Seed-like, with *long, plume-like, gray "tails"* 2" (5 cm) long.

Height: 6–16" (15–40 cm).

Flowering: Late April–July.

Habitat: Woods and prairies.

Range: Alberta east to Ontario and south to New York, Michigan, Illinois, Iowa, and South Dakota; also throughout West, except Alaska.

Comments: One of the earliest flowers to appear on the prairies, this species attracts attention when in fruit with its "feather duster" look, especially when it forms colonies. Native Americans once made a tea from its roots.

---

44 **Bowman's Root; Indian Physic**
Porteranthus trifoliatus

Description: An erect plant bearing *white or pinkish flowers with narrow petals* and almost stalkless, 3-parted leaves.

Flowers: About 1½" (4 cm) wide; sepals and petals 5 each; stamens numerous; pistils 5.

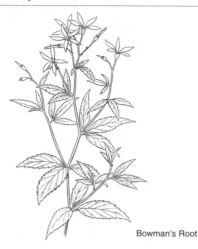

Bowman's Root

Leaves: Leaflets 2–4" (5–10 cm) long, toothed, with tiny stipules.

Fruit: Pod, opening mainly along one side.

Height: 2–3' (60–90 cm).

Flowering: May–July.

Habitat: Rich woods.

Range: Michigan east to Massachusetts, south to Georgia, west to Alabama and Arkansas, and north to Kentucky and Illinois.

Comments: The five petals of this plant project somewhat irregularly. The dried and powdered root was used by Native Americans as a laxative and emetic, hence the common names. A southern and western relative, American Ipecac *(P. stipulatus),* found from Kansas, Michigan, and New York south to Georgia and Texas, has large, sharply toothed or jagged stipules. These plants were formerly included in the genus *Gillenia.*

236 Silverweed
Potentilla anserina

Description: A prostrate plant bearing *1 golden yellow flower* on each leafless stalk and *compound, basal leaves with white-silvery hairs beneath.*

Flowers: ½–1" (1.5–2.5 cm) wide; petals usually 5, blunt; stamens and pistils numerous.

Leaves:	To 1' (30 cm) long, pinnately compound, divided into numerous sharply toothed leaflets to 1½" (4 cm) long, smaller leaflets interspersed between larger ones.
Fruit:	Dry, seed-like.
Height:	Creeper; runners 1–3' (30–90 cm) long.
Flowering:	June–August.
Habitat:	Sandy shorelines, banks, and wet meadows.
Range:	Alberta east to Newfoundland, south to New Jersey, west to Nebraska, and north to North Dakota; also throughout West.
Comments:	This plant grows as far north as the edge of the Arctic. The roots are edible; boiled, their taste resembles that of parsnips. Another species having leaves with silvery undersides is Silvery Cinquefoil *(P. argentea),* an erect perennial 6–12" (15–30 cm) high, found in dry open fields from North Carolina west to Kansas and north to Alberta and Newfoundland; it has palmately compound leaves with five wedge-shaped leaflets with rolled-down edges.

233 Canadian Dwarf Cinquefoil
Potentilla canadensis

Description:	A low spreading plant bearing *silvery-downy stems and 1 yellow flower* on each long stalk rising from axils of palmately compound leaves with 5 leaflets.
Flowers:	½–⅝" (13–16 mm) wide; sepals and petals 5 each; stamens and pistils numerous; *first flower rising from axil of first leaf.*
Leaves:	Leaflets to 1½" (4 cm) long, toothed at tip, untoothed below middle.
Fruit:	Dry, seed-like.
Height:	2–6" (5–15 cm); stems prostrate after flowering.
Flowering:	March–June.
Habitat:	Dry open soil.
Range:	Ontario east to Newfoundland, south to Georgia, west to Arkansas and Texas, and northeast to Missouri, Kentucky, and Ohio.

Comments: This species is very similar to Common
Cinquefoil *(P. simplex),* but the latter has
larger leaflets to 2½″ (6.5 cm) long, and
the first flower rises from the axil of the
second leaf; it is found throughout our
area, except the Prairie Provinces and
the Dakotas. Both species are indicators
of impoverished soil.

234 Rough-fruited Cinquefoil
Potentilla recta

Description: An erect, *hairy plant* with flat-topped,
sparse clusters of *pale yellow flowers with
notched petals.*
Flowers: ¾″ (2 cm) wide; sepals and petals
usually 5 each, petals large compared to
sepals; stamens and pistils numerous,
with anthers at least ¹⁄₁₆″ (1 mm) long.
Leaves: Compound, divided into 5–7 blunt-
tipped, toothed leaflets 1–3″ (2.5–7.5
cm) long.
Fruit: Dry, seed-like.
Height: 1–2′ (30–60 cm).
Flowering: May–August.
Habitat: Roadsides, dry fields, and waste places.
Range: British Columbia east to Newfoundland
and southward throughout United
States, except Utah, Arizona, and New
Mexico.
Comments: The forage value of this species is low,
and it is seldom eaten by livestock;
consequently this European introduction
is now considered to be one of the most
rapidly increasing weeds in some areas.
A similar weedy plant, Norwegian
Cinquefoil *(P. norvegica),* has leaves with
only three leaflets.

235 Dwarf Cinquefoil; Robbins's Potentilla
Potentilla robbinsiana

Description: A *tufted dwarf plant* with a fuzzy, hairy
appearance and bearing deeply toothed,
3-parted leaves and *1 (rarely 2) yellow
flower* on each thread-like, hairy stem.

Flowers:	To ⅜" (8 mm) wide; sepals and petals usually 5 each; stamens and pistils numerous; green bracts beneath sepals.
Leaves:	Leaflets ¼–⅜" (5–8 mm) long, wedge-shaped to ovate.
Fruit:	Dry, seed-like.
Height:	½–2" (1.5–5 cm).
Flowering:	June–July.
Habitat:	Alpine regions.
Range:	White Mountains Presidential Range of New Hampshire.
Comments:	This small plant, found only at high elevations in the White Mountains of New Hampshire and listed as an endangered species in that state, is one of the rarest in the United States. It lacks the runners characteristic of other *Potentilla* species.

430 Red Chokeberry
Pyrus arbutifolia

Description:	A spreading shrub with terminal clusters of *white or pink-tinged flowers on hairy stalks.*
Flowers:	½" (1.5 cm) wide; petals 5; stamens numerous, with conspicuous, *black or dark red anthers.*
Leaves:	1–3" (2.5–7.5 cm) long, toothed, oval to broadly lanceolate, with pointed tips, dark green and smooth above, *densely hairy* and pale beneath; glands along upper midrib visible with hand lens.
Fruit:	Bright or dull red, berry-like, ¼" (6 mm) wide.
Height:	3–12' (90–360 cm).
Flowering:	April–July.
Habitat:	Thickets, clearings, low woods, and swamps.
Range:	Ontario east to Nova Scotia, south to Florida, west to Texas, and northeast to Arkansas, Kentucky, and New York.
Comments:	A native shrub, this species forms sizable colonies and is excellent for naturalistic landscaping. A closely related, black-fruited species, Black Chokeberry *(P. melanocarpa),* has leaves that are hairless beneath; it is found

from Ontario east to Newfoundland and south to Georgia and Arkansas.
Growing in much the same range, Purple Chokeberry *(P. floribunda)*, which appears to be derived by hybridization of Red and Black Chokeberry, has purple fruit. Although chokeberry fruits persist through much of the winter, they appear to be of little importance to wildlife; they are occasionally eaten by game birds and songbirds and reportedly by bears. Chokeberry species are sometimes placed in the genus *Aronia*.

457 Prairie Rose
Rosa arkansana

Description: Small clusters of *white to deep pink flowers* on densely *prickly stems* of new growth or on short, lateral branches of older stems.
Flowers: About 2″ (5 cm) wide; sepals and petals 5 each; stamens and pistils numerous.
Leaves: Pinnately divided into 9–11 toothed, ovate to oblong leaflets to 2″ (5 cm) long, covered with *soft hairs beneath;* size variable according to moisture conditions.
Fruit: Bright red hip.
Height: 2′ (60 cm).
Flowering: June.
Habitat: Prairies, roadsides, and ditches.
Range: Alberta east to Ontario and Massachusetts, southwest to Indiana and Texas, and northwest to Montana.
Comments: The flower buds of this species are a deeper pink than the open flowers. The colorful fruit remains on the plant into the fall and winter.

202 Multiflora Rose
Rosa multiflora

Description: Clusters of many small, *fragrant, white flowers on arching stems* with flattened curved prickles.
Flowers: ¾–1½″ (2–4 cm) wide; sepals 5, lanceolate, sharp-tipped; petals 5; stamens and pistils numerous.

Leaves:	Pinnately divided into 7–9 ovate, toothed leaflets about 1″ (2.5 cm) long; *stipules fringed.*
Fruit:	Small, red, many-seeded hip.
Height:	6–15′ (1.8–4.5 m).
Flowering:	May–June.
Habitat:	Fields, woods, and roadsides.
Range:	Ontario east to New Brunswick, south to Florida, west to Texas, and north to Nebraska and Minnesota; also in far west.
Comments:	Introduced from eastern Asia, this small-flowered rose is sold as a living hedge by nurseries. An invasive pest in many areas, spreading into fields and pastures, it forms dense, impenetrable masses. In at least 10 states Multiflora Rose is considered a noxious weed. On the positive side, it provides excellent wildlife cover. In the South, the white-flowered Cherokee Rose *(R. laevigata),* an introduction from China, has flowers 2–3″ (5–7.5 cm) wide and evergreen leaves with three leaflets; it has escaped from cultivation from North Carolina south to Florida and Texas. Another introduced white-flowered species, Macartney Rose *(R. bracteata),* with 5–9 leaflets and fringed stipules, has become a pest in the South from Kentucky and Virginia south to Florida, Arkansas, and Texas.

455 Rugosa Rose; Wrinkled Rose
Rosa rugosa

Description:	Large, *rose-lavender (sometimes white) flowers on very prickly, hairy stems.*
Flowers:	2–3″ (5–7.5 cm) wide; sepals and petals 5 each; stamens and pistils numerous.
Leaves:	3–6″ (7.5–15 cm) long, pinnately compound, with toothed, elliptical to oblong, *dark green leaflets appearing wrinkled.*
Fruit:	Brick red hip; capped by long, persistent sepals.
Height:	4–6′ (1.2–1.8 m).
Flowering:	June–September.

Habitat:	Seashore thickets, sand dunes, and roadsides.
Range:	Ontario east to Newfoundland, south to Virginia, west to Missouri, and north to Minnesota.
Comments:	This large showy rose was introduced from eastern Asia. It is a plant frequently used to stabilize beaches and dunes. Sweetbrier *(R. eglanteria),* with non-hairy, prickly stems, smaller pink flowers, and highly aromatic leaves, was introduced from Europe and has spread in pastures throughout our area except the Prairie Provinces, the Dakotas, Florida, and Louisiana. Dog Rose *(R. canina),* also a European introduction, is similar but has nonaromatic leaves; it is found from Ontario east to Newfoundland and south to Kansas, Arkansas, Alabama, and North Carolina.

456 Virginia Rose
Rosa virginiana

Description:	A bushy shrub with hairy stems bearing *scattered, stout, curved prickles, pink flowers,* and pinnately compound leaves.
Flowers:	2–3″ (5–7.5 cm) wide; sepals and petals 5 each; stamens numerous.
Leaves:	Divided into 5–9 dark green, smooth, shining, oval, toothed leaflets 1–2½″ (2.5–6.5 cm) long; stipules wing-like, narrow, flaring.
Fruit:	Red hip.
Height:	1–6′ (30–180 cm).
Flowering:	June–August.
Habitat:	Clearings, thickets, and shorelines.
Range:	Ontario east to Newfoundland, south to Georgia and Alabama, and north to Tennessee, Missouri, and Illinois.
Comments:	Numerous species of rose occur in a variety of sites, from dry uplands to wetlands and sand dunes. Their fruit, the so-called hip, is rich in vitamin C and can be eaten, made into jam, or steeped to make rose hip tea. Swamp Rose *(R. palustris),* also pink-flowered, reaches a height of 7′ (2.1 m) and has

flowers 1½–2½″ (4–6.5 cm) wide, very narrow stipules, and stout hooked prickles; it is found in wet sites from Ontario south to Arkansas and east to the Atlantic Coast, except Newfoundland. Pasture Rose *(R. carolina)* is a shorter shrub, less than 3′ (90 cm) tall, with pink flowers, dull green leaves, very narrow stipules, and straight prickles; it is found in dry pastures and open woods throughout our range, except the Prairie Provinces, the Dakotas, and Newfoundland.

---

50 Swamp Dewberry; Bristly Dewberry
Rubus hispidus

Description: Trailing, woody stems bearing *weak, backward-curving bristles,* erect branches, usually *3-parted, shiny leaves, and white flowers* in loose, terminal clusters or in leaf axils.

Flowers: ¾″ (2 cm) wide; sepals and petals 5 each; stamens and pistils many.

Leaves: Leaflets to 2″ (5 cm) long, thick, ovate, toothed, mostly evergreen.

Fruit: Red or blackish, blackberry-like.

Height: Creeper; erect branches 4–12″ (10–30 cm).

Flowering: June–September.

Swamp Dewberry

Habitat: Usually moist thickets, open woods, and clearings.

Range: Ontario east to Nova Scotia, south to South Carolina, west to Tennessee, and north to Iowa and Wisconsin.

Comments: A great many species of dewberry occur, some with bristles and some with stronger prickles. These plants and the related blackberries and raspberries (both in *Rubus*) are among the most important summer foods for songbirds and game birds as well as for many mammals.

---

547 **Purple-flowering Raspberry**
Rubus odoratus

Description: An erect, shrubby plant *lacking prickles* and bearing *rose-lavender flowers* in loose clusters; new branches bristly-hairy.

Flowers: 1–2″ (2.5–5 cm) wide; petals 5, rose-like; stamens and pistils many.

Leaves: 4–10″ (10–25 cm) wide, *large, maple-like,* with 3–5 lobes, heart-shaped at base.

Fruit: Red, broad, shallow; becoming raspberry-like at maturity.

Height: 3–6′ (90–180 cm).

Flowering: June–September.

Habitat: Rocky woods and thickets.

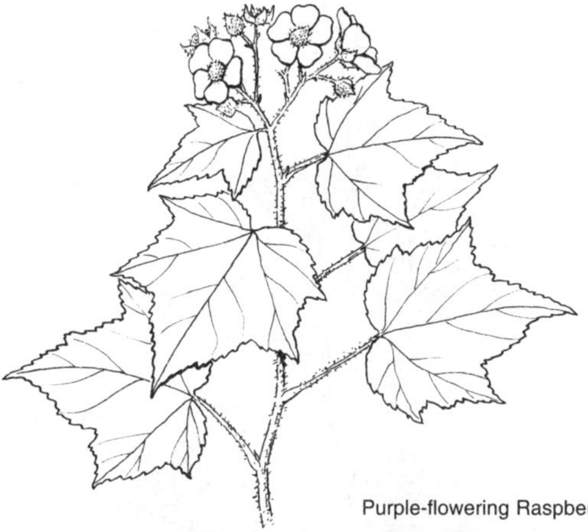

Purple-flowering Raspberry

Range: Ontario east to Nova Scotia, south to
Georgia, west to Alabama, and north to
Wisconsin.

Comments: Thimbleberry *(R. parviflorus)*, with very
similar white flowers and similar but
smaller leaves, occurs from Ontario
south to South Dakota, Illinois, and
Michigan. Baked-apple Berry *(R. chamaemorus)* is a dwarf form to only 1'
(30 cm) tall, each plant with a solitary
white flower, an amber-colored fruit,
and similar but smaller leaves;
widespread in northern North America
and Eurasia, it occurs in our area on
mountaintops in New England and in
Minnesota. All other *Rubus* species in
our range have compound leaves and
usually prickly stems.

---

105 Canadian Burnet
Sanguisorba canadensis

Description: Dense, erect, *cylindrical spikes of small
white flowers.*

Flowers: About ¼" (6 mm) wide; sepals 4, petal-
like; petals absent; stamens 4, *long;* pistil
1; spike to 6" (15 cm) long.

Leaves: Pinnately compound, with 7–15 *stalked,
oblong, toothed leaflets* 1–3" (2.5–7.5 cm)
long.

Canadian Burnet

Fruit:	Dry, seed-like.
Height:	1–5′ (30–150 cm).
Flowering:	June–October.
Habitat:	Swamps and bogs.
Range:	Manitoba; Quebec east to Newfoundland, south to Georgia, and northwest to Illinois and Michigan; also in parts of northwestern North America.
Comments:	The conspicuous stamens give the finger-like spikes a fuzzy appearance. European Great Burnet (*S. officinalis*), naturalized from Minnesota east to Pennsylvania, Maine, and Nova Scotia, has red- to purple-brown flowers, accounting for the common name burnet, which is derived from an old French word for "brown"; Garden Burnet (*S. minor*), with greenish flowers, was introduced from Europe and naturalized in our range from Ontario east to Nova Scotia and south to North Carolina and Tennessee. The genus name, from the Latin *sanguis* ("blood") and *sorbere* ("drink up"), refers to the sap of the plant, which was reputed to stop bleeding.

110 Meadowsweet
Spiraea alba

Description:	A woody shrub with a *dense, pyramidal, terminal cluster of small, white or pale pinkish flowers.*
Flowers:	About ¼″ (6 mm) wide; sepals and petals 5 each; stamens numerous; pistils usually 5.
Leaves:	1½–2¾″ (4–7 cm) long, narrowly ovate to broadly lanceolate, hairless or nearly so, coarsely toothed, pale beneath.
Fruit:	Pod, opening along one side.
Height:	2–5′ (60–150 cm).
Flowering:	June–September.
Habitat:	Meadows, old fields, and low moist ground.
Range:	Alberta east to Newfoundland, south to North Carolina, west to Missouri, and northwest to North Dakota.

Comments: The brown fruit, which persists after
flowering, is a distinctive feature of all
Spiraea. Although less spectacular than
the showy, introduced garden spiraeas,
this native species is most suitable for
naturalistic landscaping. Virginia
Spiraea *(S. virginiana),* with a rounded,
short, broad flower cluster and thin
oblong leaves, is found from Ohio and
Pennsylvania south to Georgia and
Louisiana.

487 Steeplebush
Spiraea tomentosa

Description: An erect shrub with dense, *steeple-shaped,*
branched clusters of pink flowers.
Flowers: Less than ¼" (6 mm) wide; sepals and
petals 5 each; stamens numerous; pistils
5–8.
Leaves: 1–2" (2.5–5 cm) long, oblong, toothed,
very woolly beneath.
Fruit: Pod, opening along one side.
Height: 2–4' (60–120 cm).
Flowering: July–September.
Habitat: Old fields, meadows, and sterile low
ground.
Range: Manitoba east to Nova Scotia, south to
Georgia, west to Arkansas and Kansas,
and north to Illinois and Minnesota.
Comments: A similar species, the pink-flowered
Japanese Spiraea *(S. japonica)* from Asia,
differs from Steeplebush in having flat-
topped clusters of flowers and smooth
leaves; it is found from Ontario and
Michigan east to Maine and south to
Georgia, Tennessee, and Illinois.

239 Barren Strawberry
Waldsteinia fragarioides

Description: A low, strawberry-like plant with
evergreen, basal leaves and several *yellow*
flowers on a leafless stalk.
Flowers: About ½" (1.5 cm) wide; sepals 5,
united into a cup, persistent; petals 5;
stamens many; pistils 3–6.

Barren Strawberry

Leaves:	Long-stalked, divided into 3 wedge-shaped, toothed leaflets 1–2″ (2.5–5 cm) long.
Fruit:	Dry, 1-seeded.
Height:	3–8″ (7.5–20 cm).
Flowering:	April–June.
Habitat:	Woods, thickets, and clearings.
Range:	Ontario east to New Brunswick, south to Georgia, west to Tennessee and Arkansas, and north to Illinois, Wisconsin, and Minnesota.
Comments:	Although this plant is strawberry-like, the flowers are yellow and the fruit is neither fleshy nor edible at maturity. Lobed Strawberry *(W. lobata),* found along riverbanks in Georgia and the Carolinas, has lobed and toothed leaves and narrow, yellow petals no longer than the sepals.

MADDER FAMILY
Rubiaceae

Herbs, shrubs, or trees, with flowers in branched clusters.

Flowers: Usually radially symmetrical. Sepals 4–5, or absent; petals 4–5, united at base; stamens 4–5; all these parts attached at top of ovary.

Leaves: Opposite, with bases connected by united stipules extending across node; or whorled, with stipules apparently lacking.

Fruit: Usually a berry or a 2-chambered capsule; or splitting into 2–4 seed-like sections, each 1-seeded.

There are about 450 genera and 6,500 species, primarily in tropical regions, where woody representatives are most frequent. A dye is obtained from Madder *(Rubia tinctoria),* coffee from species of *Coffea,* and quinine from species of *Cinchona. Gardenia* species are popular ornamentals in mild climates. Sweet-scented members of the genus *Galium* were once used as mattress stuffing, thus the common name bed-straw is often given to these species as well as to Rubiaceae as a whole.

182 Buttonbush
Cephalanthus occidentalis

Description: A wetland or aquatic shrub with small, *white, tubular flowers in ball-like clusters.*

Flowers: About ⅜" (8 mm) long; corolla with 4 erect or spreading lobes; stamens 4; style long, protruding; cluster about 1½" (4 cm) wide.

Leaves: 3–6" (7.5–15 cm) long, opposite or whorled, ovate, untoothed, pointed.

Fruit: Angular, seed-like; in a dense ball.

Height: 3–10' (90–300 cm).

Flowering: June–August.

Habitat: Swamps, pondsides, and streamsides.

Range: Ontario east to Nova Scotia, south to Florida, west to Texas, and north to Nebraska, Iowa, and Minnesota.

Comments: This species is noted for its ability to withstand flood conditions. The distinctive, ball-like flower and fruit heads account for the common name. The fruit has some appeal to wildlife, especially Mallard ducks.

195 Cleavers; Goosegrass
Galium aparine

Description: A weak-stemmed, sprawling plant with *backward-hooked bristles on stems and leaves* and very small, *white flowers in clusters* of 1–3 (usually 2) on stalks rising from *axils of whorled leaves.*

Flowers:	About ⅛″ (3 mm) wide; sepals absent; corolla 4-lobed; stamens 4.
Leaves:	1–3″ (2.5–7.5 cm) long, lanceolate to linear, *in whorls of 6–8.*
Fruit:	Dry, seed-like, covered with hooked bristles.
Height:	Sprawling stems 8–36″ (20–90 cm) long.
Flowering:	May–July.
Habitat:	Woods, thickets, and waste places.
Range:	Throughout North America, except Northwest Territories and Newfoundland.
Comments:	The common name Cleavers is appropriate since the bristles cause the stems, leaves, and fruit to cleave to clothes and the fur of animals. The fact that geese eat the plants accounts for the common name Goosegrass.

129   Northern Bedstraw
Galium boreale

Description:	A sometimes branched, *erect, leafy stem* bearing compact, branched, terminal clusters of *small white flowers and leaves in whorls of 4.*
Flowers:	¼″ (6 mm) wide; sepals absent; corolla 4-lobed; stamens 4.
Leaves:	¾–2″ (2–5 cm) long, lanceolate to linear.
Fruit:	Dry, seed-like, smooth or with short straight hairs.
Height:	8–36″ (20–90 cm).
Flowering:	June–August.
Habitat:	Rocky soil, shorelines, and streambanks.
Range:	Alberta east to Nova Scotia, south to Virginia, west to Tennessee, Missouri, and Nebraska, and north to North Dakota; also in much of West.
Comments:	This is a smooth species compared to some others in the genus, which have rough bristly stems. It often forms sizable patches that may smother more desirable plants.

194 Wild Madder
Galium mollugo

Description: A mostly smooth plant with an erect stem rising from a sprawling base and bearing *leaves in whorls of 6–8 and numerous small white flowers* in a loose, branched, terminal cluster.

Flowers: About ⅛" (4 mm) wide; sepals absent; corolla 4-lobed; stamens 4.

Leaves: ½–1¼" (1.5–3 cm) long, linear-oblong to lanceolate, edges rough.

Fruit: Dry, seed-like, smooth.

Height: 1–3' (30–90 cm).

Flowering: June–August.

Habitat: Roadsides, fields, and waste places.

Range: Ontario east to Newfoundland, south to Georgia, west to Mississippi, and north to Wisconsin; also in parts of West.

Comments: Naturalized from Europe, this weed has now become common throughout its range. The genus name is from the Greek *gala* ("milk") and refers to an old use of the plant to curdle milk in making cheese. At least 30 *Galium* species occur in our range, two of which are yellow-flowered: Piedmont Bedstraw *(G. pedemontanum),* with inconspicuous flowers in the leaf axils, and Yellow Bedstraw *(G. vernum),* with showy flowers in terminal clusters.

615 Bluets
Houstonia caerulea

Description: A low plant with erect, slender stems bearing *pale blue flowers with golden yellow centers.*

Flowers: About ½" (1.5 cm) wide; corolla tubular, with 4 flattish lobes; some flowers with long styles and short stamens, others with short styles and long stamens.

Leaves: Those at base to ½" (1.5 cm) long, oblong, in tufts; those on stem tiny, opposite.

Fruit: Capsule.

Height: 3–6" (7.5–15 cm).

Flowering: April–June.

Bluets

Habitat:	Grassy slopes and fields, thickets, and lawns in acidic soil.
Range:	Ontario east to Nova Scotia, south to Georgia, west to Louisiana, and north to Missouri, Illinois, and Wisconsin.
Comments:	This lovely, delicate flowering plant often forms striking patches of light blue. Star Violet *(H. pusilla),* to 4″ (10 cm) high, has a tiny, purple flower and occurs in fields and open woods from South Dakota east to Maryland and south to Florida and Texas. Large Houstonia *(H. purpurea),* a tall southern species 6–16″ (15–40 cm) high, has 3–5 ribbed, opposite, ovate leaves and white or pink flowers; it occurs from Nebraska northeast to Maine and south to Florida and Texas. These and certain other species of *Houstonia* are sometimes placed in the genus *Hedyotis.*

76, 438 Partridgeberry
Mitchella repens

Description:	A trailing, *evergreen herb* with white, fragrant, *tubular flowers in pairs.*
Flowers:	½–⅝″ (13–16 mm) long; corolla funnel-shaped, with 4 spreading lobes, fringed on inside; each pair of flowers united by ovaries; some flowers with long styles and short stamens, others with short styles and long stamens.

Partridgeberry

Leaves:	½–¾″ (1.5–2 cm) long, opposite, roundish, shiny, green, with white veins.
Fruit:	Red (rarely white), berry-like; formed by united ovaries of paired flowers.
Height:	Creeper; stems 4–12″ (10–30 cm) long.
Flowering:	June–July.
Habitat:	Dry to moist woods.
Range:	Ontario east to Newfoundland, south to Florida, west to Texas and Oklahoma, and north through Missouri to Minnesota.
Comments:	An attractive woodland creeper with highly ornamental foliage, this species can be used as a groundcover under acid-loving shrubs and in terraria. The common name implies that the scarlet fruits are relished by partridges, but they do not appear to be of much importance to wildlife. Native American women drank a tea made from the leaves as an aid in childbirth.

WILLOW FAMILY
Salicaceae

Shrubs or trees with tiny flowers in erect or nodding, plump spikes (catkins).

Flowers: Unisexual. Sepals and petals absent; 2 or more stamens and 1 pistil borne in bract axils.
Leaves: Simple, usually with stipules at stalk base.
Fruit: Small capsule.

There are 2 genera and about 340 species, found in co[l]
and temperate climates. Only willows *(Salix)* and popla[r]
(Populus) occur in North America.

---

330   Pussy Willow
Salix discolor

Description: A large shrub or small tree with *furry
catkins* appearing in spring before leaves
male and female flowers in catkins on
separate plants.

Flowers: Catkins with male flowers yellow, to 2"
(5 cm) long; catkins with female flowers
greenish, about 2½" (6.5 cm) long; both
aging to yellow-brown.

Leaves: 2–4" (5–10 cm) long, oblong to
lanceolate, bright green above, whitish
below, wavy-toothed above middle.

Fruit: Capsule.

Height: 2–20' (60–600 cm).

Flowering: February–May.

Habitat: Damp thickets, swamps, and streambanks.

Range: Alberta east to Newfoundland, south to
North Carolina, west to Missouri, and
northwest to North Dakota.

Comments: For many people, the appearance of
these flower catkins signals the arrival of
spring. The plants bearing male catkins,
with their bright yellow stamens, are
especially showy compared to the more
drab plants bearing female catkins.
Willows are represented in our area by
about 50 species, not all restricted to
wet sites. Some are large trees, some are
shrubs, and some, at high elevations and
in the Arctic, are prostrate plants.

SANDALWOOD FAMILY
Santalaceae

Trees, shrubs, or herbs, sometimes parasitic on roots of other
species, with small flowers borne singly in leaf axils or in
clusters.

Flowers: Radially symmetrical. Sepals 4–5, often petal-like;
petals absent; 1 stamen opposite each sepal; all these parts
attached at top of ovary.

Leaves: Commonly opposite, sometimes alternate.
Fruit: Berry-like drupe or small, hard, seed-like nut.

There are about 35 genera and 400 species, common in warm temperate and tropical areas. In the United States this family is best represented in the Southeast. The tropical, sweet-scented, attractive sandalwood (obtained from several species of *Santalum*) is prized for cabinet work.

174 Bastard Toadflax
Comandra umbellata

Description:	A parasitic plant with *compact, terminal clusters* of small, greenish-white, funnel-shaped flowers.
Flowers:	⅛" (4 mm) wide; sepals 5, often connected to anthers by tufts of hair; petals absent; stamens 5; pistil 1.
Leaves:	¾–1¼" (2–4 cm) long, oblong, pale beneath.
Fruit:	Small, seed-like nut.
Height:	6–16" (15–40 cm).
Flowering:	April–June.
Habitat:	Dry fields and thickets.
Range:	Throughout North America, except Alaska, Florida, Louisiana, and Arctic.
Comments:	Although a photosynthetic plant that manufactures its own food, this species is also a parasite, obtaining some of its nutrients from the roots of trees and shrubs. Usually growing in dry fields, it can also be found in bogs that dry out periodically. The genus name derives from the Greek *come* ("hair") and *andros* ("a male") and refers to the hairy attachment of the anthers to the sepals. Northern Comandra *(Geocaulon lividum),* a related plant common in Canada from Alberta to Newfoundland, is found in the United States from Minnesota east to Maine; it is smaller, has purple flowers, and orange to red, juicy, berry-like fruit.

PITCHER PLANT FAMILY
Sarraceniaceae

Carnivorous herbs with tubular leaves and large, nodding long-stalked flowers borne singly or in racemes.

Flowers: Radially symmetrical. Sepals 3–6, often petal-like; petals 5; stamens at least 12; all these parts attached at base of ovary; ovary topped by umbrella-like style and stigma.

Leaves: Basal, long; commonly with a decorative opening to a tubular base.

Fruit: Capsule, with 3–6 chambers.

There are 3 genera and 15 species, found in North America and northern South America; in the United States all species but one are in the East. A few are grown as curiosities; collecting for this purpose and habitat destruction threaten the rarest plants. Several species are classified as endangered or threatened in many states.

268 Trumpets
Sarracenia flava

Description:	A carnivorous plant bearing showy, bright yellow, drooping flowers and *erect, trumpet-shaped, hollow, inflated leaves;* flowers have a musty odor.
Flowers:	3–5″ (7.5–12.5 cm) wide; sepals and petals 5 each; stamens numerous; style large, disk-like.
Leaves:	1–3′ (30–90 cm) long; hood arching over opening that collects water, purple at constricted base.
Fruit:	Capsule.
Height:	1½–3½′ (45–105 cm); flower stalk equal to or taller than leaves.
Flowering:	April–May.
Habitat:	Wet pinelands and bogs.
Range:	New Jersey; Virginia south to Florida and west to Alabama.
Comments:	This mostly southern plant has hollow leaves that fill with water in which insects and other small organisms drown; their soft parts are then digested by the plant. A similar species, Trumpet Pitcher Plant *(S. alata),* with fiddle-shaped

petals and leaves without the
purple constriction at the base of
the hood, is found from Alabama
west to Texas; its range apparently
does not overlap with that of Trumpets.
Green Pitcher Plant *(S. oreophila),*
found in North Carolina, Georgia,
and Alabama, is classified as an
endangered species.

408 Crimson Pitcher Plant; Fiddler's Trumpet
Sarracenia leucophylla

Description: A carnivorous plant bearing nodding,
brownish-red flowers and clusters
of *erect, hollow, pitcher-like leaves;* each
leaf colored at top with *reddish-purple
veins on a white background* and topped
by an erect, roundish, wavy-edged
hood.

Flowers: 2–3″ (5–7.5 cm) wide; petals 5, fiddle-
shaped; stigma distinctive, forming a
large, reddish-green, *umbrella-like
structure in center of flower.*

Leaves: 2–3′ (60–90 cm) long.

Fruit: Capsule.

Height: 2–3′ (60–90 cm); flower stalk as tall
as leaves.

Flowering: March–April.

Habitat: Sandy bogs.

Range: North Carolina; Florida west to
Mississippi.

Comments: Insects and other small organisms
are attracted to this plant by the
colorful leaf opening and by nectar
secreted inside; they fall into the
collected water and are then
digested by plant enzymes or by
bacterial action, thereby providing
essential nutrients. Sweet Pitcher
Plant *(S. rubra),* found from North
Carolina south to Florida and west
to Mississippi, has a slender, erect
trumpet, 4–20″ (10–50 cm) tall
and green-veined with red; the flowers
are very fragrant, with the odor of
English Violet *(Viola odorata).*

269 Hooded Pitcher Plant
Sarracenia minor

Description: A carnivorous plant bearing yellow
flowers on a leafless stalk amid
clustered, *hollow, tubular leaves;* each leaf
patterned near top with *reddish veins and
pale spots* and expanding at top into an
overarching hood.

Flowers: About 2″ (5 cm) wide; sepals and petals
5 each; stamens numerous; pistil bearing
an umbrella-like style.

Leaves: 6–24″ (15–60 cm) long, winged along
one side.

Fruit: Capsule.

Height: 6–24″ (15–60 cm); leaves taller than
flower stalk.

Flowering: Spring.

Habitat: Low pinelands, marshes, and bogs.

Range: North Carolina south to Florida.

Comments: This is the most common of the Florida
pitcher plants. Because of the hood-like
dome at the tip of the leaf, rain is not
collected in this species. Instead, insects
and other small organisms are lured up a
nectar path on the wing of the leaves
and into the hood where there are
translucent spots through which the
victims try to escape. Unable to do so,
they eventually exhaust themselves and
drop to the base of the leaf. The plant
secretes a liquid that digests the
organism, and the resulting nutrients
are then absorbed by the plant.

407 Northern Pitcher Plant
Sarracenia purpurea

Description: A carnivorous plant bearing 1 large,
purplish-red flower on a leafless stalk
rising above a rosette of *bronzy, reddish-
green, hollow, inflated, curved leaves.*

Flowers: 2″ (5 cm) wide; petals 5; stamens
numerous; style expanding into an
umbrella-like structure.

Leaves: 4–12″ (10–30 cm) long; each with a
broad, flaring, terminal lip covered with
stiff, downward-pointing hairs.

Fruit:	Capsule.
Height:	8–24″ (20–60 cm); flower stalk as tall as leaves.
Flowering:	May–August.
Habitat:	Peat bogs.
Range:	Alberta east to Newfoundland, south to Florida, west to Louisiana, and north to Illinois and Minnesota.
Comments:	This striking plant has pitcher-like leaves that collect water; organisms attracted to the colored lip have difficulty crawling upward because of the recurved hairs and eventually fall into the water and drown. Enzymes secreted by the plant aid in the digestion of the insect, but much of the breakdown is passive, a result of bacterial activity. The plant absorbs the nutrients, especially nitrogenous compounds. Parrot Pitcher Plant *(S. psittacina),* a southern species found from Georgia and Florida west to Louisiana, has many prostrate "pitchers" with hooked lips like a parrot's bill.

LIZARD TAIL FAMILY
Saururaceae

Herbs, mostly of moist places, with small flowers often intermixed with colored bracts.

Flowers: Radially symmetrical; in a dense spike, raceme, or cluster often resembling 1 large flower. Sepals and petals absent; stamens 3, 6, or 8; pistils 3–4, sometimes partly joined at base.
Leaves: Simple.
Fruit: Seed-like or a fleshy capsule.

There are 5 genera and 7 species, found in North America and eastern Asia.

102 Lizard Tail
Saururus cernuus

Description:	Many tiny, fragrant, *white flowers* in a slender, tapering, *stalked spike with a drooping tip.*
Flowers:	Spike to 6″ (15 cm) long; stamens 6–8,

> each about ⅛″ (4 mm) long, showy;
> pistils 3–4, united.

Leaves: 3–6″ (7.5–15 cm) long, heart-shaped,
indented at base.

Fruit: Fleshy, wrinkled, seed-like.

Height: 2–5′ (60–150 cm).

Flowering: June–September.

Habitat: Shallow water of swamps, ponds,
streams, and ditches.

Range: Ontario and Quebec; New York and
Connecticut south to Florida, west to
Texas, north to Kansas, and northeast to
Illinois and Michigan.

Comments: This mostly southern species prefers
shaded sites. The plant grows from
rhizomes and forms small to large
colonies. The common name and the
genus name, from the Greek *sauros*
("lizard") and *oura* ("tail"), refer to the
shape of the drooping flower cluster.

SAXIFRAGE FAMILY
Saxifragaceae

Usually herbs with small flowers borne singly or in raceme-like or branched clusters.

Flowers: Radially symmetrical. Sepals 5; petals usually 5 or 10, separate; stamens 5 or 10; all these parts attached to edge of a cup-like flower base (hypanthium), with ovary in center.
Leaves: Usually alternate, basal.
Fruit: Capsule, small pod, or berry.

There are about 40 genera and 700 species, mainly in cooler regions of the Northern Hemisphere. Species of *Saxifraga, Bergenia,* and *Astilbe* are commonly grown as ornamentals.

100 False Goatsbeard
Astilbe biternata

Description: Small, *white or yellowish flowers* in
elongated clusters branching off a hairy
stalk; clusters collectively form *a large,
much-branched, terminal cluster.*

Flowers: About ⅛″ (4 mm) long; petals 4–5;
stamens 10; pistil 1, with separate
styles, splitting into 2 sections; male

and female flowers sometimes on
separate plants, female flowers with
minute petals or petals absent.

Leaves: To 2' (60 cm) wide, compound, divided
into 3 parts and again divided into 3
toothed or lobed, ovate leaflets; terminal
leaflet usually 3-lobed.

Fruit: Pair of pods, each opening along one
side.

Height: 2–6' (60–180 cm).

Flowering: May–July.

Habitat: Mountain woods.

Range: West Virginia and Maryland south to
Georgia; Mississippi north to Kentucky.

Comments: The species name refers to the double
subdivision of the leaves. The flower
masses of this southern plant are
thought to resemble a goat's beard and
are similar to those of true Goatsbeard
(Aruncus dioicus) of the rose family
(Rosaceae), which has at least 15
stamens and 3–5 pistils per flower; it is
found from Ontario and Quebec south
to Georgia, west to Mississippi,
Arkansas, and Oklahoma, and north to
Missouri, Iowa, and Wisconsin.

33 Alumroot
Heuchera americana

Description: A somewhat hairy stalk bearing
yellowish-green, bell-shaped, drooping flowers
in loose, slender, branching clusters;
usually 4–5 flowers on each branch.

Flowers: To ¼" (6 mm) long; calyx 5-lobed, cup-
shaped; petals 5, small, greenish;
stamens 5, projecting, *with orange
anthers;* pistil 1, composed of 2 united
segments.

Leaves: 3–4" (7.5–10 cm) wide, basal, long-
stalked, heart-shaped, lobed, somewhat
maple-like.

Fruit: 2-beaked capsule.

Height: 2–3' (60–90 cm).

Flowering: April–June.

Habitat: Woods, shaded slopes, and rock crevices.

Range: Ontario; New York and Connecticut
south to Georgia, west to Louisiana, and

Alumroot

north to Nebraska, Iowa, Illinois, and
Michigan.

Comments: Several similar *Heuchera* species occur in
our range, many of which are difficult to
distinguish from one another. The genus
name honors the 18th-century German
physician and botanist Johann von
Heucher.

121 Miterwort
Mitella diphylla

Description: A slender, elongated cluster of *tiny white
flowers, with 5 delicately fringed petals,
above 1 pair of stalkless leaves at midstem;*
other leaves basal.

Flowers: About ⅛" (4 mm) wide; stamens 10;
pistil 1.

Leaves: Basal leaves to 3" (7.5 cm) long, ovate,
lobed, stalked; stem leaves opposite,
mostly 3-lobed.

Fruit: Capsule, splitting open and exposing
black seeds.

Height: 8–18" (20–45 cm).

Flowering: April–June.

Habitat: Rich woods.

Range: Ontario and Quebec; Vermont and New
Hampshire south to Georgia, west to

Mississippi and Arkansas, and north to Minnesota.

Comments: The flower is a fantastic bit of geometry, especially evident when viewed with a hand lens. The single pair of leaves at midstem accounts for the species name. The common and genus names allude to the fruit, which has the shape of a small cap or bishop's miter. Naked Miterwort *(M. nuda),* a lovely smaller species, has only basal leaves and fewer, slightly larger, greenish to yellow flowers; it occurs from Alberta east to Newfoundland, south to Pennsylvania, west to Michigan, Wisconsin, and Iowa, and northwest to North Dakota.

55 Grass-of-Parnassus
Parnassia glauca

Description: *1 white flower, with petals striped with green veins,* atop a stem bearing *1 rounded, clasping leaf* at midstem; other leaves basal.

Flowers: 1″ (2.5 cm) wide; sepals and petals 5 each; stamens 5, yellow, 3-pronged, gland-tipped, alternating with petals and forming a circle around pistil.

Leaves: Basal ones to 2½″ (6.5 cm) wide, heart-shaped, ovate, or round.

Fruit: 4-parted capsule.

Height: 6–20″ (15–50 cm).

Flowering: July–October.

Habitat: Bogs, meadows, and shorelines.

Range: Saskatchewan east to Newfoundland, south to Pennsylvania, and west to Illinois, Iowa, and the Dakotas.

Comments: The delicate, green veins of the petals are the distinctive feature of this perennial. Despite its common name, it does not really resemble a grass; Parnassus refers to the Greek mountain, sacred to Apollo, where the ancient naturalist Dioscorides observed similar plants in meadows. Three other very similar species of *Parnassia* occur in the South.

347 Ditch Stonecrop
Penthorum sedoides

Description: Inconspicuous, *greenish-yellow flowers clustered on one side of slender, diverging stalks.*

Flowers: About ⅛" (4 mm) wide; sepals 5, oblong-lanceolate, erect; petals 5, small, often absent or dropping off early.

Leaves: 2–4" (5–10 cm) long, lanceolate to elliptical, sharply toothed.

Fruit: 5-horned, many-seeded, crown-like capsule.

Height: 8–24" (20–60 cm).

Flowering: July–October.

Habitat: Ditches, streambanks, and wet places.

Range: Manitoba east to New Brunswick, south to Florida, west to Texas, and north to North Dakota.

Comments: The genus name is derived from the Greek *pente* ("five") and *horos* ("mark") and refers to the 5-parted pattern of the flower. This wildflower resembles members of the genus *Sedum* in the stonecrop family (Crassulaceae), hence the species and common names. However, Ditch Stonecrop lacks the succulent leaves of stonecrops.

544 Purple Saxifrage
Saxifraga oppositifolia

Description: A low, *densely tufted plant with 1 rose-purple flower* atop each stem bearing small, opposite, purplish leaves.

Flowers: About ½" (1.5 cm) wide; sepals and petals 5 each; stamens 10; pistils 2.

Leaves: To ¼" (6 mm) long, ovate to roundish, edges hairy, with 1–3 lime-encrusted pores at tip; leaves more numerous on lower stem.

Height: ¾–4" (2–10 cm).

Flowering: May–August.

Habitat: Rocks, ledges, and cliffs.

Range: Alaska east to Greenland and Newfoundland, south to Vermont and New York; also from British Columbia and Alberta south to Oregon and Idaho.

Comments: There are other species of this family found on New England mountains. Star-like Saxifrage *(S. foliolosa)* has thin, green, basal leaves and white flowers that appear only on the larger plants; it is found in the United States only on Mount Katahdin in Maine. White Mountain Saxifrage *(S. paniculata)* has tufted, toothed, basal leaves and small white flowers; it is found on ledges and in gravel from Manitoba to Newfoundland, on Mount Katahdin, on mountains in New Hampshire, Vermont, and New York, and in Michigan and Minnesota. Yellow Mountain Saxifrage *(S. aizoides)* has bright yellow flowers and occurs from Manitoba to Newfoundland and in New York and Vermont.

320 Swamp Saxifrage
Saxifraga pensylvanica

Description: A stout, hairy, *sticky stalk* bearing branched clusters (at first compact, later elongated and loose) of *small, usually greenish-yellow flowers.*

Flowers: About ⅛″ (4 mm) wide; petals 5; stamens 10; pistils 2, united.

Leaves: 4–8″ (10–20 cm) long, basal, ovate to lanceolate, nearly toothless.

Fruit: 2-beaked capsule.

Height: 1–3′ (30–90 cm).

Flowering: April–June.

Habitat: Wet meadows and prairies, swamps, bogs, and banks.

Range: Saskatchewan east to Ontario; Maine south to North Carolina, west to Missouri, and north to Minnesota.

Comments: The young leaves of this large saxifrage can be eaten in salads or as cooked greens. The genus name is from the Latin *saxum* ("a stone") and *frangere* ("to break") and alludes either to the supposed ability of the plant to crack rocks (in the crevices where some members of the genus are found) or to the stone-like bulblets on the roots of a

European species. In earlier times, saxifrages were assumed to have medicinal value in dissolving kidney or gallbladder stones.

220 Early Saxifrage
Saxifraga virginiensis

Description: A hairy stalk rising from a *basal rosette of leaves* and bearing branched clusters of *fragrant white flowers.*

Flowers: ¼" (6 mm) wide; sepals and petals 5 each; stamens 10, yellow; pistils 2, nearly separate.

Leaves: To 3" (7.5 cm) long, broadly toothed, ovate to oblong.

Fruit: 2-beaked capsule.

Height: 4–16" (10–40 cm).

Flowering: April–June.

Habitat: Dry rocky slopes and outcrops.

Range: Manitoba east to New Brunswick, south to Georgia, west to Louisiana and Oklahoma, and north to Missouri and Illinois; Minnesota.

Comments: This early spring wildflower can be planted in shaded rock gardens. The many members of this genus grow in both wet and dry habitats. Mountain Saxifrage *(S. michauxii),* found from Kentucky east to Maryland and south to Georgia, reaches a height of 1½' (45 cm); it has coarse leaves and white petals of slightly different sizes, spotted with yellow.

115 Foam Flower
Tiarella cordifolia

Description: Small white flowers in a *feathery, somewhat elongated, terminal cluster.*

Flowers: ¼" (6 mm) wide; sepals 5; petals 5, each narrowing to a stalk-like base; stamens 10, protruding, with reddish or yellow anthers; pistils 2, of unequal size.

Leaves: 2–4" (5–10 cm) long, basal, stalked, lobed, sharply toothed, somewhat maple-like, usually hairy.

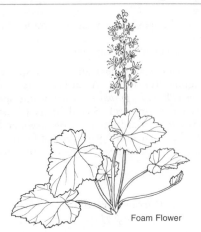

Foam Flower

Fruit:	Pair of capsules, each splitting open along one side.
Height:	6–12″ (15–30 cm).
Flowering:	April–June.
Habitat:	Rich woods.
Range:	Ontario east to Nova Scotia, south to Georgia, west to Mississippi, and north to Ohio, Michigan, and Minnesota.
Comments:	This attractive wildflower, which spreads by underground stems, forms colonies and creates excellent groundcover for shady, wooded sites. The tiny flowers and fine texture of the stamens resemble foam, hence the common name. The genus name is from the Greek *tiara,* designating a turban once worn by the Persians, and refers to the shape of the pistil.

FIGWORT FAMILY
Scrophulariaceae

Mostly herbs, sometimes shrubs, rarely trees, often with showy flowers.

Flowers: Usually bilaterally symmetrical. Sepals united, usually forming calyx with 4–5 lobes; petals usually 4–5, united, usually forming corolla with an upper and lower lip; stamens usually 4, sometimes 2 or 5, when 5 the fifth often sterile and different; all these parts attached at base of ovary.

Leaves: Alternate, opposite, or whorled; simple or pinnatel
   compound.
Fruit: Berry or 2-chambered capsule.

There are about 190 genera and 4,000 species, found
nearly throughout the world. A cardiac drug is extracted
from Foxglove *(Digitalis purpurea),* a handsome species also
cultivated as an ornamental. Snapdragons *(Antirrhinum)*
speedwells *(Veronica),* beardtongues *(Penstemon),* and slipper-
flowers *(Calceolavia)* are other plants grown for their beauty
Scrophulariaceae has also been known as the snapdragon
family.

---

475   Purple Gerardia
Agalinis purpurea

Description:	*Pink to rose-purple, bell-shaped flowers* on short stalks in axils of opposite, linear leaves.
Flowers:	About 1″ (2.5 cm) long; calyx with 5 fused sepals; corolla with 5 unequal, spreading lobes; stamens 4, with yellow anthers, attached to petals, not projecting; pistil 1.
Leaves:	1–1½″ (2.5–4 cm) long, ⅛″ (4 mm) wide.
Fruit:	Round capsule.
Height:	1–4′ (30–120 cm).
Flowering:	July–September.
Habitat:	Moist soil.
Range:	Ontario; New Hampshire south to Florida, west to Texas, and north to Nebraska and Minnesota.
Comments:	The corolla of this widely spreading, smooth-stemmed annual has dark spots on the inside of the throat. As a group, gerardias are slender, wiry-branched plants with narrow leaves. A smaller species, Seaside Gerardia *(A. maritima),* found in coastal salt marshes from New Brunswick and Nova Scotia south to Florida and Texas, has rather fleshy, linear leaves and smaller flowers. About 15 species of this genus occur in our area, all with pink to purplish, or occasionally white, flowers; many of them are difficult to distinguish from one another.

307 Smooth False Foxglove;
Entire-leaved False Foxglove
Aureolaria laevigata

Description: A cluster of *yellow, funnel-shaped flowers atop a smooth stem.*

Flowers: ¾" (2 cm) wide; corolla with 5 flaring lobes.

Leaves: 1½–4" (4–10 cm) long, opposite, lanceolate to ovate, all but lower leaves untoothed.

Fruit: Capsule.

Height: 1–5' (30–150 cm).

Flowering: July–October.

Habitat: Woods and thickets, chiefly in mountains.

Range: Pennsylvania south to Georgia, west to Mississippi, and northeast to Ohio.

Comments: The members of this group of plants are semi-parasitic on the roots of oaks and usually turn black when dried as herbarium specimens. Northern False Foxglove *(A. flava)* is very similar but has pinnately lobed leaves; it is found from Ontario east to Maine and south to Florida and Texas.

Smooth False Foxglove

308 Downy False Foxglove
Aureolaria virginica

Description: A terminal cluster of *funnel-shaped, yellow flowers,* with 1 flower in axil of each opposite bract, atop a *downy stem.*

Flowers: 1″ (2.5 cm) wide; corolla with 5 flaring lobes; stamens 4.

Leaves: 2½–5″ (6.5–12.5 cm) long, opposite, downy, lanceolate to ovate; *lower ones pinnately lobed;* upper ones with fewer lobes or unlobed.

Fruit: Capsule.

Height: 1–5′ (30–150 cm).

Flowering: June–August.

Habitat: Dry open woods.

Range: Ontario; New Hampshire south to Florida, west to Louisiana and Texas, and north to Tennessee and Michigan.

Comments: Like the very similar Smooth False Foxglove *(A. laevigata),* this plant is partly parasitic on the roots of oaks.

Downy False Foxglove

420 Indian Paintbrush; Painted Cup
Castilleja coccinea

Description: Flowers hidden in axils of *scarlet-tipped, fan-shaped bracts* and arranged in a dense spike.

Flowers: About 1″ (2.5 cm) long, greenish yellow, tubular; corolla with a long, 2-lobed upper lip arching over a shorter, 3-lobed lower lip; styles protruding beyond bracts; bracts slightly longer than corolla.

Leaves: Those at base 1–3″ (2.5–7.5 cm) long, in a rosette, elliptical, untoothed; those on stem stalkless, divided into narrow segments.

Fruit: Capsule.

Height: 1–2′ (30–60 cm).

Flowering: May–July.

Habitat: Meadows, prairies, and fields.

Range: Saskatchewan east to Ontario; New York and Connecticut south to Florida, west to Louisiana, northwest to Kansas, and northeast to Iowa and Minnesota.

Comments: The conspicuous, red-tipped bracts appear to have been dipped in paint. This genus of more than 200 species is especially common in the western United States. Purple Painted Cup *(C. purpurea),* with purple or violet bracts, occurs from southwestern Missouri to Texas. Downy Painted Cup *(C. sessiliflora),* found from Alberta east to Manitoba and south to Illinois, Missouri, and Texas, has green bracts. Pale Painted Cup *(C. septentrionalis)* has whitish or creamy bracts, often suffused with bronze or dull purple, and is found from Manitoba east to Newfoundland and south to Maine, New Hampshire, Vermont, Michigan, and Minnesota.

142 Turtlehead
Chelone glabra

Description: A smooth plant with *white (often lavender-tinged), tubular, 2-lipped flowers resembling turtle heads* in tight, terminal clusters.

Flowers: 1–1½" (2.5–4 cm) long; upper
          corolla lip arching over hairy lower
          lip; stamens 5, the fifth short and
          sterile.
Leaves: 3–6" (8–15 cm) long, opposite,
          lanceolate, sharply toothed.
Fruit: Capsule.
Height: 1–3' (30–90 cm).
Flowering: July–September.
Habitat: Wet thickets, streambanks, and low
          ground.
Range: Manitoba east to Newfoundland, south
          to Georgia, west to Louisiana and
          Arkansas, and north to Minnesota.
Comments: The distinctive shape of the flowers of
          turtleheads is reflected in the genus
          name, which is Greek for "tortoise."
          This species does well in wildflower
          gardens.

478 Lyon's Turtlehead
Chelone lyonii

Description: A tall erect plant with *pink or rose-purple,
             tubular, 2-lipped flowers resembling turtle
             heads* in compact clusters atop stems or
             in axils of opposite leaves.
Flowers: About 1" (2.5 cm) long; 2-lobed upper
             corolla lip arching over 3-lobed lower
             lip; lower lip bearded with yellow hairs
             inside.
Leaves: 3–7" (7.5–17.5 cm) long, toothed,
             ovate, base rounded; stalk often more
             than 1" (2.5 cm) long.
Fruit: Capsule.
Height: 1–3' (30–90 cm).
Flowering: July–September.
Habitat: Rich woods, wet thickets, and
             streambanks.
Range: West Virginia, North Carolina, South
             Carolina, Alabama, Mississippi, and
             Tennessee; sparingly introduced farther
             north.
Comments: This species occasionally escapes from
             cultivation in New England and
             elsewhere. The common name honors
             John Lyon, an early-19th-century
             American botanist.

637 Blue-eyed Mary
Collinsia verna

Description: A weak stem bearing whorls of 4–6 stalked, 2-lipped, *blue and white flowers* rising from axils of opposite, mostly stalkless leaves.

Flowers: ½" (1.5 cm) long; upper corolla lip 2-lobed, white; lower corolla lip 3-lobed, blue, with a folded middle lobe enveloping 4 stamens and 1 style.

Leaves: ¾–2" (2–5 cm) long, ovate.

Fruit: Capsule.

Height: 6–18" (15–45 cm).

Flowering: April–June.

Habitat: Damp open woods.

Range: Ontario and New York south to Virginia, southwest to Tennessee and Oklahoma, and north to Kansas, Iowa, and Wisconsin.

Comments: This plant is sometimes so abundant in woodlands as to form a blue carpet on the forest floor. The seeds of this delicate winter annual are shed in the summer and germinate in the fall, the seedlings persisting through the winter. The genus name honors Zaccheus Collins (1764–1831), a Philadelphia botanist. The species name is the Latin word for "spring" and describes the flowering time.

579 Eyebright
Euphrasia nemorosa

Description: A small plant with short, spike-like, terminal clusters of *pale lavender flowers* on a *hairy stem* and its branches.

Flowers: ⅜–½" (8–13 mm) long; upper corolla lip 2-lobed; lower corolla lip marked with deeper purple, large, *with 3 notched lobes;* bracts beneath flowers conspicuous, ovate, coarsely toothed.

Leaves: ¼–¾" (6–20 mm) long, coarsely toothed.

Fruit: Capsule.

Height: 4–15" (10–38 cm).

Flowering: June–September.

Habitat: Fields and roadsides.
Range: Ontario east to Newfoundland and south to Connecticut; also in Michigan and Minnesota.
Comments: There are several species of eyebright, native to the colder regions. They are partly parasitic on the roots of other plants. The common name refers to the fact that the plants were at one time used to treat eye diseases and improve vision. The genus name, from the Greek word for "cheerfulness," may allude to the same properties.

312 Butter-and-eggs; Common Toadflax
Linaria vulgaris

Description: *Yellow, 2-lipped, spurred flowers* in a terminal cluster on a leafy stem.
Flowers: About 1″ (2.5 cm) long; sepals 5; upper corolla lip 2-lobed; lower corolla lip 3-lobed, with orange ridges and a prominent spur at base; stamens 4; pistil 1, with a green style.
Leaves: 1–2½″ (2.5–6.5 cm) long, gray-green; upper ones alternate, linear, grass-like; lower ones opposite or whorled.
Fruit: Capsule.
Height: 1–3′ (30–90 cm).
Flowering: May–October.
Habitat: Dry fields, waste places, and roadsides.
Range: Alberta east to Newfoundland, south to Florida, west to Texas, and north to North Dakota; also throughout West.
Comments: This weedy European introduction is now naturalized over much of North America. It grows from creeping roots and can form small to large colonies, thriving in dry sites. In Virginia and several western states it is considered a noxious weed. An orange path on the corolla's lower lip leads to nectar contained in the long spur and serves as a "honey guide" for insects. Experiments with hawk moths indicate that the moths will try to stick their proboscises into flowers pressed between glass;

marks on the glass coincide with the orange honey guide. Even a honey guide excised and placed on other flowers will attract the moths. The name toadflax refers to the opening of the corolla, which looks like the mouth of a toad, and to the leaves, which resemble those of flax *(Linum).* The common name Butter-and-eggs alludes to the color combination of the corolla. Dalmatian Toadflax *(L. genistifolia* subsp. *dalmatica)* resembles a larger version of Butter-and-eggs, with ovate or lanceolate leaves and flowers to 1¾″ (4.5 cm) long; it is increasingly common across Canada and in the northeastern and western United States and is considered a noxious weed in at least nine western states.

96 Cow Wheat
Melampyrum lineare

Description: A low, upward-branching plant with small, tubular, *creamy white, 2-lipped flowers* on short stalks in axils of upper leaves.

Flowers: ½″ (1.5 cm) long; upper corolla lip 2-lobed, white, arching; lower lip 3-lobed, yellow; stamens 4, under upper corolla lip, 2 long and 2 short.

Leaves: ¾–2½″ (2–6.5 cm) long, opposite, linear to lanceolate-ovate, often with 2–4 bristly teeth at base.

Fruit: Capsule.

Height: 6–18″ (15–45 cm).

Flowering: June–August.

Habitat: Dry to moist woods, bogs, and rocky barrens.

Range: Alberta east to Newfoundland, south to Georgia, and northwest to Tennessee, Illinois, and Minnesota; also in Montana, Idaho, and Washington.

Comments: This small, native, woodland annual has flowers that resemble a snake's head. The genus name is from the Greek for "black" and "wheat" and refers to the black seeds found in some species.

304 Muskflower
Mimulus moschatus

Description: A *sticky, hairy, musk-scented plant with bilaterally symmetrical, tubular, yellow, flattish-faced flowers* in leaf axils on a weak, ascending stem.

Flowers: ¾" (2 cm) long; sepals 5; corolla 5-lobed, 2-lipped, with an open throat; stamens 4, attached to petals; pistil 1.

Leaves: 1–2½" (2.5–6.5 cm) long, opposite, ovate to lanceolate, sometimes toothed, short-stalked.

Fruit: Capsule.

Height: 8–16" (20–40 cm).

Flowering: June–September.

Habitat: Streambanks and pondsides.

Range: Ontario east to Newfoundland, south to North Carolina, and northwest to West Virginia; Michigan; also in much of West.

Comments: This plant has apparently escaped from cultivation over much of its present range. It can be used in wetland wildflower gardens. Two other species, both known as Yellow Monkeyflower, have smooth stems and yellow flowers: *M. guttatus* has flowers ½–1¾" (1.5–4.5 cm) long, with essentially closed throats, and is naturalized from western North America, occurring in Newfoundland, New Brunswick, New York, Connecticut, Pennsylvania, Michigan, and probably elsewhere in our range; *M. glabratus* has flowers ¼–1" (6–25 mm) long, with wide-open throats, and is found from Alberta to Quebec and from Michigan, Illinois, Iowa, and the Dakotas south to Texas.

566 Monkeyflower
Mimulus ringens

Description: *2-lipped, blue-purple flowers* rising from axils of opposite leaves clasping a *square stem.*

Flowers: About 1" (2.5 cm) long; upper corolla lip 2-lobed, erect; lower lip 3-lobed,

with 2 yellow spots inside; corolla throat white, nearly closed; stamens 4; stalk ⅜–2½″ (1–6 cm) high.

Leaves: 2–4″ (5–10 cm) long, unstalked, oblong to lanceolate.

Fruit: Capsule.

Height: 1–3′ (30–90 cm).

Flowering: June–September.

Habitat: Wet meadows and streambanks.

Range: Saskatchewan east to Nova Scotia, south to Georgia, west to Texas, and north to North Dakota; also in parts of West.

Comments: The flower looks something like a monkey's face, hence the common and genus names, the latter from the Latin *mimus* ("a buffoon"). The variety *colpophilus,* found from Quebec to Maine on tidal muds, is classified as endangered in Maine. The lavender-flowered Sharp-winged Monkeyflower *(M. alatus)* has flower stalks less than ½″ (1.5 cm) long, stalked leaves, and a winged stem; it occurs from Ontario east to Massachusetts, south to Florida, west to Texas, and north to Nebraska and Iowa.

---

580 Blue Toadflax; Old-field Toadflax
Nuttallanthus canadensis

Description: *Small, light blue-violet, 2-lipped, spurred flowers* scattered in an elongated cluster on a slender stem.

Flowers: ¼–½″ (6–13 mm) long; sepals 5; upper corolla lip 2-lobed; lower corolla lip 3-lobed, with 2 small white ridges and a long, thread-like spur projecting at base.

Leaves: Those at base small, opposite, on trailing stems forming a rosette; those on stem to 1½″ (4 cm) long, alternate, linear, smooth, shiny.

Fruit: Capsule.

Height: 6–24″ (15–60 cm).

Flowering: April–September.

Habitat: Open, dry, shady or rocky sites and usually sandy, abandoned fields.

Range: Ontario east to New Brunswick, south to Florida, west to Texas, and north to North Dakota and Minnesota.

Comments: This delicate, attractive, wide-ranging
native toadflax is found locally even on
the Pacific Coast. Once in the genus
Linaria, this species has recently been
placed in *Nuttallanthus.* The genus name
honors English-born Thomas Nuttall
(1786–1859), a botanical explorer of
North America in the early 1800s.

425   Wood Betony; Lousewort
Pedicularis canadensis

Description: A hairy plant with a *short, dense, terminal
cluster of tubular, 2-lipped flowers,* all red,
all yellow, or yellow and red.

Flowers: ¾" (2 cm) long; upper corolla lip
arching, with 2 small teeth; lower
corolla lip shorter, 3-lobed, spreading;
stamens 4, attached to upper lip, 2 long
and 2 short; *leaf-like bracts beneath flowers.*

Leaves: 3–5" (7.5–12.5 cm) long, mostly basal,
oblong-lanceolate, deeply divided into
toothed lobes.

Fruit: Capsule.

Height: 6–18" (15–45 cm).

Flowering: April–June.

Habitat: Woods and clearings.

Range: Manitoba east to New Brunswick, south
to Florida, west to New Mexico, and
north to North Dakota.

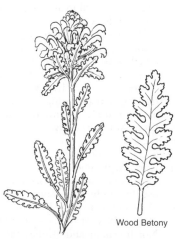

Wood Betony

Comments: *Pedicularis* species are low, semi-parasitic plants that get some of their nourishment from the roots of other plants. The variable flower color and the finely cut foliage of this species are distinctive. The genus name, from the Latin *pediculus* ("a louse"), and the common name lousewort refer to a superstition that livestock would become infested with lice if they ate this plant. Swamp Lousewort *(P. lanceolata),* with many opposite leaves on a stem 1–3' (30–90 cm) tall, has light yellow flowers and usually occurs in wet meadows from Saskatchewan east to Massachusetts and south to Georgia, Tennessee, Arkansas, and Nebraska. Furbish's Lousewort *(P. furbishiae)* is similar but has finely cut, alternate leaves; it is found on the banks of the Saint John River in New Brunswick, and in northern Maine, where it is classified as an endangered species.

578 Gray Beardtongue
Penstemon canescens

Description: *A downy stem* topped by a loose cluster of *showy, tubular, violet-purple to pinkish flowers* with darker violet-purple lines inside corolla.

Flowers: 1–1½" (2.5–4 cm) long; 2-lobed *upper corolla lip erect;* 3-lobed *lower corolla lip projecting forward;* stamens 5, the fifth sterile.

Leaves: Those at midstem 3–6" (7.5–15 cm), ovate to ovate-lanceolate; upper ones clasping stem; basal ones stalked, broadly ovate, in a rosette.

Fruit: Capsule.

Height: 1–3' (30–90 cm).

Flowering: May–July.

Habitat: Dry woods and thickets.

Range: Illinois east to Pennsylvania, south to Georgia, west to Alabama, and north to Kentucky.

Comments: This is one of numerous beardtongues, which are most common in the western

United States. The common name
beardtongue refers to the tuft of hairs
found on the sterile stamen of many
species, including this one. Cobaea
Beardtongue *(P. cobaea),* found on
prairies and rocky bluffs from Nebraska
east to Ohio, southwest through
Missouri to Texas, and north to Kansas,
reaches a height of 2′ (60 cm) and has
downy, clasping leaves and white to
deep purple flowers to 2″ (5 cm) long.

577 Large-flowered Beardtongue
Penstemon grandiflorus

Description: Large, *lavender, horizontally arranged,*
tubular flowers on a *smooth stem* above
opposite, blue-green, clasping leaves and
in axils of similar leafy bracts.

Flowers: To 2″ (5 cm) long; corolla tube flaring
out abruptly into 5 lobes above calyx;
stamens 5, the fifth sterile but minutely
hairy at tip.

Leaves: 1–2½″ (2.5–6.5 cm) long, opposite,
broadly ovate, usually with whitish
bloom.

Fruit: Capsule.

Height: 2–4′ (60–120 cm).

Flowering: May–June.

Habitat: Woods and thickets.

Range: North Dakota east to Michigan, south
to Ohio, southwest to Missouri,
Oklahoma, and Texas, and north to
North Dakota; also in parts of West.

Comments: This handsome plant is especially
spectacular when growing in masses. It
occasionally escapes from cultivation in
the East. At least 15 species of *Penstemon*
occur in our area, and there are many
more in the western United States.

576 Hairy Beardtongue
Penstemon hirsutus

Description: *A woolly-stemmed plant* with open stalked
clusters of *lavender, trumpet-shaped, white-*
lipped flowers.

Flowers: 1" (2.5 cm) long; upper corolla lip 2-lobed, erect; lower corolla lip 3-lobed, arching upward, more or less closing mouth of tube, projecting forward; stamens 5, the fifth sterile but hairy.

Leaves: 2–5" (5–12.5 cm) long, opposite, light green, oblong to lanceolate, toothed or almost toothless.

Fruit: Capsule.

Height: 1–3' (30–90 cm).

Flowering: June–July.

Habitat: Dry or rocky ground.

Range: Ontario east to Maine, south to Virginia, west to Tennessee and Illinois, and north to Wisconsin.

Comments: The beardtongues are a very large, taxonomically complex group, and separating the species is often difficult. The genus name, from the Greek *pente* ("five") and *stemon* ("thread"), refers to the slender, sterile fifth stamen.

311 Yellow Rattlebox
Rhinanthus crista-galli

Description: A sometimes branched, erect stem bearing stalkless, *yellow flowers in a leafy, 1-sided spike; calyx highly inflated when in fruit.*

Flowers: ½" (1.5 cm) long; calyx 4-toothed, at first flattened vertically, later becoming

Yellow Rattlebox

nearly round; *upper corolla lip arching,* with a low tooth on each side; lower corolla lip 3-lobed; bracts with bristle-tipped teeth beneath flowers.

Leaves: ¾–2½" (2–6.5 cm) long, opposite, stalkless, triangular-lanceolate to oblong, toothed.

Fruit: Flattened, circular capsule.

Height: 4–31" (10–80 cm).

Flowering: May–September.

Habitat: Fields and thickets.

Range: Alberta east to Newfoundland, south to New York and Connecticut; Wisconsin; North Dakota; also in parts of West.

Comments: As the common name implies, the seeds rattle in the capsule at maturity. The plant, though able to make its own food through photosynthesis, is semi-parasitic, obtaining some of its nutrients from the roots of other plants.

377 Maryland Figwort
Scrophularia marilandica

Description: A 4-sided, grooved stem bearing a branching, somewhat pyramidal, terminal cluster of small, erect, *sac-shaped, greenish-brown flowers with magenta-brown interiors.*

Flowers: About ¼" (6 mm) long; upper corolla lip 2-lobed, projecting forward; lower

Maryland Figwort

corolla lip 3-lobed, middle lobe bent
downward; stamens 5, attached to
petals; fifth stamen brownish-purple,
gland-like, sterile.

Leaves: 4–16″ (10–40 cm) long, opposite, ovate
to lanceolate, toothed, stalked.

Fruit: Many-seeded capsule.

Height: 3–8′ (90–240 cm).

Flowering: June–October.

Habitat: Rich woods and thickets.

Range: Ontario and Quebec; Vermont and New
Hampshire south to Florida, west to
Texas, and north to South Dakota and
Minnesota.

Comments: Figworts are tall plants with brownish
or greenish flowers in a large branched
panicle. The common name figwort
refers to the early use of the plants in
treating hemorrhoids, an ailment once
known as "figs." The plants were also
used as a tonic; in the 1800s an infusion
of the roots was given as a treatment for
insomnia and anxiety. Hare Figwort *(S.
lanceolata),* similar to Maryland Figwort,
has shiny flowers and a greenish-yellow
fifth stamen; it is found from Alberta
east to Nova Scotia, south to North
Carolina, northwest to Ohio and Illinois,
southwest to Oklahoma, and north to
North Dakota. Figwort *(S. nodosa),* a
very similar Europoan species, has
become established in New York,
Massachusetts, Rhode Island,
Connecticut, Pennsylvania, and New
Jersey; it has a brownish-purple sterile
stamen and usually finishes flowering in
June.

152, 310 Moth Mullein
Verbascum blattaria

Description: *Yellow or white flowers with rounded petals,*
their backs marked with brownish
purple, in a slender, open, spike-like
cluster on an erect stem.

Flowers: 1″ (2.5 cm) wide, nearly radially
symmetrical; petals 5, united; stamens
5, with orange anthers and *violet hairs* on

Leaves: filaments; pistil 1; stalk longer than
capsule.

Leaves: 1–5″ (2.5–12.5 cm) long, triangular to
oblong or lanceolate, coarsely toothed,
clasping stem.

Fruit: Many-seeded capsule.

Height: 2–4′ (60–120 cm).

Flowering: June–September.

Habitat: Old fields and roadsides.

Range: Ontario east to Nova Scotia, south to
Florida, west to Texas, and north to
North Dakota; also in much of West.

Comments: Moth Mullein is naturalized from
Europe. Its fuzzy filaments resemble
moth antennae, hence the common
name. Also known as Moth Mullein is
V. virgatum, with flower stalks shorter
than the capsule; it is found locally from
Ontario east to Nova Scotia and south to
Florida and Texas. White Mullein *(V.
lychnitis),* with yellow (rarely white)
flowers only ½–¾″ (1.5–2 cm) wide and
leaves to 1′ (30 cm) long, is found
sporadically from Ontario and New
Hampshire south to Virginia and Iowa.

---

309 Common Mullein
Verbascum thapsus

Description: An erect, woolly stem rising from a
rosette of *thick, velvety, basal leaves* and
bearing a *tightly packed, spike-like cluster
of yellow flowers* and white-woolly stem
leaves.

Flowers: ¾–1″ (2–2.5 cm) wide, nearly radially
symmetrical, very short-stalked or
stalkless; petals 5, united; stamens 5;
pistil 1.

Leaves: Basal ones to 1′ (30 cm) long, oblong,
stalked; upper ones smaller, stalkless,
with bases continuing down stem as
thin ridges or wings

Fruit: Many-seeded capsule.

Height: 2–7′ (60–210 cm).

Flowering: June–September.

Habitat: Fields, roadsides, and waste places.

Range: Throughout North America, except
Yukon and Northwest Territories.

Comments: Naturalized from Europe, this biennial with very velvety leaves has long been used for many purposes. Roman soldiers purportedly dipped the flower spikes in grease for use as torches, and the leaves are still sometimes used as wicks. Native Americans lined their moccasins with the leaves to keep out the cold, and colonists used them in their stockings for the same purpose. A tea made from the leaves was used to treat colds, and the flowers and roots were employed to treat various ailments from earache to croup. The leaves are sometimes applied to the skin to soothe sunburn and other inflammations. Similar to Common Mullein is Orange Mullein *(V. phlomoides),* the leaves of which do not continue down the stem as thin ridges or wings (or only slightly so); its flower stalks are at least ¼″ (5 mm) long, and its flowers are 1–1½″ (1.5–4 cm) wide.

629 Corn Speedwell
Veronica arvensis

Description: A low, hairy, much-branched plant with *1 minute, nearly stalkless, deep blue flower* in each upper leaf axil.

Flowers: Less than ¼″ (5 mm) wide; sepals 4, of unequal length; petals 4, united, lowest petal narrower; stamens 2.

Leaves: Lower ones to ½″ (1.5 cm) long, opposite, rounded or oval, with low teeth; upper ones alternate, unstalked, lanceolate.

Fruit: Capsule.

Height: 2–16″ (5–40 cm).

Flowering: March–August.

Habitat: Waste places, pastures, open woods, and cultivated sites.

Range: Ontario east to Newfoundland, south to Florida, west to Texas, and north to South Dakota; also in much of West.

Comments: The species name of this originally European plant is from the Latin for "belonging to plowed land" and indicates that the weed is a frequent

invader of lawns and gardens. Another weedy speedwell with nearly stalkless, minute flowers is the white-flowered Purslane Speedwell *(V. peregrina);* its species name, meaning "wandering," refers to the fact that this native North American plant was long ago naturalized in Europe. The speedwells are a large group, with more than 20 species in our area. The common name speedwell reflects the rapidity with which these plants spread.

151, 585   **Common Speedwell**
Veronica officinalis

Description: *A prostrate, mat-forming, hairy plant with spike-like clusters of pale lavender, blue, or white flowers* rising from leaf axils.
Flowers: About ¼" (5 mm) wide; petals 4, united; stamens 2.
Leaves: ¾–2" (2–5 cm) long, opposite, elliptical, toothed, downy.
Fruit: Capsule.
Height: Creeper; flower stalks to 3–10" (7.5–25 cm).
Flowering: May–July.
Habitat: Dry fields and open woods.
Range: Ontario northeast to Greenland and Newfoundland, south to Georgia, and northwest to Tennessee, Kansas, and North Dakota; also in parts of West.
Comments: This weed is native to the United States, the British Isles, Europe, and Asia. The species name means "of the shops" and probably indicates that it was at one time sold for its reputed diuretic and astringent properties.

150   **Thyme-leaved Speedwell**
Veronica serpyllifolia

Description: A mat-forming plant bearing *short, erect, narrow clusters of white or pale blue flowers* with darker stripes arising from creeping stems.
Flowers: About ⅛" (4 mm) wide; petals 4,

united, 3 rounded, lowest petal narrower; stamens 2.

Leaves: ½–⅝″ (13–16 mm) long, mostly opposite, ovate, minutely toothed.

Fruit: Capsule.

Height: 2–10″ (5–25 cm).

Flowering: April–July.

Habitat: Roadsides, meadows, damp open woods, and lawns.

Range: Alberta and Saskatchewan; Ontario to Newfoundland, south to Georgia, west to Arkansas, north to Kansas and North Dakota.

Comments: This small plant, naturalized from Europe, is often found in lawns. Its leaves resemble those of thyme, hence its common name. The variety *humifusa,* a North American native found from Ontario east to Newfoundland and south to Massachusetts and Minnesota, is distinguished by its bright blue flowers. The genus name is thought to be derived from the Latin *vera* ("true") and the Greek *eicon* ("image"), alluding to the legend that the true image of Christ was received by Saint Veronica, for whom the genus was named.

101 Culver's Root
Veronicastrum virginicum

Description: Several long, tapering, erect, *dense spikes of small, white or purplish flowers.*

Flowers: About ¼″ (5 mm) wide; sepals and petals 4 each; stamens 2, projecting; spike 2–6″ (5–15 cm) long.

Leaves: Lanceolate to narrowly ovate, mostly in whorls of 3–7, sharply toothed, short-stalked.

Fruit: Ovoid capsule, opening at tip.

Height: 3–7′ (90–210 cm).

Flowering: June–September.

Habitat: Rich woods, thickets, roadsides, and prairies.

Range: Manitoba and Ontario; Maine south to Florida, west to Texas, and north to South Dakota.

Comments: Culver's Root has been used as a

medicine because of its cathartic and emetic qualities. There are only two species in the genus; the other is found in Siberia. The genus name, a combination of *Veronica* and the suffix *astrum* ("false"), describes the plants' resemblance to those of the genus *Veronica*.

CATBRIER FAMILY
Smilacaceae

Vines, usually prickly, or erect plants, with broad leaves and umbels of greenish flowers; male and female flowers on separate plants.

Flowers: Unisexual or bisexual, radially symmetrical. Sepals 3, petal-like, united; petals 3, united; stamens 3–9; all these parts attached below ovary.

Leaves: Simple, untoothed, usually with tendrils rising at base of leafstalk; 3–7 main veins interconnected by a network of smaller veins; evergreen or dropping off.

Fruit: Berry.

There are 12 genera and about 330 species, most in the genus *Smilax,* found on all continents except Antarctica. Sarsaparilla, extracted from the roots of various *Smilax,* is a flavoring agent. These plants are sometimes placed in the complex lily family (Liliaceae).

34 Carrion Flower
Smilax herbacea

Description:	A vine with broad leaves and stalked round clusters of *small, green, putrid-smelling flowers* in leaf axils.
Flowers:	About ½″ (1.5 cm) wide; sepals 3, petal-like; petals 3, greenish; stamens 6.
Leaves:	To 5″ (12.5 cm) long, pale green, ovate, parallel-veined.
Fruit:	Few-seeded, blue berry.
Height:	Vine; stems 3–9′ (90–270 cm) long.
Flowering:	May–June.
Habitat:	Moist woods, thickets, and meadows.
Range:	Ontario east to New Brunswick, south to Georgia, west to Louisiana and Oklahoma, and north to Kansas, Iowa, and Minnesota.

Comments: This attractive vine climbs over other vegetation by means of tendrils. The unpleasant-smelling flowers attract insects, especially carrion flies (hence the common name), which serve as pollinators. There are at least six species of *Smilax* in the East; all are thorny, green-stemmed, often evergreen vines that form tangled thickets. The most common are Greenbrier *(S. rotundifolia),* with heart-shaped leaves and stout thorns; Sawbrier *(S. glauca),* with heart-shaped leaves, a whitish bloom beneath, and weak spines; and Bullbrier *(S. bona-nox),* a southern and midwestern species with triangular leaves, stout thorns, and 4-sided stems.

NIGHTSHADE FAMILY
Solanaceae

Herbs, shrubs, vines, or trees with often showy flowers, generally in branched clusters.

Flowers: Usually radially symmetrical. Sepals 5, united; petals 5, united; stamens usually 5, sometimes fewer; all these parts attached at base of ovary.
Leaves: Alternate or rarely opposite; usually simple, sometimes compound.
Fruit: Berry or 2-chambered capsule.

There are about 85 genera and 2,800 species, found in tropical and warm temperate regions, especially in Central and South America. Several are poisonous, but others supply food such as chiles and bell peppers *(Capsicum),* tomatoes *(Lycopersicon esculentum),* potatoes *(Solanum tuberosum),* eggplant *(Solanum melongena),* and groundcherries (also known as husk tomatoes or tomatillos, in *Physalis).* Commercial tobacco is obtained from *Nicotiana tabacum.* Painted Tongue *(Salpiglossis sinuata),* petunias *(Petunia),* and butterfly flowers *(Schizanthus)* are grown as ornamentals. Solanaceae has also been known as the potato family.

75 **Jimsonweed**
Datura stramonium

Description: A tall, stout, smooth plant with a greenish or purplish stem and *trumpet-shaped, white or violet flowers.*

Flowers: 3–4″ (7.5–10 cm) wide; calyx 5-lobed, angular, tubular, green; corolla 5-lobed funnel-shaped, about twice as long as calyx.

Leaves: To 8″ (20 cm) long, ovate, irregularly lobed.

Fruit: *Prickly, egg-shaped capsule, 2″ (5 cm) wide*

Height: 1–5′ (30–150 cm).

Flowering: July–October.

Habitat: Waste places, fields, and barnyards.

Range: Alberta and Saskatchewan; Ontario east to Nova Scotia, south to Florida, west to Texas, and north to North Dakota; also throughout West.

Comments: This rank-smelling plant, introduced from tropical America, is easily distinguished by its large, trumpet-shaped flowers and prickly fruit. All parts of the plant are very poisonous. Cattle and sheep have died from grazing on it, and humans have been poisoned by eating the fruit for its narcotic properties. Touching the leaves or flowers may cause dermatitis in susceptible individuals. The common name is a corruption of "Jamestown," where the plant grew near the colonists' homes. Two southern species are Angel Trumpet *(D. wrightii),* also known as Southwestern Thorn Apple, with white flowers to 8″ (20 cm) long, occurring along Florida roadsides, and Entire-leaved Thorn Apple *(D. metel),* with violet-tinged, often double flowers, one within the other; the latter reaches a height of 7′ (2.1 m) and is found from Florida west to Texas.

---

258 Clammy Groundcherry
Physalis heterophylla

Description: *A sticky-hairy plant* bearing 1 stalked, *bell-shaped, greenish-yellow flower* with a purplish-brown center in each leaf axil.

Flowers: ¾″ (2 cm) wide; corolla 5-lobed; stamens 5, with yellow anthers.

Leaves: 1–4″ (2.5–10 cm) long, ovate to heart-shaped, with few teeth on edges.

Fruit:	Yellow, tomato-like berry; enclosed in an *inflated, papery, green calyx.*
Height:	1–3′ (30–90 cm).
Flowering:	June–September.
Habitat:	Dry woods and clearings.
Range:	Ontario east to Nova Scotia, south to Florida, west to Texas, north to North Dakota; also in much of West.
Comments:	The leaves and the unripe fruit of this plant are poisonous, but the ripe fruit can be made into jams or pies. Animals have been poisoned by feeding on the plants but generally avoid them unless other forage is scarce. The groundcherries, with about two dozen species in our area, have bell-like flowers with colored centers and inflated bladders around the fruit. The cultivated Chinese Lantern Plant *(P. alkekengi)* has white flowers and a showy, inflated, orange calyx in fruit.

41 Horse Nettle
Solanum carolinense

Description:	*Star-like, white or pale lavender flowers* with yellow centers in lateral clusters on a *prickly, erect stem.*
Flowers:	¾–1¼″ (2–3 cm) wide; petals 5; stamens 5, with *yellow, elongated anthers forming a central cone.*
Leaves:	3–5″ (7.5–12.5 cm) long, rough, elliptical-oblong, coarsely lobed, covered with prickles.
Fruit:	Yellow, tomato-like berry, ¾″ (2 cm) wide.
Height:	1–3′ (30–90 cm).
Flowering:	May–October.
Habitat:	Fields, waste places, and cultivated sites.
Range:	Ontario east to Maine, south to Florida, west to Texas, and north to South Dakota; also in much of West.
Comments:	This coarse, native, deep-rooted perennial is considered a weed by some, yet the flowers are attractive. Deep hoeing is needed to eradicate the underground stems, and gloves must be worn while handling this prickly plant.

Its foliage is not eaten by cattle. Despite the common name, *Solanum* nettles are not related to true nettles (Urticaceae). White Horse Nettle *(S. elaeagnifolium),* very similar plant with silvery foliage, occurs in the western United States east to Missouri and is spreading eastward from Missouri and Illinois south to Louisiana, Florida, and North Carolina. Buffalo Bur *(S. rostratum),* an annual with bright yellow flowers and a prickly calyx enclosing the berry, is naturalized from the western United States as a weed in fields throughout our area, except the Maritime Provinces, Newfoundland, and Florida.

604   Bittersweet Nightshade; Climbing Nightshade; Deadly Nightshade
Solanum dulcamara

Description: *A climbing vine* with loose flattish clusters of *drooping, blue or violet, star-shaped flowers* with yellow centers.

Flowers: ½″ (1.5 cm) wide; corolla 5-lobed; stamens 5, with *yellow anthers forming a beak-like, central cone.*

Leaves: To 3½″ (9 cm) long, halberd-shaped, with 2 basal lobes.

Fruit: Shiny, green, tomato-like berry, turning bright red.

Height: Vine; stems 2–8′ (60–240 cm) long.

Flowering: May–September.

Habitat: Thickets and clearings.

Range: Alberta east to Newfoundland, south to Florida, northwest to Tennessee, Missouri, and Kansas, and north to North Dakota; also in much of West.

Comments: This vine, introduced from Europe, has distinctive leaves. The leaves and unripe fruit contain the poisonous alkaloid solanine. Although the plant is sometimes called Deadly Nightshade, its toxin is not fatal; however, the berries are attractive to children and can cause poisoning if eaten in a large quantity. The species is called bittersweet because portions of the plant first taste bitter,

then sweet. Long ago the plant was used in England to counteract witchcraft.

42 Common Nightshade
Solanum ptychanthum

Description: A smooth plant with few-flowered, lateral umbels of *small, white, star-like, drooping flowers.*

Flowers: ⅜" (8 mm) wide; petals 5, curving backward; stamens 5, with *yellow anthers forming a central cone.*

Leaves: 2–4" (5–10 cm) long, thin, ovate, pointed, wavy-toothed.

Fruit: Green berry, turning black.

Height: 1–2½' (30–75 cm).

Flowering: June–November.

Habitat: Cultivated and disturbed areas and open woods.

Range: Alberta east to Newfoundland, south to Florida, west to Texas, and north to North Dakota; also in parts of West.

Comments: This native species, sometimes called *S. americanum* or *S. nigrum,* often appears in open areas. The leaves and berries contain the poisonous alkaloid solanine; although the toxic quality of the berries seems to disappear with ripening, it is best not to eat them. Other similar nightshades with small white flowers include the western and Great Plains species Cut-leaved Nightshade *(S. triflorum),* with deeply dissected leaves, which occurs in our area from Minnesota, Iowa, and Missouri occasionally eastward, and Hairy Nightshade *(S. villosum),* with very hairy stems and yellow or red berries, which occurs sporadically from Maine south to Florida.

BUR REED FAMILY
Sparganiaceae

Aquatic or marsh herbs with grass-like leaves and densely crowded, round heads of small flowers in or above axils of bract-like leaves.

Flowers: Unisexual. Sepals and petals absent, or represented by few scales; stamens usually 5; pistil 1; male and female flowers in separate heads, with male heads above female heads.

Leaves: Alternate, on opposite sides of stem in 2 vertical rows, with bases sheathing stem.

Fruit: Seed-like; together forming bur-like heads.

There is only 1 genus with about 13 species, found in temperate and cool regions of the Northern Hemisphere, Australia, and New Zealand.

36 Bur Reed
Sparganium americanum

Description:	An erect, *grass-like, rhizomatous aquatic* with *zigzag stalks* bearing *ball-like heads* of tiny green flowers.
Flowers:	Sepals and petals represented by scales; female flowers with 1 stigma, in heads 1″ (2.5 cm) wide; male flowers with 5 stamens, in 5–9 smaller heads above female heads, withering and dying after pollen shed.
Leaves:	To 3′ (90 cm) long, 2–4½″ (5–11.5 cm) wide, flat, softly textured, underside ridged along center, partly submerged.
Fruit:	Seed-like, beaked; in green (turning brown), bur-like heads.
Height:	1–3′ (30–90 cm).
Flowering:	May–August.
Habitat:	Shallow water and muddy shorelines.
Range:	Ontario east to Newfoundland, south to Florida, west to Texas, and north to Kansas, Iowa, and Minnesota.
Comments:	The bur reeds represent an important group of emergent plants that are partly in and partly out of the water; they frequently form dense stands along edges of shallow lakes and ponds. The seed-like fruits are eaten by waterfowl and marsh birds, and muskrats feed on the entire plant. Great Bur Reed (*S. eurycarpum*) reaches a height of 7′ (2.1 m) and has two stigmas rather than one, as in the rest of the group; it is widely distributed in our area except from Texas and Arkansas east to North

Carolina and Florida. Floating Bur Reed (*S. fluctuans*) has a floating stem and floating, ribbon-like leaves; it is found in cold ponds and lakes from Ontario east to Newfoundland and south to Pennsylvania and Minnesota.

CATTAIL FAMILY
Typhaceae

Aquatic or marsh herbs with creeping rhizomes, long narrow leaves, and minute flowers crowded in terminal spikes.

Flowers: Sepals and petals represented by hair-like bristles; male flowers with 2–5 (usually 3) stamens; female flowers with 1 stalked ovary; male and female flowers in separate spikes, with male spikes above female spikes.
Leaves: Sword-like, on opposite sides of stem in 2 vertical rows, with bases sheathing stem.
Fruit: 1-seeded follicle, opening along one side.

There is only 1 genus with 10 species, found in temperate and tropical regions worldwide.

382 Common Cattail
Typha latifolia

Description: A tall stiff plant bearing a *yellowish, cylindrical spike* of tiny male flowers extending directly above a brownish spike of female flowers; usually no bare stem between male and female spikes.
Flowers: Sepals and petals represented by bristles; male and female spikes each to 6″ (15 cm) long; female flowers with 1 stalked pistil; male flowers with usually 3 stamens, dropping off after pollen shed, leaving stalk bare.
Leaves: To 1″ (2.5 cm) wide, taller than stem, sword-like, flat, sheathing stem.
Fruit: 1-seeded follicle, opening along one side.
Height: 3–9′ (90–270 cm).
Flowering: May–July.
Habitat: Freshwater marshes, ditches, and shorelines.
Range: Throughout North America, except Arctic.

Comments: Spreading by its creeping roots, this typical marsh perennial forms dense stands in shallow water and provides a favorable habitat for red-winged blackbirds, as well as other marsh birds and muskrats. The latter can engage in extensive "eat outs," creating areas of open water in the marsh. The root is mostly starch; it was ground into meal by Native Americans, and early colonists also used it for food. Most of the plant is edible: The young leafy shoots, as they emerge in spring, can be cooked and eaten like asparagus; the immature pollen spikes can be boiled and eaten like corn on the cob; and the sprouts at the tip of the rootstock can be used in salads or boiled and served as greens. The closely related Narrow-leaved Cattail *(T. angustifolia),* which may have been introduced from Europe, grows from Alberta east to Nova Scotia, south to South Carolina, west to Tennessee, Arkansas, and Louisiana, and northwest to North Dakota; it has narrower leaves to ½" (1.5 cm) wide, a narrower fruiting head less than ¾" (2 cm) wide, and a gap between the male and female flower spikes. In both species the hairs on the long stalk of the fruit aid in wind dispersal. If the fruit lands in water, it soon splits open and releases its seed.

NETTLE FAMILY
Urticaceae

Leafy herbs, or shrubs or trees in tropical regions, often with stinging hairs, watery sap, and small, greenish, clustered flowers often in leaf axils.

Flowers: Bisexual or unisexual. Sepals 4–5, separate or sometimes united; petals absent; stamens as many as sepals; all these parts attached at base of ovary.
Leaves: Mostly opposite, simple, toothed.
Fruit: Seed-like.

There are about 45 genera and 700 species, widely distributed but most common in tropical regions.

17 **False Nettle**
Boehmeria cylindrica

Description: *Small, head-like clusters of tiny, greenish flowers in continuous or interrupted spikes* in axils of opposite leaves; plant lacks stinging hairs.

Flowers: Less than 1/16″ (2 mm) long; male flowers with 4 sepals and 4 stamens, usually in interrupted spikes; female flowers with 4 united sepals, mostly in continuous spikes to 1½″ (4 cm) long, often terminated by clusters of leaves.

Leaves: 1–3″ (2.5–7.5 cm) long, opposite, ovate to ovate-lanceolate, coarsely toothed.

Fruit: Seed-like.

Height: 1½–3′ (45–90 cm).

Flowering: July–October.

Habitat: Moist or shady ground.

Range: Ontario east to New Brunswick, south to Florida, west to Texas, and north to South Dakota and Minnesota.

Comments: This species differs from Clearweed *(Pilea pumila),* another member of the nettle family lacking stinging hairs, in that it does not have a translucent stem and is taller.

19 **Wood Nettle**
Laportea canadensis

Description: Clusters of *small greenish flowers in axils of alternate leaves* on a *stout stem with stinging hairs;* female flowers in loose, elongated clusters in upper axils, male flowers in shorter clusters in lower axils.

Flowers: About 1/8″ (4 mm) long; female flowers with 4 sepals and 1 pistil; male flowers with 5 sepals and 5 stamens.

Leaves: 2½–8″ (6.5–20 cm) long, thin, ovate, long-stalked, coarsely toothed.

Fruit: Dry, seed-like, crescent-shaped.

Height: 1½–4′ (45–120 cm).

Flowering: July–September.

Habitat: Low woods and streambanks.

Range: Saskatchewan east to Nova Scotia, south to Florida, west to Mississippi and Oklahoma, and north to North Dakota.

Comments: Wood Nettle is one of the nettles that
           really stings; it can cause severe pain to
           hapless passersby who touch it. The
           flowers of the similar Stinging Nettle
           (Urtica dioica) are in tighter, slender
           clusters in axils of opposite leaves with
           heart-shaped bases.

20 Clearweed
Pilea pumila

Description: A small, *translucent-stemmed* annual with
              *short curved clusters of inconspicuous,
              greenish-white flowers* in axils of opposite
              leaves; plant lacks stinging hairs.
   Flowers: About ⅛" (4 mm) long; female flowers
              with 4 sepals and 1 pistil; male flowers
              with 4 sepals and 4 stamens.
   Leaves: 1–5" (2.5–12.5 cm) long, opposite,
              ovate, conspicuously veined, coarsely
              toothed.
   Fruit: Dry, seed-like, green, often marked with
             black.
   Height: 4–20" (10–50 cm).
Flowering: July–October.
  Habitat: Moist shaded places.
    Range: Throughout East, except Prairie
            Provinces and Newfoundland.
Comments: The common name refers to the
           distinctive clear stem, soft and with a
           watery look. Lesser Clearweed *(P.
           fontana),* very similar but with dull
           black, seed-like fruit, occurs from
           Ontario and Quebec south to Florida,
           west to Alabama, northwest to Illinois
           and Nebraska, and north to North
           Dakota. Clearweeds are restricted to
           shady areas, where they may form a
           continuous cover over moist soil.

18 Stinging Nettle
Urtica dioica

Description: A 4-sided stem covered with many
              bristly, stinging hairs and bearing slender,
              branching, *feathery clusters of minute,
              greenish flowers* in axils of opposite leaves;

male and female flowers on separate plants, or on same plant with male flowers in axils of upper leaves and female flowers in axils of lower leaves.

Flowers: About $1/16''$ (2 mm) long; sepals 4; stamens 4.

Leaves: 2–4" (5–10 cm) long, opposite, ovate, with heart-shaped bases, coarsely toothed, bearing stinging bristles.

Fruit: Seed-like.

Height: 2–4' (60–120 cm).

Flowering: June–September.

Habitat: Waste places and roadsides.

Range: Throughout much of North America, except Arctic.

Comments: This nettle should not be handled, as it contains a fluid (dispensed through hairs that function like tiny hypodermic needles) that can cause a severe, burning skin irritation. However, the very young shoots and upper leaves may be cooked and served as greens or used in soups and stews. The family and genus names are derived from the Latin *uro* ("I burn").

VERBENA FAMILY
Verbenaceae

Herbs, shrubs, or trees, usually with flowers in spike-like or branched clusters or in heads.

Flowers: Bilaterally symmetrical. Sepals 5, united; petals 5, united, forming corolla with a slender tube and an abruptly flared top; stamens usually 4; all these parts attached at base of ovary.

Leaves: Opposite or whorled, simple.

Fruit: Often separating into 4 hard sections (nutlets), each 1-seeded.

There are about 100 genera and 2,600 species, mostly in tropical and warm temperate regions. A highly prized furniture wood is obtained from Teak *(Tectona grandis)*. Vervains *(Verbena)*, lantanas *(Lantana)*, lippias (also known as frog fruits, in *Phyla*), and Chaste Tree *(Vitex agnus-castus)* are grown as ornamentals. Verbenaceae has also been known as the vervain family.

146 Lopseed
Phryma leptostachya

Description: Pairs of small, *white or pinkish-lavender flowers in slender, elongated, spike-like clusters* along top of stem and its diverging branches.

Flowers: About ¼" (6 mm) long; corolla 2-lipped, lower lip much longer than upper; stamens 4; cluster to 6" (15 cm) long.

Leaves: 2–6" (5–15 cm) long, opposite, coarsely toothed; upper ones short-stalked.

Fruit: Dry, seed-like; enclosed in *calyx hanging down against stem.*

Height: 1–3' (30–90 cm).

Flowering: July–September.

Habitat: Moist woods and thickets.

Range: Manitoba east to New Brunswick, south to Florida, west to Texas, and north to North Dakota.

Comments: This species also occurs in Asia. The downward-hanging fruit, which accounts for the common name, makes the plant easily recognizable. Three of the calyx teeth are hooked at the tip, which may assist in dispersal by attachment to animals. This species is sometimes placed in its own family, the Phrymaceae.

499 Rose Vervain
Verbena canadensis

Description: An erect or reclining plant with a hairy stem and a dense, terminal, *flat-topped cluster of pinkish-lavender or white, tubular flowers with flaring corolla lobes.*

Flowers: ½–¾" (1.5–2 cm) wide; corolla with 5 notched lobes; stamens 4; pistil 1, with 4-lobed ovary.

Leaves: To 3" (7.5 cm) long, opposite, palmately veined, ovate to lanceolate, coarsely toothed or lobed, stalk partly winged.

Fruit: Separating into 4 hard, seed-like sections.

Height: 6–18" (15–45 cm).

Flowering:	April–October.
Habitat:	Sandy or rocky prairies and roadsides.
Range:	Minnesota east to Connecticut, south to Florida, west to Texas, and north to Nebraska.
Comments:	This showy vervain is especially good for rock gardens; although it is a southern species, it is tolerant of northern climates. The somewhat similar Small-flowered Verbena *(V. bipinnatifida)* has a bristly-hairy stem and finely divided leaves with stiff hairs; it occurs in fields and along sandy roadsides in Quebec and from South Dakota and Wisconsin south to Florida and Texas. Stiff Vervain *(V. rigida),* with toothed, lanceolate leaves and a more elongated flower cluster, occurs from Virginia south to Florida and west to Texas and Oklahoma.

145 Slender Vervain
Verbena halei

Description:	An erect, rough, hairy, square-stemmed plant with *long narrow spikes of small, white, tubular flowers.*
Flowers:	About ¼″ (6 mm) wide; corolla 5-lobed; stamens 4; pistil 1, with 4-lobed ovary.
Leaves:	To 4″ (10 cm) long, opposite, coarsely toothed or cut, sharp-pointed.
Fruit:	Separating into 4 hard, seed-like sections.
Height:	2–4′ (60–120 cm).
Flowering:	June–September.
Habitat:	Rich thickets and woodland borders.
Range:	North Carolina south to Florida, west to Texas, and north to Oklahoma and Missouri.
Comments:	Often considered a weed, this species is not as attractive as its blue counterpart, Blue Vervain *(V. hastata).* The very similar Pink Vervain *(V. scabra),* found from West Virginia and Maryland south through the Atlantic and Gulf Coast states to Texas, has pale pink flowers.

591   Blue Vervain
Verbena hastata

Description: Stiff, *pencil-like spikes of numerous small,*
tubular, blue-violet flowers atop a square
grooved stem and its branches.

Flowers: ⅛" (3 mm) wide; corolla with 5 flaring
lobes; stamens 4, in 2 pairs of different
lengths; pistil 1, with 4-lobed ovary.

Leaves: 4–6" (10–15 cm) long, opposite,
lanceolate, doubly toothed, rough-
textured.

Fruit: Separating into 4 hard, seed-like
sections.

Height: 2–6' (60–180 cm).

Flowering: July–September.

Habitat: Damp thickets, shorelines, and roadsides.

Range: Throughout United States and Canadian
provinces, except Alberta and
Newfoundland.

Comments: An attractive perennial, this species has
showy, candelabra-like flower spikes.
Bumblebees are among its important
pollinators. In ancient times some
European verbenas were thought to be
cure-alls among medicinal plants; the
genus name is the Latin for "sacred
plant." Hoary Vervain *(V. stricta),* to 10'
(3 m) tall and with flowers ½" (1.5 cm)
long, occurs from North Dakota,
Ontario, Quebec, and Vermont south to
Georgia and Florida. Narrow-leaved
Vervain *(V. simplex)* has narrow leaves
and lavender flowers ⅜" (8 mm) long; it
occurs from Nebraska, Ontario, and
Vermont south to Florida and Texas.

VIOLET FAMILY
Violaceae

Herbs with often colorful flowers in the United States, but
often shrubby and less showy elsewhere.

Flowers: Bilaterally or radially symmetrical. Sepals 5, separate; petals 5, separate, lower petal often largest and bearing a backward-projecting spur; stamens 5, loosely
united around ovary; all these parts attached at base of
ovary.

Leaves: Simple, sometimes deeply lobed.
Fruit: Berry or explosively opening capsule.

There are about 16 genera and 800 species, found nearly throughout the world. Many species of *Viola* are cultivated for their attractive flowers.

5 Green Violet
Hybanthus concolor

Description:	*Greenish, drooping, bilaterally symmetrical flowers* in groups of 1–3 on short recurved stalks rising in leaf axils.
Flowers:	¼" (6 mm) long; sepals 5, linear, about as long as petals; petals 5, lateral ones narrow, lower petal longer and somewhat swollen at base; stamens 5, united around ovary; pistil club-shaped.
Leaves:	3½–6½" (9–16.5 cm) long, elliptical, tapering at both ends, untoothed or slightly toothed.
Fruit:	Capsule.
Height:	1–3' (30–90 cm).
Flowering:	April–June.
Habitat:	Rich woods and ravines.
Range:	Ontario; Michigan east to Vermont, south to Florida, west to Mississippi and Oklahoma, and north to Kansas and Iowa.
Comments:	This species, the only member of the genus in the East, only vaguely resembles other violets, but its five united stamens and club-like pistil are characteristic of the family. The genus name is from the Greek *hybos* ("hump-backed") and *anthos* ("flower") and probably refers to the drooping flowers. The species name means "of one color," reflecting the green of both the sepals and petals.

91 Sweet White Violet
Viola blanda

Description:	Leaves and *fragrant white flowers* on separate, *reddish stalks* rising from an underground stem with runners.

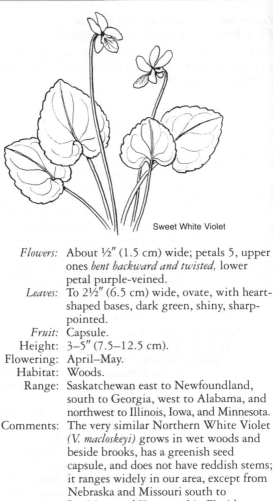

Sweet White Violet

Flowers: About ½″ (1.5 cm) wide; petals 5, upper ones *bent backward and twisted,* lower petal purple-veined.

Leaves: To 2½″ (6.5 cm) wide, ovate, with heart-shaped bases, dark green, shiny, sharp-pointed.

Fruit: Capsule.

Height: 3–5″ (7.5–12.5 cm).

Flowering: April–May.

Habitat: Woods.

Range: Saskatchewan east to Newfoundland, south to Georgia, west to Alabama, and northwest to Illinois, Iowa, and Minnesota.

Comments: The very similar Northern White Violet *(V. macloskeyi)* grows in wet woods and beside brooks, has a greenish seed capsule, and does not have reddish stems; it ranges widely in our area, except from Nebraska and Missouri south to Louisiana and Texas, and in Florida.

92 Canada Violet
Viola canadensis

Description: *Slender, purplish stalks bearing fragrant white flowers* and heart-shaped, finely toothed leaves.

Flowers: ¾–1″ (2–2.5 cm) wide; petals 5, white inside, purple-tinged outside, base yellow.

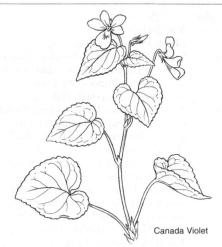

Canada Violet

Leaves:	2–4″ (5–10 cm) long.
Fruit:	Capsule.
Height:	8–16″ (20–40 cm).
Flowering:	April–June.
Habitat:	Woods.
Range:	Alaska south and east across Canada to Newfoundland, south to Georgia, west to Arkansas, and north to Illinois, Iowa, Nebraska, and North Dakota; also from New Mexico and Arizona northwest to Washington.
Comments:	This violet is found mainly along southern Canada, the northern United States, and in mountains elsewhere. It grows well in wildflower gardens if planted in a cool spot.

562 Dog Violet
Viola labradorica

Description:	A low plant with leaves and *light bluish-violet flowers* on same stalk.
Flowers:	About ¾″ (2 cm) wide; petals 5, lateral ones slightly bearded, lower petal with purple veins and a spur ⅛–¼″ (4–5 mm) long.
Leaves:	1¾″ (4.5 cm) long, round, heart-shaped, weakly scalloped; *finely toothed,* leaf-like stipules at base of stalks.
Fruit:	Capsule.

Height: 2–6″ (5–15 cm).

Flowering: March–July.

Habitat: Meadows and damp woods.

Range: Saskatchewan east to Newfoundland, south to Florida, west to Alabama, and northwest to Illinois, Wisconsin, Minnesota, and North Dakota.

Comments: The very similar Long-spurred Violet *(V. rostrata)* has pale blue flowers with darker blue centers and spurs ½–1″ (1.5–2.5 cm) long; it is found from Ontario and Quebec south to Wisconsin, Illinois, Alabama, and Georgia. Prostrate Blue Violet *(V. walteri),* a southern species growing from Ohio south to Texas and Florida, is densely hairy. Also very similar, Hooked-spur Violet *(V. adunca)* is a northern species occurring as far south as South Dakota, Iowa, Wisconsin, and New England in dry rocky habitats.

561 Birdsfoot Violet
Viola pedata

Description: A smooth plant with *deeply cut leaves and blue-violet flowers* on separate stalks.

Flowers: To 1½″ (4 cm) wide; petals 5, beardless; lower petal whitish, veined with violet, grooved, spurred; stamens 5, with conspicuous *orange anthers* in throat of flower.

Leaves: 1–2″ (2.5–5 cm) long, *fan-shaped,* with linear, toothed segments.

Fruit: Capsule.

Height: 4–10″ (10–25 cm).

Flowering: March–June.

Habitat: Dry sandy fields and open woods.

Range: Ontario; Maine south to Georgia, west to Texas, and north to Nebraska, Iowa, and Minnesota.

Comments: Larger than most violets, this beautiful plant of dry upland sites, with its showy, blue-violet flowers and distinctive bird's-foot-shaped leaves, is easy to identify. It is pollinated by bees and butterflies. A bicolored form of this species, with deep violet upper petals

and lilac lower petals, is one of the
loveliest violets.

---

301 **Downy Yellow Violet**
Viola pubescens

Description: *A softly hairy plant* with leaves and *yellow
flowers* on same stalk.
Flowers: ¾" (2 cm) wide; petals 5, lower ones
with dark purple veins, lateral ones
bearded.
Leaves: 2–5" (5–12.5 cm) wide, heart-shaped,
hairy, scallop-toothed; usually 1 basal
leaf.
Fruit: Capsule.
Height: 6–16" (15–40 cm).
Flowering: May–June.
Habitat: Woods.
Range: Throughout East, except Alberta,
Newfoundland, and Florida.
Comments: The hairiness of this species makes it
distinctive among the numerous yellow
violets. Prairie Yellow Violet *(V.
nuttallii),* with lanceolate leaves, occurs
from Alberta east to Manitoba and south
to Minnesota and Kansas. Our only
yellow violet with flowers and leaves on
separate stalks is Round-leaved Yellow
Violet *(V. rotundifolia),* with a small
flower and roundish, basal leaves; it
occurs from Ontario and Quebec south
to Maine, Ohio, Tennessee, and Georgia.

563, 625 **Common Blue Violet**
Viola sororia

Description: A smooth low plant with leaves and *blue
or purple to white flowers* on separate
stalks.
Flowers: ½–¾" (1.5–2 cm) wide; petals 5,
sometimes white with purple veins,
lateral ones bearded, lower petal longer
and spurred.
Leaves: To 5" (12.5 cm) wide, heart-shaped,
with scalloped edges.
Fruit: Capsule.
Height: 3–8" (7.5–20 cm).

Flowering: March–June.
Habitat: Damp woods, moist meadows, lawns,
and roadsides.
Range: Throughout East, except Alberta.
Comments: Many violets also produce flowers near
the ground that fail to open but
nevertheless produce vast quantities of
seeds. Violet leaves are high in vitamins
A and C and can be used in salads or
cooked as greens. The flowers can be
candied. Marsh Blue Violet *(V. cucullata)*, a similar species of very wet
habitats, has flowers with dark blue
centers borne well above the leaves; it
occurs from Ontario east to
Newfoundland and south to Georgia
and Arkansas.

MISTLETOE FAMILY
Viscaceae

Mostly evergreen shrubs, lacking roots and growing parasitically on trees, with inconspicuous flowers borne singly or in clusters in leaf axils or at branch ends.

Flowers: Unisexual, usually radially symmetrical. Sepals 3–4; petals absent; all these parts attached at top of ovary.
Leaves: Opposite or whorled, simple, untoothed, mostly leathery; sometimes reduced to scales.
Fruit: 1-seeded berry or drupe.

There are about 7 genera and 350 species, widely distributed in tropical and temperate areas. Viscaceae was once included in Loranthaceae.

232   Mistletoe
Phoradendron leucarpum

Description: *A semi-parasitic, epiphytic shrub* with *tiny, yellow flowers* in short, interrupted
clusters in leaf axils on smooth, *green, jointed stems.*
Flowers: About ⅛″ (3 mm) wide; sepals 3; petals
absent; male and female flowers on
separate plants.
Leaves: ¾–5″ (2–12.5 cm) long, opposite, ovate
to lanceolate, thick, leathery.

Mistletoe

Fruit: White, berry-like, 1-seeded, less than
¼" (6 mm) wide.

Height: 1' (30 cm).

Flowering: September–October.

Habitat: On branches of deciduous trees in open
areas.

Range: New York south to Florida, west to New
Mexico, and northeast to Kansas,
Missouri, Illinois, and Ohio.

Comments: This is the common mistletoe used at
Christmastime. It is sometimes called *P.
serotinum* or *P. flavescens.* The genus name
derives from the Greek *phor* ("a thief") and
dendron ("tree") and refers to the fact that
the plant gets at least some nourishment
from the tree on which it grows. Its sticky-
coated fruit is poisonous to humans but
relished by birds such as cedar waxwings
and bluebirds. The birds spread the
seeds through their droppings and by
wiping the sticky seeds off their beaks
onto branches, where a new plant may
become established. The small northern
Dwarf Mistletoe *(Arceuthobium pusillum)*
has short, yellow-green stems 1"
(2.5 cm) long, with leaves reduced to
thin brown scales; it grows only on
spruces and is found in northern
forests and bogs from Alberta east to
Newfoundland, south to New Jersey and
Pennsylvania, and west to Minnesota.

CALTROP FAMILY
Zygophyllaceae

Herbs or shrubs, rarely trees, with flowers borne singly or in branched clusters.

Flowers: Usually bisexual, radially symmetrical. Sepals usually 5, separate; petals 5, separate; stamens 5, 10, or 15, often with scale-like appendages on stalks; all these parts attached at base of ovary.
Leaves: Opposite, pinnately compound.
Fruit: Usually a 5-chambered capsule.

There are about 30 genera and 250 species, mostly in warm temperate or tropical regions. Creosote Bush *(Larrea tridentata)* is a common shrub in southwestern deserts. The densest of well-known commercial woods, lignum vitae, is obtained from tropical trees in the genus *Guaicum.*

---

255 **Puncture Weed;**
Goat's Head; Caltrop
Tribulus terrestris

Description: A trailing plant with *yellow flowers* on short stalks in axils of *opposite, pinnately compound leaves.*
Flowers: ½" (1.5 cm) wide; sepals and petals 5 each; stamens 10.
Leaves: ¾–2½" (2–6.5 cm) long, in pairs of unequal length; with 3–7 pairs of leaflets, each to ⅝" (16 mm) long.
Fruit: Separating into 5 segments, each ending in a *sharp spine.*
Height: Creeper; stems 1–3' (30–90 cm) long.
Flowering: June–September.
Habitat: Dry waste places and open ground.
Range: Ontario; New York south to Florida, west to Texas, and north to North Dakota; also throughout West.
Comments: Naturalized from Europe, this plant is a troublesome weed, especially in the West. The spines on the fruits are very sharp and will injure animals if present in hay. These spines are the source of the common name Puncture Weed; the plant is also sometimes called Puncture Vine. In addition, there appears to be a toxic substance in the

plant that causes animals eating it to become sensitive to sunlight and develop swellings and dermatitis on unpigmented portions of the body. Puncture Weed is considered a noxious weed in Iowa, Virginia, and many western states.

PART III
APPENDICES

GLOSSARY

Achene   A small, dry, hard, seed-like fruit that does not open and contains one seed.

Adventive   A plant that has been introduced from one region into another but has not become fully naturalized. *See also* Introduced.

Air plant   A plant growing on another plant but deriving no nutrition from it; an epiphyte.

Alternate leaves   Leaves rising singly along the stem, not in pairs or whorls.

Annual   Having a life cycle completed in one year or season.

Anther   The sac-like, pollen-containing part of a stamen.

Aquatic   A plant growing in water.

Axil   The angle formed by the upper side of a leaf and the stem from which the leaf grows.

Banner   The broad upper petal in a pea flower; also called the standard.

Basal leaves   Leaves at the base of the stem.

Bearded   Bearing a tuft or ring of long or stiff hairs.

Berry   A fleshy fruit with one to many seeds, developed from a single ovary.

Biennial   Growing vegetatively during the first year and flowering, fruiting, and dying during the second.

Bilaterally symmetrical   A flower that can be divided into equal halves by only one line through the middle; often called bilateral or irregular. *See also* Radially symmetrical.

Bisexual   A flower with both female (pistil) and male (stamen) parts.

Blade   The flat portion of a leaf, petal, or sepal.

Bloom   A whitish, powdery or waxy coating giving a frosted appearance, usually easily rubbed off (e.g., the bloom on a plum).

Bract   A modified leaf, usually smaller than the foliage leaves, often situated at the base of a flower or an inflorescence.

Bractlet   A small bract.

Bud   An undeveloped leaf, stem, or flower, often enclosed in scales; an incompletely opened flower.

Bulb   A short, underground stem, the swollen portion consisting mostly of fleshy, food-storing, modified leaves (e.g., an onion).

Bulblet   A small bulb; most often referring to one borne in a leaf axil or in an inflorescence.

Calyx   Collective term for the sepals of a flower.

Capsule   A dry, usually thin-walled fruit with one or more compartments, splitting open along two or more lines.

Carnivorous   Subsisting partly on nutrients obtained from the breakdown of animal tissue; with regard to plants, usually referring to insect tissue.

Catkin   A scaly-bracted, deciduous spike composed of very small, unisexual flowers.

Clasping leaf   A leaf with its base wholly or partly surrounding the stem.

Claw   The narrow, stalk-like base of a petal.

Compound leaf   A leaf divided into leaflets.

Compound umbel   A flower cluster consisting of small umbels joined by their stalks to a common point. *See also* Umbel.

Corolla   Collective term for the petals of a flower.

Corona   A crown-like structure between corolla and stamens on some flowers.

Creeper   Technically, a trailing shoot that takes root at the nodes; used here to denote any trailing, prostrate plant.

Cross-pollination   The transfer of pollen from one plant to another.

Deciduous   Shedding leaves seasonally; the shedding of certain parts after a period of growth.

Disk   The fleshy development of the base of the flower around the base of the ovary; in reference to members of the aster family, the swollen, often dome-like top of the flower stalk, bearing the disk flowers.

Disk flower   Each of the small, tubular, radially symmetrical flowers making up the central part of the flower head in many members of the aster family, or making up the entire head in some members.

Dissected leaf   A deeply cut leaf, the cleft not reaching to the midrib; same as a divided leaf.

Divided leaf   A deeply cut leaf, the cleft not reaching to the midrib; same as a dissected leaf.

Drupe   A fleshy fruit with a single seed enveloped by a hard covering (e.g., a peach); also called a stone fruit.

Emergent   An aquatic plant with its lower part submerged and its upper part extending above water.

Epiphyte   A plant growing on another plant but deriving no nutrition from it; an air plant.

Escaped   A plant that has spread beyond the confines of a deliberate planting, as from a garden.

Family A group of closely related genera.

Female flower A flower with one or more pistils but lacking stamens; a pistillate flower.

Fertile stamen A stamen with a pollen-producing anther.

Filament The stalk of a stamen, usually slender and thread-like.

Follicle A dry, one-chambered fruit developed from a single ovary, usually opening along one line (e.g., a milkweed fruit).

Fruit The seed-bearing, ripened ovary or pistil, often with attached parts.

Genus (plural, Genera) A group of closely related species.

Gland A small structure secreting some substance, usually oil or nectar.

Glandular Bearing glands.

Head A crowded cluster of flowers on very short stalks or without stalks; in reference to members of the aster family, the composite of ray and disk flowers resembling a single flower.

Herb A plant producing little or no woody tissue, as opposed to a shrub or a tree.

Humus A brown or black, complex, variable material resulting from partial decomposition of plant or animal matter and forming the organic portion of soil.

Hypanthium A cup- or saucer-shaped or tubular base to certain flowers, composed of the united and modified bases of calyx, corolla, and stamens; sepals, petals, and stamens grow from the rim.

Inflorescence A flower cluster on a plant or, especially, the arrangement of flowers on a plant.

Introduced A plant that has been either accidentally or deliberately brought from one region into another; may or may not become naturalized.

Involucre A whorl or circle of bracts beneath a flower or flower cluster.

Irregular flower A flower with petals that are not uniform in size or shape but often form an upper and lower lip; usually used in reference to a bilaterally symmetrical flower.

Keel A sharp ridge or rib; in a pea flower, the two lowest petals joined by lower edges and shaped like the prow of a boat.

Lanceolate Lance-shaped, much longer than wide and pointed at the end, usually with the widest portion below the middle.

Leaflet One of the leaf-like parts of a compound leaf.

Linear Long, narrow, with parallel sides.

Lip petal The lower petal of some bilaterally symmetrical flowers, often larger and/or more showy than the other petals.

Lobed Indented on the edges, with the indentations not reaching to the center or base.

Local A plant occurring sporadically but sometimes common where found.

Male flower   A flower with stamens but lacking pistils; a staminate flower.

Naturalized   A plant that has been introduced from one region into another where it has become established in the wild and reproduces as though native.

Node   The place on a stem from which a leaf or a branch grows.

Obovate   More or less egg-shaped; in reference to a leaf, one with the stalk attached at the narrow end of the leaf.

Opposite leaves   Leaves occurring in pairs at a node, with one leaf on either side of the stem.

Ovary   The swollen base of a pistil, within which seeds develop.

Ovate   More or less egg-shaped, pointed at the top, and broadest near the base or below the middle; in reference to a leaf, one with the stalk attached at the broad end of the leaf.

Palmate leaf   A leaf with three or more divisions or lobes, much like the outspread fingers of a hand.

Panicle   A branched, open inflorescence in which the main branches are again branched.

Pappus   Bristles, scales, hairs, or a crown atop the seed-like fruits of various members of the aster family.

Parasite   A plant deriving its nutrition from another organism.

Pea flower   A bilaterally symmetrical flower with the corolla consisting of one broad upper petal (banner or standard), two lateral petals (wings), and two joined bottom petals (keel).

Perennial   Present at all times of the year; in reference to a plant, one that lives for more than two years, usually producing flowers, fruits, and seeds annually.

Perianth   Collective term for the calyx and corolla of a flower; in a flower lacking either sepals or petals, simply the outer whorl.

Petal   The basic unit of the corolla; flat, usually broad, and brightly colored or white.

Petiole   The stalk-like part of a leaf, attaching it to the stem.

Pinnate leaf   A leaf with leaflets along the sides of a common central stalk, much like a feather.

Pistil   The female organ of a flower, composed of an ovary, style, and stigma.

Pistillate flower   A flower with one or more pistils but lacking stamens; a female flower.

Pith   A spongy material present in the center of stems of certain plants.

Pod   A dry fruit that opens at maturity to release its seeds.

Pollen   The mass of dust-like grains produced in the anther of a stamen.

Pollen sac   The terminal, pollen-containing portion of a stamen; the anther.

Pollination   The transfer of pollen from an anther to a stigma by various agents (insects, birds, wind, water, etc.).

Raceme   An unbranched, often elongated flower cluster in which each flower is attached by its stalk directly to a central stem; flowers bloom in sequence from bottom to top.

Radially symmetrical   A flower with the symmetry of a wheel; often called radial or regular. *See also* Bilaterally symmetrical.

Ray flower   Each of the bilaterally symmetrical flowers around the edge of the central disk in many members of the aster family, or making up the entire head in some members; each ray flower resembles a single petal.

Recurved   Curving backward or downward.

Reflexed   Abruptly bent backward or downward.

Regular flower   A flower with petals and/or sepals of equal size and shape arranged around the center, much like the spokes of a wheel; always radially symmetrical.

Rhizome   A horizontal, underground stem, often enlarged by food storage, distinguished from a root by the presence of nodes and sometimes scale-like leaves.

Root   A specialized structure that absorbs water and nutrients from the soil and transports these substances to a plant's stem; lacks nodes.

Rose hip   A smooth, rounded, fruit-like structure consisting of a cup-shaped calyx enclosing seed-like fruits in certain members of the rose family.

Rosette   A crowded cluster of leaves; usually basal, circular, and appearing to grow directly out of the ground.

Runner   A stem that grows on the surface of the ground, often developing leaves, roots, and new plants at the nodes or tip.

Sap   A general term for the liquid contained within the parts of a plant.

Saprophyte   A plant lacking chlorophyll and living on dead organic matter.

Scale   A small, flattened, thin, usually green structure; the scales of a grass spikelet, among which the flowers develop, or the scales (much reduced leaves) in a flower cluster.

Self-pollination   The transfer of pollen from a stamen of one flower to the stigma of the same flower or of another flower on the same plant.

Sepal   The basic unit of the calyx; often green, sometimes colored and petal-like.

Sessile   Without a stalk; in reference to a leaf, one lacking a petiole, with the blade attached directly to the stem.

Sheath   A more or less tubular structure surrounding a part, as the lower portion of a leaf surrounding the stem.

Shoot   A young stem or branch with its leaves and flowers not yet mature.

Shrub   A woody, relatively low plant with several to many stems arising from the base.

Simple leaf   A leaf that is not compound.

Spadix   A dense spike of tiny flowers, usually enclosed in a spathe.

Spathe   A bract or pair of bracts, often large, enclosing the flowers.

Spatulate   More or less spatula- or spoon-shaped, with a rounded tip and tapering to the base.

Species (plural, Species)   A fundamental category of taxonomic classification, ranking below a genus; individuals within a species usually reproduce among themselves and are more closely related than to individuals of other species.

Spike   An elongated, unbranched flower cluster in which each flower lacks a stalk.

Spikelet   A tiny spike; in reference to members of the grass family, a structure consisting of overlapping scales enclosing small flowers lacking petals or sepals.

Spur   In reference to a flower, a slender, usually hollow projection.

Stalk   A general and less precise term for the stem; used here to describe a supporting structure, such as a leafstalk or flower stalk.

Stamen   The male organ of a flower, composed of a filament topped by an anther; usually several in each flower.

Staminate flower   A flower with stamens but lacking pistils; a male flower.

Standard   The broad upper petal in a pea flower; also called the banner.

Stem   The main axis of a plant or of its branches, responsible for supporting the leaves and flowers.

Sterile stamen   A stamen that does not produce pollen; usually lacks an anther.

Stigma   The tip of the pistil where the pollen lands and begins its development in the style.

Stipule   A small, often leaf-like appendage on either side of some petioles at the base.

Style   The narrow part of the pistil, connecting ovary and stigma.

Succulent   Fleshy and thick, storing water; a plant with fleshy, water-storing stems or leaves.

Tendril   A slender, coiling structure that helps support climbing plants.

Toothed   Having a sawtooth edge.

Tuber   A fleshy, enlarged part of an underground stem, serving as a storage organ (e.g., a potato).

Umbel   A flower cluster in which the individual flower stalks grow from the same point, much like the ribs of an umbrella.

Unisexual   A flower with only female (pistil) or male (stamen) parts.

Whorl   A circle of three or more leaves, branches, or flower stalks at a node.

Wing   A thin flat extension or ridge found at the edges of a seed or leafstalk or along the stem; in a pea flower, each of the two lateral petals.

PHOTO CREDITS

1 Angelina Lax/Photo Researchers, Inc.
2 Bill Beatty
2 (inset) Kevin Adams
3 Wolfgang Kaehler
3 (inset) Eda Rogers
4 Rob & Ann Simpson
5 Emily Johnson
5 (inset) Emily Johnson
6 David Liebman
7 Alan & Linda Detrick/ Photo Researchers, Inc.
7 (inset) Alan & Linda Detrick/ Photo Researchers, Inc.
8 Kevin Adams
8 (inset) Kevin Adams
9 Rob Curtis/The Early Birder
9 (inset) Rob Curtis/The Early Birder
10 Bill Beatty
10 (inset) Bill Beatty
11 David Dvorak, Jr.
12 Mark Turner
12 (inset) Mark Turner
13 Gilbert Twiest/Visuals Unlimited
13 (inset) John Serrao
14 David Cavagnaro/Visuals Unlimited
15 John Sohlden/Visuals Unlimited
16 David Cavagnaro
16 (inset) Glen M. Oliver/ Visuals Unlimited
17 Jessie M. Harris
17 (inset) Jessie M. Harris
18 Jessie M. Harris
18 (inset) Jessie M. Harris
19 Dave Spier/Visuals Unlimited
20 Joseph G. Strauch, Jr.
20 (inset) Joseph G. Strauch, Jr.
21 David Cavagnaro
21 (inset) David Cavagnaro
22 David Cavagnaro
22 (inset) David Cavagnaro
23 William J. Weber/Visuals Unlimited
23 (inset) William J. Weber/ Visuals Unlimited
24 Greg Gorel/Visuals Unlimited
24 (inset) Greg Gorel/Visuals Unlimited
25 Dick Scott/Visuals Unlimited
25 (inset) Brian F. Jorg
26 Jennifer Thieret Westermeyer
26 (inset) Jennifer Thieret Westermeyer
27 Jennifer Thieret Westermeyer
27 (inset) Jennifer Thieret Westermeyer
28 Jennifer Thieret Westermeyer
29 Rob & Ann Simpson
30 Jerry Pavia
31 Harry Ellis
32 E. R. Degginger/Color-Pic, Inc.
33 Jessie M. Harris
33 (inset) Jessie M. Harris
34 John D. Cunningham/ Visuals Unlimited
35 David Liebman
36 E. R. Degginger/Color-Pic, Inc.
36 (inset) E. R. Degginger/ Color-Pic, Inc.
37 Alan & Linda Detrick/ Photo Researchers, Inc.
38 Rob & Ann Simpson

39   Jessie M. Harris
40   Stephen G. Maka
41   David Liebman
41   (inset) David Liebman
42   Noble Proctor/Photo
     Researchers, Inc.
42   (inset) Noble Proctor/
     Photo Researchers, Inc.
43   Paul Rezendes
44   Rob & Ann Simpson
45   David Ransaw
46   Joseph G. Strauch, Jr.
47   Rob & Ann Simpson
48   John A. Lynch
48   (inset) John A. Lynch
49   Rob & Ann Simpson/
     Visuals Unlimited
50   Bill Johnson
51   Rob & Ann Simpson
52   Jessie M. Harris
53   Jessie M. Harris
54   George J. Wilder/Visuals
     Unlimited
55   Harry Ellis
55   (inset) Jakub Jasinski/
     Visuals Unlimited
56   Carol Gracie
57   Don Eastman
57   (inset) Don Eastman
58   Pat Lynch/Photo
     Researchers, Inc.
59   Rob & Ann Simpson
59   (inset) Rob & Ann Simpson
60   Kevin Adams
60   (inset) Kevin Adams
61   Andrew J. Martinez
62   Jeff Lepore/Photo
     Researchers, Inc.
62   (inset) Jeff Lepore/Photo
     Researchers, Inc.
63   Don Eastman
64   J. Paul Moore
65   Henry Aldrich
66   David Dvorak, Jr.
66   (inset) David Dvorak, Jr.
67   Jerry Pavia
68   Michael P. Gadomski/
     Photo Researchers, Inc.
69   Joseph G. Strauch, Jr.
70   Alan & Linda Detrick
71   Kevin Adams
71   (inset) Kevin Adams

72   E. R. Degginger/Color-Pic,
     Inc.
73   Rob & Ann Simpson
74   Joy Spurr
74   (inset) Stephen G. Maka
75   Jessie M. Harris
76   Kevin Adams
76   (inset) Kevin Adams
77   E. R. Degginger/Color-Pic,
     Inc.
78   Gail Jankus/Photo
     Researchers, Inc.
78   (inset) Gail Jankus/Photo
     Researchers, Inc.
79   E. R. Degginger/Color-Pic,
     Inc.
80   John Serrao
81   Mary M. Thacher/Photo
     Researchers, Inc.
82   Walt Anderson
83   E. R. Degginger/Color-Pic,
     Inc.
84   David Sieren
85   Gail Jankus/Photo
     Researchers, Inc.
85   (inset) John Bova/Photo
     Researchers, Inc.
86   John A. Lynch
87   Rob & Ann Simpson
87   (inset) Rob & Ann Simpson
88   Joseph G. Strauch, Jr.
89   Jessie M. Harris
90   David Dvorak, Jr.
90   (inset) Rob Curtis/The
     Early Birder
91   Rob & Ann Simpson
92   Kevin Adams
93   David Cavagnaro
93   (inset) Gerald D. Tang
94   John Bova/Photo
     Researchers, Inc.
95   John Bova/Photo
     Researchers, Inc.
95   (inset) John Bova/Photo
     Researchers, Inc.
96   Frederick D. Atwood
97   Joseph G. Strauch, Jr.
98   Jessie M. Harris
98   (inset) Jessie M. Harris
99   Joy Spurr
99   (inset) Joy Spurr
100 John A. Lynch

271   Bill Johnson
271   (inset) Bill Johnson
272   Paul Rezendes
273   Kevin Adams
273   (inset) David Dvorak, Jr.
274   Michael P. Gadomski/
      Photo Researchers, Inc.
275   John Bova/Photo
      Researchers, Inc.
276   David Dvorak, Jr.
276   (inset) David Dvorak, Jr.
277   Gene Ahrens/Bruce
      Coleman, Inc.
278   Deneve Feigh Bunde/
      Unicorn Stock Photos
279   Jessie M. Harris
280   Jessie M. Harris
280   (inset) Jessie M. Harris
281   Joseph G. Strauch, Jr.
282   David Liebman
283   Jerry Pavia
283   (inset) Jessie M. Harris
284   Rob & Ann Simpson
284   (inset) Rob & Ann Simpson
285   David Cavagnaro
286   Gail Jankus/Photo
      Researchers, Inc.
287   Kenneth M. Highfill/
      Photo Researchers, Inc.
288   E. R. Degginger/Color-Pic, Inc.
289   Michael Lustbader/Photo
      Researchers, Inc.
290   E. R. Degginger/Color-Pic,
      Inc.
291   Ronald J. Taylor
292   Joseph G. Strauch, Jr.
293   Emily Johnson
294   Jessie M. Harris
294   (inset) Jessie M. Harris
295   Robert P. Carr/Bruce
      Coleman, Inc.
295   (inset) Robert P. Carr/
      Bruce Coleman, Inc.
296   Michael P. Gadomski/
      Photo Researchers, Inc.
297   Gilbert S. Grant/Photo
      Researchers, Inc.
298   Carol Gracie
298   (inset) Carol Gracie
299   Don Eastman
299   (inset) Don Eastman
300   Jessie M. Harris

300   (inset) Jessie M. Harris
301   Kevin Adams
301   (inset) Kevin Adams
302   Ann E. Geise
302   (inset) John A. Merkle
303   Rob & Ann Simpson
303   (inset) Rob & Ann Simpson
304   Jessie M. Harris
304   (inset) Jessie M. Harris
305   Bill Beatty/Visuals
      Unlimited
306   Rob & Ann Simpson
307   Kevin Adams
307   (inset) Kevin Adams
308   William J. Weber/ Visuals
      Unlimited
308   (inset) William J. Weber/
      Visuals Unlimited
309   Jerry Pavia
309   (inset) Jerry Pavia
310   David Liebman
310   (inset) David Liebman
311   Jessie M. Harris
311   (inset) Jessie M. Harris
312   David Ransaw
312   (inset) David Ransaw
313   William J. Weber/Visuals
      Unlimited
313   (inset) William J. Weber/
      Visuals Unlimited
314   Carol Gracie
315   Caroline R. Dean
315   (inset) Caroline R. Dean
316   L. West/Photo Researchers,
      Inc.
316   (inset) L. West/Photo
      Researchers, Inc.
317   Rod Planck
317   (inset) Rod Planck
318   Bill Beatty/Visuals
      Unlimited
319   Bill Beatty
319   (inset) Bill Beatty
320   Jessie M. Harris
320   (inset) Jessie M. Harris
321   Paul Rezendes
322   Pat Lynch/Photo
      Researchers, Inc.
323   Harry Ellis
323   (inset) Harry Ellis
324   Alan & Linda Detrick/
      Photo Researchers, Inc.

589 Joy Spurr
590 Gerald D. Tang
590 (inset) Gerald D. Tang
591 Frank Oberle
591 (inset) Frank Oberle
592 Ronald J. Taylor
592 (inset) Ronald J. Taylor
593 Kevin Adams
593 (inset) Kevin Adams
594 Walter S. Judd
594 (inset) Walter S. Judd
595 Joseph G. Strauch, Jr.
595 (inset) Joseph G. Strauch, Jr.
596 Joseph G. Strauch, Jr.
597 Terry Livingstone
598 David Cavagnaro
598 (inset) Jakub Jasinski/
       Visuals Unlimited
599 J. Paul Moore
599 (inset) Carol Gracie
600 Kevin Adams
601 Jessie M. Harris
601 (inset) Jessie M. Harris
602 Jessie M. Harris
602 (inset) Jessie M. Harris
603 Terry Livingstone
603 (inset) Mark Turner
604 Mark Turner
605 Kevin Adams
605 (inset) Kevin Adams
606 E. R. Degginger/Color-Pic,
       Inc.
606 (inset) E. R. Degginger/
       Color-Pic, Inc.
607 Bill Beatty
608 Joseph G. Strauch, Jr.
608 (inset) Joseph G. Strauch, Jr.
609 Frank Oberle
609 (inset) Frank Oberle
610 Kevin Adams
610 (inset) Kevin Adams
611 E. R. Degginger/Color-Pic,
       Inc.
612 J. Paul Moore
612 (inset) J. Paul Moore
613 Rob & Ann Simpson
613 (inset) Rob & Ann Simpson
614 Rick Cech
615 John K. Gates

616 Jim Roetzel
617 Rob & Ann Simpson
617 (inset) Rob & Ann Simpson
618 Jerry Pavia
618 (inset) Jerry Pavia
619 Jessie M. Harris
620 Scott T. Smith
620 (inset) Scott T. Smith
621 Pat & Tom Leeson/Photo
       Researchers, Inc.
622 Alan & Linda Detrick/
       Photo Researchers, Inc.
622 (inset) Alan & Linda Detrick/
       Photo Researchers, Inc.
623 Mary S. Shaub
623 (inset) Mary S. Shaub
624 Ronald J. Taylor
625 Bill Beatty
626 Kevin Adams
627 John K. Gates/Visuals
       Unlimited
627 (inset) John K. Gates/
       Visuals Unlimited
628 Frank Oberle
628 (inset) Frank Oberle
629 Nigel Cattlin/Photo
       Researchers, Inc.
629 (inset) Nigel Cattlin/Photo
       Researchers, Inc.
630 Jessie M. Harris
630 (inset) Jessie M. Harris
631 Bill Beatty
631 (inset) Bill Beatty
632 E. R. Degginger/Color-Pic,
       Inc.
632 (inset) E. R. Degginger/
       Color-Pic, Inc.
633 E. R. Degginger/Color-Pic,
       Inc.
634 Steven & Lisa Peake/Photo
       Researchers, Inc.
634 (inset) Steven & Lisa Peake/
       Photo Researchers, Inc.
635 Harry Ellis
636 Stephen P. Parker/Photo
       Researchers, Inc.
637 Jessie M. Harris
638 Paul Rezendes
638 (inset) Paul Rezendes

STAFF

Prepared and produced by
Chanticleer Press, Inc.

Founding Publisher: Paul Steiner
Publisher: Andrew Stewart

Staff for this book:

Associate Publisher: Alicia Mills
Executive Editor: George Scott
Senior Editor: Miriam Harris
Editors: Lisa Lester, Lisa Leventer, Pamela Nelson,
Mary Sutherland, Marian Appellof
Editorial Assistant: Mee-So Caponi
Art Director: Drew Stevens
Designers: Bernadette Vibar, Jennifer Dahl, Michiyo Uno
Photo Editors: Ruth Jeyaveeran, Jennifer McLanaghan
Associate Photo Editor: Meg Kuhta
Photo Assistants: Jean Lee, Jennifer Braff
Production Assistant: Megan Lombardo
Color Correction: Katherine Thomason
Production Interns: Alyssa Okun, Carlin Fier
Office Manager: Sui Ping Cheung
Map: Ortelius Design
Silhouettes and Illustrations: Bobbi Angell

Original series design by Massimo Vignelli

All editorial inquiries should be addressed to:
Chanticleer Press
665 Broadway, Suite 1001
New York, NY 10012

To purchase this book or other National Audubon Society
illustrated nature books, please contact:
Alfred A. Knopf
299 Park Avenue
New York, NY 10171
(800) 733-3000
www.randomhouse.com